TOUGH ISSUES
STRAIGHT ANSWERS

DR. RICHARD K. THOMAS

© 2009 by Dr. Richard K. Thomas
All rights reserved.
Printed in the United States of America
ISBN: 1-4392-4748-X
EAN13: 9781439247488
Visit www.booksurge.com to order additional copies.

DEDICATED

To all the men and women of
National Association of Nouthetic Counselors (NANC)
who freely share what God has taught them
and have recorded those truths in book form
so that the next generation of counselors
can draw sweet refreshment for
themselves and those they counsel.

A special thank you

to

Dave Thomas

whose valuable editing skills, and knowledge of his father's preaching and teaching style, helped shape this volume.

CONTENTS

1. I'm a Teacher, Not a Referee   9
    The Classroom as a Counseling Center   9

2. I'm Not an Addict. I Can Stop Anytime!   15
    Addictions: When and How to Help   15

3. Practically Perfect in Every Way—Part 1   21
    Pouncing on Perfectionism   21

4. Practically Perfect In Every Way—Part 2   31
    Pouncing on Perfectionism   31

5. How to Help Someone Who Complains   43
    The Life of Joseph   43

6. Helping Those Who Use People and Those Who Feel Used   49
    Lessons from the Life of Jephthah   49

7. The Bible Is Not a Textbook on Mental Health   59
    In Defense of Biblical Counseling—Part 1   59

8. The Bible is not a Textbook on Mental Health   69
    In Defense of Biblical Counseling—Part 2   69

9. My Doctor Says I Have a Chemical Imbalance   81
    The Human Brain, Chemical Imbalances, Truth,
    Assumptions and Biblical Counsel   81

10. I Can't Shut My Brain Down. My Mind Is Always Racing.
From Where are These Thoughts Coming?   91
    Destructive Thoughts and How to Control Them   91

11. I Can't Do That! What Does God Expect from Me?   99
    Helping Someone Who Says They Can't   99

12. Spiritually Slim for Life: Cutting out the Devotional
Ding Dongs   113
   **Helping the Counselee Develop a Strong
Spiritual Life**   **113**

13. If I Could Ask God, I Would Ask…   127
   Four of Life's Greatest Questions   **127**

14. Nowhere to Run, Nowhere to Hide   133
   Are You Running Away from God?   **133**

15. Well, I Was Baptized…   145
   Are You Saved?—Part 1   **145**

16. I'm a Member of Down the Road Community Church   151
   Are You Saved?—Part 2   **151**

17. I Believe in God…   159
   Are You Saved?—Part 3   **159**

18. I'm So Confused. Whom Can I Trust?   189
   Be Careful to Whom You Listen   **189**

19. I'm Not Sure This is What God Wants Me To Do   199
   Second Guessing God   **199**

20. Dear God, Please…   209
   Be Careful What You Ask For   **209**

21. Fearfully and Wonderfully Made   217
   **Helping Caregivers Care for Crack
Cocaine Babies**   **217**

22. It Seems I Can't Remember Anything Anymore   237
   **Dementia: Understanding Dementia and
Counseling Those Who Provide Care**   **237**

23. Bashful, Doc, Dopey, Grumpy, Happy, Sleepy, Sneezy   261
   Helping Someone Who Grumbles   **261**

24. *Fail, Phail, Flop*	273
Helping Those Who Feel They Are Failures	**273**
25. *I Never Saw It Coming*	279
The Warning Signs of Temptation	**279**
26. *Just can't Seem to Lick This Problem*	287
Fifteen Biblical Ways to Tame Temptation	**287**
27. *My Family Doesn't Know How to Do Anything without Fighting*	297
Developing Family Unity	**297**
28. *What Kind of Person Am I? What Kind of Person Should I Be?*	305
My Heart—Christ's Home or Time Share?	**305**
29. *I Can't Handle Another "Let's Be Friends" Talk*	313
Navigating the Landmines of a Breakup	**313**
30. *Okay, God, I've Got a Few Questions I'd Like to Ask You*	337
Asking God the Tough Questions in Life	**337**
31. *I Can't Handle One More Thing on My Plate*	347
Stripping Stress of Its Destructive Power:	
Biblical Life Skills for Stress Management	**347**
32. *Satan: You and Your Crew Have Been Served*	371
The Power of Biblical Counseling:	
The Demoniac	**371**
33. *Wildest Police Chases*	377
The High Cost of Rebellion	**377**
34. *There's Just Not Enough Time*	395
Getting the Most out of Your Twenty-Four	
Hours: Biblical Life Skills for Time Management	**395**
35. *I'm at My Wits' End!*	413
What Can You Do When You Can't	
Do Any More?	**413**

36. Smack Down, Tap Out   425
    **Wrestling with God: "I Will Not Let You
    Go Until You Bless Me"**   **425**

37. I Can Count on One Hand How Many of My Friends Don't ...   441
    The Case for Abstinence   **441**

38. It Seems Like Nothing Is Going Right for Me   463
    What to Do When Surrounded by Suffering   **463**

39. No One Cares. No One Understands Me!   489
    Cutting, Self-Mutilation   **489**

Epilogue   501

FOREWORD

As I read this book, I don't think a chapter went by that I didn't think, "I could have used this when I was counseling that couple," or "I can use this now as I counsel," or "This chapter really would be helpful for the one with whom another counselor in our church is working." Doctor Thomas's commitment to biblical counseling rings true in every chapter and gives the counselor practical insights and tools to use in a myriad of situations. From dealing with addictions, perfectionism, grumbling, or caring for crack babies or those suffering from dementia, the range of topics and answers from God's powerful Word gives hope, direction, and the power to effect change for the glory of God in life's most difficult of circumstances. I thank God for the work Dr. Thomas has done in equipping helpers on the front lines with these insights into His Word.

Kerry Francetich, M.Div., Counseling Pastor
Southwest Hills Baptist Church, Beaverton, Oregon

PREFACE

Many counseling issues have arose; it is painfully difficult to keep up. In fact, I do not believe any counselor can know and understand all the contemporary counseling problems. From a human perspective, it looks very dim and hopeless. How can we help so many people who have so many different problems?

For the biblical counselor, these are bright days. These days are filled with hope. The biblical counselor has a great deal of confidence and assurance in the midst of today's kaleidoscope of counseling troubles. Solomon summarized it well when he penned these words,

> "That which has been is that which will be, and that which has been done is that which will be done. So there is nothing new under the sun. Is there anything of which one might say, 'See this, it is new?' Already it has existed for ages which were before us" (Ecc. 1:9–10).

Francis Bacon (1561–1626) wrote, "Some books are to be tasted, others to be swallowed, and some few to be chewed and digested. I hope that this volume will be food for you, the reader, to chew and digest. These chapters address, "See this, is it new?" Under the *sun*, nothing is new. It is merely a manikin draped with the latest fashion diagnoses. But under the *Son*, this material will help you strip away the naked facades of the medical and psychological communities. You will discover tools that can help you clothe the counselee in the precious robes of Christ's righteousness to live victorious as a child of the King. My prayer is echoed in the words of A. W. Tozer (1897–1963), who wrote, "The things you read will fashion you by slowly conditioning your mind."

I'm a Teacher, Not a Referee

The Classroom as a Counseling Center

"But she said I wasn't her friend!" said the little voice. I was listening to a second grade student tell me of her great trouble at lunch. She explained how distressed she was that one of her friends told her she was not her best friend any longer.

After lunch, I found her and her former' friend at my desk waiting. They knew the classroom policy: "You may tell Miss Thomas about problems with another student; however, the other student *must* come with you." In an effort to reduce childhood tattling, I put this policy into effect. They solemnly looked up at me and choked out, "Miss Thomas, we need to talk about a problem with you." Walking with them into the hallway, affectionately called my office, I prayed for wisdom to understand their situation and relationship. Using *Kipling's Men of Renown* as a guide, I asked the basic questions. Each explained to me, in turn, how Katie* had witnessed Tammy* being unkind to another student by not playing with them. Katie was really sad that Tammy had been mean. So, she decided that she wouldn't be Tammy's friend anymore.

Tammy and Katie both looked up at me earnest for my response. It was then I saw the deeper issues.

The History of Education

There continue to be several schools of thought prevailing upon education. While we have "learned" much from the ideas of behaviorism, post-modernism/relativism, and humanism, the Truth has remained unchanged, unlike these schools of thought.

Behaviorism
John B. Watson (1878–1958) is considered the father of modern behaviorism. He followed the lead of Ivan Pavlov, who became famous for his behavioral experiments on the salivation of dogs. Watson "postulated that psychology should stop studying what people think

and feel, and begin to study what people do" (Knight, p. 127). As a result, he believed that the environment was the primary molder of children.

B.F. Skinner, the eldest son of modern behaviorism, continued Watson's beliefs through his influence on education by his numerous works on behavioral psychology. His contributions to the educational field include the understanding that because a human being does not have any special dignity as a human, the task of an educator is then to study and discover the laws of behavior in animals for application to humans. Therefore, human beings become simply a product of their environment or behavioral engineering (Knight, p. 128–129). As a result, behaviorism can be defined in this statement: "Men and women are neither innately good nor bad; they are complex animals, an integral part of nature—and nothing else" (Layman, p. 87).

Post-Modernism/Relativism
This philosophy is a conglomeration of men's musings regarding the relationship between humans and knowledge. Originally, David Hume heaped discredit onto the question of cause and effect and the human ability to truly know the external world. Then Immanuel Kant sought to resolve Hume's philosophy but ended up by claiming that the human mind could not know things in and of itself. While it was Hume and Kant who laid the groundwork for the postmodern mindset, Friedrich Nietzsche fleshed out the ideas (Knight, p. 87).

Nietzsche's basis for his beliefs is that there is no foundation on which to rest beliefs. According to him, truth is dead; thus, knowledge became a human construct based in the subjective use of language. "Morality," he contended, "is relative to one's particular upbringing, not an eternally valid code of principles derivable from human nature or reason" (Higgins, p. 433).

The impact on education begins with the complete discarding of absolute truth given to us by a sovereign, transcendent Being. The ripple effects are seen in small children who do not understand why some things are wrong and some are right. Children understand that adults make occasional exceptions, but are confused when absolutes are not consistent. This is also seen in the manner in which information is chosen and then taught by the teacher.

Humanism
The proponent of this theory, John Dewey (1859–1952), who is the father of progressive education, was "born into a God-fearing family in Vermont." He attended church and Sunday school with faithfulness, but he rejected the doctrine because of the hypocrisy he saw running rampant in their ranks (Gibbs, p. 173).

The main tenet to his philosophy is that man is innately good. This stems from his previous education with G. Stanley Hall, who was educated by Wilhelm Wont, who espoused the idea of man being good in and of himself. First, this illustrates the fact that belief does influence actions. Second, this demonstrates Dewey's premise that the "teacher's role is that of advisor, guide, and fellow traveler, rather than that of authoritarian and classroom director" (Knight, p. 101).

Humanism hit education with a peculiar force. It was eagerly enveloped into the existing curriculum. In some cases, the old curriculum was completely tossed out in favor of this new progressive educational theory. Therefore, "this resulted in a shift from content, order, and discipline, to permissiveness, neglect of scholarship and trivializing of the curriculum" (Layman, p. 98).

This is clearly illustrated in the "open classroom" movement in the 1930s to 1950s. This movement put the theory of humanism to the test. As the grades declined in new progressive schools and classrooms, the general public returned to a conglomerate method, seeming to reject the theory of humanism.

Compare and Contrast
Behaviorism presupposes that children can be shaped through behavioral stimulation for the purposes of the engineer. This denies the fact of each child's uniqueness. We are stamped with God's image and cannot be uniformly engineered for whoever desires such things (Genesis 1:26). Behaviorism also wipes out the fact of God's creativity in each person He has created. The world around us is filled to the brim

with examples of God's humor, wisdom, and sovereignty. He has created each child for a specific purpose; even if just to bring glory to Himself.

We as teachers must strive to know our students and see them as God sees them. Since He has made each child a "little theologian," teaching their wonderful little minds for the sole purpose to acknowledge the mystery of God's ways and love Him is first priority.

Post-Modernism/Relativism follows in its denial of an absolute Truth source on which we build our houses of beliefs. It denies the very existence of God which is the true reason for human existence, and the wonder of reality in Christ. God was, is, and will always be (Hebrews 13:8; John 1:1–3). As a result, there is an absolute basis on which to base absolute, unchanging Truth—God Himself! In this world of uncertainty, we can be sure of one thing—God's Word is absolute Truth. It is absolutely true in every time, in every place, for every person, and in every situation.

End of story.
Nietzsche contended the purpose of human beings was to make the best of individual intelligence. He could have gone just one step further and said that God has given everyone individual talents for Him to command (dare I say it?!) for the glory of God!

Teachers are challenged to demonstrate how important each child is to God and likewise to us. We are to teach each child that his individual talents were given to him by an all-knowing, all-powerful Creator.

Humanism's great emphasis is that "humans are greater than even God." This philosophy disputes the fact that humans are totally depraved. Small children prove this at the first inklings to crawl. This view mirrors the Post-Modernism/Relativism philosophy in that it decapitates the idea of there actually being absolute, objective Truth that does not change. Human beings are totally and inherently depraved, but at the same time, they have inherent dignity and worth because of their Creator.

We, as educators, must emphasize to our students the idea that we do not live for ourselves. We live every day for an eternal record—not for the here and now. Immediately resulting from such a thought will be classroom discipline. This concept will require less "forest fires" incidents and transform them into minor infractions. Selfless living is obviously not a cure-all for the world's educational ills, but it is definitely positive movement towards Christ-like classrooms.

As part of the *Methods I* class in college, I was required to come up with a classroom discipline philosophy in as few sentences as possible. The following philosophy still holds true for me as I teach today:

> The biblical pattern of authority indicates that the parents are to raise their children in a Godly manner; therefore, as a teacher, when the children come to school that responsibility is transferred to my shoulders. I must uphold biblical discipline that enforces the fruits of the spirit, encourages biblical repentance, and shows as well as demonstrates biblical forgiveness. Through these, it is my goal as a teacher to disciple the children in my charge to be godly men and women.

The above assertion flies in the face of the educational theories previously stated. It holds to an absolute Truth that can never change because of the Giver of Truth. It demands obedience from the children, yet is tempered with gentleness. It models biblical forgiveness and repentance so the children may learn by example. It upholds parental authority and will not usurp said authority through inappropriate punishments. Thus, the fruit of the spirit will have a firm beginning in each child's heart.

Remember the two second grade students? As I looked into their innocent faces, the issues seemed suddenly clear. I explained that we are to love one another and build one another up, not tear one another down. Their countenance fell immediately. I continued by asking Tammy what she had done that was wrong. Tammy told me that she had been mean to another student. She acknowledged her guilt. I looked at Katie and asked her the same question. Katie explained to me that she had not built Tammy up. I also reminded her that if someone offends you, then it is your responsibility to approach that person and resolve the issue.

The next step for them was forgiveness. First, each of them needed to petition God for His forgiveness. As they clasped their hands in prayer, I inwardly thanked God for giving me the words to explain the issue.

Next, they have to patch up the relationship between the two of them. My personal policy is derived from scripture. God does not tell us to say "sorry," and then He will forgive our sins and cleanse us from all unrighteousness. As a result, I have made "sorry" a semi-bad word in my classroom. God commands us to confess our sins.

My students know they must say, "I was wrong for _____. Will you please forgive me?" The person being asked must reply, "Yes, I forgive you." Each student knows that "I forgive you" means "I choose not to remember."

God doesn't say, "It's okay," or "Don't worry about it"; He makes it very clear—He forgives us of our sin. By the way, He doesn't forget our sin either. God doesn't forget anything. He's God! It is so crucial to remember this piece of doctrine. God chooses to put our sin as far as the east is from the west—simply because of His love for us.

Each time that I have a session out in the hallway, I go over each of the points above and remind the children of the meaning of what they are saying. It can be extremely tedious and time-consuming, but so is building precept upon precept, line upon line (Psalm 119). Following God's principles is always fruitful.

*names changed for privacy.

Bibliography

Gibbs, Eugene S. *A Reader in Christian Education—Foundations and Basic Perspectives.* Grand Rapids, MI. Baker Book House: 1992.

Higgins, Kathleen Marie. "Friedrich Wilhelm Nietzsche" *Philosophy of Education—An Encyclopedia.* 1996 ed.

Knight, George R. *Philosophy & Education—an Introduction in Christian perspective.* Berrien Springs, MI. Andrews University Press: 1992.

Layman, George. *Philosophy of Christian School Education.* Colo. Springs, CO. ACSI: 1998.

Mrs. Ruth (Thomas) Verkaik, a graduate of Moody Bible Institute, and a former second grade teacher at Christian Liberty Academy, Arlington Heights, Illinois, now resides in Michigan with her husband, Mike, and three lovely children.

I'm Not an Addict. I Can Stop Anytime!
Addictions: When and How to Help

Ed Welch, in his book *Addictive Behavior*, defines addiction as a worship disorder. "Instead of worshipping the divine king, addicts worship idols that temporarily satisfy physical desire. Addiction is bondage to the rule of a substance, activity, or state of mind, which then becomes the center of life, defending itself from the truth so that even bad consequences don't bring repentance."

During recent counseling of addicts and their spouses, one passage of Scripture, more than any other, surfaced repeatedly. This chapter will share with you *how and when to help someone with an addiction*. The principles in this chapter are derived from Luke 15's prodigal son. Luke 15 is such a familiar passage that I was astonished by its clear teaching on addiction as I restudied it. My prayer is that you will learn as much as I have from this it.

Describing the Addict

DISRESPECT FOR HUMAN AUTHORITY—15:12

It was not uncommon for a father to bestow a "gift" on one of his children prior to the division of the inheritance (Gen. 25:6). But it is highly irregular and brash of a child to demand "the share of the estate that falls to me." The estate was divided upon the death of the testator. In reality, this young man wished for his father's death so he could gain access to his inheritance. This young man valued his freedom more than the loving care and advice of his father.

Addicts are no different. They demand their own way. They live for their own agenda. Everyone surrounding them are pawns to be moved to achieve a state of self-centered pleasure. People are incidental resources for a greater personal fulfillment. The addict has no regard for the hurt or pain inflicted by his egocentricity. Self-interest rules. Personal fulfillment is always the ultimate goal in the life of the addict. The addict says, *"I know what's best for me."*

DISRESPECT FOR DIVINE AUTHORITY—15:13

The father divides up the estate and the young man receives his legal portion of one-third (Deut. 21:17). Several days later the boy leaves. How is disrespect for divine authority seen here? How did the boy dishonor his father through the inheritance? The inheritance, at least a large portion of it, was commodities. The boy liquidated the land, livestock, and grain to get cash. He sold his portion of the inheritance. Is this so bad? Wasn't he free to do with the inheritance as he wished?

No! According to Leviticus 25:23 and Numbers 36:7, the inheritance was to remain within the family. God said don't sell or trade it. If it was used to pay debts, the Year of Jubilee (every fifty years) returned the family inheritance. One reason for this law was to prevent monopolies. An example of this principle is found in 1 Kings 21:3 where King Ahab solicits Naboth to part with his family inheritance.

The addict acts in kind. They take the riches and goodness of God (that are designed to produce repentance, Rom. 2:4) and exchange them for the paltry pickings of the world's pleasures for a season (Rom. 1:23). They often assert that they have the right do act as they wish, and what they spend their money on or how they live is their business. Anyone who challenges them is sticking their nose in where it doesn't belong. They assume God's position as owner rejecting the responsibility of stewardship. The addict says, *"I can do what I want."*

SQUANDERING RESOURCES—15:13

The boy packs everything up. He has no plans of returning. There is no looking back. He wants his freedom. He is convinced this is the only way to find happiness.

The text says, "he squandered his estate with loose living." Remember that he received one-third of what his father had. From the context, it appears that the father was a wealthy man. The word "squandered" is rendered "winnow." To winnow means to take grain and toss it up in the air, allowing a breeze to blow away the light chaff while the heavier grain falls back to the ground.

This boy was throwing his father's estate to the wind. The word "loose" explains how he did this. "Loose" means wasteful. Whatever the boy wanted, he bought. If he were hungry and he had a choice between a hamburger and filet mignon, he bought the filet mignon—and then wouldn't eat it all! If he was window shopping and saw the latest silk tunic from Persia, he bought it—even though he had twenty changes of clothes in his travel trunk. He had no concept of money, its value, or its fleeting nature.

The addict, because he lives for the now and is driven by momentary pleasures, takes the family inheritance and casts it to the winds of lust. He cannot produce anything of lasting value from his investment. His purchases are wasteful, either upon himself or others who live for the same cravings. The addict says, *"I'm not hurting anyone."*

DESTITUTE—15:14

How long did it take this boy to exhaust his inheritance? We do not know. But consider the child who is given $10 to spend at the beginning of a day's vacation. More than likely, the money is gone by noontime, or sooner. Then he is destitute (and whines) for the rest of the day.

This boy is no different. The good times suddenly stop. He is without friends because he is without money. He is alone. He experiences isolation. He is left with his thoughts, which accuse him of being foolish and careless. He feels the pressure within. Like Esau, he weeps, but the weeping is worldly sorrow (Heb. 12:16).

The addict feels remorse and sorrow. It is a sorrow that is filled with regret (2 Cor. 7:10). If the addict could do it all over again, he would not be as free with "drinks are on me," or "I would have bought a twenty-four inch television and not the eighty-six inch one!" It is never, "This is sinful," but it is all about how to sin differently or who can the addict find to blame for his present difficulty. The addict says, *"Next time, I'll…"*

CIRCUMSTANCES—15:14

The text is clear that a famine occurred. It was no ordinary famine, but a severe famine. It was not a localized famine where the boy could relocate and continue his loose living, but a prevailing and penetrating famine. Every hollow, village, and town was hit. We know that famines were one of God's way to discipline His rebellious people (see the books of Judges and Ruth).

Without exception, God creates a "famine" in the life of the addict. It may be termination from a job, impending eviction, mechanical failure of a car, health issues, a spouse leaving, or an arrest. The addict is given an opportunity to make a choice in that circumstance—make a wise decision and repent or a foolish decision and continue headlong in stubbornness living under the disciplining hand of God (Cain). The addict says, *"Why is this happening to me?"*

IMPOVERISHED—15:14

This young man has a lucid moment in his thinking. He begins to realize his situation is serious. He begins to see he is impoverished. The word means to come late, be behind, come short or be in want. He becomes conscious that he is broke. There is no one to lend him aid because everyone is experiencing the famine. He has lost all of his friends. This realization has come a bit too late.

The addict comes to realize a bit too late how much time, energy, and money he has wasted. He catches a small glimpse of how his relationship with his spouse, employer, children, and church are impacted by his willfulness. The addict has regret. The addict says, *"If only I had…"*

CONNIVING—15:15

You would think that this boy has reached bottom. He sees his condition, yet he connives to maintain control of his lifestyle. He seeks employment. Instead of turning to God, he relies upon himself.

But his plan will only complicated his life. His plan heaps more sin and consequences on his shoulders—shoulders already stooped by the heavy burden of previous sinful choices.

He finds employment, and his job assignment is feeding pigs. He hopes to start generating income. If he can do this, he can weather the financial storm, get back on his feet, and return to his lifestyle. His situation, so he thinks, is only temporary.

His solution complicates his life. No Jew was to be in contact with pigs. God called them unclean, and everyone who came in contact with them became unclean (Lev. 11:3–8).

The addict may seem like he comprehends his situation, may shed tears, and may speak in terms of seriously seeking intervention, but he continues to connive to alleviate the hardships of his sin. His determination is not to change, but to adapt to the pressing circumstances and hang tough until they pass. The addict says, *"If I do this...."*

FATALISTIC—15:16

This young man is desperate. His plan is not working. He thinks all is lost. In desperation, he contemplates eating the food he fed the pigs. If you have ever "slopped" pigs, like I have, you must be pretty desperate to even think about eating what pigs eat.

He is still not broken. You continue to see his conniving as he begs for food. God closed the windows of Heaven and the hearts of men. The boy only displays remorse for his circumstances. There is no repentance for his sin.

The addict operates in much the same fashion. The despair overwhelms them. Nobody cares. They may talk of suicide. The plan they enacted against counsel is backfiring. They feel out of control. But they are not broken. Like the prodigal, they are still looking for someone else to "feed" them solutions. They are reluctant to assume their responsibility for change. The addict says, *"Nobody understands or cares."*

Counseling the Addict

If you are living with someone who is an addict, counseling an addict, or know of someone as described above, let me offer you a word of caution. I believe we make the mistake of rushing in when we see the person destitute, or we see their circumstances increasing in difficulty, or they can't pay the rent. Proverbs 19:19 addresses the personal consequences of rescuing a man given to anger. In principle, you can replace anger with any life-dominating sin. "A man given to cocaine shall bear the penalty, for if you rescue him, you will only have to do it again." Or, "A man given to alcohol (gambling, adultery, etc.) shall bear the penalty, for if you rescue him, you will only have to do it again." Psychology calls this enabling the person to remain in the life-dominating sin. I believe the following must be evident so our counsel will have the greatest effect.

AN AWAKENING—15:17

The word "but" in the Bible is fantastic. The word signals hope in the midst of impossibility. "*But* when he came to his senses," signals a change of perspective. Before, when the boy was impoverished, his viewpoint was how to deal with the externals, the pressures he was experiencing. Here, the idea is coming to his senses. It means arriving at a correct self-estimation, or personal evaluation, or consciousness. The perspective is inward.

The addict must take personal inventory. He must take stock of his life, not solely based on what surrounds him, but what lies within him. How did he get where he is? How have his actions impacted his life? The lives of others? What harm has he caused to others and himself? I liken this to Isaiah's experience with God. When Isaiah saw God for who He was, Isaiah saw himself for who he was. When the addict is able to see God for who He is, then the addict should have little problem seeing himself as he really is.

REALISTIC THINKING—15:17

The prodigal, until this very moment, had no hope. As he begins to think about what he selfishly walked away from, the foolish decisions he made, and the hurt he caused, he becomes hopeful. He knows his father treats the slaves with respect and makes full provision for them. He thinks he has lost his "sonship," but is confident that his father will show kindness and allow him to return as a slave.

The addict must know there is hope when he returns. A *lot* is lost, but not *all* is lost! Life was better under authority, counsel, and divine patterns of living. Freedom did not turn out to be all it was cracked up to be. The serpent offered autonomy, but only produced slavery.

AN INITIAL GODLY DECISION—15:18

Clear thinking produces godly decisions. The prodigal decides he will return home. He had enough of the "good" life. But he also makes another decision—to assume full and complete responsibility for his actions. He is willing to own up to the hurt and pain his selfishness caused. Going back would be easy. Biblically "owning up" to what he did is humbling.

The addict must act in kind. He must make a godly decision to return. He must return to his home, to a spouse, job, church. But he must "own up" to his actions in his home, to his spouse, boss, or church. *Before assimilation comes humiliation (brokenness).* The addict cannot merely return home and resume playing house. In fact, I advocate, if the one with the life dominating sin has left the home, it is mandatory that a biblical restoration strategy be put into place prior to allowing the person back in the home.

APPROPRIATE ACTIONS—15:20

Like the Prodigal, the addict must follow through with this clear thinking. He must act on what he has been thinking. He must arise and return with the intention to act upon the illumination in his heart.

CONFESSION—15:21

The prodigal confessed his sin to God and to his father. Notice the order: first, upward (God), then outward (father). The best way to demonstrate humble repentance, removing doubt of insincerity, is for the addict to first start with God. When God breaks the addict, the addict will always look up into the face of the one he offended with humility (see the publican and the Pharisee—Luke 18:10–14).

RESTORATION—15:22-24

The father restored the prodigal. Symbols of fellowship were bestowed. The restoration was not private. It was conducted with great celebration. The prodigal did not walk on eggshells. The slate was clear and clean.

Likewise, the addict must receive symbols of restoration as trust is rebuilt (2 Cor. 2:7–8). The addict must know he is forgiven and that there is a desire by those he offended to rebuild the relationship.

Until the addict stops saying: "I know what's best for me," "I can do what I want," "I'm not hurting anyone," "Next time, I'll ..." "Why is this happening to me?" "If only I had ..." "If I do this ..." "Nobody understands or cares," you will not be able to counsel effectively.

Here are some resources I recommend that can help you work with an addict.
Addictions: Banquet at the Grave. Ed Welch
The Heart of Addictions. Mark E. Shaw
Divine Intervention. Mark E. Shaw

Practically Perfect in Every Way—Part 1

Pouncing on Perfectionism

A clip in the family movie, *Mary Poppins*, shows Mary, played by Julie Andrews, unpacking her carpet bag as she is employed by Mr. Banks to become Jane and Michael Banks's nanny. She removes some pretty ridiculous articles. One article is her hand held tape measure. The camera zooms in as Mary Poppins draws out the tape measure. At the end of the tape it reads: "Mary Poppins—Practically Perfect in Every Way." She smiles. All is well with the world—and Mary!

Do you feel like what you accomplish is never quite good enough? Do you often put off tasks waiting to get them just right? Do you feel you must give more than 100 percent in everything you do or else you will be mediocre or even a failure? Have you ever thought or said, "None of my accomplishments ever meet my standards." Or, "I avoid answering questions or even giving opinions because I may say something dumb." What about, "If I don't get all As (100% correct or the best grade in the class) that tells me that I am a failure." Or, "I delay completion of projects because I cannot get them just right (like they should be)." These are questions or thoughts that the modern Mary Poppinses entertain. Most of the modern-day Poppinses are not smiling!

Defining or Describing Perfectionism[1]

- Perfectionism can be defined as a personality trait characterized by a compulsive effort to eliminate all flaws and blemishes from one's behavior and the product of that behavior.
- According to Webster, it is a disposition that regards anything short of perfect as unacceptable.
- Perfectionism is not the healthy pursuit of excellence, as most people tend to believe, but rather it is the compulsive striving toward unrealistic goals.

- Perfectionism is a learned internal motivation to strive for perfection based on the belief that self-worth is equated with performance.
- Perfectionism is a set of beliefs, feelings and behaviors aimed at excessively high and unattainable goals.

The American Psychological Association says there are at least three different types of perfectionism: other-oriented, self-oriented, and socially prescribed.

The other-oriented involves demanding that others meet exaggerated and unrealistic standards. The self-oriented involves exceedingly high, self-imposed unrealistic standards and intensive self-scrutiny and criticism in which there is an inability to accept flaw, fault, or failure within oneself. The socially prescribed perfectionist holds the belief that others maintain unrealistic and exaggerated expectations that are difficult, if not impossible, to meet, but one must meet these standards to win approval and acceptance.

Linda Kreger Silverman defines perfectionism differently when she writes that perfectionism is the result of excellence. The root of excellence is perfectionism. She writes that all gifted people are perfectionist. She cites Nobel laureates, Olympians, and world-class scholars and artists.

Other Descriptions

- An irrational belief that you or your environment must be perfect.
- You must strive to be the best, reach the ideal, and never make a mistake.
- There is an all-pervasive attitude that whatever you attempt in life must be done letter-perfect with no deviation or mistakes.
- There can be no slip ups or inconsistencies, a habit developed from youth that keeps you constantly alert to the imperfections, no failing, and no weakness in yourself and others.

- A level of consciousness that keeps you ever-vigilant to any deviations from the norm, the guidelines or the way things are "supposed to be."
- The underlying present motive is the fear of failure, fear of rejection by others, which is why you may be fearful of success with a rigid, moralistic outlook that does not allow for human mistakes or errors.
- An inhibiting factor that keeps you from making a commitment to change habitual, unproductive behavior out of fear of not making the change "good enough."
- Finally the belief that no matter what you attempt, it is never "good enough" to meet your own or others' expectations.

Proposed Causes[2]

According to Bauer and Anderson (1989), perfectionism can be traced to eating disorders. Psychologist Dr. Sidney J. Blatt, Ph.D. (Yale) cites that perfectionism is a result of deep-seated feelings of inferiority and vulnerability forcing the individual into an endless cycle of self-defeating over-striving in which each task and enterprise becomes another threatening challenge. Carl Jung (1875–1961) has suggested that perfectionism is the result of some punitive childhood experience as a toddler, which creates distortions. Alfred Adler (1870–1937) suggests that because the child was made to feel incompetent and ineffective, the child over compensates to regain this innate "will to power." Others say that it may be caused by a parental style characterized by authoritarianism combined with conditional love.

How a Perfectionist Thinks

1. Everything in life must be done perfectly. The perfectionist oftentimes is frustrated because the standard of perfection is very random. The standard varies from person to person that the perfectionist attempts to please.
2. It is unacceptable to make a mistake. The perfectionist's life is stringent, hyper-structured, lacking spontaneity, and perhaps

legalistic. These are ways that a perfectionist insulates themselves from personal disappointment and having to deal with perceived failure.

3. You must always reach the ideal no matter what. Here the perfectionist places themselves in harm's way to attain the ideal. The total makeup of the perfectionist striving to achieve the ideal is subject to levels of self-destructiveness.

4. If those in authority say this is the way it is supposed to be, then that is the way it is supposed to be. Any creativity on the perfectionist's part, and subsequent rejection, would be viewed as a failure. The perfectionist disappointed the authority figure by not completely complying with their wishes.

5. You are a loser if you cannot be perfect. The perfectionist's value and worth are dependent upon the approval of others. If perfectionists do not get the approval or what they perceive as adequate praise, they feel like losers.

6. It is what you achieve rather than who you are that is important. Satisfying goals are vital. The intensity of the goal for the perfectionist, the expenditure of energy, and high of emotions are more important than the development of character through the goal.

7. The perfectionist thinks: "There is no sense in trying to do something unless I can do it perfectly."

8. "I have no value in life unless I am successful. I am successful if I complete the project not only on time but ahead of schedule. I am valuable because I earn more money for the company than anyone else. I am valuable because they awarded me the promotion to senior vice president of marketing."

9. "If I have a failure or experience a setback in my efforts to change, then I should give up." Perfectionists struggle with modification. Change bothers them. Adjustments challenge their self-esteem.

10. "The ideal is what is real; unless I reach the ideal I am a failure." A perfectionist can dream, but struggles with wrapping his or her mind around the dream in such a way that brings the dream to fruition because the dream is an ideal. The dream is something

that could be but is not certain because it lacks substance for the perfectionist.

11. "There are so many roadblocks and pitfalls to keep me from succeeding. It is better just to give up and forget my goal." Perfectionists are more than capable. They usually are the cream of the crop in their field. They are creative geniuses. Their racing creative minds also stall from unfounded obstacles of "What if."

12. "Unless I am Number One, there is no sense in trying. Everyone knows what Number Two is. To win is the only acceptable goal." An A- is unacceptable if someone else got an A+. A "Well done" is interpreted as failure if the perfectionist does not hear, "Wow! What a terrific job! We could not have done it without you."

13. "If you fail in your efforts to achieve a goal, just give up. It must be too hard to achieve." Some perfectionists will undertake a project, but the moment a change is presented, the perfectionist immediately resigns. The perfectionists often come up with plausible excuses for removing themselves from the project, but inside it is because they viewed a modification as a failure. They construe criticism as a failure.

14. "You must always strive to reach the ideal in everything you do because it is in the achievement of the ideal that you give meaning to life." This thought process finds the perfectionist on the "project treadmill." They move from project to project. They may mentally accept the accolades of the boss or spouse, but vow to do better on the next project. Perfectionists are relentless and tireless in their efforts. They can be exhausting to be around, to watch, to work with, or to work for.

15. "Don't ever let anyone know what goal you're working on. That way they won't consider you a failure if you don't reach it." This self-secrecy is a time bomb. Usually, this mentality does not diffuse the impending explosion. Often, the explosion others witness confuses them. The explosion often appears to be related to an insignificant event, but the perfectionist knows what it is related to.

16. "It you can't do it right the first time, why try to do it at all?" The committed perfectionist is a procrastinator. Often, it is related to

25

the fear of the unknown. They are concern about the outcome. Perfectionists believe they should be able to control the outcome, but they can't.

17. "There is only one way to reach a goal: the right way." The right way is the perfectionist's way. This "right way" eliminates others' assistance because their way may be different. The "right way" often is biased, and creates tension when a group must work together toward the common goal.

18. "It takes to much effort and energy to reach a goal. I save myself the aggravation and discouragement by not setting goals for myself." This is the perfectionist's fear. The perfectionist wants to avert others' rejection and disapproval.

19. "I'll never be able to change and grow the way I want to, so why try?" The perfectionist often seeks to imitate another's success, achievements, and accomplishments. Another's success becomes the perfectionist's standard. Failure to be like their example means failure. The perfectionist is imitating is the tool of measurement, and the tape measure says, "Not perfect."

20. "I am a human being prone to error, frailty and imperfections; therefore, I won't be able to accomplish things in a perfect or ideal way. I'll just give up on achieving any of my goals or desires."

Examining Our Findings through a Biblical Lens

First, I think we would agree that being perfection is a myth. It just doesn't exist. Only the Sovereign Lord of the universe and our Creator is perfect—without flaw, always accomplishing His goals (creationism: it was good, it was very good), flawless in character, and always presents to His creatures reasonable, attainable goals. The value and worth of creation is intrinsic, and not contingent on His performance (worthy of all worship and adoration); He welcomes the impossible for Himself in His power, empowers His creation to face the impossibilities (our perspective and usually under the sun), and is gracious, forgiving, and merciful to His creation when it falls short of His glory.

Second, after reading how the world defines and describes perfectionism, it is imperative that we evaluate these descriptions using the Bible. I see the following biblical issues.

- Perfectionism changes the God-given personality God breathed into every human being at birth (how God has created me as a person in will, emotions, intellect). This occurs through the imputation of the Adamic nature and the cultivation of that Adamic nature through nurture.

- Perfectionists either compare themselves to or are dissatisfied with God's creative and redemptive work. The psalmist reminds us that we are fearfully and wonderfully made. God cannot be charged with what we perceive as a "birth defect"! The perfectionist tries to charge God with short-changing them, which in turn hampers them from being successful.

- Perfectionists struggle with accepting God's creative work and therefore are lazy in working in concert with the sovereignty of God to develop these God-ordained qualities. The perfectionist who believes they cannot achieve or do things perfectly becomes unwilling to try. This fear or stubbornness is an excuse to be uncooperative with God's will. The perfectionist says, "I feel I cannot, so I will not." God says, "You can do all things through me, who strengthens you."

- A perfectionist has developed a thought process that critically reflects in judgment upon God, others, or self. The perfectionist often blames others or themselves (which is an attack upon God) for their failures and lack of success. It is much easier for the perfectionist to point the finger at others than to accept personal responsibility for their unbiblical thought life and subsequent sinful actions.

- Perfectionism is an ungodly measuring device for a person's value, worth and identity. The thought life of the perfectionist is their value, worth, and identity is found in what others think and say about them. Man's evaluation of a fellow human being is arbitrary and subjective. Ask any five people their opinion on a matter, and you will get more disagreement than consensus. Therefore, the perfectionist is usually living with emotional and mental imbalance in their equilibrium.

- Perfectionists refuse to accept the divine revelation that they live in a sin-sick and cursed world that is waiting for its redemption when the sons of God are revealed (Rom. 8:22–23). Their refusal to accept this divine truth impedes their personal journey of sanctification including all of their life's struggles, victories, and lessons to be learned between the struggles and victories (Rom. 7:1–13). Much of what impedes the perfectionist from "success" cannot be controlled. Changes may occur because those authorizing the project secured more information that warrants a change. Or a product for the project did not arrive on time through no fault of the perfectionist. There was a snowstorm on the eastern seaboard. The perfectionists that blame themselves for things not in their control or under their authorized control in essence are attacking God's sovereignty. The perfection says, "I could have done better if I were in charge."

- Perfectionists become transfixed with the approval of others rather than hearing the approval of God, "Well, done thou good and faithful servant" (Luke 19:17). This is the fear of man. The fear of man is the antithesis of the fear of God. The fear of God can be understood as every thought, word, and deed is done in the presence of a holy God who hears and judges. If the fear of man is the opposite, then the perfectionist's thoughts, words, and deeds are done in the presence of another human being who hears and judges. The perfectionist both fears and craves the approval of this fellow human being. This is idolatry.

- Perfectionism creates abominable, unreasonable, and illogical scales between success and failure. The scale is abominable because the tool for measurement is finite and subjective as opposed to God's objective, compassionate, and infinite measurement. The scale is unreasonable because the measuring tape is arbitrary and unmerciful. There is no grace and forgiveness. There is only condemnation and guilt. The scale is illogical because what is used for one situation becomes different for another situation. This scale is a form of mental torture.

In this chapter, we defined or described perfectionism. We looked at what psychology claims are the causes of perfectionism. We took considerable space to examine how a perfectionist thinks. Most importantly, we examined these findings through a biblical lens.

In the next chapter we will discover how Jesus interacted with the perfectionists of His day—the Pharisees—and we will discover timeless principles for the perfectionist today.

Sources Cited:
[1] various Web locations cited below:
www.spicewoodgroup.com
www.gifteddevelopment.com
www.couns.ucis.edu
www.counseling swt.edu
www.usfweb.usg.edu
www.coping.org
www.apa.org
www.clarocet.com
www.bestyears.com
[2] ibid.

Practically Perfect in Every Way—Part 2
Pouncing on Perfectionism

In the previous chapter, we began to explore the myth about perfectionism, and it's just that—a myth! We took time to define perfectionism from several perspectives. We invested an extensive amount of time to understand how a perfectionist thinks. Then we waded through the volume of material to examine our findings through a biblical lens. What we concluded in our last chapter were the following eight points.

1. Perfectionism changes the God-given personality (soul) God breathed into every human being at birth.

2. Perfectionists either compare themselves to or are dissatisfied with God's creative and redemptive work.

3. Perfectionists struggle with accepting God's creative work and therefore are lazy in working in concert with the sovereignty of God to develop these God-ordained qualities.

4. A perfectionist has developed a thought process that critically reflects in judgment on God, others, and self.

5. Perfectionism is an ungodly measuring device for a person's value, worth, and identity.

6. Perfectionists refuse to accept the divine revelation that they live in a sin-sick and cursed world. Their refusal to accept this impedes their personal journey of sanctification including all of its struggles, victories and lessons to be learn between the struggles and victories.

7. Perfectionists become obsessed with the approval of others rather than desiring the approval of God.

8. Perfectionism creates abominable and unbalanced scales for evaluating success and failure.

This chapter deals with how to help the perfectionist. Counsel from the medical-social-psychological-religious communities suggests the following ways to help a perfectionist.

- Give yourself credit for the small accomplishments you make every day.
- Give yourself permission to make mistakes.
- Accept yourself as a human being.
- Forgive yourself for mistakes or failing.
- Love yourself.
- Learn to focus on your successes rather than perceived failure.
- Set realistic and reachable goals.
- Focus on the process of doing an activity, not just on the result.
- Set strict time limits on tasks. When the time limit is up, move on to something else.
- When you make a mistake, ask yourself, "What is the worst thing that could happen if I don't do this task perfectly?"

And many other suggestions. Some may be helpful, while others are psychological and unbiblical.

As I mulled over how I would counsel a perfectionist, my mind was drawn to our Lord. He dealt with perfectionists nearly every day of His life on earth! Who were those perfectionists? The Pharisees! It was their way or the highway!

I began to review the passages in the Gospels where Jesus encountered the perfectionist and how He counseled them. From this cursory study (someone can always expand on your original work, and I welcome others to do so—we can all learn more from each other), the following principles surfaced.

Matthew 9:9–13
This passage records the calling of Matthew as a disciple. Matthew was a tax-collector. His brethren despised him because of his occupation. A tax-collector inflated the amount collected in order to make a living. Rome did not care provided the base amount was collected

and submitted. A tax-collector could become quite wealthy, like Zaccheus. Matthew "follows Jesus," and he invites some other colleagues to a dinner party so he can introduce them to Jesus. The Pharisees are shocked that Jesus, who claims to be the Messiah, is associating with such unsavory characters.

The Pharisees measured their status in life by standing upon the shoulders of others who did not measure up. They pointed to "what they did," not who they were and what they should be "becoming." Their elevation was based on a self-righteous standard. This resulted in a superior attitude over whom they deemed as inferior. Therefore, Jesus was inferior because He did not meet their preconceived qualifications. This would result in a conflict.

Jesus' response provides insight on counseling someone who is like this. Christ stated that He desired (*thelo*) that they learn and practice compassion. Our Lord's desire for these perfectionists is not a mere longing. Christ desired that they would *will* or *determine* to look at situations from a divine viewpoint, not their rigid, "it has to be this way" viewpoint. The compassion necessary to avoid perfectionism is described as *mercy*. Mercy refers to kindness or goodwill towards the miserable and the afflicted, joined with a desire to help them. Rather than imposing self-judgment based on a human standard, a perfectionist must examine each and every situation from a divine viewpoint. This promotes humility and debases pride.

Matthew 12:14–17
The disciples of John ask Jesus' disciples why they were not fasting like they or the Pharisees did. Each group practiced fasting as a ritual. Any deviation from this practice was viewed dimly.

Jesus explains the deviation from what is understood as normal. He uses three illustrations to clarify what the Pharisees perceived as inappropriate conduct by His disciples: that of the bridegroom, the garment, and the wineskin.

The perfectionist becomes obsessed by a procedure. Any deviation from that procedure (deemed right in his own eyes) can produce conflict.

What can help the perfectionist is to be taught that new or different ways may be preferable and even superior to former things. Paul said that old things have passed away (past tense, and they remain passed) and behold all things are becoming new (present tense). Proverbs reminds us that there is a way that seems right to a man, but the end leads to death (14:12, 16:25). Help the perfectionist to accept change. Look at change from God's point of view, not a personal affront to what they believe is right.

Matthew 12:1–8
Jesus and His disciples traveled through a grain field on the Sabbath and they became hungry. While passing through, they picked some of the grain, broke away the husk, and enjoyed the morsels inside. This practice was acceptable according to the law.

However, the Pharisees deemed the situation as unlawful. They interpreted the disciples's actions as working on the Sabbath by threshing, grinding, and preparing. Jesus confronts these perfectionists, using logic to address their illogical accusation. He cites what Ahimelech the priest did for David, and how the priest themselves are violating the Sabbath by exchanging the Consecrated Bread.

Jesus points out that human relationships are more important than upholding a notion or idea that rests on misinformation or tradition. I find it interesting as you review the Gospel accounts regarding the healings of Jesus that the Pharisees never once rejoiced when a man, woman, or family was restored to health and wholeness. The joy produced by grace was soured by legalism unless it was done their way. They majored in the minor.

Matthew 12:24–37
When a perfectionist gets "outdone," they often resort to illogical accusations because of their pride. For example, when Christ was near the zenith of His ministry. Picture this: the crowds grew. Each miracle brought the crowds to their feet, and they lifted their voices in praise. When the Pharisees heard and saw these miracles and could not refute what was happening, they charged Christ with using the power of Satan to perform these miracles.

Jesus used logic in addressing this problem. "How can Satan war against himself? Why would Satan grant power to the Son of God to accomplish an act of righteousness?"

There may be times when a perfectionist intensifies his aggressive ways in order to cling to a position that is senseless. Arguments escalate over insignificant and non-eternal matters of life. The discussion becomes heated in order [1] to be heard because he doesn't feel like he is being heard (another words he is not getting his way), or [2] to bully and manipulate another into submission, claiming he is only trying to help the other person see the error of *their* way.

We can help the perfectionist by employing a logical presentation. Stated differently, you must not resort to using the inflamed emotional approach. Logic must prevail. Using logic, however, is no guarantee that the person will subdue his emotion, but using the alternative can be likened to the devastation of September 11. The persistent display and communication of truth will set some perfectionists free, but for others, like the Pharisees, they retreat, regroup, and find something else to argue about.

Matthew 12:38–45

A perfectionist is seldom satisfied. The Pharisees asked Jesus for another sign. Up to this point, according to Ryrie's Study Bible, Jesus had performed thirteen miracles and preached the Sermon on the Mount along with several sermons. Nicodemus interviewed him, and I can only image that information spreads like wildfire among the Pharisees.

Jesus strongly rebuked them for seeking additional signs. He said that such pursuits can be considered evil and adulterous. The word "evil" carries two significant implications.

First, there is a concept of some action bringing great toils, hardships, or labors. It implies harassment, annoyance, being pressed in upon, causing pain and sorrow. Second, it reflects the nature or character of something or someone. The impossible standards the Pharisees placed upon others proceeded from within. Adulterous means unfaithful. One who commits adultery is more concerned with seeking personal fulfillment than pleasing another (spouse, God).

A perfectionist must learn to accept what cannot be changed or what is already done. The lack of acceptance pushes limits, creates fractured relationships, and promotes unbearable pressure for the perfectionist and those who live with them. Jesus tells them the evidence is ample. Rejecting the evidence only makes the future inevitably ominous. What a perfectionist needs is to learn contentment. Paul said, near the end of his life, that he had learned to be content in whatever phase of life he found himself. His satisfaction was not another book written, not another conciliatory meeting, or the like. His satisfaction and contentment was marveling at the work of God through Him and to Him in whom he makes his boast.

Matthew 15:1–9
Perfectionists have "laundry lists." If a proselyte performed perfectly nine religious observations, the perfectionist (Pharisee) always something else to add to the list of "do's and don'ts."

In this passage, the Pharisees were bewildered as to why Christ's disciples did not wash their hands before eating. It is not that the disciples were not washing their hands, but that they were not washing their hands according to the traditions of the elders (perfectionists!). According to the Law, the disciples did not need to wash their hands, but only the priests (Lev. 22:1–16). Again, it was not "did they wash their hands," but "how" they washed their hands.

Jesus recognized what the Pharisees were attempting to do. Christ revealed the wickedness of their heart by reminding them of the Law in contrast to the tradition of the elders. He pointed to the Law commanding the children to care for their parents. However, He continued, if the child could be persuaded that a greater good would be achieved by donating that money to the synagogue, the child would be absolved from the Law's penalty. The Pharisees misused the Scriptures for their own personal gain and advantage.

The perfectionist is prone to supporting notions and preferences by using Scripture out of context. They do this because they desire personal pleasure more than pleasing God. For some perfectionists, it is a matter of receiving rather than giving, of being served rather than serving. Scripture explains scripture. Therefore, counsel through the complete Word.

Matthew 15:12–14
There is no direct confrontation with a Pharisee (perfectionist). What is interesting to note from this passage is the disciple's observation of how the Pharisees reacted to Christ's instruction about serving rather than being served. The disciples asked Jesus if He recognized that the Pharisees were offended by what He said. The word "offend" means "to be offended in one, to see in another what I disapprove of and what hinders me from acknowledging his authority or to cause one to judge unfavorably or unjustly of another." The Pharisees judged Jesus with disapproval because He did not support or endorse their traditions. In fact, Jesus' honest and open remarks were viewed as opposing them. This created antagonism.

A perfectionist can be stubborn and hard-headed. They can become so thoroughly convinced that they are right and ruin relationships when they feel others oppose them (when they do not agree with them). When a perfectionist stoops to such depths, Jesus says, leave them alone. God alone is able to convict and correct. Attempting any further assistance may result in the person helping the perfectionist to be captivated by the perfectionist's blindness as to also follow (Proverbs 26:4)

Matthew 19:3–9
The Pharisees were legalists, and so are many perfectionists. The Pharisees were looking for "loop-holes." They sought Jesus out and asked an ambiguous question that improperly answered would impugn the character of God (similar to what Satan did in Genesis 3 with Eve: "Hath God said…"). The Pharisees do not run the gamut as so many perfectionists do. "What about…" Or "Then how about…" Or "Well, maybe if…." They asked an open-ended ambiguous question.

In such an atmosphere of "what ifs," it can be very easy to become emotionally embroiled that the heart of the issue is lost. Jesus remains focused and responded using known biblical facts to answer their question.

A perfectionist presses against the truth of God's Word, rather than yielding to it. You see how the Pharisees used "association data," that is focused on one aspect of the dialogue and responding to that area moving further away from the issue. This means when working with a perfectionist guard, against being removed from the issue. This verbal exchange is exhausting. A person usually says, "Whatever…" to avoid continuation of a meaningless conversation. No one matures or deals with the character deficiencies by resigning.

Luke 5:21–24

The scribes and the Pharisees joined ranks to search for some accusation against that young rabbi who was growing in popularity. Christ was heralded as one who spoke with authority, unlike the religious leaders. They witnessed Christ's proclamation to forgive sins. They reasoned among themselves that God alone forgives sins—not man.

These religious leaders had constructed in their minds, and thus had taught the people, a prototype of who and what the Messiah would be like. They concluded that Christ did not measure up to their ideals. The Pharisees and scribes were critical and misinformed because of their self-imposed perceptions.

A perfectionist must look at the obvious, not what might have been, could have been, or should have been. Something different is acceptable. That which is unexpected is permissible. Just because something does not fit the mold or falls short of the pattern is not reason to be judgmental or critical. The creativity of God must receive praise, not punitive pronouncement. Every good and perfect gift comes down from the Father of lights who promotes diversity and variety as the God of creativity.

Luke 6:6–11

The two main objections against Jesus by the Pharisees were performing miracles on the Sabbath and breaking the traditions of the elders.

This passage found the watchdogs of legalism barking about a miracle on the Sabbath. They were looking for a reason to accuse Jesus.

A man with a withered hand attended synagogue. Christ was teaching. Christ knew there was hypocrisy between what He was teaching and how this man was being treated. He was unproductive to the Jewish society, he was deformed (probably due to some sin), and he was a financial drain on the community.

Jesus wanted to teach the Pharisees a lesson. He asked if it were lawful to heal or do harm on the Sabbath? No answer—duh! What do you expect?

Perfectionists, when confronted with biblical truth, are often unable to answer without implicating themselves. But their silence loudly condemns them.

A perfectionist must be taught to see the greater good outside themselves. A perfectionist may often uphold a tradition, belief, custom, or practice that is harmful to relationships. They must be shown how to tear down the walls of self, tradition, and pride to build relationships. Right becomes wrong when perceptions destroy relationships. A sidebar: You can tell the perfectionist heart posture by their response—here it is rage and a murderous heart.

Luke 11:37–44
Jesus was invited to dine with a Pharisee. The Pharisee was shocked at what he observed. Jesus sat down to lunch and didn't ceremonially washed his hands! It was not as if Jesus did not wash His hands, but it is a case of "how" He washed His hands. Remember, the Pharisees had a ritual for washing hands. Evidently, Jesus did not do exactly as they required.

What words did Jesus provide for this Pharisee? He reminded him that all the externals might have been in place, lined up in nice little rows, nothing out of place, but the inside could still be full of distain, evil, and taking away instead of giving. This man was willing to settle for reformation, but avoid transformation. He looked for a procedure rather than a process.

The key verse is 41. Our Lord demands that the perfectionist offers himself first, foremost, and all that he does in love. Then what flows from this wellspring will be acceptable. Love is more interested in the moral condition of the heart than the moral condition of unwashed hands. The way one does things is acceptable when the motivation for doing those things come from a heart of love for the object served.

Luke 15:1–32

Here we read the famous parable regarding the lost things. There are three divisions, but only one parable. We have the lost sheep, lost coin, and the lost son. This parable was given in response to the accusation of the Lord fellowshipping with certain types of people who were unsavory—less desirable for one of such stature to spend time with.

After reading and pondering this parable, one nearly concludes that the Pharisees' attitude toward people were that they were expendable. They did not go out of their way to pursue broken or hurting relationships. Neither did they see the need to mend relationships. Their joy seemed to be in the "good riddance" philosophy—that these troubling people (so deemed by them) were dismissed, shunned, and rejected. They were made to feel inferior.

As you read, you see a stark contrast between their outlook on troubled people and what Jesus described. Christ described the festive joy and celebration over the lost item. These perfectionists were willing to reject God's purpose and calling in their lives towards other for the sake of appearance. Their holiness and piety were measured by what they did and how others viewed them. The condition of their persona before men was more valued than the condition of their heart before their Creator God. Their measurement was inferior because it left out God—what God thought of them. In fact, the Pharisees attempted to justify their spiritual superiority by citing the numerous items performed and at times exceeding what the law required.

The perfectionist must learn how to rejoice instead of finding fault, be glad instead of revealing the sins of others, and seek instead of being sought.

Let's summarize this chapter. We want to get a handle on all that we have learned so we will be able to help the perfectionist with biblical accuracy and insight. God wants all of us to work toward holiness, not perfection. Only God is perfect. He does not lower the bar, but clarifies the bar that has been maligned. His standard is obedience, which allows for progressive growth and maturity.

Here are a series of questions derived from the central passages in this chapter. They can provide additional data for helping the perfectionist.

1. How would God want me to view this situation?
2. In what ways can this new way of doing something make me more efficient and bring God greater glory?
3. Will my attitude or actions help or hinder this relationship?
4. Why is this so important to me? Do I feel like I'm not being heard or understood?
5. Am I trying to get my own way?
6. Am I listening to what is being said?
7. Am I frustrated and allowing my mind to go in search of something else to substantiate my side?
8. What would I change? Would the change help me to honor and obey God?
9. Do I really understand what God's Word has to say? Is this what the passage really says?
10. Have I recently lost any relationships? Am I experiencing strained or damaged relationships?
11. What might I have done to contribute to this situation? What would God want me to do to resolve this matter? What would God want me to do to avoid this matter in the future?
12. Do I ever resolve problems with people? If not, what are the reason(s) I do not?

13. Am I a person of praise, or would others say of me that I am critical?

14. How would this help to achieve the greater good, the larger picture?

15. Is my love totally free and unconditional? What can my spouse (friend, etc.) do to place a strain on our relationship?

16. By desiring this (person, place, thing), am I rejecting God's purpose and calling on my life?

How to Help Someone Who Complains

The Life of Joseph

A man decided to join a monastery. The monastery regulations allowed him to speak two words every ten years. At the end of ten years he said, "Bad food!" Ten more years went by and he said, "Hard bed!" Finally, on his thirtieth anniversary with the brothers, he thundered, "I quit!" The priest in charge quipped, "You might as well. All you do is complain anyway."

Maranatha Magazine carried the following humorous story about criticism. "The wife of a hard-to-please husband was determined to try her best to satisfy him for just one day. 'Darling,' she asked, 'what would you like for breakfast this morning?' He growled, 'Coffee and toast, grits and sausage, and two eggs—one scrambled and one fried.' She soon had the food on the table and waited for a word of praise. After a quick glance, he exclaimed, 'Well, if you didn't scramble the wrong egg!'"

We chuckle, but complaining, grumbling, or murmuring is part and parcel of American fabric. Many of us are tone deaf to the chirping of our children. Many are blind to the reality of deeply inbred complaining. From the constant murmuring of our children to the folly of our co-workers, we simply convince ourselves this is the social norm. Many of us have adopted an indifference to complaining by explaining, "Oh, that's just Dad."

How does the Bible describe and define someone who complains? The Bible uses four different Hebrew words to express the meaning of "complain." They are:

> **ANAN**—Num. 11:1, means murmur.
>
> **RIB**—Jud. 21:22, Job 33:13, means to rub, strive, contend, argue, find fault, and quarrel or to judge.
>
> **ZAAQ**—2 Sam. 19:28, means to cry out, draw attention to oneself or plight.

SIACH—Job 7:11, Ps. 55:17, means to muse, meditate, think about, and contemplate.

The Bible uses one Greek word for complain. It is **STENAZO**—Js. 5:9, which means to groan within, sigh heavily.

If the Holy Spirit were a police sketch artist, what kind of composite would He draw?

- Someone who complains is negative in speech, attitudes, and body language. If it is a beautiful day outside, they say, "It's too hot." If you found a bargain, they say, "It'll probably break before you get it home."

- Someone who complains finds the faults of others easily. They are argumentative. They harp and nag on issues. They are irritable and rub people the wrong way. They often bring out the worst in themselves and others.

- Those who complain are highly opinionated, selfish, and focused on themselves and having conversations with themselves. They display destructive self-talk.

- Someone who complains spends a lot of time thinking on negative things, rehashing scenarios; his or her mind is preoccupied with the problem regardless of the hope, answers, or solutions in his or her possession.

Here are some addition descriptions of those who complain.

- They always need to know what is going on. They have control issues.

- They often are lonely, feeling isolated, and claiming to have no friends.

- They may struggle with anger, fear, and worry.

- They are likely disobedient in an area of their life and living with guilt. It may be that the area they complain about so vehemently is their area of sin.

- They may be lazy. They are willing to show you the problem, describe the problem, and tell you what to do about the problem.
- They often lack involvement; hence, they lack commitment, diligence, and perseverance.
- Complainers are not unlike the people in the Bible. The Israelites complained about not having water to drink and food to eat. They complained about the obstacles to overcome to enjoy God's blessings, blaming others for their sinful choices.
- Complainers may be compared to the hired men who grumbled that those hired near the end of the day received the same wages as they did without working as hard. Complainers often have a distorted sense of fairness and justice.
- Complainers even grumble about the Bible and what it has to say like the Pharisees in Jesus' day.
- Complainers are rebels because they complain against divinely appointed authority. In effect, someone who complains is really saying, "*I know I can do better!*"

How do I know if I am complaining or expressing a viewpoint?

1. A person who complains attacks a person, but someone who expresses a viewpoint is attacking a problem.
2. A person who complains hurts people with their words, while someone who expresses a viewpoint wants to help people with what they say.
3. A person who complains constantly looks at the problem, whereas a person who expresses a viewpoint is searching for a solution.

The Story of Joseph—Genesis 37–44

Joseph never complained when he was asked to do something.

> Israel said to Joseph, "Are not your brothers pasturing the flock in Shechem? Come, and I will send you to them." And he said to him, "I will go" (Gen. 37:13).

Joseph never complained when his brothers displayed jealousy, hatred, and even spoke of death.

> When they saw him from a distance and before he came close to them, they plotted against him to put him to death (Gen. 37:18).

Joseph never complained when the Midianites led him off into slavery.

> Then some Midianite traders passed by, so they pulled him up and lifted Joseph out of the pit, and sold him to the Ishmaelites for twenty shekels of silver. Thus, they brought Joseph into Egypt (Gen. 37:28).

Joseph never complained when he was purchased as a slave by Potiphar.

> Judah said to his brothers, "What profit is it for us to kill our brother and cover up his blood?" (Gen. 37:36).

Joseph never complained when he was falsely accused by Potiphar's wife.

> So Joseph's master took him and put him into the jail, the place where the king's prisoners were confined; and he was there in the jail (Gen. 39:20).

Joseph never complained when people did not keep the promises they made.

> Only keep me in mind when it goes well with you, and please do me a kindness by mentioning me to Pharaoh and get me out of this house. "For I was in fact kidnapped from the land of the Hebrews, and even here I have done nothing that they should have put me into the dungeon" (Gen. 40:14–15).

Joseph never complained during the two years he was imprisoned unjustly—41:1–16.

Joseph never complained even when given the chance to get even with his brothers—chapters 42–44.

Consider this:
Is your life anywhere close in comparison to Joseph's? Has your life gone the distance comparable to Joseph? If your life is easier by comparison than Joseph's, then you have more motivation to learn how to do all things without complaining and grumbling.

If you believe your life is just as bad as Joseph's, you still have the greater advantage to live a complaint-free life like Joseph. Why? Because of the resources Joseph used. They are available to you now, today!

What Resources Did Joseph Use to Avoid a Complaining Spirit?

How can I help someone who complains?

Joseph knew that God was always with him. Joseph was never alone. No one else observed the difficulties of Joseph's life, but God did. Joseph was more concerned about pleasing God than escaping his difficulties.

> The Lord was with Joseph, so he became a successful man. And he was in the house of his master, the Egyptian. Now his master saw that the Lord was with him and how the Lord caused all that he did to prosper in his hand. But the Lord was with Joseph and extended kindness to him, and gave him favor in the sight of the chief jailer (Gen. 39:2, 3, 21).

This resource is the Sovereignty of God. The resource is used by trusting God, not complaining.

Joseph viewed all of the hard times as God's way of preparing him for a very special assignment.

> As for you, you meant evil against me, but God meant it for good in order to bring about this present result, to preserve many people alive (Gen. 50:20).

This resource is the purging and preparing work of God. This resource is used by submitting to God, not complaining.

Joseph remembered God's Word to him in the dreams.

> Then Joseph had a dream, and when he told it to his brothers, they hated him even more. He said to them, "Please listen to this dream which I have had; for behold, we were binding sheaves in the field, and lo, my sheaf rose up and also stood erect; and behold, your sheaves gathered around and bowed down to my sheaf." Then his brothers said to him, "Are you actually going to reign over us? Or are you really going to rule over us?" So they hated him even more for his dreams and for his words. Now he had still another dream, related it to his brothers, and said, "Lo, I have had still another dream; and behold, the sun and the moon and eleven stars were bowing down to me." He related it to his father and to his brothers; and his father rebuked him and said to him, "What is this dream that you have had? Shall I and your mother and your brothers actually come to bow ourselves down before you to the ground?" (Gen. 37:5–10).

This resource is the faithfulness of God. This resource is used by obeying God, not complaining.

> Do all things without grumbling or disputing; so that you will prove yourselves to be blameless and innocent, children of God above reproach in the midst of a crooked and perverse generation, among whom you appear as lights in the world, holding fast the Word of Life (Philippians 2:14–16a).

*Helping Those Who Use People and
Those Who Feel Used*

Lessons from the Life of Jephthah

Bill was a graphic designer and works for one of Chicago's leading firms. When he was first hired, the Human Resource department was impressed with his resume, portfolio, and outstanding knowledge of "the business" at such a young age. His skill rivaled those in the industry who had ten years of experience. He thought he had a bright future with the company.

During the first few years, Bill faced a number of difficult adjustments. He chalked it up to being "the low man on the totem pole." Bill believed those initial years of being overlooked, lightly esteemed, and passed over were handled successfully. He refused to allow his emotions and a runaway mindset affect his attitude or the quality of his performance.

"But those initial years of adjustments should have ended," he said to himself. *"I bring the largest amount of sales to the company. My production level exceeds the number of other designers combined."* The quality of his work earned him praises by his colleagues, industrial awards, and the admiration of his clients. Appreciative clients gave him paid vacations to their time shares.

But despite his successes, Bill's boss was generally stiff and unfriendly towards Bill. It troubled him that his boss was not this way with other co-workers. Yet, when his boss wanted a favor, when a special project or task was at hand, he always turned to Bill. He approached Bill with a smile, friendly voice, upbeat, back-slapping attitude and comment, "You are the only one that can do this for us!" Once the project was done, the customer was satisfied, and the company has deposited the fat check, it was … well, you know!

Bill was being used, and his boss was the user. The tidal waves of frustration, anger, bewilderment, and confusion rocked Bill's life. He came close to capsizing a number of times. He thought to himself, and even told his wife, "Why bother? Why try? Why do my best? They don't seem to appreciate me! Maybe I should look for another job." At this point, Bill was confident that he should be at this job. But he wonders how to avoid being used, taken advantage of, feeling like a doormat? He struggle with his Christian responsibility toward his circumstances, the company, and especially his relationship to his boss.

A person using people is not something new. It is as old as the Bible itself. Consider the following biblical examples.

- Balak used Balaam to curse the nation of Israel and Balaam used Balak to increase his bank account (Num. 22:5f).
- Abner used Ish-bosheth to advance his political career and when he failed to achieve the desired results he was willing to betray Ish-bosheth by defecting to King David (2 Sam. 3:6–10).
- Jacob used Esau to gain the birthright in Genesis 25:27–31.
- Judas used Jesus hoping to gain a powerful position in the Kingdom. When he realized Jesus' mission was spiritual and not political, he betrayed Jesus for thirty pieces of silver. (Luke 22:4–6).
- Adonijah used Bathsheba by requesting to marry Abiahag in order to usurp the throne from Solomon (1 Kings 1:5–9, 2:19–22).
- Jezebel used worthless men to accuse falsely Naboth of blasphemy in order to siege Naboth's family inheritance that her husband Ahab wanted for a vegetable garden just outside his window (1 Kings 21:2–3, 5–16).
- Haman used King Ahasuerus to advance his own political career (Esther 3:8–11).
- Simon attempted to use Peter to purchase the gift of the Holy Spirit so he could continue to maintain power over the people (Acts 8:9, 13, 18–19).
- King Herod used the Magi to secure information so he could eliminate Jesus whom he viewed as a threat to his monarchy (Matt. 2:7–8, 16).

- Sarah used Hagar to secure God's promise of a son (Gen. 16:1–2).
- James and John's mother tried to use Jesus to secure positions of prominence for her sons (Matt. 20:20).
- Samson used his parents to fulfill his lust by marrying a wife from the uncircumcised Philistines (Judges 14:2–3).
- Nabal used people to increase his profit and loss statement by defrauding his workers and reneging on his contracts (1 Sam. 25:3).
- Sisera used Jael to hide him and provide safety from the pursuing Israeli armies (Judges 4:18).
- Zaccheus used his own brethren to live a life of luxury by over taxing them (Luke 19:7).

Characteristics of a User

What are some characteristics of a "user"? What characteristics can be drawn from this infamous list?

It may be hard to admit, but saints can be users. Many of the people just cited were God's covenant people, under the sign of circumcision. Nevertheless, they used other believers for their own personal gain. Such relationships are superficial and rooted in selfishness.

Many times users take advantage of subordinate relationships such as the employer-employee, husband-wife, parent-child, or pastor-congregation. This type of using reflects tyrannical leadership in its worst form, especially when it occurs within the family of God. These actions are an abuse of power. Such abuse erodes the fabric of oneness in the family of God.

Users are selfish. They often have ulterior motives when they show kindness. Conditional love is often the only affection they show. They are more interested in dominating people rather than partnering with them. They are often consumed with self rather than controlled by service. Users are prone to being critical rather than commending.

Those who are used swindle themselves into thinking each time will be different; change is just around the corner. The renewed warmth and friendliness sparks inward hope in the person being used. They hope for a better relationship only to be disappointed and once again left feeling abused.

Sometimes those who use others are often times themselves being used. They create a seemingly endless cycle of sin leaving a path cluttered with broken relationships.

Users may be lazy, disorganized, or irresponsible. They know they can control others and simply delight in doing so.

Many times this using is mutual. I call it a parasite relationship, bottom-feeders! "You scratch my back, and I'll scratch your back." I never really saw this before until I considered the life of Jephthah as recorded by the Holy Spirit in Judges 11. What can we learn from this great man of faith that would help us help those who use others and those who are being used?

When we use people, we close them out. The user attempts to limit others from fully using their gifts and talents. This type of person restricts the used by deliberately ignoring his responsibility to fulfill the "One Another" commandment. What the user attempts to close out, God places his mighty hand upon to keep open and flourishing. Jephthah's name means, "God will open" (v.1). When God's hand is upon the person being used, he will be exalted in due time with tremendous splendor. From seemingly nowhere, God may open the place or position like the one He did for Joseph and Daniel.

Jephthah was the son of his father's adultery (v 2). He was viewed as a threat to the biological son's inheritance, similar to the near kinsman redeemer's reason for not redeeming Ruth (Ruth 4). The user often creates hurtful situations that others may have to live with and under. It is beyond the control of the one being used. Something happened to them—something they can't change, something in the past, but something they are willing to deal with and use profitably. But many times the user will hinder them from rising above.

Used people usually know they are being used. At first, the person being used may overlook the sudden change in disposition of the user. However, if the relationship continues forward and the same behavior is displayed, the person being used knows what the real score is about. Denial gives way to anger. Suppression fades into disgust. What is bewildering to the used is how to stop the cycle of being used. The used longs for a warm friendship. Dying embers are fanned by the renewed posture of the user only to be quenched once again by the user's requests.

Using people promotes separation, emotionally, mentally, socially, and physically, and furthermore promotes isolation. Notice how the actions of Jephthah's brothers forced him to flee. Running away can foster an ungodly circle of influence. Worthless men gathered around Jephthah (v. 3). Those who observe the departure and isolation stand by and complained, "Well, why does s/he do such n' such?" A deep, honest examination reveals the used are not accepted unless they perform or act a certain way. This is clearly seen in Christ's parable of the Pharisee and publican, not to mention the entire Pharisaical system of thought and practice as recorded in the Synoptic Gospels.

When a problem occurs that leadership is unable or unwilling to manage, they often reenlist the isolated person. The Elders of Israel blatantly continued their form of using. They informed Jephthah that they wanted him to deliver them from the enemy's hand. Please notice the absence of his brethren wanting him to return. It appears they were still clinging to their pride. The Elders called, not the family (vs. 5–6).

The person who is used often asks serious soul-searching, biblical questions. Jephthah wanted the Pharisees to explain why they had come to him. He reminded them that they hated him (emotions). He tells them they viewed him as an enemy. They turned against him. They drove him away (expelled, divorced). Now they were in trouble (bind, a narrow place). But they remained brazened and blunt. These religious leaders only wanted Jephthah to rescue them because he possessed something they didn't. He was a valiant warrior (vs. 7-8).

Someone who is being used is skeptical and seeks a genuine commitment in the form of an oath, vow, or promise. Being wounded and burned before, Jephthah wanted assurances that the Pharisees would not go back on their word. The Pharisees presented their case and vowed he would be inaugurated as their ruler. Jephthah seems to make them fulfill their promise before even entering into negotiations with the King of Ammon (vs. 9–10).

Help for the User
What help can counselors provide for those who use others? What does God require of them?

First, the user must be reminded that those they use are made in the image of God. When they abuse them, they are abusing and dishonoring God. James writes these words.

> Listen, my beloved brethren: did not God choose the poor of this world to be rich in faith and heirs of the kingdom, which He promised to those who love Him? But you have dishonored the poor man. Is it not the rich who oppress you and personally drag you into court? Do they not blaspheme the fair name by which you have been called? (James 2:5–8).

Coming to the proper understanding of these verses demands repentance and confession. The contrition of heart is vertical (towards God) and horizontal (towards those used). Neglecting the horizontal reveals a King Saul heart in his dealings with David.

Second, users must be taught that people are more important than tasks, agendas, success, or advancement. It is hard to consider that the great missionary statesman, the Apostle Paul, may have used young John Mark. When John Mark failed (as determined by Paul), Paul's attitude in Acts 15 was more concerned for the task of missions than why John Mark left them! Not until much later in Paul's life did he commend John Mark and call for his services. Tasks come and go, tasks are achieved, and new ones take their place. Tasks are endless. There is no shortage of them. However, relationships are priceless and valuable. It is from relationships that we grow and mature.

Third, the user must move beyond the past and look for the inward God-given talents, abilities, skills, and spiritual giftedness that God has placed within the person. Paul reminded Philemon to do so with the runaway slave Onesimus. What qualities did Jephthah possess?

- Jephthah had great historical knowledge. When confronting the King of Ammon, he knew the history of events. He was a historical scholar.
- Jephthah had great ability to communicate truth systematically. Jephthah rehearsed carefully the events in their proper order.
- It appears that Jephthah dealt with his anger because he was able to demonstrate patience toward the elders of Israel and to the sons of Ammon.
- Jephthah was a man of courage and convictions. When the necessity arose to stand firm, he boldly did so.
- Jephthah stood for truth, not self.
- Jephthah was a man of dedication and commitment. He followed through and brought freedom and victory to Israel.

Help for the Person Who Feels Used

How can we help those who are or have been used? What insights can we provide to those who feel used so they can maintain a holy walk before their God?

1. Help them to take their eyes off the user. Their focus must be on pleasing God in all things. Teach them to look unto Jesus who is the author and finisher of their faith, who is recording every single act of service they perform and eagerly waits to bestow upon them, "Well done thou good and faithful servant," and Who will not forget their labor of love.

   > [F]ixing our eyes on Jesus, the author and perfecter of our faith, who for the joy set before Him endured the cross, despising the shame, and has sat down at the right hand of the throne of God (Heb. 12:2).

> "And he said to him, 'Well done, good slave, because you have been faithful in a very little thing, you are to be in authority over ten cities'" (Luke 19:17).
>
> For God is not unjust so as to forget your work and the love which you have shown toward His name, in having ministered and in still ministering to the saints (Heb. 6:10).

2. Teach them about the power of prayer and *how* to pray for the person that they feel is using them. Teach them they are commanded to pray for those who despitefully use them (Luke 6:28). Have them consider in what specific areas they could lift the user before the throne of grace. Have them consider the life of the Lord Jesus Christ. Ask them to list the benefits that could result from their effectual prayer.

3. Follow the counsel of Christ in Luke 6: 27–37. Christ instructs His disciples that when treated unfairly, they are obligated to maintain a certain confident spiritual posture toward the user. What does our Lord say the disciples of Christ should do? They are to love their enemies (v. 27). Brainstorm with the counselee about how this would look in their situation. They are to do good to those who hate them. Ask the counselee to list how this might be done in their situation. They are to bless those who curse them (v. 28). Role play with the counselee about how this might look in their situation. They are to pray for those who mistreat them. Ask the counselee to write out some prayers for the abuser. They are to meet legitimate needs (v. 29). Have the counselee make a list of the user's needs and another list of resources that might fit those needs. Brainstorm with the counselee on this would look in their situation. They are to avoid partiality, the very thing they are feeling (v. 31). Unpack these concepts with the counselee. They are to show mercy and avoid a judgmental attitude (v. 37). Brainstorm with the counselee on how this would look in their situation.

4. Help them gain a sober-minded assessment of their strengths and strengthen their weaknesses. Often inaccurate perspectives overwhelm the person being used so that they begin to believe what they see, hear, or feel.

5. If appropriate to teach them how to confront the abuser (Luke 17:3ff).

6. Encourage them with Jephthah's name, "The Lord will open." They must believe that no one can close them out. God will open!

No one likes being used. It is degrading. It often breaks the human spirit. Whatever mistreatment we may experience in our short-lived lives is under the control of a sovereign God who uses all things for His glory. Each sovereign act can become a blessing to the user and the used as we respond biblically. May we appropriate these truths and continue to imitate Jesus, our example, Lord and Redeemer.

The Bible Is Not a Textbook on Mental Health

In Defense of Biblical Counseling—Part 1

In this chapter, I want to answer the questions and assertions critics of biblical counseling raise. "What makes biblical counseling superior to other counseling systems? Such a claim is arrogant, boastful, and prideful. The Bible cannot speak to the deepest, darkest mental and emotional needs of man. It is archaic and outdated. Only modern psychology is qualified to help such people because these men and women are trained to study human behavior."

Can you answer such assertions and attacks? Or do you find yourself uncomfortable and perhaps even intimidated? Do you think that if you said the wrong thing you could ruin the person's life forever? Let's see what the major differences are between contemporary counseling systems and biblical counseling. Let's grow in our confidence that all other counseling systems that are not rooted in the sufficiency of the Word and the supremacy of Christ are inferior and will fail in addressing man's deepest and darkest emotional, mental, and spiritual condition.

Why should I be interested in this subject? First, it is close to the heart of our Lord Jesus, who is known as the Wonderful Counselor in Isaiah 9:6. What is close to the heart of God must be upon our hearts. God shows concern about holiness, and so should we. God is concerned about sinners and their eternal destinations, thus we should be. God is concerned about freeing people from bondage, as we should be concerned.

Second, counseling is not reserved for the professionally trained. Every Christian counsels. It goes like this: "John, here is my situation. What do you think I should do?" The minute you open your mouth you are counseling. For the Christian, the counsel we provide has eternal ramifications. Paul writes in Romans 15:14 that he was utterly confident that the saints in Rome were competent to counsel.

Third, the Church and her saints are the keepers of the oracles of God. We possess the only truth that sets people free from their bondage and captivity. There is no truth outside of God's truth, the absolute truth. And it is because of this truth that Jesus said if you know the truth, the truth will set you free.

I want to establish a line of reasoning with you before we go on. I will be employing the term *contemporary counseling systems*. I chose this term in contrast to biblical counseling or Nouthetic counseling system. Contemporary counseling systems will include both secular counseling systems and Christian counseling systems. Biblical counseling or Nouthetic counseling is distinctively different.

The three reasons that biblical counseling is superior are the following: its belief system (doctrine), its authority (the Bible), and its treatment goal (transformation). In this chapter, we will discuss the first reason biblical counseling is superior. In the following chapter, we will discuss the remaining two distinctions.

One: Biblical counseling is superior because of its belief system. *What evidence would I suggest that contemporary counseling has failed to solve man's problems?*

First, the discord and disagreement within the branches of counseling today. For example: There are over 200 different counseling systems just within the Freudian approach. There is little agreement on the patient's problems. There is disagreement as to the etiology of the patient's malady. There is still further disparity on how to help the patient solve his/her problems.

This could be likened to a group of auto mechanics diagnosing why a particular vehicle is performing poorly. One says it is the carburetor, while another says it's the spark plug wires. A third says it is a foul spark plug, and a fourth says it is the fuel injectors. One could literally spend hundreds of dollars trying to resolve the problem and still have a vehicle that does not perform as it was intended.

This is a common result in counseling. People spending, or perhaps insurance companies remitting, hundreds of dollars for countless sessions only to produce a product that does not function as God created it to function.

Second, the discord and disagreement within contemporary counseling itself. The Freudians disagree with the Rogerians, the Rogerians differ with the Jungites, and the Jungites dispute with the Maslowites.

Freud claimed man's basic problem is he has failed to adjust sexually during early childhood. Jung argues man's basic problem is he has failed to achieve self-realization, rejecting Freud's hypothesis. Adler asserts man's basic problem is he has failed to understand himself and others, has faulty goals, and cannot gain perfection and productivity. Horney (pronounced "horn-eye") proposes man's basic problem is he fails to give up defending his idealistic self, and this illusion hinders him from realizing his full potential. Sexual problems, self-actualization, idea self, failure to understand myself, dominant or recessive traits, *ad infinitum*.

Third, contemporary counseling is developed on biases. Many contemporary counseling systems today are a reaction to Freud's bias that all problems are related to sexual maladjustment. Many recognized Freud's flawed thinking and rejected that every one of man's problems was rooted in some sexual problem.

But those men and women who developed subsequent systems are equally biased. How you ask? Repeatedly, reviewers of counseling textbooks on contemporary counseling today used two key words in describing contemporary counseling system: empirical and hypotheses.

"Empirical" means data gathered through observation. The gathering and understanding of such data is subjective. "Hypotheses" means something considered true. A test to prove or disprove it is developed. The bias is further advanced through numerous trait and personality tests developed by such people as Cattell, Esyneck, and Allport—tests still used today in contemporary counseling.

Fourth, the self-declarations from both secular and Christian counselors that the best help they can offer is to help the counselee *learn how to cope*. If you read the counseling literature with discernment or ask pointed questions to the counselor, they tell the counselee they will never be cured. They will be on medication the rest of their life. A cursory reading of the counselor's bible (DSM 4) speaks this way exactly on innumerable diagnoses. On a personal note, the psychiatrist informed me that my sister could only learn how to cope. A Christian counselor told several members of the church I served as pastor the same.

Fifth, the astronomic rise in the past several decades in the development, sale, and distribution of antidepressant and antipsychotic drugs. This is not to mention the insurance statistical information on the increase of hospitalizations for depression, panic attacks, and other mood disorders.

What is the reason contemporary counseling systems have failed? The answer, I think, is simple and basic. However, the answer should not be devalued or minimized. The reason for the failure of contemporary counseling is its belief system. The belief system of contemporary counseling is humanistic theology. What exactly do I mean?

Theology Proper (Belief about God)
The secular counselors never consider God because they are evolutionists. Most hold no endearment for religion. They view religion oftentimes as a complicating problem. It is a crutch that must be discarded if the counselee expects to make any progress.

For Christian counselors, God is asked to fit into an existing system where His counsel is part and parcel with Freud, Skinner, and Rogers. Christian counseling is often polytheistic by practice and eclectic, meaning the blending of the best from a variety of sources. This is because of the basic belief that the Bible does not address the deep emotional and psychological needs of humanity.

It could be likened to the All-Star baseball game—bringing the best from all the league teams to form one team. If God is involved, He is redefined in loving, compassionate, tender, merciful, and nonjudgmental terms. God is the grandfather who understands your struggles. He wants you to try harder. He hopes you succeed. If God is involved, it is enough that

He provides some warm spiritual feelings, but not enough to warrant radical amputation of sinful behavior.

Wilbur Reese writes with biting sarcasm:

> I would like to buy $3 worth of God, please. Not enough to explode my soul or disturb my sleep, but just enough to equal a cup of warm milk or a snooze in the sunshine. I don't want enough of him to make me love a black man or pick beets with a migrant. I want ecstasy, not transformation. I want the warmth of the womb not a new birth. I want about a pound of the eternal in a paper sack. I'd like to buy $3 worth of God, please.

Anthropology (Belief about Man)

For the secular counselor, man is not created in the image of God. He is a product of evolution. He is the strongest species. He is the fittest. If man is created in the image of God, God played a terrible trick on such people as the alcoholic, homosexual, the angry man or woman. God made them this way. Or it remains God's fault because God allowed me to be born into this family, at this time, and in this place.

Man is not responsible for he is a product of his environment, heredity, genetics, or the product of liberal or stringent family and church morés. Because man is not responsible, he is a victim or has an addiction, disease, illness, disorder, or another -ism.

Harmartiology (Belief about sin)

Contemporary counseling does not address the heart of the problem but the behavior or symptoms. They want to change the behavior so the person is socially acceptable or fits into a family structure without hurting or offending.

A man who has a sexual relationship outside of marriage had an affair. He did not commit adultery. A woman who is fearful is told she is having a panic attack. A child who lacks discipline and structure both at school and home is diagnosed as having ADD or ADHD. A person with anger is now told he has intermittent explosive eisorder (IED). Parents of a rebellious child are told the child has oppositional defiant disorder. A person who has suffered a great tragedy, such as a job threatening disability or memories of a war, is diagnosed with post-traumatic stress disorder. And the reclassification of a person's actions by contemporary counseling systems is nearly endless.

Contemporary counseling rarely cites sin as the original problem. If it did, it implies the counselee must accept responsibility, and, for the Christian, there is only one way in dealing with that issue … or sin.

Soteriology (Belief about Salvation)
Man must save himself. Man must do something about his situation. No one else can but him/her. Man is responsible for his own self-actualization. Man must do what he thinks is best for him/herself. Man must set boundaries so he can be happy. If he/she is made to feel uncomfortable or threatened, he/she is free to act in ways of self-preservation. In the end, man remains autonomous, independent, and in control.

Sanctification
Man must do for himself what makes him happy. Obedience is not an issue, for there is no objective standard. Man himself is the standard. Whatever he/she deems right in his/her own eyes to secure and maintain happiness is free for him/her to act to accomplish. What pleases man therefore, regardless of its effects upon others, personal pleasure becomes the goal.

So what can we conclude as to the reason contemporary counseling is failing today? Can we sum it all up in a sentence?

Contemporary counseling is failing today because of what and how it believes. What makes biblical counseling the alternative? The answer again, I think, is simple and basic. But, again, it should not be devalued or minimized. The reason biblical counseling is the best alternative is its belief system. It is biblical!

What Biblical Counseling Believes about Theology Proper
We believe God is holy, just, righteous, and sovereign. We believe that man is made in His image and has the ability to think, feel, and act.

We believe that God is compassionate, kind, tender, loving, and merciful. But God is also holy, just, righteous, and unchanging toward man's sinful behavior. To have an accurate portrait of God, the counselor must always keep in balance God's complete profile of attributes. God loves, because God is holy. God is merciful, because God is just.

An examination of Christ, our Wonderful Counselor, shows that when appropriate, He was gentle, kind, merciful and loving. Equally, when appropriate and it was what the person needed, He was frank, bold, just, and holy.

What Biblical Counseling Believes About Anthropology

We believe that God created man perfect and holy. Man has the image of God stamped upon his life. Man was given intellectual, emotional, and volitional abilities. This image was to reflect his Maker's glory, not his own.

We deny that man is a product of evolution. If man does not have a Creator, man is not responsible to anyone but himself. Because creationism is the easier theory to embrace, man has an accountability relationship. He is not independent. He cannot do what he wants to. He is designed to live for God, not himself.

We believe that man was and is created for fellowship with God. His greatest need is for God, nothing or no one else can complete man or fill that void.

We deny that his greatest need is self-actualization, self-realization, or to love himself as advocated by secular counselors or Christian celebrity figures.

What Biblical Counseling Believes About Harmartiology

We believe, according to biblical revelation, that man willfully chose to disobey God. This rebellion resulted in separation from God and his fellow man.

We deny that man's current state of affairs is due to environment, heredity, illness, or disease, for our Lord, the prophets, disciples, and apostles lived obediently despite their environment.

We believe that the current state of man must be attributed to the issue of sin unless medical evidence genuinely proves otherwise. Man's problems are clearly and repeated stated by God in Jeremiah as twofold: you have no fear of Me before you, and you have left or forsaken Me.

God made man with a free will. God did not create robots. Because of this concept, like Adam, man continues to make choices. The current condition of man is man's choice to walk away from God. The action declares, "I do not fear you."

Again God speaking through Jeremiah reminds Judah that,

> "Have you not done this to yourself by forsaking the Lord your God?" 2:17

> "Your own wickedness will correct you, and your apostasies will reprove you." 2:19

> "Because you have rebelled against Me, your ways and your deeds have brought these things to you. This is your evil. How bitter. How it has touched your heart." 4:17b–18

What Biblical Counseling Believes about Soteriology

We believe that the only remedy for man is completely provided through the shed blood of Jesus Christ on the cross of Calvary.

We believe this shedding of blood is for the remission of sins. Without it, no one will see God, and without it there is no hope of the future or the present.

We deny that man can [1] develop a standard to impress God or [2] live by that standard to impress God.

We believe the death, burial, and resurrection of Christ did away with the power of the devil.

In Defense of Biblical Counseling—Part 1

> The Son of God appeared for this purpose, to destroy the works of the devil. 1 John 3:8

We believe the death, burial, and resurrection of Christ did away with the ruling power of sin.

> For sin shall not be master over you. Rom. 6:14

Biblical salvation provides hope to all situations.

- Hope given to the woman caught in the very act of adultery
- Hope given to the woman at the well who lived through five bad marriages and now was shacking up
- Hope given to the demon possessed man in the tombs
- Hope given to those without hope and cast off by society such as the lepers, tax collectors, and prostitutes
- Hope of change for the angry disciples James and John
- Hope for change offered to Judas Iscariot, who refused
- Hope offered to the rich young ruler, who refused
- Confident declaration that there is hope for the alcoholic
- Confident declaration that there is hope for the marriage broken by adultery
- Confident declaration that there is hope for the wayward rebellious child
- Confident declaration that there is hope for the gambler, the person involved with pornography, the homosexual, the sexually abused, the sexual abuser—there is no hopeless person or helpless situation!

No other system of counseling provides hope that is rooted in another's all-sufficient, efficacious accepted work like Jesus Christ and Him alone!

The Bible Is Not a Textbook on Mental Health
In Defense of Biblical Counseling—Part 2

In the previous chapter, we discussed the first distinction that makes Nouthetic (biblical) counseling superior to contemporary counseling systems today. The first distinction is doctrine. In this issue, we will discuss the remaining two distinctions, namely biblical counseling is superior because of its authority (the Bible), and because of its treatment goal (transformation).

Attacks on the Authority of Scriptures

The authority of the Scriptures were never so challenged and universally undermined until the late 1800s and early 1900s. German biblical scholars sought confirmation from independent sources to confirm the biblical historical record of such things as Adam and Eve, ex-nihil (creationism), Noah and the flood, the parting of the Red Sea, the collapse of Jericho, and other historical biblical accounts.

The German biblical scholars were guided in their quest for confirmation by the strong influence of the Enlightenment (if it meant something to you, then okay) and the Rationalists (if it doesn't make sense, it certainly cannot be true). Their efforts resulted in a discipline called "higher criticism" that migrated to England and then to North America. In England, Rudolf Bultmann used higher criticism to "demythologize" the Bible of its supernatural record.

The evangelical church did not know how to respond to legitimate questions, so it either [1] embraced higher criticism, or [2] ignored it hoping it would go away. Higher criticism did not go away, but infiltrated Bible colleges and seminaries in England and America. It was inevitable how the erosion of the Bible's authority would impact nearly every major offered from education to theology to pastoral to counseling.

Today, in the field of counseling you will hear such statements as:

- All truth is God's truth.
- Psychology provides insights into man's mind and behavior that the Bible cannot provide.
- The Bible doesn't address the gamut of man's psychological problems.
- To believe the Bible is to be naïve and simplistic.
- The Bible is limited in scope in offering counsel for the serious mental and emotional problems of man.
- Those who believe the Bible is sufficient need to step aside and allow the experts who are specifically trained to deal with the deep mental and emotional disturbances of humanity.

Contemporary counseling systems are based on a human theology of God, man, sin, salvation and sanctification. This foundation naturally leads to establishing an authority for counseling that is human. The human authority is the expert who has studied in this field.

This is evident through the training the counselor receives. The majority of his training is in psychology courses, with little to no training in the area of biblical theology. He will study introduction to psychology, developmental psychology, history of psychology, abnormal psychology, child psychology, clinical psychology, general psychology, experimental psychology, educational psychology, psychology of women, psychology of religion, family psychology and adolescent psychology to name a few of nearly sixty different subjects.

This training leads to flawed testing procedures. This system starts with empirical data (gathering facts through observations). Hypotheses are formulated from these observations. Tests are developed to prove these hypotheses. Conclusions are drawn from the tests.

The problems with this basis of authority are twofold. First, because it is empirically based, nothing outside itself but itself, the data is subject to change, thus altering the outcome. The change of data may come in months or years. Second, the conclusions drawn lead to methods that are restricted to dealing with the counselee's behavior. A more sure and certain authority must be acknowledged. That authority is the Word of God. The Bible is God's inspired Word to His creation (2 Timothy 3:16–17; 2 Peter 1:20–21).

The authority of the Bible directed men of God to act—even contrary to culture, family, and friends. Consider the following examples.

- Noah and the building of the Ark.
- Gideon and the conquest over the Midianites.
- David and Goliath.
- Peter and James before the Sanhedrin.

The prophets verify the authority of the Scriptures.

- "Thus says the Lord"—used 417 times
- "And the Word of the Lord came to me"—12 times
- "The Lord said"—232 times

Jesus affirmed the authority of the Scriptures by quoting them, using them, and teaching them. Remember He is the perfect Son of God. The Apostles affirmed the authority of the Scriptures in the same way as our Lord.

Let's consider the contrast between the psychologist's authority and the biblical counselor's authority.

1. Cain's problem would be labeled intermittent explosive disorder, but God called it anger and gave him the prescription on how to deal with it.
2. Saul's problem would be labeled paranoid schizophrenia undifferentiated, but we are clearly instructed in God's Word that his problem was rebellion, disobedience, and pride.
3. David would be classified as delusional as he allowed his saliva to run down his beard and he scratched the walls of King Achish. But we know that David ran ahead of God out of fear.

4. Elijah would be classified as bipolar but it is clear from Scripture that Elijah's problem was a sinful response to God's sovereign operation.

5. Nebuchadnezzar's problem was pride, which he was forewarned about and even knew what to do about his animal like characteristics.

6. Society and friends left the demoniac helpless, isolated, bound, and suicidal but only the power of the Living Christ could break his chains and produce a new man—one who was calm, sitting, clothed, and talking rationally. And the list could be endless.

This Creator has intimate knowledge of what He created. The Creator would be the One who would best know what went wrong with man and how to 'fix' him.

Let me provide two illustrations. First, if I drive a 2006 Infiniti M35X valued at $43,340, do you think I would take it to the local Chevy or Ford dealer for repairs? Second, my wife likes to purchase items with a lifetime warranty. There is a company called William Sonoma, and she has a lifetime warranty on a spatula! A spatula! Now she cannot go to Wal-Mart, Kmart, Target, or anywhere else because they will not honor William Sonoma's warranty.

Likewise, man has a lifetime warranty on him by his Creator—God! No one else can come close to fixing God's product line. They may try, but try as they may it will never be as God intended. God is the only one that can repair man to the original design for which man was created.

Biblical counseling is the sole uniqueness missing in contemporary counseling today. Consider a brief survey of Psalm 119. We will quickly walk through this Psalm to find encouragement to the premise I have presented. Consider these topics Psalm 119 provides counsel for.

- Dealing with immorality—v. 9
- Addictions—v. 11

- Guilt and shame—v. 22
- False accusations and slander—v. 23
- Intense sorrow—v. 25
- Overwhelming grief—v. 28
- Lying and deceit—v. 29
- Pride and selfishness—v. 37
- Afflictions—v. 50
- Scorn and mockery—v. 51
- Persecution—v. 61
- Willful sin v. 67
- Health issues—v. 83

Biblical counseling is based on the theology of the Bible. This theology provides divine, undisputable, objective, and absolute data about God, man, man's problems, avoidance of problems, and solutions of such problems. This inspired data has been tested throughout history for its diagnosis, and treatment has never failed when properly applied.

Listen to the words of Joshua and Elijah.

Joshua:

> "If it is disagreeable in your sight to serve the Lord, choose for yourselves today whom you will serve: whether the gods which your fathers served which were beyond the River, or the gods of the Amorites in whose land you are living; but as for me and my house, we will serve the Lord" (Joshua 24:15).

The people in Joshua's day vowed they would follow Jehovah, but we know from the Book of Judges they did not. The impact of their decision was devastating. Likewise, if we say we believe in the theology of the Bible and that the Bible is our sole authority and yet practice contemporary counseling systems, the seeds sown will yield a harvest unlike any the church has ever seen.

Elijah came near to all the people and said,

> "How long *will* you hesitate between two opinions? If the Lord is God, follow Him; but if Baal, follow him." But the people did not answer him a word (1 Kings 18:21).

The people in Elijah's day abstained from voting. They did not answer him. They hedged their bets. What if by some chance Baal was mightier than Jehovah? They wouldn't want to be on the wrong side at the wrong time. But in fact, they were on the wrong side at the wrong time. Given an opportunity, they failed to seize it. I beseech you not to hedge your bets on contemporary counseling systems. Those you seek to serve will be robbed of hope, forgiveness, and the means to live a God-honoring, victorious life.

The third distinctive of Nouthetic counseling is its treatment goal (transformation).

Do you remember the story of King David and his desire to return the Ark of the Covenant to Jerusalem? In 1 Samuel, Eli's sons took the Ark into battle and used it as a good luck charm. The Philistines capture the Ark when they defeated Israel. Divine humor removed the Ark from the Philistines where it came to rest nearly twenty years at Kiriath-jearim in the house of Abinadab.

David discovers where the Ark is and greatly desires to bring it to Jerusalem. What a marvelous idea! There was nothing wrong with returning the Ark to Jerusalem. His intentions were noble and good. There was no evil motive or selfishness on his part. Yet when we read the account, Uzzah is struck dead by the Lord. David was angry and fearful! What went wrong? The desire was good, but David's plan to obtain the Ark was sinful. David transported the Ark the way the pagans did when they sent it out of their territory—on a cart drawn by oxen. This is how David attempted to do a good thing the wrong way.

Likewise, contemporary counseling systems may very well have a deep desire to see people free from their problems. But how they go about helping people is wrong. Like David and Uzzah, oftentimes it brings disastrous results to the counselee and their family.

Methodology is as equally important as the goal. When the goal becomes more important, we are in danger. And that is where counseling in the twenty-first century is today! This is known as pragmaticism.

How the problem is diagnosed: Contemporary counseling systems
In a general observation, the diagnosis is made based on the subjective reporting of the counselee. The counselor will carefully take notes of what the counselee describes. There may be certain tests prescribed to evaluate the person's mental and emotional condition such as the MMPI, T-JTA, and other personality and psychological tests. Questionnaires have been developed that solicit how the counselee feels or thinks about a situation, which is not challenged and becomes the subjective means of evaluation of the counselee's problems (note: you can access many of these questionnaires, which are based on a subjective numerical rating scale online).

There may be blood tests that are taken for the purpose of ruling out an organic cause for the feelings and behaviors. Then the counselor formulates a diagnosis. The problem with this approach is the counselees believe what is being describing is the cause of their problems. In reality, what counselees hear is the result of their previous actions.

The counselor assigns a medical/psychological label (DSM IV) without evidence to support such a diagnosis. Medication is often used to treat physical causes for an unsubstantiated mental/emotional/spiritual cause.

How the problem is diagnosed: Biblical counseling
Biblical counseling operates from basic principles. Since the cause of the problem cannot be scientifically or medically proven, the biblical counselor operates from the understanding that the counselee is not living as God intended, whether the counselee is a believer or not.

We further believe that the counselee is unable to biblically identify the cause for the behavior; otherwise, they would have the ability to correct the problem. The counselee's descriptions must be questioned as to what was done, or not done, resulting in such behavior.

The biblical counselor also understands that the counselee has three levels to their problem: [1] Presentation: what the counselee thinks is the problem when asked; [2] Performance: how the counselee is disobedient to biblical standards; and [3] Preconditioning: how the counselee has learned to avoid responsibility and unpleasant structure and discipline.

Biblical counseling works hard at gathering data and measuring that data through the grid of Scriptures, not humanistic theology or authority based on experience, education, or collective assumptions.

For example, consider someone who is labeled bipolar. How was the diagnosis determined? What specific tests did the doctor perform to reach this conclusion? Did the doctor order blood work, and if so, what were the results of those tests? Is the patient on medication? If so, what is the name? How many mgs? How often is the instruction to take it? Does the patient take it as prescribed? Does he or she find the medication helping? In what specific ways? Are there any side affects? If so, what are they? What does he or she feel when he or she had an episode? When was the last time an episode occurred? Please describe exactly what occurred. Who was there? What was going on just prior to the episode? How long did the episode last? What brought the patient out of the episode? How frequently are these episodes? Does the patient know when he or she is about to have an episode? Can he or she ward them off, and if so, how?

Then the biblical counselor examines the data through a biblical lens. In a general statement, bipolar is a spiritual problem that often encompasses fear. The Bible has a lot to say about fear and what to do with it. Also, by gathering concrete data and examining it through the Word of God, one can find encouragement through the Scriptures (Rom. 15:4; Ps. 130:5; 31:14; 56:3–4).

How a problem is treated: Contemporary counseling system
If you examine contemporary counseling treatment options today, they are limited in scope. There is medication therapy. This means

an antidepressant or antipsychotic drug will be prescribed to bring relief from the symptoms. Such treatment is subject to change as to the type of drug offered and the strength prescribed. One thing that usually does not change is the belief that apart from this type of treatment, the counselee will relapse. A reason that medication therapy is sought is the motivation of the counselee—relief! The counselee does not like the bad feelings. Guilt results in more bad feelings and is related to sinful choices. They want to "feel" better.

The reason for the development of new antidepressant and antipsychotic drugs is that they lose their effectiveness or the immediate relief the counselee is looking for is achieved. As a rule, counselees will be forced to wait three to six weeks for the antidepressant to begin working. Because the counselee wants immediate relief, after several days they call their doctor saying the medication is not working. What do the doctors do? Increase the dosage.

The second type of treatment is group therapy. This may take a variety of forms. Essentially, it is talk therapy. These are groups of people with similar problems who gather to "talk" out a solution. The belief is "I can learn from someone else who is struggling with the same issues." Also, this can be individual therapy. This type of treatment is non-directive, in that the counselor believes the answers lie somewhere in the counselees and the counselor's job is to help them realize their potential. In extreme cases, hospitalizations where shock treatment is performed is recommended.

<u>How a problem is treated: Biblical counseling</u>
We believe, unless the medical community can demonstrate a change in tissue or a chemical imbalance, the problem is spiritual in nature and therefore demands the use of the Bible.

Relevant studies today are admitting that the so-call chemical imbalance has been a placebo. Knowing they cannot measure serotonin levels in the brain, new studies have proposed brain imaging that can pinpoint imbalances in the brain. However, the jury of doctors and psychologists do not agree that this is an effective diagnostic tool. Nouthetic counseling is not bothered by bizarre behavior. The

Bible describes people with bizarre behavior such as Nebuchadnezzar, David, Saul, and others. And in each case the issue was sin, not a chemical imbalance.

Because there is no scientific or medical evidence indicating a bodily malfunction, we must ask how is the counselee's life reflecting a broken relationship with God and/or with another human being? What does this counselee want more than to please and obey God? In what way does this behavior help to avoid dealing with the present situation?

Our treatment takes the counselee to the Bible to biblically identify the root causes, provide hope in Christ Jesus, discover biblical solutions that please God, develop discipleship in the counselee's life, and identify and instruct on preconditioning factors.

The prognosis of the problem: Contemporary counseling system

The prognosis' buzz word is "coping." Contemporary counseling systems can only offer coping techniques. "Cure" is seldom heard. The singular hope for the counselee is to learn how to cope. The result is often a counselee will spend a lifetime in counseling in which any noted progress pales in comparison to the investment of time and money. The counselee often lives in fear. This fear may be self-imposed (fearful of a relapse) or imposed by the therapist (reminding the counselee of what life was like before medication and therapy).

The prognosis of the problem: Biblical counseling

Biblical counseling results in a transformation, not a reformation. This transformation is assured through the faithful, compassionate instruction by the counselor based on the data gathered. With skill and insight, the counselor addresses the idols of the heart by contrasting the joy and peace that comes from obeying Christ. We are thoroughly convinced of the freedom awaiting the counselee. The counselee's freedom is not related to any magical number of sessions or some prescribed time. The counselee's freedom is directly proportionate to their unswerving faith and total obedience to the kergama (declaration of God's unchanging Word).

Summary of biblical counseling's distinctive features

The perspective of the present-day counseling systems is erroneous. It is based on humanistic theology, not biblical theology. The core issue then is which theology should be employed to help man solve his problems? *This is a call for biblical theology.*

Every counseling system is established upon an authority. Every counseling system that is not biblical has for its authority sinful man's deductions drawn from empirical data, by which sinful man has developed a set of hypotheses and tests, ending with a sinful man's conclusions. What makes biblical counseling distinct is its authority. That authority is infallible, inerrant, trustworthy, truthful, and inspired. The source is 2 Corinthians 5:18– 21—the word of reconciliation—The Bible. *This is a call for biblical authority.*

The heart of God and the mandate of the Church is reconciliation. In order to reconcile man to God, we are obligated to use the ministry of reconciliation (2 Cor. 5:18–21). Effective counseling will please God. Biblical counseling is effective counseling. Biblical counseling pleases God! *This is a call to biblical methodology.*

My Doctor Says I Have a Chemical Imbalance

The Human Brain, Chemical Imbalances, Truth, Assumptions, and Biblical Counsel

Over the years, we have heard the term "chemical imbalance." It is used to describe hundreds of diagnoses in the DSM IV. It is cited as the cause of abnormal and bizarre behavior. Doctors and psychiatrists write that one of two chemicals in the brain (serotonin and dopamine) register unusually high or low in a synaptic junction. When this occurs, peculiar behavior occurs because of this imbalance. To regulate the brain's function and to restore someone to a semblance of normalcy, antidepressants or antipsychotic medications are prescribed to restore equilibrium to the brain. Chemical imbalance implies that a balance can be restored. Medication therapy is believed to restore the imbalance.

By way of disclaimer, I am not a medical doctor, nor am I a licensed professional in the area of psychology or psychiatry. However, I, like you, am a rational and observant individual concerned with the rise of the number of counselees, friends, family, and members of the local church who have been told or who have come to believe they have a chemical imbalance. And I am further alarmed by the claims the pharmaceutical companies make that have little to no significant changes in those using their products.

The thrust of this chapter is to: 1. Provide some working definitions of terms that are hurled at us from the medical community, terms that are intimidating because they come from professionals we have elevated to "experts" who should not be questioned; 2. Share my research on the concept of the synaptic junction and how it functions, and the improbability of the medical/psychological counseling world ever really determining this theory as cause; 3. Provide some biblical guidelines on counseling someone on antidepressant or antipsychotic drugs and what may be occurring in the counselee's mind, and 4. Share why the counselee and family members may cling so desperately to the hope of the medication and become fearful to ever think about reducing or eliminating the use of the drug.

LANGUAGE: KNOW IT, DON'T FEAR IT

Serotonin
In the central nervous system, serotonin is believed to play an important role in the regulation of anger, aggression, body temperature, mood, sleep, vomiting, sexuality, and appetite. Low levels of serotonin may be associated with several disorders, namely increase in aggressive and angry behaviors, clinical depression, obsessive compulsive disorder (OCD), migraine, irritable bowel syndrome, tinnitus, fibromyalgia, bipolar disorder, anxiety disorder, and intensive religious experiences.

This chemical was isolated and named in 1948 by Maurice M. Rapport, Arda Green, and Irvine Page of the Cleveland Clinic. Serotonin is a chemical produced by nerve cells. The serum serotonin level is a blood test to measure the amount of serotonin in your body. Serotonin is synthesized extensively in the human gastrointestinal tract (about 90%), and the major storage place is platelets in the blood stream.

Dopamine
Dopamine was discovered by Arvid Carlsson and Nils-Ake Hillarp at the Laboratory for Chemical Pharmacology of the National Heart Institute of Sweden, in 1952. Dopamine functions as a neurotransmitter.

Dopamine has many functions in the brain, including important roles in behavior and cognition, motor activity, motivation and reward, sleep, mood, attention, and learning. Dopamine can be supplied as a medication that acts on the sympathetic nervous system, producing effects such as increased heart rate and blood pressure. However, since dopamine cannot cross the blood-brain barrier, dopamine given as a drug does not directly affect the current central nervous system.

Synaptic Junction
Chemical synapses (you also have electrical synapses) are specialized junctions through which the cells of the nervous system signal to

each other and to non-neuronal cells such as those in muscles and organs. Chemical synapses allow the neurons of the central nervous system to form interconnected neural circuits. They are thus crucial to the biological computations that underlie perception and thought. They provide the means through which the nervous system connects to and controls the other systems of the body.

The human brain contains a large number of chemical synapses; young children have about 10^{16} synapses (10 quadrillion). This number declines with age, stabilizing by adulthood. Estimates for adults vary from 10^{15} to 5×10^{15} (1–5 quadrillion) synapses. The word "synapse" comes from "synaptein," which Sir Charles Scott Sherrington and his colleagues coined from the Greek "syn" (together) and "haptein" (to clasp).

Neurotransmitters
Neurotransmitters are chemicals that are used to relay, amplify, and modulate signals between a neuron and another cell. There are many different ways to classify neurotransmitters. Often, dividing them into amino acids, peptides, and monoamines is sufficient for many purposes.

What are the effects of these neurotransmitters? Some examples of neurotransmitter actions:

- Acetylcholine—voluntary movement of the muscles
- Norepinephrine—wakefulness or arousal
- Dopamine—voluntary movement and motivation, "wanting"
- Serotonin—memory, emotions, wakefulness, sleep, and temperature regulation
- GABA (gamma aminobutyric acid)—inhibition of motor neurons
- Glycine—spinal reflexes and motor behavior
- Neuromodulators—sensory transmissions, especially pain

SOME PRELIMINARY OBSERVATIONS

- The chemicals spoken of are real, not scientific illusions. God has "wired" us with these chemicals, and they serve a purpose. God has allowed some purposes to be discovered by scientists, while other purposes God has concealed.

- Estimates for adults vary from 10^{15} to 5×10^{15} (1–5 quadrillion) synapses. This, for me, raises a scientific question (although I am not a scientist but a seeker of truth). How then, since there is no measurable device for chemicals in the brain, do they determine which of the 1–5 quadrillion synaptic junctions is too high or too low on serotonin?

- Serotonin is synthesized in the human gastrointestinal tract (about 90%), and the major storage place is platelets in the blood stream. God designed serotonin to be manufactured in the human body, stored in platelets, and measured by blood work. What does that say about chemical imbalance in the brain especially after blood work is tested and the results come back "clean"?

- How can the medical/psychological communities believe that these chemicals play an important role in "mood disorders"? Is this belief substantiated with scientific data, or is it founded on the subjective reporting of feelings by the patient?

- Since rarely can a medical cause be found, why is it that the condition (something that cannot be measured, proved, or disproved) is treated with medication?

According to medical historical development, change in or damage to tissue must be proven to establish an organic cause for a chemical imbalance. Yet, mental disorders are common in the United States and internationally. An estimated 26.2% of Americans, ages eighteen and older, (about one in four adults), suffer from a diagnosable mental disorder in a given year. When applied to the 2004 U. S. Census residential population estimate for ages eighteen and older, this figure translates to 57.7 million people. Even though mental disorders are widespread in the population, the main burden of illness is concentrated in a much smaller proportion, about 6%. That means 1 in 17 suffer from a serious mental illness. In addition, mental disorders are the leading cause of disability in the U.S. and Canada for ages fifteen to forty-four. Many people suffer from more than one mental disorder at a given time. Nearly half (45%) of those with any mental disorder meet criteria for two or more disorders, with severity strongly related to co-morbidity.

The prevalent tool used to diagnose who has and who does not have a mental illness is the DSM IV. The Diagnostic and Statistical Manual of Mental Disorders (DSM) is a handbook for mental health professionals that lists different categories of mental disorders and the criteria for diagnosing them, according to the publishing organization the American Psychiatric Association. Clinicians and researchers as well as insurance companies, pharmaceutical companies, and policy makers use it worldwide.

Is the American public being treated with truth or assumptions? A recent article I read included in its declaration that there was no etiology (cause) but their assumptions were the best option available. Is it possible then that in this particular area (mood disorders), those making these diagnoses are not keeping with scientific theory and methodology? Is it possible in this field they are truly "practicing" medicine?

I propose that the medical/psychological communities have built a super structure on assumptions and "hope so"s (we think so, we conclude, it appears, it may, and we think so." Even if there is a database to support the scientific findings, the data is limited in scope, confined to a restricted populace, and limited by geographic area.

HOW TO COUNSEL BIBLICALLY

1. Remember you are not a medical doctor. You are not qualified to instruct anyone to reduce or stop taking the prescribed medications. *If* what we have said is true, then the likelihood of the medication having any significant affect is little to none. Perhaps the greatest impact is in the mind of the person who is taking the medication. They claim to "feel" better. Like the original diagnosis made by the

doctor based on the counselee's subjective reporting, the improvement is rooted in the same subjective reporting of feelings. Stated differently, you and I cannot measure improvement from such reports. Under no circumstance should you instruct the counselee to stop taking their medications.

2. I think it is wise to know the type of medication (name), the dosage, and the frequency. A simple Internet search can provide some insight as to what the medication was given for, the various dosage levels (could tell you if the counselee is on the high or low end), and how often he/she is to take the medication as well as side effects. Most medication is prescribed for consumption on a daily basis.

Some medications are prescribed for twice a day. All medication should be taken with food to allow for better absorption. I want to know this information so I can talk intelligently. I ask them if they are taking the medication as scheduled. Many times, they are not. I instruct them to take the medication as prescribed by their doctor. If they think it is too much, then they are encouraged to speak with the prescribing doctor.

3. Ask them how their diagnosis was determined. What specific medical tests were ordered to determine their diagnosis? What lab or blood work was performed? It is not uncommon for the counselee to respond that no lab or blood work was ordered. The diagnosis was determined by the doctor on what the patient told the doctor. Often counselees will report that they were asked a series of questions. At the conclusion of the interview, the doctor would comment that the patient has a majority of the criteria for _____ .

These diagnostic questionnaires can be located on the Internet. I want to ask these questions to provoke the counselee's thought and ultimately provide hope in that Christ did not die for mood disorders but for man's sin. Biblical truth addresses these issues (often seen in physiological symptoms as displayed by Cain, David, King Saul, and Elijah) and that truth sets the captive free.

4. Do a thorough historical timelines of events in the counselee's life. Have them use a piece of paper (landscape). Draw a line down the middle and have them record each incident of occurrence, who was involved, what was happening, what made it so significant, and how did they attempt to resolve it. This provides the counselor with vital data, will reveal the idol (s) of their heart (what they want more than pleasing God), will show preconditioning patterns, and lays a foundation for biblical counseling.

5. Take each issue, identifying that issue using biblical terminology, work hard at helping them put off that sin, and work as diligently with them to put on the biblical replacement.

6. Assign appropriate, measurable, attainable, and reasonable homework. Remember the third law of teaching that the student cannot go to the next truth until the first one is firmly in place. Insure you are seeing a heart for God and the effort of consistent change. Avoid the mentality that you covered the material while the counselee has not embraced or incorporated the truth.

7. Remind the counselee that freedom does not mean spiritual insurgents will not attempt a spiritual overthrow. Teach them to be on the alert, vigilant, watchful, and on their guard for the devil, who is like a roaring lion seeking to devour them. I am becoming more convinced as I counsel that the enemy is more than willing to allow a few days. weeks, or even months of spiritual victory. Why? He knows the average Christian G.I. Joe will declare amnesty, go on "peace time status," and then bam! Counselees wonder why they find themselves in the revolving door once again.

8. Teach the counselee to serve others. For so long, most of those labeled with a DSM IV diagnoses are being served. They are told they have a disease, an illness, and they are not responsible for their condition. They liken the condition to getting the flu. So they are served by medical community (pills), the psychological community (it's not your fault, blame others counseling systems), and the religious community (God loves you and has a wonderful plan for your life). The focus is on them. Once they begin to recognize that what they

presently are living under is a result of previous sinful decisions, they will need to learn to serve others. The focus needs to be on others.

9. Other: I am sure you can add numerous other counseling issues, as wide as the variety of data gathered.

WHY COUNSELEES ARE FEARFUL OF REDUCING OR ELIMINATING THE MEDICATION

Jim was making significant progress. He came to me with a "label." However, during our time together, Jim began to recognize his sinful fear, worry, and lack of faith and trust in a sovereign God. Jim began to ask me about his medication. I encouraged him to see the prescribing doctor. I even went with him on a number of occasions for moral support. Over the next several months, his medication was reduced. The day after his last pill, he returned to my office. He was worse than when we first began. I was stunned, shocked, and bewildered. The Lord taught me that more than likely there was no physical addiction. But there was a mental and emotional addiction.

This addiction develops several ways. First, the patient is told of the medication's power to relieve suffering and discomfort. Second, the patent is warned (I call it intimidation) that he will need to be on the medication the rest of his life. If he stops taking the medication, the doctor often paints a morbid picture reminding the person of what he was like before. "Do you want to feel the way you did before? Do you want to subject your family to that again?" Third, if the counselee is not biblically taught, they will return to the medication (out of fear of the feelings returning), or if they do not resume taking the medication, the probability of a hospitalization that results in loss of job and approval from others (family, spouse, church/friends) is overwhelming. With each failure of coming off the medication, the despondency often deepens. Now the counselee is "hooked"—not physically, but mentally and emotionally. I learned a profound, painful, and valuable lesson that day with Jim. We had to go back to square one, and it was my fault!

A POSTSCRIPT: WHY DO COUNSELEES OFTEN REGULATE THEIR MEDICATION?

Here are some thoughts. I am using the word "toxicity" with the understanding that it is a buildup of a chemical in the body. Like someone using drugs, sooner or later, the initial "hit" wears off, and the same amount does not produce the desired effects. So more is taken. Likewise, the body builds up a toxicity to antidepressant medication. The body cannot absorb any more. The "fumes" of the "feel good" medications build up and the patient feels wonderful. They are cured. Some doctors even instruct the patient to take the medication when they start to feel bad. But as the body uses the stored "fumes," the old feelings return. The body, like a car running on fumes, comes to a grinding halt on the side of the road of life. Hospitalization, mega dosages to stabilize, and strong warnings to take their medication and to return to group therapy restarts the cycle. The toxicity builds, bad feelings leave, good feelings appear, medication is halted, and fumes dissipate, bad feelings return and bam— again!

God built us with these chemicals. They are real. Doctors are required to do their due diligence to diagnosis properly. If they are unable to determine the etiology of the patient's problems, they should go back to square one and dig deeper. Many who wear a DSM label could throw away the crutches the medical/psychological communities have prescribed and walk in freedom. Why? The Great Physician never makes a wrong diagnosis, and His remedies always work!

I Can't Shut My Brain Down. My Mind Is Always Racing. From Where Are These Thoughts Coming?

Destructive Thoughts and How to Control Them

The human mind is astounding. This part of the human body is an absolute wonder. Scientists cannot fully appreciate, comprehend, or fathom its operation. They have not fully grasped its full capabilities; it is incomprehensible. A kid's health pamphlet, attempting to explain the intricacy of the brain says: "Your brain is the boss of your body. It runs the show and controls just about everything you do, even when you're asleep."

Did you know that the brain controls breathing, heart rate, and blood pressure at the same time it performs a mental task? In some cases, the brain has "built-in backup systems." If one pathway in the brain is damaged, there is often another pathway that will take over this function of the damaged pathway.

The brain is capable of imagination. The brain is the site of reason and intelligence, which include such components as cognition, perception, attention, memory, and emotion.

The brain is responsible for control of posture and movements. It makes possible cognitive, motor, and other forms of learning. The brain can perform a variety of functions automatically, without the need for conscious awareness, such as coordination of sensory systems (e.g., sensory gating and multisensory integration), walking, and homoeostatic body functions such as blood pressure, fluid balance, and body temperature.

The human brain is a marvel; its capabilities are indescribable. But the marvels of this organ can be destructive to mental health and spiritual vitality. It can have a dark and ugly side. The power of the human brain turned inward reaps a whirlwind of human destruction. Unbridled, the mind can destroy families, relationships, and even one's self.

Unrestrained, it can alter a person's feelings and weaken and enslave the person's will.

Consider the destructive thinking of King Saul. The Bible describes Saul as insignificant and unworthy (1 Sam. 15:17). However, the people wanted a king, and they chose Saul. Samuel was commanded by God to listen to the people and anoint Saul (1 Sam. 8:7). Saul made his first public appearance after being lured out from hiding among the baggage. He had to be brought out before the people to be crowned (1 Sam. 10:22). Saul started his reign well, stirring the people to victory against the Ammonites (1 Sam. 11). Sadly, his life ended in defeat and despair (1 Sam. 31:4).

What went wrong? He allowed destructive thoughts to control, direct, and ultimately sabotage his life. Let's trace the thought pattern of King Saul's life and discover some valuable lessons on the downward spiral that uncontrolled thoughts can have. Then we will look at some ways to help a counselee control their thought life. Recommendations of several counseling resources will be noted for further help.

For King Saul, it began with his desire to hang on to the kingdom. The possession of the throne was his idol (1 Sam 15:8). We read, "What more can he have but the kingdom," referring to David and his popularity. Immediately in the next verse, we read that Saul viewed David with suspicion from that day forward (15:9).

In 1 Sam. 15:10, we read that God removed the Holy Spirit and allowed a tormenting spirit to come upon Saul. This could represent an actual demon or this could be the torment of unconfessed sin (1 Sam. 13:8, 15:12–14). Nevertheless, Saul experienced the real sense of lost fellowship with God.

This led to forms of aggressive behavior and violence (15:11). Saul's fear intensified because David's goodness exposed his wicked, evil heart (15:12). Such exposure led to isolation and separation (15:13). Because of this isolation, he dreaded David even more (15:15).

In chapter 18, we see how Saul begins to use people to accomplish his own evil desire of preserving the throne for Jonathan, his son (18:17). He enlists his own daughter, Michal, as a snare to rid himself of David by enticing David to marry her (18:21–25). His dread deepens when David is loved by the people and his own daughter (18:29).

In chapter 19, Saul spreads his hatred and contempt for David to others (19:1). Saul will use Michal's marriage to David to eliminate David. He sends soldiers to David—even on his sick bed—to be murdered (19:11). When this manipulative act fails, he turns on his daughter accusing her of letting his enemy go (19:17). The family relationship becomes distorted because of Saul's thought life.

In chapter 20, Saul continues his preoccupation of preserving the kingdom and monarchy for his son Jonathan (20:31). In verse 33, Saul continues turning on and away from family members.

In chapter 22, Saul manipulates others based on tribal nationality. His fellow Benjamites are verbally attacked. Following which, they are verbally incited with the lures of lands if they would just tell Saul where David is (22:6–8). Saul accuses them of conspiring against him. He continues spreading these accusations against others (22:13).

In chapter 23, Saul is informed as to David's whereabouts. He misuses his position, time, energy, and resources by assembling all the men of war (age twenty and up) to pursue David to kill him.

This must have been quite a sight to see thousands of men on a search-and-destroy mission, which was impossible to achieve because God was for David and against Saul (23:8).

We see Saul blessing anyone who aids and sides with him in his pursuit. Those who cooperate with Saul's plans are praised (23:21). After being led away to care for government business, he again locates David and selects three thousand men of war (24:2). Saul is confronted with the truth of his behavior. He even acknowledges that David is correct in his declaration, but Saul remains committed to his falsehoods and lies he has cultivated in his mind (24:9–22). He superficially agrees with David but emotionally and volitionally is driven by his destructive thoughts.

Again, in chapter 26, he gathers three thousand chosen men to search for and destroy David (26:2, 18–26).

Near the end of his life, Saul returns to kingdom business—although in the wrong fashion. He consults with the witch of Endor, seeking some spiritual guidance from Samuel about the affairs of state (28:15). The senseless end of King Saul's thought life was destruction—self-destruction. Saul committed suicide (31:4).

So—how can you help someone control his or her thought life? Does the Bible have a solution? Is it really possible to have the peace of God that passes all understanding? Can I really believe that the strong hand of God can stay my mind? Can I really think differently (Phil. 4:8)?

Teach biblical absolutes
The counselee needs encouragement to know he or she can control their thought life. The counselee often refers to their mind as "racing," "I can't control my mind," or "can't shut the mind down." Counselees feel helpless and hopeless that their situation can or will change. The good news is that counselees can control their thought life. Ephesians 5:18 can be used to show the counselee that allowing this situation to continue reflects on their relationship to Christ.

The counselee proclaims a faith-based life, but their rampet thought life testifies that God is not center in their particular situation. Daniel 1:8 instructs the counselee to premeditate the pressure points before they occur. Daniel purposed in his heart not to defile himself with the king's food. He gave serious consideration to the immediate future. What pressures would he face and how would he respond? When the thought life is out of kilter, most decisions are driven by emotions—the spur of the moment, what feels right. Teach the counselee to think ahead, be driven by facts, predetermine how to respond, and if a situation arises the decision is already made.

See if the counselee is living in the past
Isaiah 43:18 is a powerful verse of hope and encouragement. God commands Judah to stop dwelling in the past. Why? Because one cannot change the past. A person dwelling on the past is completely lost. How? A person thinking about the past cannot properly respond to the present situation. The present situation is daunted and controlled by the past. As a result, the future becomes misshapen. If the future is going to be like the present, then why try—why bother?

Now, God encourages those dwelling in the past to look for the active hand of God's divine intervention. But when someone looks at the past, he or she cannot see God's operative hand. A wild thought life believes that the situation is impossible. God says that what the counselee calls impossible is not. God pictures the possibilities of the impossibilities as roadways in the wilderness and rivers in the desert (Isa. 43:18).

Search for that with which the counselee may be preoccupied
Dominating destructive thoughts are reoccurring destructive thoughts. These thoughts have become lodged in the mind. They become fixed, immoveable, hard and fast, and permanent (Jer. 4:14). Solomon struggled with his thought life for a period of time. You can read about it in the book of Ecclesiastes. Here we support the principle of evaluating what the counselee is setting his mind upon and how it dominates his thoughts (Eccl. 1:3, 17; 2:3; 7:25; 8:9).

Effective data gathering will show the counselor what the preoccupation of mind may be—finances, worry, fear, anger, relationships, disappointments, etc.

Provide measurable and attainable homework
A few suggestions would be in order.

- Have the counselee develop a praise list—things he or she can praise God for and write specifically how that particular praise helps them view their situation in a God-honoring fashion.

- Have the counselee memorize appropriate Bible verses that address the destructive thoughts and record how these verses address their circumstances.

- Have the counselee search for, write out, and apply biblical promises for the specific condition.
- Assign Christian biographies that provide principles the counselee can adapt to change their thought processes.
- Carefully work through Philippians 4:6–8. This is one of the clearest passages on how to control the thought life from a practical standpoint. Teach the counselee how the different words in verse 6 climax in a crescendo with the peace of God. Verse 6 doesn't direct the counselee to pray merely about these destructive thoughts. It is an escalator toward that peace that stands as a sentinel to protect his or her emotional and mental state. Strive to understand each Greek word Paul uses.

Dissect and apply 2 Corinthians 10:4, 5

Here is another powerfully inspired portion of God's Word directed toward destructive thoughts.

Speculations or imaginations (English words) is the Greek word *logismos* from where we derive the English word logic or logistics. Destructive thoughts are the result of the investment of time on the wrong ideas.

Let's say we have a counselee overwhelmed with sorrow. He recently lost his job after eighteen years. His health is beginning to break. His wife leaves him for another man. The bank is foreclosing in his home. He barely qualifies for SSI (Social Security Disability Benefits). His social security doesn't kick in for another four years. He has depleted his savings, 401(k), and retirement accounts. With each successive tragic event, he wonders where God is in his life. He tries to convince himself that God loves him. He attempts to maintain the belief that God is in control—that God does care. But he measures his circumstances by the ineptitude of God.

The logic of his situation concludes otherwise. He is convinced that God does not love him, otherwise God would not have allowed all these things to happen. His mind influences him that God is not in control, that God does not really care for him—he is but a speck in the larger picture of life. God must be busy!

The attacks on God's character and attributes come from his logic. This is what Paul writes—that the logistics lead to lofty thoughts raised up against the knowledge of God.

But Paul doesn't stop there. It is a bleak scenario, but against such darkness shines the light of hope, grace, and mercy. We have powerful weapons, unlike any weapons we might have used before (10:4). These weapons are so powerful they can utterly destroy those destructive thoughts.

The counselee must desire to incarcerate these thoughts. He must take each thought captive to the obedience of Christ.

For example: "God must not love me because of all that I am enduring" (ungodly thought). A biblical thought might be, "God indeed loves me so thoroughly and completely that He is allowing these trails to come into my life for His preordained purpose in my life and to magnify His glory."

Well, we have briefly traced King Saul's destructive thought life and recorded the undesirable end. We have offered biblical suggestions on how to begin helping someone banish those destructive thoughts.

In conclusion, here are two resources you will find extremely helpful. They are: Paul VanderGriff's *In the Arena of the Mind*, and Kriss Lundgaard's *The Enemy Within*.

I Can't Do That! What Does God Expect from Me?
Helping Someone Who Says They Can't

How do you help someone who says, "I can't"? The wife who says she can't live another moment with her husband. The parents who claim they can't control their rebellious teenager. The employee who bemoans he can't work another day for his harsh boss. The depressed person who cries she can't get out of bed in the mornings because she is weighed down by her fears. What about the person who argues he can't control his anger? And the person who argues she can't forgive the person who wounded her so deeply, or the person who claims he can't stop drinking? The person who asserts she can't stop being afraid, or the person who can't control his tongue?

Here are some prevalent ideas and classifications of human responses to those who claim, "I can't." These are misguided words of encouragement some think will help the person refrain from saying "I can't."

The Disposable Generation. This is the philosophy that espouses if a situation is not working out as you thought or wanted, then change situations. If your marriage partner is a disappointment, get a new marriage partner or live single. Relationships that do not meet one's needs can be discarded. The disposable mentality now includes relationships.

The Little Engine That Could. This old children's story describes many people's counsel to those who claim they can't. Just try harder. Like the little engine climbing the steep mountain trying to get to the top, that little engine needed to think positive thoughts. The little engine needed to focus on its inherit ability to succeed. Just push aside all the negative and simply work harder, work faster, or work longer. In the end, things will improve, but it's up to you.

The Eeyore Syndrome. Eeyore is that loveable character in Winnie the Pooh stories. He is the donkey with the pessimistic approach to life. Eeyore is the one who forecasted doom and gloom. His attempts at living could be summarized as "Grin n' Bear It." Rarely, if ever, do you see Eeyore smiling, cheerful, positive, or enjoying life. Those trying to cheer up the "I can't" person will say things like, "That's just the way he is, honey." Or, "You can't teach old dogs new tricks." Or, "You just got to love him." Or, "You could have done worse if you married so and so."

<u>JP in Angels in the Outfield.</u> This Walt Disney picture is about a young boy, Roger, who believes in his last place baseball team, the California Angels. As the boy spent his years living in short-term foster care, his father's infrequent visit yields a quip from him that if the Angels can end the season in first place they could become a family again. JP becomes a close friend to Roger. JP's catch-phrase is, "It could happen." JP is a positive thinker. He has the faith of a mustard seed. He has child-like faith. Many try to encourage the "I can't" naysayer with "It could happen." You have to believe. You have to have faith. You must believe more—harder.

A powerful passage to help the "I can't" person is found in 1 Corinthians, chapter 10, verse 13.

> No temptation has overtaken you but such as is common to man; and God is faithful, who will not allow you to be tempted beyond what you are able, but with the temptation will provide the way of escape also, so that you will be able to endure it.

Before unpacking this verse, to appreciate fully its content, we need to examine briefly the historical setting.

The first twelve verses describe Israel's journey to the Promised Land. This journey is described for us in the books of Exodus and Numbers. Take time to note the numerous references to the word "all" (verses 2, 3, 7). Also, note the specific mention of displeasure with "most" in verse 5. Conversely, observe the obvious that there were some that were pleasing to God. Carefully observe that this specific time, and all of the Old Testament, was recorded *as examples for us* (10:6, 11). We can learn such great biblical truths from the Old Testament.

From the moment these Israelites were redeemed from the bondage of the Egyptians, a life of complaining, grumbling, and rebellion to authority displayed itself. In spite of blood redemption, in spite of divine promises, in spite of daily provisions, guidance, and protection, they said, "We can't" (Num. 13). They even went further and desired to go back into slavery. They cried against Moses and demanded to know why he brought them out into the wilderness to die. They wanted to return to the meager existence of making bricks, building pagan monuments, and "when we sat by the pots of meat, when we ate bread to the full: (Ex. 16:3, 17:3; Num. 14:2–4, 20:5, 21:5).

Preliminary Conclusions

The nature of the temptation is undefined so we do not miss the point of the passage—that *yes, we can*. When we say "We can't," we are telling God He is a liar and His promises are untrustworthy. When we say "We can't," we return to the same sins the children of Israel committed. What are some of the "I can't" sins?

- Craving evil things. Remaining in the past, learning coping devices, making adjustments for the purpose of stagnation. They wanted to return to Egypt, which is a picture of the world.

- Idolatry. Wanting a pleasant life rather than a disciplined life. The easy way out. They wanted a god that wouldn't demand so much of them, like the Golden Calf.

- Immorality. Wanting to feed the flesh and justifying immediate gratification, often at another person's expense. Wanting to handle the situation as the world would handle it.

- Testing God. Direct and deliberate disobedience as displayed at Kadesh-barnea.

- Grumbling. Verbal abuse towards others and God, as seen when they wanted food, water, and deliverance from their enemies.

- Pride. Cyclical failure due to self-righteousness. This is recorded in the Book of Judges. The Judges cycle is sin, servitude, supplication, salvation.

There are four promises that can help someone change their speech from "I can't" to "Yes, I can." These four promises are found in 1 Corinthians 10:13.

First promise is: <u>Yes, I can, because someone before me has experienced the same difficulties</u>. When I believe, say, and act upon "Yes, I can," I am moving in a biblical direction to fulfill God's intended purpose for my life. I am performing the good works He ordained for me to walk in before the foundations of the world (Eph. 2:10). I am doing God's will. Consider the following biblical examples.

Satan attempted to discredit and disqualify Jesus as the Holy One, Messiah, and Promised Deliverer. Satan presented three distinct allurements to Christ. If Christ acted upon any of the temptations, He would sin and negate His purpose of being the sinless Lamb of God that takes away the sins of the world. Jesus never said, "I can't." The temptations He faced were real and genuine. He was tempted in all points like man, but He never sinned. Christ proclaimed, "I can" and used the Scriptures to defeat each of Satan's temptations to remain holy and undefiled.

Because Jesus was made in the likeness unto His brethren (Heb. 2:17), we have a sympathetic high priest who completely understands our infirmities (Heb. 4:15). Christ is our example of removing the spiritual debilitating "I can't," replacing it with "I can" (Heb. 4:16), living in obedient holiness, and enjoying victory.

The Bible addresses a myriad of everyday situations that influence a person to herald, "I can't."

Relational problems—Abraham/Lot
Abraham could have thrown up his hands toward Heaven and muttered to himself about the ingratitude of his nephew Lot. "How ungrateful! I didn't have to take you along, but I did. But now you are haggling with my herdsmen, complaining there is not sufficient land for grazing to support both of our large herds, not enough water." Abraham could have said, "I can't continue living with this spoiled brat anymore." But he didn't. He met with Lot, and let Lot look over the vast land expanse and selected where he wanted to live.

Was Abraham disappointed in Lot? Yes! Was Abraham frustrated with Lot? More than likely. Would Abraham like to have gone back to the day he and Sarah left and "uninvited" Lot to go with them? He very well may have had second thoughts. The point is, Abraham did not succumb to self-pity by saying, "I can't." His "I can" allowed God to rightly separate them, bringing peace. When Lot got into trouble, Abraham became actively involved in prayer for Lot's sake.

Marriage Problems—Adam/Eve
If any man might have had the right to balk at the outcome of his wife's conversation and decision, Adam would be the man. I mean, Adam did not ask for this helpmate. Nowhere in Scripture does it say he looked toward Heaven and wanted to know why he was alone. He knew he was different from the animals, but there is no record of his complaining.

God graciously met the human factor in Adam's life. She was perfect. She was the perfect helpmate. She was specially crafted to be with Adam. Eve was Adam's companion. She was Adam's complement. They were a unit. There was oneness between them.

While Eve was deceived, Adam acted willfully. He directly violated the clear command of God not to eat of the Tree of the Knowledge of Good and Evil. Adam and his descendents would be forever held responsible for the entrance of sin upon God's creation.

The Holy Spirit accurately, clearly, and with brutal honesty, records the words, attitudes, and deeds of God's creatures. Do you not find it interesting there is no recorded subsequent conversation between Adam and Eve about the tragic Garden episode or expulsion from Paradise? Adam and Eve were restored to fellowship with God, maintained that fellowship, and sought to raise their sons in the ways of God. Had either one said, "I can't," we might have witnessed the first divorce and wondered which one would have remarried and to whom.

We all know the statistical information on divorces in the United States. The average divorce rate per any given year for the past three decades hovers between 48–52%. So, one out of two marriages end in divorce. Divorce stats increase significantly with each subsequent marriage after a divorce.

Why? A spouse says, "I can't." A mate receives poor counsel from biased parents that solidifies, "I can't." When a person says "I can't" in a divorce, they are saying in effect that they want their own way. They want to be free. They have come to believe that freedom means their happiness. Remaining married to their mate will only mean unhappiness. This person, if they are a saint, is also saying that they do not want God's will. They are claiming that God's will is not good, perfect, and acceptable.

The mate who says "I can" says "I want God's will. I want to glorify God. I know it will be difficult, but with God's strength, I can."

This particular chapter can be excessively long as I look at the other areas that weigh people down and who in turn will say, "can't." Consider examining the Scriptures on how each of these daily circumstances was approached by the biblical character who said, "Yes, I can."

- Financial problems—Paul
- Employment problems—Daniel
- Illness—Job
- Sibling hatred—Joseph
- False accusations—David
- Sinful father—Jonathan
- Antagonistic culture—Corinth, Ephesus, Rome
- Temper—John
- Adultery—Hosea
- Envy—Asaph (Ps. 77)
- Discouragement—Elijah
- Fear—Gideon
- Worry—Disciples

- Sexual pressures—Timothy
- Church problems—Paul

Second promise is: <u>Yes, I can, because God is faithful.</u> God's promises are my anchor. This anchor fastens me to the rock of truth so when I am buffeted by the winds and waves I can say, "I can." What are some of these promises? Here are four precious promises. But a preliminary thought first.

How do we know if someone is faithful? Ah, you say—by their promises; by what they say. This is only partially true. Mankind is full of good intentions, thoughts and words. But you can know if people are faithful, if they will keep their word, primarily by their track record of "kept" promises; the promises they have spoken and fulfilled.

God is a promise-maker. Throughout Scripture, we read of promises He made to His creation. We also know from the Scriptures God has never broken a promise. He keeps His word. God is the truth-teller and the promise-keeper. Man is a liar (Rom. 3:4).

Heb. 13:5

> Make sure that your character is free from the love of money, being content with what you have; for He Himself has said, "I will never desert you, nor will I ever forsake you."

We can say "I can," because no matter what our circumstances may be, God is with us. He promises never to desert us. He pledges He will never forsake us. God says He will never allow us to sink. Remember Peter? He nearly sank while trying to walk on water. Jesus grasped his hand and did not allow him to sink. He promises to uphold me. I am upheld by the righteous powerful right arm/hand of God. When God says He will not forsake me, God is saying He will never leave me in a strait. He pledges never to leave me helpless. He vows that I will never be totally abandoned, or utterly forsaken. "Yes, I can," because I am assured of His power.

Isa. 41:10

> Do not fear, for I am with you; do not anxiously look about you, for I am your God. I will strengthen you, surely I will help you, surely I will uphold you with My righteous right hand.

"Yes, I can," because I am confident of God's power. This verse reminds me that I am able to vanquish fear by recognizing and using God's power. God's presence again is significantly mentioned at the beginning of this verse. Notice what follows. We are commanded not to look anxiously about us. We are not to gaze, stare off, or be distracted at what is happening around us. A person's focus influences their heart. The strength of a person's courage to say "I can" is found in what they have regard for; what they look at.

People, pressure, stress, worries, and a plethora of other circumstances and problems tend to magnify themselves. Comparatively, the sun looms down on a small object and can enlarge that object to overwhelming unrealistic measurements. But the object is miniscule without this outside effect. This is why God commands us to know He is God. Knowing He is God opens our hearts to be strengthened by Him alone. Otherwise, the inferior things we become distracted by appear to be stronger than God is.

Because of who God is, He alone will make me stout, make me strong, and make me alert and bold, so I can continue to say, "Yes, I can." His righteous right hand supports me. This powerful hand is what I must grasp and to which I must cling. His right hand is one of power, justice, strength, and dominion. Because of who He is and what He can do, I do not need to fear or be anxious. Because of who God is, I can.

Isa. 43:2

> When you pass through the waters, I will be with you; and through the rivers, they will not overflow you. When you walk through the fire, you will not be scorched, nor will the flame burn you.

Isa. 43:18, 19

> Do not call to mind the former things, or ponder things of the past. Behold, I will do something new, now it will spring forth; will you not be aware of it? I will even make a roadway in the wilderness, rivers in the desert.

Many times "I can" changes quickly to "I can't" because of our past. We parade across our minds and pull things from the dusty memory box things that dishonored our Savior. We review our sinful and abominable actions. We call to mind the former things and ponder the things of the past. Israel could do this. Isaiah tries to encourage them with the words of God not do dwell on the past. They were idolaters. They intermarried. They refused to remain in the Promised Land. They made faulty alliances with pagan nations. They erected statues to Baal and Asteroth. They robbed the widows. They cheated their neighbors by using unjust balances. God had punished them for these wicked deeds. But there is a side of humanity that returns to these matters as if to make personal atonement for them; to perform some religious ritual to appease God. We try to sooth our conscience by some act of penance or charity.

God says that He is going to do something so shocking it will catch everyone's attention. Man often thinks that his deeds are so terrible God cannot use him. Because of man's terrible rebellion, God is so disgusted with man that God shelves man. But God says He is going to do something new. And God asks a question. Will those He is speaking to even notice?

If you do not accept God's terms of forgiveness, you will perpetually be looking for ways to accomplish your own self-atonement. God says you and I must be looking for His activities, not orchestrating our own. God says that through your sins are like scarlet, though they are as dark as night, what He will do is near impossible—except it is not, because it is God who is doing it. God will straighten out crooked roads in the most barren land; He will insure a river flows through it.

The counselee who says they can't is one who continues to remember the past. They may be rejecting God's way of forgiveness. They may be absorbed in a type of Martin Luther self-flagellation to atone for their sins. They certainly are not looking at the roadway in the wilderness and the river in the desert. The person who admits, confesses, repents and seeks forgiveness is the person who can go on saying "Yes, I can" because his or her next steps, the journey forward from then on, is all about Him and his or her obedience to following Jesus. Yes, I can!

Can you make a list of God's fulfilled promises in the past? What God stood for in the past is what He stands for now and for all eternity.

Third promise is: <u>Yes, I can, because God doesn't give me more than I can handle.</u> Have you ever thought, felt, or said, "I just can't take anymore"? Maybe you feel like a cup that just cannot take one more droplet of water without overflowing. Or a balloon that will burst if another breath of air is exhaled into it. Or a rubber band stretched to its limit near the verge of snapping.

Feelings and thoughts like these are usually because someone else is in control. Someone else is influencing the outcomes of our lives. Someone else is calling the shots. Someone else is making decisions for their own good, not considering how those decisions impact our lives.

Here is a great thought. Someone else may make decisions that influence our lives, but behind every "someone else" is God. It may seem like we cannot take any more, but God says we can because God knows exactly how much we can endure. His wisdom and love for us tempers the extent and intensity of what we can bare up underneath. We refer to this as the sovereignty of God. What is the sovereignty of God?

- Complete Control. God is completely in control. He controls all things real and potential. He controls the length of all events. He controls the duration of all events. He controls the intensity of all events. Because He is in control, He knows when an event will begin and when the event will stop. Nothing can elude the notice of God. Nothing happens spontaneously. No event catches God by surprise. God is never frustrated because of the deeds of men. God is never stymied by the plans of His creation. Therefore, because God is completely and thoroughly in control, I know with confidence and assurance that God will never give me more than I can bear up underneath. God will not add another thing to my plate that He knows I cannot handle through His strength.

- Infinite in Wisdom. I like Bill Gothard's definition of wisdom. He simply defines wisdom as "skillful living." God imparts knowledge to me so I can live in a way that pleases and glorifies Him. With skill, I am able to handle each of life's situations through Him who strengthens me. If Job were invited into the presence of God on the day God and Satan dialogued about Job, I wonder if Job might have interjected something like, "Hey, guys, I'm not really that great of a guy. I do have my faults. God, you are just being to gracious. Remember, I bite my fingernails. Remember the day I hit my thumb with the hammer and I had to stifle what I wanted to say? Satan may be right after all. I'm not sure how I might react if some terrible things happened to my family or me!" I do not know personally of another human being who endured such great, terrible, complete devastating loss like Job. Job did not know the extent. He did even know he was the target of this conversation. Yet, with each servant's report, with each casket and burial, with each declining profit and loss statement, Job said, "Yes, I can trust God, Maker of Heaven and Earth." Job said, "Naked I came from my mother's womb, and naked I shall return there. The Lord gave and the Lord has taken away. Blessed be the name of the Lord." Through all this Job did not sin nor did he blame God.

- Perfect in Love. God's love for me is perfect. His love is always for my best. His love is directed to my wellbeing. His love is for my welfare. His love is unselfish. Because His love is characterized like this, the tokens of His love are perfect. His gifts of love are designed to mature us. They are assigned as avenues to perfect us. When He showers me with love, the intention of His gift is based on His complete knowledge base of me. Every good thing given and every perfect gift is from above and is given at this precise time in my life as the unsurpassed way for me to develop in a particular area of my life.

Fourth promise is: <u>Yes, I can, because God provides the way through, not out.</u>

When I was the pastor of family ministry, my church undertook a remodeling project in the sanctuary. It called for new carpeting and reconfiguration of the sanctuary pews. A number of pews were going to be removed. A church in Wisconsin purchased the pews, but would not be able to pick them up for several weeks. This required a number of men to remove the extra pews down two flights of stairs, around immoveable hand railings, and beneath low ceilings. After numerous attempts with the first pew, we figured out the best way to move the remaining ones. There was only one way to navigate the stairs, hand railings, and low ceilings. Only one way.

When you read the last few words of this verse, many people stop short of the complete contents. Just like when people quote Ephesians 2:8–9, they forget to include verse 10. People quote, "but with the temptation will provide the way of escape." But that's not the complete sentence. God provides the way of escape *so that you will be able to endure it.*

Many translations have taken the liberty of replacing the definite article "the" with the indefinite article "a." Let me illustrate the significance of this. Suppose I had one penny, two nickels, four dimes, and two quarters. I place these coins on the table before you and tell you to take a coin. You would be at liberty to take any coin you wished. If I were you, I would take the quarter. But if I lay those same coins before you and tell you to take the penny, you choices are limited to "the" penny. Only once choice.

Likewise, when God days He will provide "the" way of escape, there is only one way out of the problem. That way is not to escape the problem and or its consequences, but the escape is to insure that you "endure" the process. "Escape" means the way out, result, or outcome. To know the outcome is to experience the process. The word "endure" means to bear up by being under. The idea is a weight on one's shoulders that the person bears up underneath. There is no escape, running away from, or even lightening the load. The concept is to carry the full load from start to finish, to endure.

Most of us when we are experiencing the "I can't" events want to have the way of escape, not endurance. We want the situation to end quickly. We want the consequences to go away. We want relief, comfort, and solace. Left to ourselves, we would choose the pathway that is the easiest, most convenient, and with the least amount of hardships. We would choose the pathway of escape through expedience. And when this occurs, we miss the lessons of the "I can" person. There was a way in, there is *the* way out. Satan is not permitted to block up the way out.

An Acrostic to help those who say they can't: **TOP.**

- **"T"**—Trust—in what area do you need to trust God? In what way will you show you are trusting God? Ps. 37:3.
- **"O"**—Obey—believing that good will come forth no matter how you feel or what your circumstances are.
- **"P"**—Preserve—keep doing what is right no matter if your situation changes. Right is always right in every situation.

Spiritually Slim for Life: Cutting out the Devotional Ding Dongs

Helping the Counselee Develop a Strong Spiritual Life

A number of years back, I was unable to attend church with my family. So what do you do on a Sunday morning when you're not at church? You channel surf. I was amazed at the lack of real intelligent programming. I skimmed by *Face the Nation* and other political line-ups. Then of course, I spun by the info commercials. These are paid television-advertising segments with the usual air time of thirty minutes. There was the "Rocket Chief," a revolutionary discovery in cooking. And one of my favorites was, "The Ab Machine."

These info commercials paraded former sports celebrities, health trainers, and fitness experts to sing the praises of this new innovative exercise process. The camera crew zoomed in on the California beaches where sand-walkers tested the machine and testified to its immediate results. I found it interesting the "experts" looked like they just won the Mr./Miss Universe contest! To boot, none of those sand-walkers were overweight!

Getting into shape takes more than the latest fitness machine, diet, or fad; it takes devotion, discipline, and diligence. Likewise, becoming spiritually strong will not happen with Mobile Daily Devotions for your cell phone, Christian Devotions for Busy Women, 365 five-minute devotions for men, or one-year devotional readings. That is why Paul recorded 2 Timothy 2:3–8. We will examine three metaphors Paul uses to instruct Timothy on how to have a strong spiritual life.

What is the historical backdrop of this passage? A good student of the Word should always examine the surrounding context to understand the flow of the author's thoughts. Look behind and ahead of the passage in question. What do we know?

- Paul established the church at Ephesus on his second missionary journey.
- He spent three years in this city and saw the power of God overcome witchcraft and sinful, licentious lifestyles.
- He later wrote a letter called Ephesians to the church in which he praises this church for their fervent love.
- We know of a second letter written to the church at Ephesus by the Apostle John, in which he chides them for leaving their first love.

What happened between Pastor Paul and John? 1 and 2 Timothy fill in the missing years.

Timothy was the pastor of the church at Ephesus. The church was slipping into carnality. There were issues of discord regarding woman's role in the church. There was a dilemma over who should be appointed to leadership and what would be the qualifications for those seeking leadership positions. There was the presence of false teaching that was creeping into the church and disrupting the church's unity and fellowship. The church was mixed economically. This led to difficulty with the rich, who were abusing their positions with wealth. Additionally, caring for the widows became a renewed controversy.

In 2 Timothy, Paul writes a very personal letter. In chapter 1, Paul reminds Timothy of his godly heritage and how Timothy was set apart for ministry. In chapter 2, Paul uses three metaphors to encourage Timothy to press forward in his Christian walk, service, ministry, and leadership as a pastor.

These three metaphors are instructive for us today. With all the pressures surrounding the Christian and the Church, it is easy for Christians and the Church to compromise, lose fervor, dilute beliefs, and redefine Christianity to coincide with a lifestyle of comfort and pleasure. What are these three metaphors and what instructive lessons can we learn in order to have a strong spiritual life as a Christian wife, mother, husband, father, grandparent, teen, student, single, employer, or employee? The soldier, the athlete, and the farmer are all used by Paul in order for us to learn anew how to persevere.

The Soldier

There are several truths to consider from this first metaphor. Every Christian is involved in a war. History reveals that since the inception of the United States, we have spent more time at war than at peace. Based on the computation in the *Moscow Gazette*, Gustave Valbert, in his day, could report, "From the year 1496 BC to AD 1861 in 3,358 years there were 227 years of peace and 3,130 years of war, or 13 years of war to every year of peace."

Yet, the war spoken of here is not a physical battle but a spiritual battle. Every Christian is engaged in a struggle with the world, flesh, and devil. Read what God's Word says about this war.

The world:

> If the world hates you, you know that it has hated Me before it hated you. If you were of the world, the world would love its own; but because you are not of the world, but I chose you out of the world, because of this the world hates you (John 15:18–19).

And again,

> These things I have spoken to you, so that in Me you may have peace. In the world you have tribulation, but take courage; I have overcome the world (John 16:33).

The flesh:

> For we know that the Law is spiritual, but I am of flesh, sold into bondage to sin. For what I am doing, I do not understand; for I am not practicing what I would like to do, but I am doing the very thing I hate. But if I do the very thing I do not want to do, I agree with the Law, confessing that the Law is good. So now, no longer am I the one doing it, but sin, which dwells in me. For I know that nothing good dwells in me, that is, in my flesh; for the willing is present in me, but the doing of the good is not. For the good that I want, I do not do, but I practice the very evil that I do not want. But if I am doing the very thing I do not want, I am no longer the one doing it, but sin which dwells in me. I find then the principle that evil is present in me,

the one who wants to do good. For I joyfully concur with the law of God in the inner man, but I see a different law in the members of my body, waging war against the law of my mind and making me a prisoner of the law of sin which is in my members. Wretched man that I am! (Romans 7:14–24).

The devil:

> Be of sober spirit, be on the alert. Your adversary, the devil, prowls around like a roaring lion, seeking someone to devour. But resist him, firm in your faith, knowing that the same experiences of suffering are being accomplished by your brethren who are in the world.

But the resources of a good soldier are not of this world.

> For the weapons of our warfare are not of the flesh, but divinely powerful for the destruction of fortresses (2 Cor. 10:4).

We have a Commander-in-Chief who has wholly outfitted the saint to wage war successfully. The saint is arrayed from head to toe with an armor that is invincible, impenetrable, and indestructible. God has issued the saint a complete military provision to wage war successfully.

> Take up the full armor of God, so that you will be able to resist in the evil day, and having done everything, to stand firm. Stand firm therefore, having girded your loins with truth, and having put on the breastplate of righteousness, and having shod your feet with the preparation of the gospel of peace; in addition to all, taking up the shield of faith with which you will be able to extinguish all the flaming arrows of the evil one. And take the helmet of salvation, and the sword of the Spirit, which is the word of God (Eph. 6:13–17).

War creates hardships. Pain is a by-product of war. War brings suffering. Death is inevitable. Disease and causalities are inevitable during battle. Soldiers often deal with fear and loneliness.

Paul's statement of "suffering hardship with me as a good soldier" describes Timothy's mental, emotional, and spiritual condition. Timothy was scared, tired, fearful, and ashamed. In 2 Tim. 1:8–12, Paul admonished Timothy not to be ashamed of Paul in prison. This statement indicates that Timothy was considering going AWOL—absent without leave. Seeing his fellow soldiers and brethren suffering, Timothy wanted to escape and flee the hardship. Timothy did not want to stay on the front lines and fight his share of the battle. He wanted a "desk job." This is what happened when John Mark deserted Paul on the first missionary journey. If Timothy had deserted Paul, Timothy would have been deserting God as well.

The level of devotion to a fallen comrade or fellow soldier under fire is directly proportioned to our devotion to God.

As soldiers, we are on active duty. A Roman soldier usually served between seven to sixteen years, and his active duty was around the clock, much like our military service people today. He was always on call. He could be moved from one outpost to another at a moment's notice.

As a former MP, I could be rousted to leave immediately for anywhere in the U.S. for an assignment. If home on furlough, I could be recalled and be expected to return to base immediately.

However, an active soldier also implies alertness while serving. Paul states that a soldier on active duty does not entangle himself in everyday affairs. This allows for a pure thought process for the job at hand.

A soldier couldn't be daydreaming while on active duty. He couldn't be thinking about how "short" he was, the current "Dear John" letter, problems at home, loneliness or fear, soggy fungi-rotten boots, snakes, heat, or insects.

"Active duty" means mental alertness, which is critical to survival and life. In the Vietnam conflict, the Vietcong was known as the "unseen enemy" because of their booby traps. They used trip wires. This wire triggered crossbows or boards with nails that flew up from the ground, piercing the soldier's body. They employed Punji spikes. "Punji traps" were sharp spikes made of bamboo and hidden in pits. These fields could easily disable an enemy soldier. Punjis were often deliberately contaminated to increase the risk of infection. Toe poppers were another means of guerilla warfare that the Vietcong used. Toe poppers were a booby trap that the VC had used to maim and kill many a Marine. They would dig a little hole in the ground about the length of a 50-caliber round, fashion a small piece of wood with a nail in it, and place the board in the hole first. Vietcong soldiers would then drop a Chinese 51-caliber round down the hole. Finally, another flat piece of wood was placed above the round, and covered with dirt and brush. When someone stepped on the contraption, the bullet would shoot upward, taking toes, a good part of a leg, or even kill the victim. The point man was constantly surveying the terrain for these hidden devices. Careful observations and subsequent warnings by a soldier could save the life and limb of a fellow GI.

Christians are on active duty. We often forget we are in a war. The enemy goes underground. The skirmishes are infrequent. Someone declares a "D" day, and the saint celebrates amnesty. The war is not over until the King returns with His sword coming out of His mouth to destroy every enemy that stood against His rule.

This war is real. It is for today. The saint is not in high school ROTC practicing routines with a plastic or wooden rifle. We are not in the National Guard where once a month we "drill" and two weeks out of the month we go off and have "maneuvers." The saint is neither a weekend warrior nor a reservist.

We are to be ready in and out of season. We are to be alert. We are to be watchful. Paul writes,

> Be on the alert, stand firm in the faith, act like men, be strong (1 Cor. 16:13).

> There is no time for sleeping. Paul commands, "so then let us not sleep as others do, but let us be alert and sober (1 Thess. 5:6).

Christians on active duty desire to please their commanding officer. Obie Milner was a supply sergeant when I was stationed at Ft. Hood, Texas. Sergeant Milner had 7–8 hash marks, which represented approximately 28–32 years of active service. But Obie was only an E-6. Milner was just a lowly staff sergeant.

Helping the Counselee Develop a Strong Spiritual Life

Obie was entangled into the affairs of the world. He was always seeking to make a buck on GI surplus such as flight jackets, sun glasses, and K-rations. He was an opportunist. The only metal on his dress green was a Distinguished Service Metal given to everybody. No battles, no metals of honor, valor, or the Purple Heart. Milner was just getting by playing soldier.

If you never enter the battle, because you consider yourself a civilian, then you will never have any metals. If you never engage the spiritual enemy, form convictions, stand up for what you truly believe, and live life in a powerful holy way, you will have no crowns to present to your commanding officer, Jesus Christ.

Are you on spiritual furlough? When is your military furlough up? When are you going to return to active duty? Have you gone AWOL at home or work? Do you flee under the aerial assault of the enemy? Are you in the spiritual infirmary because you were daydreaming and did not see the spiritual booby traps? Can you recognize the booby traps of the enemy and avoid becoming causality? Are you devoted?

Devotion flows from your love life for God to others.

The Athlete
The second metaphor Paul encourages Timothy with is the athlete. Paul seems to be the only writer who uses the metaphors from the Olympics. In 1 Cor. 9:24, he refers to running the race. "Do you not know that those who run in a race all run, but only one receives the prize? Run in such a way that you may win. Everyone who competes in the games exercises self-control in all things. They then do it to receive a perishable wreath, but we an imperishable" (9:24–26). In 1 Cor. 9:26, he writes about boxing in such a way as to win. I box in such a way, as "not beating the air." In 1 Cor. 15:32, he refers to the gladiators.

In our verses, Paul reference to the Isthmian or Olympian Games conducted at Corinth or Ephesus. In fact, over the course of biblical history of 1,000 years, there were four known games: the Isthmian, Nemean, Pythian, and the Olympian Games that were held every four years even during war. The Games began around 765 BC and continued until Constantine ended them in mid 350s AD due to Christian objections and protests.

Like today, there were several qualifications for each competitor.

- Birth: they had to be a Greek-born citizen.
- Training: they had to commence training at least ten months prior to the Games.
- Residence: all competitors were to reside in the same place under close supervision thirty days prior to the Games.
- Diet: each competitor had to comply with a strict diet.
- Competition: each had to complete according to the specific rules of the event.

Failure to meet these requirements, to pretend that the requirements were met, or to act in a deceptive fashion would not only result in the contestant being disqualified, but the contestant would be beaten and branded in disgrace.

An athlete is involved in a competition. Competition implies participation, similar to a soldier on active duty. This is not an athlete who is on waivers. This is not an athlete who is a pre-season hold-out. This is not an athlete who is on the DL (disable list). This is not an athlete who is in the coach's dog house, warming the bench. This is not an athlete who is a former figure of glory and fame such as Robert Parrish, former great of the Boston Celtics, warming the Chicago Bull's bench in their final championship of the six-peat.

This athlete is actively involved in a struggle to be the best in a particular event. This means the athlete observes training and discipline routines. The athlete puts forth effort, adheres to the coach's schedule, and shows up for every practice. This preparation involves strength training, performance training, and skill refinement.

Training for competition may mean making personal adjustments in order to shave a split second off, which will result in the gold rather

Helping the Counselee Develop a Strong Spiritual Life

than the bronze. It will mean trial meets to practice newfound skills and to test the body and mind of the athlete.

Like the soldier, the athlete must set aside everything to train. He or she cannot be concerned with the senior prom, gir friends, or latest fads. The athlete is usually tutored in the morning after an early practice. Then in the afternoon, they have a second practice, and the evening hours are devoted to homework and preparation for the upcoming day. This routine is repeated day in and day out. For some Olympians, this routine lasts nearly four years, and for many Olympians the competition itself may last less than one minute.

Wilma Rudolph suffered from polio as a child, which left her with a crooked left leg. She wore metal braces and had to have treatments for over six years. At age eleven, through sheer diligence and determination, she forced herself to walk without braces for the first time. Her older sister was a good runner, and, at age twelve, Wilma started to think about running. What a decision! She then presented herself with diligence to be a runner. She talked to the coach and asked for a special time. The coach agreed. In two years, she outran every other girl in her high school in Clarksville, Tennessee. Two years later, in 1956, she ran in the Olympics in Melbourne, Australia, and won the bronze medal. Four years later, in 1960, in Rome, she was ready. She had paid the price. She won, and she won big. She won the 100-meter dash. She won the 200-meter dash. She anchored the U.S. relay team and won three gold medals. A lovely, little, disabled girl reached for the gold.

One 3-meter Olympian relocated 2,500 miles away to live with her coach to qualify. Another left family behind and for the next seven years did nothing but the 3-meter and 10-meter platform.

An athlete must compete according to the rules. In researching this chapter, many of the rules you have in the present-day Olympics are derived from the very first events. An athlete is involved in daily practice, but this practice is governed by the rules of the game. Practicing by the rules simulates the actual event and provides realism for the athlete's preparation. Practicing and competing by the rules provides equal opportunity for anyone from anywhere to stand on the winner's platform. It now becomes a matter of training, desire, and developed ability.

Vince Lombardi once said, "The difference between a successful person and others is not a lack of strength, not a lack of knowledge, but rather a lack of will."

An athlete competes for a prize. What purpose would training and practice have if upon entering an event there were no prize, medal, recognition, acclaim, symbol of victory, or commercial endorsement contracts?

The athlete in Bible times received a prize. It was an olive branch, which later was replaced by the laurel wreath decorating the Olympian's head. This crowning designated him as the best in that event.

Paul reminds us that our prize is temporary.

> Everyone who competes in the games exercises self-control in all things. They then do it to receive a perishable wreath (1 Corinthians 9:25).

Paul also reminds us that we pursue a higher calling, an upward call of the Lord Jesus Christ.

> I press on toward the goal for the prize of the upward call of God in Christ Jesus (Philippians 3:14).

Because there is Heaven, because there is the soon return of Christ with all who have gone before us, because there is the residency work of the Holy Spirit, because we have a unique fellowship among the saints, we run our race with endurance. We are assured of victory!

Have you met the qualifications to compete? Have you experienced the spiritual new birth Christ told Nicodemus he must have to see the Kingdom of God? If you have a personal relationship with Christ, when was the last time your coach saw you at practice? For what exactly are you competing? Are you losing spiritual meets because you do not follow the rules? Does the prize elude you?

As soldiers, you and I must work at devotion, and like the athlete, we must work at discipline. Are you disciplined? You cultivate discipline through training and practice.

The level of victory is related directly to your efforts in practice.

The Farmer
The farmer is diligent. Though the majority Paul's work took place in the metropolis, the roots of Jewish work was agrarian. They were farmers. They planted figs, olives, and vineyards.

Jesus often used the farmer as an analogy to teach spiritual truth. The farmer with the seed and soils, the farmer whose enemy sowed tares in his field, or the farmer who sent servants and then his son to collect the first fruits as payment from the tenants were all used as examples by Christ.

The farmer is characterized as hard working. The Greek "work" means to labor to the point of exhaustion, to work until you sweat, and to toil long hours no matter the weather conditions. With the onslaught of technology today, farming is comparatively easier than yesteryear. We have stereos, TV, satellite farming, and AC in giant combines that can cover huge pieces of farmland in a matter of hours or days.

The biblical farmer knew little of modern conveniences. Everything pertaining to farming was performed by hand. There were untold hours of preparing the soil by hand, removing rocks, weeds, and thistles. Then he would set the seed, always by hand. Then he would wait and see.

Living in Colorado, because of the limited rain fall (average perhaps fifteen inches annually), the farmers would "set water." This had to be done every 3–4 hours around the clock as long as the water was flowing. As the snows melted in the higher elevations, it would accumulate in large reservoirs. In the early spring, these reservoirs would be opened and the water would "run." Then the farmers could "set water" in the ditches that surrounded their crops.

The farmer is always busy. His occupation is not clamorous such as the soldier preparing for battle or the athlete preparing for a race. The farmer has no crowds to cheer him on or to herald his latest bumper crop. Each and every day the farmer lives a life of mundane, tedious chores, tirelessly performing them in hope.

Out of all three metaphors, the farmer is the one who lives most by faith. In the most brutal sense, there is little skill in farming. It is all up to God. In a twinkling of an eye, an entire farm can be devastated by a sudden hailstorm pelting the beans to a pulp. It is too late to plant another bean crop or to replant the destroyed crop with other seed. Day in and day out, with little recognition, the farmer remains diligent to the fundamentals and trusts God for a bountiful harvest.

The farmer is guaranteed participation from his efforts. Proverbs talks about the diligence and the reward for tireless efforts.

> *Poor is he who works with a negligent hand,*
> *However, the hand of the diligent makes rich.*
> *The soul of the sluggard craves and gets nothing,*
> *But the soul of the diligent is made fat.*
> *The plans of the diligent lead surely to advantage,*
> *But everyone who is hasty comes surely to poverty.*

We must remember that our labor is never in vain in the Lord. He takes notice of our efforts, and if we do not faint, we will reap. God honors faithfulness. Remember the commendation to the faithful stewards? They received their reward.

Am I faithful in the mundane things of life? Am I faithful in the tedious things of life? What am I sowing? How hard am I working? Am I taking too many coffee breaks? Am I diligent? Do I call in sick? Am I on strike?

You cultivate diligence by believing that what you are doing is the single most important thing God wants you to do.

Paul summarized his life in 2 Timothy 4:7 when he wrote that he had fought the good fight (soldier), he had run the race (athlete), and he had kept the faith (farmer).

Vince Lombardi made a film, which drums an important principle into the heads of football players. The film is entitled *Second Effort*. It arouses players to do more than memorize plays, faithfully train, and work hard. It urges them to keep going when everything within them says, "Stop," and to pick up the extra necessary yards after they have been tackled.

The soldier, despite fear, goes on. The athlete, despite fatigue, goes on. The farmer, despite possible failure, goes on.

If I Could Ask God, I Would Ask…
Four of Life's Greatest Questions

Have you ever wondered about the great questions in life? Have you pondered those questions that could make a difference in a person's life? For example, Oral Hershicher was recently asked when he thought the Cubs would bring a World Series to Chicago. Other questions might be: Will the Bears win the division? Who gives Ann Lander's advice? Does Dudley Do Right ever get Nell? What is 911's emergency number?

On a more serious note, people of all ages ask: What is the purpose of life? Why am I here? What am I suppose to be doing? Why does God allow suffering? Why does God permit evil?

Funny thing about questions—some are not worthy of an answer. Some questions you will never find an answer to on this side of life. For some you can find the answers, but it takes a great deal of faith to live with the answer.

There are four questions recorded in Scriptures for us from Romans 8:31–39 I would like to attempt to unpack. Understanding these questions can make a world of difference. They can improve the quality of Christian living. What are these questions?

- If God is for us, who can be against us?
- Who will bring a charge against God's elect?
- Who is the one who condemns?
- Who can separate us from the love of Christ?

They can be slightly rephrased without injustice to capture the minds of men and women today.

- I know I am saved, but will God help me a live holy life in an unholy world?

- I know I disappoint God more than I dazzle Him. I wonder if He will ever change His mind about my salvation?
- I know Christ died on the cross for my sin, but does that include *all* my sin?
- I feel like Pigpen, Charles Shultz's character, who always has a cloud of dirt following him. Are all my troubles a sign that God has abandoned me?

Before we begin, there are some crucial areas of observation. First, each question contains the word "who." Second, two out of the four questions contain the present tense verb "is" and relate to God's omnipotence and Christ's Substitutionary atonement. Third, the remaining two verses contain the future tense verb "will" and relate to God's justice and Christ's everlasting, unconditional love.

<u>Question One</u>
If God is for us, who can be against us? Or paraphrase, "I know I am saved, but will God help me live a holy life in an unholy world?"

The word "if" is not the classical first or second condition. It is not, "If it is true, but it might not be," or "If it is not true but it could be." It is a third class conditional statement that can be legitimately translated using the words "since" or "because." You can read the first sentence of this verse as, "Because God is for us…" or "Since God is for us…"

"For us" means God is proactive not only on our behalf but for every saint. God's kind intention of His will is directed toward us as a grace gift (Eph. 1:5, 9). We are the benefactors of His plans. All of God's might, power, purposes, and resources have us in mind. We have become His most precious and valued recipients.

We need to pause and understand the phrase, "who is against us?" "Against us" means that someone or something is opposing, challenging, or is in direct opposition to us. We must raise the logical question, "Who or what is greater than the omnipotence of God, Maker of Heaven and Earth? Who sustains the world? Who is the Creator of all, before all, in all, through all and above all?"

The world thinks it can stand against God with its philosophies and belief-value systems. The flesh thinks it can stand against God with its enticements, allurements, and allusions. The devil thinks he can stand against God with his covert and overt operations of deceptions, lies, and cunning delusions. Man thinks he can stand against God with his human reasoning, policies, and traditions.

With each of these rhetorical questions, Paul supplies the answer. God's eternal decrees insure us of His daily involvement in my life. God didn't space his Son but delivered Him over for us all. There were other ways God sought to stand for us. God ordained the priesthood, prophets, Moses, the Law, the sacrificial system, kings, and a monarchy. All failed miserably to stand before the people representing an unshakable God.

God gave His very best. God gave us His only begotten Son. Why would He wimp out on anything less? Compared to the matchless Christ, those things are indeed inferior. But since God gives the very best, it is unfathomable to think He would withhold such lesser blessings.

I have Christ by faith and I have what Christ has. I am told that I am a joint heir (8:17). It is spiritually insane to think, believe, or entertain the thoughts that God would suddenly become a miser on lesser things. To withhold a lesser spiritual blessing is to devalue the finished work of Jesus Christ. We make the vicarious work of Christ pale by withholding an inferior blessing.

Let me try and provide two examples. The first is a negative example. You go to your local car dealer. You inform the salesperson you want to buy a new car. You have never had a new car before. The dealer begins to let you know the following options come with the purchase of your new ride. You can have a satellite radio combination CD player stereo system. Instead of vinyl seat covers, you can have leather seats. Rather than develop your quadriceps and triceps, you can have power steering. Power locks, power mirrors, power seats, tilt steering wheel, and undercoating are all available. But you decline these options. Your new ride has been reduced to four wheels, one seat, two-doors, a glove compartment, and a rear view mirror. Likewise, many Christians only see their salvation as a stripped down model.

Here is a positive example. You purchase a one-day pass to Great America. All the rides are included with the purchase of one ticket. You have access to unlimited rides. Everything in the theme park is available to you for the purchase price of a single ticket. Understand, loved ones, God has given us access to all of the tools and supplies to live a holy life in an unholy world. Knowing that God is for me and nothing can stand against me is possible because God did not give us a "stripped-down" version of salvation. He gave us access to everything!

Question Two
The second question is "Who will bring a charge against God's elect? I know I disappoint God more than I dazzle Him. So, I wonder sometimes if He will ever change His mind about my salvation?"

The word "accusation" means to bring forth a charge, to come forth and accuse someone of something. The word is mostly used in the book of Acts. Let's identify a few sources that may accuse us.

People can accuse us. They can find fault with us and point it out. The accusation may be true and real, or it may be based on their perception. *My conscience* can accuse me. My conscience can hit certain keystroke combinations and bring back to mind confessed and cleansed sinful actions. *Satan* can be the accuser of the brethren. The accusation is against the "elect," those redeemed by the blood of Christ and justified by God based on His Son's atonement.

What are the elect accused of and does the accuser implicate God Himself? The basic accusation is against the elect's manner of living. The accuser implies God made a mistake in His role as justifier. God is on the "take." His system of justification is prejudicial, inferior, and leaning towards an elite group. However, God's justification is certain and sure because of the work of Christ. Paul writes in Romans 3:23–26:

> For all have sinned and fall short of the glory of God, being justified as a gift by His grace through the redemption which is in Christ Jesus; whom God displayed publicly as propitiation in His blood through faith. This was

> to demonstrate His righteousness, because in the forbearance of God He passed over the sins previously committed; for the demonstration, I say, of His righteousness at the present time, so that He would be just and the justifier of the one who has faith in Jesus.

Who is the one who condemns? The word "condemns" means to judge worthy of punishment. Someone has violated a rule or regulation. The evidence is clear, convincing, and invocating a condemnation that includes the appropriate punishment.

Prior to salvation, I stood condemned before God. I knew through conscience, creation, and the Law that I willfully transgressed. However, that condemnation is removed because of my faith in Christ (Rom. 8:1 says, "Therefore there is now no condemnation for those who are in Christ Jesus").

After salvation, saints still sin. The Apostle John wrote in his first Epistle, "My little children, I am writing these things to you so that you may not sin. And if anyone sins, we have an Advocate with the Father, Jesus Christ the righteous" (1 John 2:1–2).

Did Christ's death cover *all* my sin? Notice the divine ascriptions to Christ's Work and Person. He died for all my sin. This was one of the purposes for His crucifixion. He was raised for our justification. This is His Resurrection. God His Father raised Christ from the dead as a testimony of Jesus' death paying the full penalty for my sin. The resurrection is proof for my justification and God's complete pleasure in His Son's atonement (Gal. 1:1; Eph. 1:20; Col. 3:1). Jesus now sits at the right hand of His Father. This is His ascension. Because He has been raised and has ascended, Christ exercises power, position, acceptability, and honor. He intercedes for those that are His (Heb. 7:25). The only one who can condemn me took my place and takes my place when accused. *He cannot lie!*

Who will separate us from the love of Christ? The word "separate" means to divide, part, pull asunder. The separation has to do with Christ's love for me. Note it speaks of love (*agape*), not any other level of love, which is subjective and conditional. Christ's love is unconditional. Christ is committed to me (John 1:12, Rom. 5:6, 8).

Nothing that I can see or those things that reside in the physical realm can turn off Christ's love directed towards me. Not tribulation—distress, affliction; nor distress—narrow or tight place, extreme affliction. Not persecution—harassment, opposition, nor famine—without food. Neither can nakedness—without clothing or peril—danger, harm, physical. Nor can the sword—death, violence.

Christ's committed love insures my victory in an overwhelming, dominating sense because His love provides everything I need in any one of those situations. I lack nothing!

Nothing that cannot be seen or those things in the spiritual realm can turn off Christ's love toward me. Not death—cessation of the body; not life—the continuance of life; not angels—God's agents in the Heavens; not principalities—Satan's agents in the underneath; not things present—uncertain future; not things to come—uncertain events of today; nor power—human or governmental. Neither can height—that which is above me; depth—that which is below me; or any other created thing—just in case we forgot something.

Yes. God will help me live a holy life each day, every day, until He returns on that day.

No. God will never change His mind about saving me from my sins. God never thinks or believes He made a mistake in saving me.

Yes. The death of Christ covers mankind's sin. It covers my sin. It covers all my sin. Christ's atonement is complete, all-encompassing, effectual, and thorough.

No. God has not forsaken you because you are having difficult times. God has not abandoned you because life is hard. God has not left you. God trusts you enough to respond properly to this valley of growth.

Nowhere to Run, Nowhere to Hide

Are You Running Away from God?

Have you ever heard or read the parable entitled, "The Job Nobody Did"?

> Once upon a time, there were four men named Everybody, Somebody, Anybody, and Nobody. There was an important job to be done, and Everybody was asked to do it. But Everybody was sure that Somebody would do it. Anybody could have done it. But Nobody did it. Somebody got angry about it, because it was Everybody's job. Everybody thought that Anybody could do it, and Nobody realized that Everybody wouldn't do it. It ended up that Everybody blamed Somebody, and Nobody did the job that Anybody could have done in the first place.

This describes the myth of the volunteer church member. I cannot find the origins of this well-established thought process that riddles the church today. However, there is an abundance of Scripture that addresses this false concept of volunteerism. Yes, indeed, the Scriptures declare that we are conscripted into service. Every saint is drafted. In the military sense, conscription (also known as compulsory service, the draft, the call-up, or national service) is a general term for involuntary labor demanded by an established authority. It is most often used in the specific sense of government policies that require citizens, male and female, to serve in the armed forces. It is known by various names—for example, the most recent conscription program in the United States was known colloquially as "the draft."

There is a spiritual selective service. Consider these words from holy writ.

- Every saint is called to serve and our service is motivated and performed in love.

   > For you were called to freedom, brethren; only do not turn your freedom into an opportunity for the flesh, but through love serve one another (Gal. 5:13).

- Christ, the second person of the Trinity, established the example of conscripted service when His disciples failed to do common household tasks.

  If I then, the Lord and the Teacher, washed your feet, you also ought to wash one another's feet. For I gave you an example that you also should do as I did to you (John 13:14–15).

- The believer's service is for the common good of the Body of Christ. The Body needs my skills, talents, and gifts. Failure to use them to build up the Body hampers the growth and maturity of the Body.

  But to each one is given the manifestation of the Spirit for the common good (1 Cor. 12:7).

- When God chose us to be saved, He also chose, at that same moment, acts of service only we can and should do.

  For we are His workmanship, created in Christ Jesus for good works, which God prepared beforehand so that we would walk in them (Eph. 2:10).

- The Bible speaks of gain or loss of rewards directly attributed to the deeds we have done in the flesh since our conversation. Why would there be a Bema Seat if we were not expected to serve? (1 Cor. 3 and 2 Cor. 5).

The old church adage states that 10% of the people are doing 90% of the work. There is a plethora of excuses. When I served as a pastor and even now in a teaching/counseling role, I have heard these excuses and a few more.

- I've tried in the past and it was a total disaster.
- I wouldn't have the foggiest idea on what to say or do.
- I would feel embarrassed if they didn't respond to me.
- I don't feel qualified. I have no degree or training in that area.
- I don't want to serve. I've been burned before in church work and I just plan to sit and soak!

Moses had similar excuses. Does the average saint really understand that God wants us to serve Him and He will not accept excuses? God's resources remove my excuses.

Excuse #1: I've tried to serve, but I failed. This excuse is offered because of problems of the past (Exodus 3:11–12).
In this text, Moses fled to the wilderness from Egypt. Why did Moses flee? The daughter of Pharaoh adopted him after discovering baby Moses in a basket floating among the reeds in the Nile. Moses was raised in the palace. He had access to the finest teachers. Moses was a technician of the Egyptian language, culture, and customs. He was fluent and influential.

Moses knew that his ethnic background was Jewish. One day, "he went out to his brethren and looked on their hard labors" (Ex. 3:11). He saw a Hebrew slave being beaten by an Egyptian. The text says he first looked one way and then the opposite way, and then he killed the Egyptian and hid him in the sand (3:12).

Moses recognized the harshness and cruelty of slavery. He could not understand why one nation had to enslave another into bondage. He greatly desired to bring equality, but the way he went about achieving this goal was wrong.

When a similar situation occurred between two Hebrews, Moses asked, "Why are you striking your companion?" The vocal Hebrew rejected Moses' position of authority. "Who made you a prince or a judge over us?" The vocal one continued challenging Moses when he said, "Are you intending to kill me as you killed the Egyptian?"

Moses did not know that anyone saw his previous actions. He did not realize that there was a witness to his crime. His position and power to help, used in his own feeble effort, would be exposed. He might lose everything: position, power, and life. Indeed, when Pharaoh heard what Moses had done, he tried to kill Moses. Thus, Moses fled to the wilderness and settled in the land of Midian.

Forty years later, after helping Jethro as a herdsman, Moses saw a bush on fire but not consumed. There, in the midst of the burning bush, he met Jehovah. On that hallowed ground, Jehovah enlisted Moses into service. In that encounter, Moses gave his first excuse. "I tried to serve, but I failed. Lord, you know how I tried to serve you and the outcome. That's why I am here, hiding out."

God selected Moses because Moses was the right fit for the assignment. Moses asked to whom should he go. But, God said, "I know who you are, and you are the precise one who can go tell Pharaoh to let My people go."

"Moses," the Lord might have said, "you lived in this man's house, ate his food, probably sat on his knee as his adopted grandson, received gifts from him, clothed by him, exalted in his house, and learned from the finest scholars Egypt had, all because you were accepted by the Pharaoh."

As true as these things were, God told Moses he was chosen because God would "certainly be with [him]." God assured Moses that His presence would aid Moses when he delivered the people. The presence of God would be evidence to the assembly of the redeemed sons and daughters of Abraham, Isaac, and Jacob returning to the mountain where Moses received his commission and where God's people would worship Jehovah.

The book of Acts adds a colorful commentary to Moses' calling and mindset. Moses assumed his Hebrew brethren would understand that Jehovah had commissioned him to deliver them. But Dr. Luke, the historian, writes that those who came to be delivered did not recognize nor accept Moses as the Deliverer. This was verified from the moment Moses first returned to Egypt and lasted until the day he went up into the mountain to view the Promised Land and die.

Yes, Moses saw, felt compassion, and attempted to serve God. But Moses' attempts to serve were not energized by the Spirit of God. He sought to free God's people by means of the flesh. He tried using his might and strength, but failed to depend utterly on the Spirit's anointing. He did not wait on God's timing. He did not use God's power, and the results were disastrous. Pharaoh wanted to kill him (2:15), and the Israelites did not respect him (2:14). Even if a person has been called to serve, without God, the results are disastrous!

Moses needed to know God. He needed to spend time with God alone. Moses needed to be retrained from the self-reliant ways of Egypt. God had to prepare him to see His awesome power defeat and destroy the Egyptian gods, then humble and amaze the priests and magicians. Time matured Moses.

Our failure in serving God is dispelled as we return to service. Moses lingered long enough in the wilderness. It was time to dispel the power of negative thinking, which wrapped itself around Moses. God reminded Moses of His presence.

Excuse #2: I wouldn't know what to say. This is the problem of the message (3:12–22).

This is the first of several hypothetical situations Moses offered God. "What if's" are often rooted in the fear of man. Moses needed to equate the covenant-keeping name of God with God's self-existent, eternal name I AM.

Moses believed it would be a grave error for him to attempt to persuade God to send another in Moses' place. Moses has to approach the Hebrews and tell them he has been sent to deliver the Hebrew nation. Now, why wouldn't the Hebrews know the God of Abraham, Isaac, and Jacob? A worried Moses throws up a straw man. Moses claims the Children of God will test him by asking the name of God. Could Moses be religiously ignorant? Has all of the Egyptian training removed his knowledge of his ancestry, altars, miracles, and traditions passed from one generation to another? What is he to say if he is asked who this God is?

God instructs Moses to reply, "I AM WHO I AM sent you." In fact, this name is associated with Abraham, Isaac, and Jacob. This name is an eternal name. This name was given as a memorial name to all generations. I AM is self-existent, eternal and forever. None of the patriarchs outlived I AM. This name orders Moses to remind the elders of certain things only a God who calls Himself I AM would know. I AM has complete knowledge of Israel's past and their bright future.

I AM says He is faithful. None of the patriarchs, if called to bear witness, could find fault with God. He kept His promises made to Abraham, Isaac, and Jacob. His covenant-keeping power is the guarantee that promises yet to be fulfilled cannot fail. They too will be kept.

I AM says He is tender. He says, "I am concerned about you and what has been done to you in Egypt." For the prophesized time given to Abraham of four hundred years, God has restrained the wickedness of the Egyptians upon Israel. When first entering, the small band of seventy were sheltered and protected by the king Joseph served. Joseph found favor with this Pharaoh. Joseph's family was given land in Goshen, away from the general Egyptian populous and culture. But Scripture says that another Pharaoh who did not know Joseph and who was convinced by his advisers that this growing multitude could become a threat to Egypt's borders, enslaved the Hebrews, placing them in bondage and servitude. The word "concern" means to attend to, to return to visit with the intention of punishment, to look after, or to care for. Although Israel was in great distress, God wanted them to be reminded that He took note of everything that was done to them, and He would repay.

What else does God tell Moses to remind the elders of about His name, I AM? Moses was to remind them that I AM is the deliverer, not Moses. God promises to bring His children into a land flowing with milk and honey. This land was occupied. But God delivered them from the power of Egypt and would equally deliver them from the Canaanites, Hittites, Amorites, Perizzites, Hivites, and Jebusites. These enemies might be entrenched, fortified, aggressive, trained in military warfare, seasoned, and decorated warriors; however, I AM will deliver, because I AM is always!

Moses was to remind the elders that I AM is powerful. The black magic of the Egyptian sorcerer priests was no match for I AM. Many of those Egyptian gods were afterthoughts or established in connected with certain events as a good luck charm so that event would not reoccur if that god were appeased. I AM is always. I AM has no beginning and no end. I AM was not established because of some unforeseen event. The power of I AM was seen in all ten plagues, but especially when the staff of Aaron became a serpent and swallowed the magician's staffs that had turned into serpents. The traumatic miracles of I AM would dismantle the Egyptian's belief in their gods, and cause many of the priest and servants to plead with Pharaoh to let the Israelites go.

Moses reminded the elders that I AM is gracious. What did the Israelites have in Egypt? What would they take out from Egypt with them? Ill and lame family members. No money, little possessions, and a small bundle of clothes. Perhaps they would take some livestock or plants. And they would go to a land occupied and overrun with those who would fight to keep their property. The Israelites were farmers who were heading into a lopsided fight. But I AM promised that the Hebrews would plunder and spoil the Egyptians. I AM said, "I will grant this people favor in the sight of the Egyptians and it shall be that when you go, you will not go empty-handed" (3:21).

God warned Moses of the circumstances associated with his new assignment. God did not promise a walk *in* the park, but a walk *through* the park! The name of God was Moses' message to the elders.

Excuse #3: What if they don't respond? This is the problem of results (4:1–9).

Moses is concerned about his brethren's response. Pessimistic and obstinate were brutal character flaws of the Israelite people. Moses' authority was challenged prior to leaving (2:14). He was concerned about the conflict between himself and nation of Israel, and the growing conflict between himself and Pharaoh. He understood the nature of the challenges. There would be a great spiritual engagement between the gods of Egypt and I AM. Moses braced for the opposition. After a number of miracles, Pharaoh revised the method for making bricks. This increased the Hebrews labor while maintaining the daily quota of bricks required. There would be tough times.

God provided three miracles to encourage Moses. First, I AM asked what Moses had in his hand. Moses responded that it was a staff, and I AM commanded that he throw it on the ground. Immediately, the staff became a serpent. I AM instructed Moses to grab the serpent by the tail, and it returned to a staff. I AM was showing His power over inanimate objects, which comprised a large portion of the world Moses lived in.

Second, God then told Moses to place his hand inside of his robe next to his bosom and to pull it out. Moses' hand was leprous. Moses was commanded to return his hand inside his robe, next to his bosom, and when he pulled it out the second time the flesh was restored. I AM showed Moses He has power of terminal disease. No flesh can stand against Moses.

Finally, I AM prepared Moses just in case the people did not believe the evidence of I AM in the first two signs. Moses was to take some water from the Nile and pour it on dry ground. The water poured on the dry ground would turn to blood. I AM showed His power over the Egyptian god. No black magic or slight-of-hand would stand against Moses and God's plans for deliverance.

Moses predicted the problem of the twenty-first century church in that we are prone to a result-oriented Christian culture rather than a faithful-oriented Christian culture. Was Noah successful? Jeremiah (1:18–19)? Isaiah (6:11)? Christ? By current standards of success, Jesus might be considered a failure. Let's look at how Jesus measured up to these standards: Was he popular? No. He was not well-liked. In fact, after one of his sermons, all of his followers deserted him, except for the Twelve Apostles. Did he have political power? No. He was a political failure. All levels of government openly rejected him. Then they conspired to kill him. Did he have lots of friends? No. His friends often hurt him, eventually abandoned him, and one of them betrayed him to death. Did he have money and possessions? No. No house, no "wheels," no world headquarters, no Christian amusement park. Did his peers respect him? No. His professional peers, the Pharisees, rejected his work.

Results are not always evident when one is obedient. Obedience is the goal of the Christian life, not results. Results can be fabricated, but obedience can't. Failure to enter into service because we cannot see the results or want a guarantee of results is disobedience.

Excuse #4: I don't feel qualified. This is the problem of ability (4:10–12).

When called to obey God in a form of serving, we become more aware of our limitations. One might reason, "I could never learn a foreign language." Or, "I would never be able to adjust to a new culture—all those bugs, or men and women running around naked!" Such excuses could be used along with other vocalizations of our self-perceptions.

Moses offered yet another excuse. He believed he had a legitimate inadequacy. Knowing himself as he did, he believed he did not have the ability to communicate like an ambassador negotiating for a nation's freedom must speak. He reminds I AM that he is not eloquent in speech; he is slow to speech and slow of tongue. Irony strikes as the clay is telling the Potter a mistake has been made.

Let's examine the Hebrew words for eloquent, slow to speak, and slow of tongue. "Eloquent" means, "I have not been a man who has spoken regarding business affairs, matters of society, religious dialogue, or legal matters." Moses may not have taken the lead in such events, but he certainly observed them. "Slow to speak" means speaking is difficult, burdensome, a hardship. Moses appears to be the type of person who—if he were at a party and did not have to speak—would not be egregious and outgoing. You would find Moses in a corner or perhaps acting like the strong, silent type. It is not that Moses had a speech impediment or couldn't speak. Moses did not like to talk! "Slow of tongue" means he was not quick witted, ready with great come-backs. One would not consider Moses to be a silver-tongued orator. He carefully crafts his response when forced to think. Words did not rush out of Moses like a stampede.

Who created Moses? God asks Moses this question. "Who made man's mouth? Who makes him mute or deaf or seeing or blind?"

I AM says "I did." Introspection of one's physical limitations clouds a person's obedience and judgment of God's call and why he or she was created with a purpose. God will use everything up to this point in Moses' life, and the I AM will do the same for each believer. God assures Moses that I AM is with his mouth, his words, and his thoughts. I AM will teach Moses what to say, how to say it, and when to say it.

Moses is a man of deliberation. Imagine God sending someone like David or Paul to proclaim the message, "Let my people go." If David or Paul engaged Pharaoh to release the Israelites, the First World War would have occurred thousands of years ahead of schedule. Moses knows the "ins and outs" of Egypt. He was an insider. All of his experience and training would be used to the fullest by I AM to fulfill I AM's purposes. Remember that God uses the weak things to shame the things that are strong (1 Cor. 1:26–29). God uses our flaws to His favor.

Excuse #5: I don't want to serve. This is the problem of the heart (4:13–17).
After all of Moses excuses and I AM's gracious, tender and compassionate encouragement, Moses flat out says, "Please, Lord, now send the message by whomever you will" (4:13). This is exactly what God has been trying to do. The "whomever I AM wishes" is Moses! "Moses, do you see anyone else on this mountain range? You are the man, Moses. Your problem is not that you tried to serve in your own strength, nor you do not know the exact message I want you to speak. Neither is it that you do not need to see results, nor do you have a fatal flaw that disqualifies you. Moses, the problem is your heart." If you still offer God excuses, it is your *heart*!

God has had enough of Moses' dodging. No more excuses. God's plan is sure and certain, and it includes Moses. God's anger burned against Moses. Literally, the nostrils of God were inflamed. The phrase, "anger of the Lord" is used thirty-five times in the Old Testament. It is a serious response from I AM to His people, who are dull of hearing, are slow to obedience, and fail to perform His will. God makes one last concession. God provides Moses' brother as the mouthpiece. Moses would still be forced to witness the rejection by his brethren and deal with the anger of Pharaoh. But Moses will simply hear from God and speak to Aaron. With no more excuses to offer to God, Moses departs to serve.

Here are two thoughts to consider at this juncture. From God's viewpoint, we see His enduring patience, tender compassion, undying love, and persistence in recruiting Moses for His purposes. From Moses' vantage point, how much time, energy, thinking, and emotions did he waste in trying to finagle his way out of doing God's will? Unlike Jonah, Moses had no place to go!

As this chapter comes to a close and perhaps so does your reading, where does it leave you? When you depart from this book, will you depart to serve? Is God impressing upon you an area in which to serve Him? What area of service have you been offering God excuses in? Maybe church. Maybe as a husband, father, wife, mother, son, or daughter. Isn't it time you were a participant and not a spectator?

His *presence* will dismiss your *failure*. His *name* will provide your *message*. His *power* will produce your *results*. His *creativity* will compensate for your *inabilities*. His *discipline* will change your *heart*!

Well, I Was Baptized…
Are You Saved?—Part 1

For so many years, people have been confronted with a choice between the teachings of Karl Marx and Jesus Christ. I don't mean choosing between communism and capitalism. The choice is between following a leader like Karl Marx and others, who reject God and the Bible, and receiving Christ as Savior. Let's compare the two.

Karl Marx, the man who wrote the "bible" for communism, possessed neither the power to save people from their sins nor the character to be a suitable example. His biographers, even those who are sympathetic to communism, use terms like "isolated and bitterly hostile," "irritable," "insensitive," and "jealously suspicious" to describe him. He had no place in his thinking for concepts like God, purity, love, and gentleness. Nor did he have any hope of Heaven.

How different Jesus Christ is! He was kind—even to despised people like tax collectors and harlots. He held small children in His arms. He touched lepers and healed them. He prayed for His enemies. He was so devoted to His mother that He told John to take care of her while He was hanging on the cross. He spoke lovingly to a criminal being crucified next to Him. But best of all, by His perfect life, atoning death, and glorious resurrection, He brings salvation to all who trust in Him.

This illustration comes from Jesus' own teachings in Matthew 7 where He set a choice before those who listened to Him: either thinking one is righteous, or knowing one is righteous. The difference is eternity. The difference is Heaven or Hell.

Before we begin, we are obligated to make some historical observations to help us understand the context as the author intended.

These verses conclude Christ's first sermon, known as the Sermon on the Mount. His audience was the disciples. The enormous crowds following Jesus were eavesdropping. Jesus instruction is designed to dispel the confusion about who is righteous and who will see the Kingdom of God.

The pivotal point of His sermon is Matthew 5:20, where He instructs His listeners that their righteousness must exceed that of the Pharisees and the scribes or they would not see the Kingdom of God.

What type of righteousness did the Pharisees and scribes have that was inferior? What was it about their righteousness that would prevent them from entering into the Kingdom of Heaven? Their righteousness was merely external, all for show. Their brand of righteousness was self-centered. It was legalistic. Only those who fully and completely adhered to their standard of righteousness were included in their circle. Their righteousness was exclusive and resulted in them being separatists. Consider the commentary by our Lord about their righteousness in Matthew 5:21, 27, 33, 38, 43; 6:1, 2, 5, 16, 19, 25; 7:1, 12.

This entire message is built around contrasts and comparisons. Jesus unmasks the superficial attitude and behavior of the religious sect. But more importantly, He presents an accurate portrait of how a true Kingdom saint will look and act.

In His concluding remarks, Jesus offers one final push and invitation by providing a series of "pairs" or "couplets" as contrasts. They are: two pathways, two animals, two trees, two professions, and two people. Stemming from these couplets, I ask you, "Are you saved?" Jesus is asking the very same question of those who are listening to Him. And my dear reader, there is a right answer.

In this chapter, we will examine the two pathways. Please observe from the text carefully. Jesus is commanding those listening to Him to "enter through the narrow gate." Jesus does not present two gates from which to select. The command is singular. The acceptable gate is the narrow gate. Jesus says there is only one gate to pass through that leads to life. He also speaks plainly that only a few will find that gate. The emphatic emphasis upon the narrow gate is a glimpse of other emphatic spiritual statements Jesus makes such as, "I AM the way, the truth and the life," "I AM the bread of life," "I AM the living water," and "I AM the resurrection and the life."

Are You Saved?—Part 1

The narrow gate has several characteristics. First, it is narrow, which means there is just enough room for a single person to pass through. Only a single individual, void of all the world's possessions, can fit through such a gate.

Second, notice that the narrow gate leads to life. Life spoken of is not present living, but life after life. Life after death. Life that can be given only by one Jesus Christ who said that He came that they might have life and have life more abundantly.

Third, the narrow gate is found by only a few. The staggering statistical information generated by surveys of George Barna reveal approximately 41% of Americans claim to be born-again evangelical, while another 60–70 million claim to be non-evangelicals who use the title of "born again." But Jesus said the gate is narrow and few find it. Jesus refers to disciples as His little flock. Jesus later says that not everyone "who calls me Lord, Lord will enter the Kingdom of Heaven."

Physically speaking, Jerusalem had many gates leading into the city. The main entrance to the Old City is the Jaffa Gate. The name in Arabic, *Bab el-Halil* or Hebron Gate, means "The Beloved," and refers to the beloved of God, Abraham, who is buried in Hebron. The gate on the western side of the Old City marked the end of the highway leading from the Jaffa coast and now leads into the Muslim and Armenian quarters. A road allows cars to enter the Old City through a wide gap in the wall between Jaffa Gate and the Citadel. This passage was originally built in 1898 when Kaiser Wilhelm II of Germany visited Jerusalem. The ruling Ottoman Turks opened it so the German Emperor would not have to dismount his carriage to enter the city. Herod's (Flowers) Gate is the entrance into the Muslim quarter through the northern wall. Damascus Gate is located on the northern wall; it is the busiest and most magnificent of all Jerusalem's gates. It consists of one large center gate originally intended for use by persons of high stature, and two smaller, side entrances for commoners. The New Gate is so named because it was constructed relatively recently, in 1889; the New Gate was built with permission of Sultan Abdul Hamid

II. The gate is located near the northwestern corner of the city and leads into the Christian quarter.

The Zion Gate is located in the south, this gate was used by the Israel Defense Forces in 1967 to enter and capture the Old City. The stones surrounding the gate are still pockmarked by weapons fire. This entrance leads to the Jewish and Armenian quarters. The Dung Gate is found in the south wall, this gate is closest in proximity to the Temple Mount. Since the second century, refuse has been hauled out of the city through this gate, hence the name. The Lions' Gate is located in the east wall; the entrance leads to the Via Dolorosa. Near the gate's crest are four figures of lions, two on the left and two on the right. Legend has it that Sultan Suleiman placed the figures there because he believed that if he did not construct a wall around Jerusalem he would be killed by lions. Israeli paratroops from the 55th Paratroop Brigade came through this gate during the Six-Day War and unfurled the Israeli flag above the Temple Mount.

The Triple Gate dates back to the pre-Ottoman era, the three arches of this gate are located in the south wall and are sealed shut. The Double Gate is this entrance to the south wall is sealed shut and dates back to the pre-Ottoman times. The Single Gate was constructed prior to the Ottoman period along the southern wall, the now sealed gate led to the underground area of the Temple Mount known as Solomon's Stables. The Golden (Mercy) Gate faces the Mount of Olives on the eastern side of the Old City; this gate was constructed in the post-Byzantine period. According to Jewish tradition, the Messiah will enter Jerusalem through this gate. To prevent this, the Muslims sealed the gate during the rule of Suleiman.

There were many gates to enter Jerusalem. There were many gates to pass through to go to the Temple to offer sacrifices. But Jesus said, "Enter through the narrow gate."

Jesus contrasts the narrow gate with the board gate and provides some characteristics of the board gate. The board gate is wide. Unlike the narrow gate, one did not have to stoop to enter the gate. One could bring a variety of items with him through the gate. And unlike

Are You Saved?—Part I

the narrow gate, many could walk through this wide gate in groups. Second, the vast majority will find the wide gate. It is easy to locate and enter. It is popular, contemporary, non-threatening, and non-abrasive. It is welcoming and wants people to feel at ease. Third, the wide gate leads to destruction. It brings about eternal ruin—a ruin that is often recognized too late. It is destruction in that it often hides in the deception of its own popularity.

Members of false religions who experience crisis want answers. When I served as pastor in a predominately false religious community, many women attending a women's Bible study underwent personal and family crises—a mates dying, children rebelling, and marital infidelity. They would seek out the teacher of the women's Bible study, looking for answers. On numerous occasions, they were directed to me. I would listen and instead of spoon feeding them, I would have them crystallize their questions and direct them back to their religious leaders for the answers. I think without exception their religious leaders were unable to give them any biblical answers or hope. I was then able to share God's remarkable love, the Savior, and hope. Many, late in life, became believers. They often remarked afterwards, "Why weren't we taught this?" If we did not intervene, they would have experience certain ruin.

Have you entered the Kingdom through the narrow gate? Have you come to realize that your lifestyle was an affront to the holiness of God and there was nothing you could do to improve? Have you prayed a prayer in Sunday school because someone told you about sin and the Savior who could remove your sin once for all? You were told that lying, stealing, cheating on a test, premarital sex, disobeying your parents, anger, jealousy, and envy were sin, and no one with sin in their lives will enter into the Kingdom of God. You came to a point in your life that being baptized as an infant meant nothing, attending special instructional classes provided knowledge but not a relationship, taking your first communion did not make you a child of God, working and giving to the church made you "feel good," but you were still dead in your trespasses and sin, and God does send people to Hell today because those He created make a choice to accept or reject His free gift of eternal life by faith.

Or are you still on the broad pathway heading toward the broad gate? You know you are not living like God wants you to do, and you resolve to do better. Or you remember praying a prayer during Sunday school because your friends raised their hands and you did not want to be "different." You were told that what you were doing is wrong, you were making mistakes, and you could get to Heaven by being better. You believed you would go to Heaven because you were baptized as an infant in the church; or you attended special instructional classes; or you made your first communion; or you worked in the church or gave to the church; or you were a good person. God doesn't send people to Hell today.

We will continue this series in the next chapter. God wants to remind you of what a true Kingdom saint is so you can appreciate God's grace, mercy, and love and because of this appreciation be more effective as the light of the world and the salt of the earth. This chapter is also to help you see that perhaps many of those you love are not saved. They will not enter the Kingdom of God. You have no hope of reunion if they were to die or if the Lord comes back today. Do you need to make a decision today? Does someone you love need to make a decision today?

I'm a Member of Down the Road Community Church

Are You Saved?—Part 2

Our spiritual standing should not be measured by what others see. Others can see what they want. Others can misunderstand and misinterpret the actions of others. No one is perfect. What matters about our spiritual condition is what God sees. Only He is omniscient. He alone sees our entire spiritual condition; perfectly, compassionately, honestly, fairly, lovingly, and justly.

Let's pause for a moment to review the previous chapter. In that chapter, we outlined this section of Scriptures. The outline consists of two gates, two directions, two destinies, and two groups of people. We concluded the previous chapter with this bottom line, "Are you sure you are Heaven bound?"

I would like to introduce this chapter with an illustration. I remember coming across this illustration in a book that I used when I worked with a group of junior high students at Moody Church. It was very effective and apropos to begin this chapter. It is called "Lying Labels."

I took two cans of vegetables, one corn and the other green beans. I carefully soaked the cans so the labels could be removed without tearing them. Then, after the labels were sufficiently dried, I switched the labels and glued them to the cans. The corn can became the green bean can and vice versa.

The label said one thing but what was inside was something totally different. I had one student come forward and I asked him several times if he was confident that the what the label said were the contents of the can was what was really inside. He responded affirmatively each time asked. I handed him a can opener and instructed him to open one of the cans. He concluded that the labels had been switched and the label lied. What he saw was not really what was inside.

Likewise, this illustration fits well to explain this chapter. Wolves trying to act like sheep, thorn bushes trying to be grape vines, and thistles pretending to be figs: these analogies represent people who are living a spiritual lie. They think they are saved, but are not.

The word "beware" is used twenty-four times in the Bible, with the majority of those usages in the New Testament. The word calls for alertness, caution, discernment. It is used of a soldier on active duty on the front lines of a small platoon detail. It applies to a surgeon performing a very delicate operation that is mishandled and would leave the person paralyzed.

To what was Jesus referring? Who or what was the object of such caution? Jesus was referring to the false prophets in sheep's clothing. He referred to people who tried to look spiritual but were pretenders. Jesus uses this analogy to alert His disciples to the numerous false prophets in their day.

Wolves are the natural predator of sheep. A stray sheep, if not destroyed by the hidden troubles of the unknown places it walked, would certainly fall prey to the wolves. Wolves, according to this verse, are ravenous. The word "ravenous" means dangerous, presenting an imminent threat of harm and destruction. The word in the Greek also means swindler. A swindler is one who takes advantage of another.

To whom is Jesus applying this analogy? The false prophets are being addressed. Note first of all the plurality of the word "prophet." There are many false prophets. Matthew 24:11 says many false prophets will arise in the end times to lead people astray. Note the word "false" in contrast to "true." False prophets fall into three categories. Heretics are those who openly reject the Word of God and teach that which is contrary to divine truth. The second category is apostates. Apostates are those who once followed the true faith but have turned away from it, rejected it, and are trying to lead others away. The third category is deceivers. Deceivers are those who give the appearance of orthodoxy, frequently with great declarations and fanfare. These deceivers are not liberals or cultists, but those who speaks favorably of Christ, the cross, the Bible, the Holy Spirit, and whom associate with true believers. From looks to vocabulary, they give considerable evidence of genuine belief. But, the evidence is not genuine. They are

Are You Saved?—Part 2

false prophets. Jesus is reminding His disciples that false teachers can be heretics, apostates, and deceivers.

God recorded specific instructions about false prophets in Deuteronomy 13:1. False prophets can declare things that could come true. False prophets, even if what they said came true, led astray their follows to serve other gods. False prophets were to be stoned, not because of what they said, but because they draw people away from the faith.

The false prophets Jesus' warned about are the Pharisees. He states in 5:20 that their brand of righteousness was insufficient to usher any convert into the Kingdom, let alone themselves. Jesus went so far as to state that they were blind guides to the blind (Matt. 15:14). He called them children of the devil (John 8:44).

What were their false teachings? First, they espoused an errant theology on what it meant and how one became righteous. They taught a works/righteousness faith. A person earned righteousness by keeping the commandments and the law. Second, they espoused an errant theology on forgiveness. The Pharisees taught that one only had to forgive someone three times and no more. This prevalent ideology help coerce Peter to ask Christ questions on forgiveness. To prove His point, Christ generously doubles the legal requirements and adds one more time (Matt. 18:21). Third, they espoused an errant theology on sin. Sin was what another could observe on the outside. Sin was restricted to a person's behavior. The heart could remain filled with deceit, hatred, lust, and envy. But if someone could control their behavior, sins of the heart were inconsequential. Fourth, they espoused an errant theology on prayer and giving. The religious activity of prayer and giving indicated a person was spiritual. The louder the depository of coins in the Temple were, the more spiritual the person. The longer and louder the prayers of a person showed how close to God they were. Fifth, they espoused an errant theology on the poor and widow. Their conscience was dull to the mistreatment of the poor, elderly, and widowed. The injustice and abuse of these people lined the coffers of the Pharisees. They had no remorse. Their conscience was dead to such exploitation. Sixth, they espoused an errant theology on money. They believed that to have some accumulation of money was a sign of God's favor. To amass much was a sign of divine blessing, spirituality, and standing before God. God only blessed those in a right standing with Himself, and only blessed those in right standing materially. To be poor was a sign of God's disfavor.

Christ said the Pharisees would travel halfway around the world to make one convert and by making a convert made that person twice the son of Hell as they were (Matt. 23:15).

Many people living today honestly think they are saved. When asked about their salvation, you hear comments such as:

- I was baptized as an infant.
- I was raised in a Christian home.
- I serve in the church.
- I am a member of Down the Road Community Church.
- I always believed in God.
- I read my Bible and pray.
- My father was a minister, elder, deacon, or trustee.
- I remember going forward at an evangelistic crusade and saying some prayer.
- I promised God if He got me about of the fix I was in, I would believe in Him.
- I raised my hand along with some other friends at a summer camp.
- I ...

These dear people base their salvation on the teachings of false prophets and religions advocating something "they" must do to "earn" their way to Heaven. Often people are deceived by the cults. These false teachers deny Christ's virgin birth, humanity, death, burial, and resurrection. They rebuke the trinity, worship idols, and pray for the dead.

Are You Saved?—Part 2

But remember, Jesus is saying these false prophets wear sheep's clothing. They look and sound like the real deal. They speak the language of the Bible. They want to blend in. They have a Christian vocabulary. They hangout with other Christians. They carry a Bible and sing hymns. The old adage proclaims, "If it looks like a sheep, smells like a sheep, acts like a sheep, and sounds like a sheep—then it must be a sheep!" But Jesus says they are wolves pretending to be sheep.

False teachers or wolves in sheep's clothing promise you can do anything you want; lifestyle doesn't matter. Sincerity is the only attribute that matters. If you are sincere, then you can live the way you want. Anything and everything is possible. False teachers tell people there is no problem or situation that cannot be solved. Success awaits the man who will never say never. Others will tell you they are saved because they believe in positive thinking. Jesus' ministry was positive. The good news is news that makes you feel good. Other "good news" that makes you feel bad is not the message Jesus preached.

False teachers will tell you that God's will for you is clear. God wants you to succeed. God wants you to be rich, have good health, and enjoy life. False teachers will say that self-love is the ultimate will of man. What you need more than anything else in the world is the awareness that you are a worthy person, you have a wholesome self-esteem, and you love yourself so you can love others.

Some false teachers advocate that only what Jesus says is most important, more important than any other parts of the Bible. False prophets assert that you are saved by the blood, not by the Book.

Some false teachers define sin as the failure to see the lack of self-dignity as the core of the problem. Man's problem is that he was born non-trusting, and that is why he feels he is not good enough to approach a holy God. Man is basically good. He was born with a disability; that handicap is low self-esteem or lack of trust.

Others speak of salvation as God's ultimate objective to turn you into a self-confident person. They define the Gospel as preaching that results in making people happy. If you do not make people happy, you have not preached the Gospel. Still other say Jesus death on the cross was not enough to save us. There is a god class of beings. Or, Jesus has a beginning and an end. Still some say Jesus has not remained the same, he has changed. Jesus was reborn in the pits of Hell. Jesus was the biggest failure in the whole Bible. False prophets tell Christians that they are little gods. "Health, Wealth, and Prosperity" Gospel advocates say poverty comes from Hell and prosperity comes from Heaven. Some even proclaim that God draws no distinction between Himself and us. When accusations are made against these false teachers and their lifestyles, they say that Jesus had an expensive ministry and a nice, big house.

False teachers teach that Christ's physical death on the cross was not enough to save us. They lure gullible disgruntled Christians into their para-church organization and tell them to forget your church. "Being poor is a sin! You can have anything you want; just name it and claim it. Don't you know? You cannot glorify God if you are sick." These are a some of the lies being spread in the body of Christ and false teachings.

These are the voices, writings, sermons, video tapes, and television broadcasts of false prophets in sheep's clothing. This is popular contemporary Christian culture. You will find their books, cassettes, DVDs, MP3s, and CDs in churches and Christian bookstores. But Jesus declared a warning. "Beware." Later, Jesus will say, along with the Apostle John, "If you have an ear to hear, then listen to what the Spirit says."

Have you been deceived by the teachings of a church or a public "Christian" figure? Have you heard the phrases, "That's not what it means," or "That's not for today"? Often these phrases are used to justify instruction given by a leader who has undergone an education at liberal colleges or seminaries. These are deceptive phrases used to avoid the truth found in the Word of God.

Let's consider a real life example taken from the sacred writings of Scriptures. The premise is this: A religious person must hear and heed the words of our Lord Jesus Christ to Nicodemus.

In the Book of John, chapter 3, a ruler of the Jews, Nicodemus, sought an interview with Jesus late at night. After paying the customary

Are You Saved?—Part 2

salutations, Jesus immediately tells him, "You must be born again." How utterly startling! How shocking to tell this esteemed religious official these words. This Pharisee should have understood what Jesus said. Yet, Jesus chides him for being a religious ruler of the Jews and not understanding the spiritual truths Christ told him.

What specifically does this phrase "You must be born again" mean? It means that you have come to understand that you have sin in your life, which means your actions and attitudes are offensive to a holy God. One must come to understand that Jesus Christ, the perfect son of God, came to earth, born of a virgin, lived a sinless life, and took the penalty of your sins upon Himself while on the cross. After which, He arose on the third day and returned to Heaven. No amount of good works or self-reformation can earn you a place in Heaven. Only by placing your total belief in the finished work of Christ Jesus will you see Heaven. And, by accepting Christ as your personal Savior, you will be given power to live on earth in a pleasing way to Him until He returns. If you reject Christ's atonement, upon death you will face Him once and for all eternity, and you will be separated from Him in a place called Hell. One must understand, on a personal and individual level, that you have to make this commitment by asking Christ to cleanse you of your sin, to live in and through your daily life until He comes for you. Paul says that if an angel or anyone else preaches a different Gospel he is to be accursed.

Are you sure you are saved? Is what I described your personal experience? If not, what prevents you from committing your life to Him right now?

If you are saved, perhaps you know someone that this chapter describes. Will you make yourself available to the Holy Spirit to be used as a vessel of illumination and clarification so your friend or loved one can have the same assurance and confidence you have? Not everyone who says they are saved are saved! But anyone who desires to be saved can be saved. Jesus said, "For whosoever will may come."

Have you truly come? If not, will you come? If so, will you invite others to come?

I Believe in God…

Are You Saved?—Part 3

This chapter will conclude this mini-series entitled, "Are You Saved?" This chapter will address those people who profess salvation and those people who confess salvation. There is a stark difference, which matters in light of eternity. There is an austere distinction if I will spend the rest of my eternal state in Heaven fellowshipping with God or the rest of my eternal state in Hell fellowshipping with the devil.

I wonder how long it took Jesus to preach the Sermon on the Mount. I suppose you can read through these 111 verses in 20–30 minutes. Speaking 111 verses may have taken twice as long. But nonetheless, this is a powerful closing section and message. Christ's first sermon is concise, pointed, direct, and without fluff.

I can almost imagine that as Jesus neared the end of His very first sermon, when He presented these final thoughts found in 7:13–27, He was slow and methodical. The final destination of all those who listened to Him hung in the balance of these final verses. Will those who listened to Him spend eternity with Him or apart from Him? There is no weightier decision humanity must face. The decision is either made this side of eternity or on the other side! "Where will I spend eternity and why?" The majority of people, when facing death, reflect upon their lives and if what they have been proclaiming all along will be sufficient to enter into the Kingdom of God.

Jesus lovingly has shown two gates and two roadways for people to travel. He provided warning about being deceived by the teachings of wolves which dress like sheep. He furnished instruction on how to look for someone is truly saved—their fruit, which is to blossom.

Now, Jesus alerts us that profession is not the same as confession. A professor lies and dies, but the confessor dies and lives. It's not what a person says, but what a person does.

Comments on Verse 21

"Not everyone" means there are some who will enter the Kingdom of Heaven. The contrast to the phrase, "not everyone" is there are many (v. 13) who will not enter the Kingdom of Heaven.

Jesus says that there will be those who say, "Lord, Lord" expecting to walk the streets of gold and be escorted to their mansion. When you think of the phrase, "Lord, Lord" several thoughts come to mind. The person who says, "Lord, Lord," is one who is reverent—they do not take the Lord's name in vain. The phrase also implies an air of orthodoxy, religious phraseology, or repetition of creeds. It carries the connotation of enthusism, by being repeated twice. It is also a phrase used publicly to show respect to a person. Jesus says, "You may revere me, have a form of godliness, be enthusiastic, and even talk of the things of God publicly, but you will not enter into the kingdom of heaven."

But why does Jesus utter what seems to be such a harsh statement? Because Jesus says, "Only those who do the will of My Father, who is in heaven will enter the kingdom of heaven." First, the phrase "does the will" is in the continual tense. Only the one who continually does the will of the Father will enter into the Kingdom of Heaven. This is in keeping with our Lord's previous description of the two trees. The fruit of a tree bears witness to the root. For a while, a bad person can profess to be a believer. He may attend church, sing praises, tithe, and even serve. But the root resides with his father the devil. Sooner or later, the one professing will be exposed for what he truly is—unregenerate.

What does it mean, "The will of my Father in heaven"? "Will" means the directive heart of God. A will is a statement of directives to be carried out by the testator. God the Father is the testator and His written Word is His will. The will of God is revealed in the Word of God.

What is the will of the Father? Consider these select verses.

> For this is the will of My Father, that everyone who beholds the Son and believes in Him will have eternal life, and I Myself will raise him up on the last day (John 6:40).

Are You Saved?—Part 3

> For the sorrow that is according to the will of God produces repentance without regret, leading to salvation, but the sorrow of the world produces death (2 Cor. 7:10).
>
> For this is the will of God, your sanctification; that is, that you abstain from sexual immorality; that each of you know how to possess his own vessel in sanctification and honor, not in lustful passion, like the Gentiles who do not know God (1 Thess. 4:3–5).
>
> For such is the will of God that by doing right you may silence the ignorance of foolish men (1 Peter 2:15).
>
> So as to live the rest of the time in the flesh no longer for the lusts of men, but for the will of God (1 Peter 4:2).

The confessor lives a pure, holy, unblemished, sanctified, and sensitive to sin, repentant, faith life. The professor won't.

There is another thought in this phrase, "the will of my Father." Christ is claiming a direct relationship to Jehovah, as His Father. He is claiming deity. But there is another father that humanity is related to prior to conversation. Jesus expounds.

> You are of your father the devil, and you want to do the desires of your father. He was a murderer from the beginning, and does not stand in the truth because there is no truth in him. Whenever he speaks a lie, he speaks from his own nature, for he is a liar and the father of lies (John 8:44–45).

Confessors are related to their Father who is in Heaven. Professors are related to their father, the god of this world, Satan.

Comments on Verse 22

Now the professor raises objections to such bold statements. He protests! The professor points to religious activities he has done. This dialogue takes place on "that day." What is "that day"? It is the Day of Judgment. What does the professor say?

Again, the professor begins with that reverent, enthusiastic, orthodox, public phrase, "Lord, Lord." First, these men and women prophesized. They declared God's Word. They stood before others and proclaimed what they thought they understood God to say and mean. But we are reminded in verse 15 that false prophets look orthodox. Jeremiah reminds us of God's viewpoint on the professors and their teaching ministry. The prophets prophesy falsely, rule in self-appointed authority, and those who listen to them love it (5:31). The professors point to special revelation as the authority of their message. They are given dreams, and only they can understand and explain them to others (23:25, 26). God says that if you listen to the words of these professors, you will be removed from your land. The prophesies are lies. The utterances of these false teachers contain no truthfulness. Those who listen, believe, and act will experience great loss (27:10, 14–15). What is taking place is the belief that if I associate a name with the message, the name validates the erroneous message.

They said that they cast out demons in His name. But how do you explain what appears to be the record of such if they are only professors? If they are not true believers, how can they accomplish such spiritual feats in the world of spiritual warfare?

God allowed them to do so, as He did with Balaam (Num. 23:5) and Saul (1 Sam. 10:10) and Caiaphas (John 11:51). The casting out of demons may have been acts accomplished using Satanic powers (Matt. 24:24 and Acts 19:14). And some of the claims of casting out demons were false, fake, and contrived.

They conclude by pointing to the fact that "in Your name they performed miracles." We know that professors can perform miracles because of Acts 8:9–11. The imitation of supernatural powers is recorded with Pharaoh's magicians through the end of time, marked by the Beast and False Prophet in Revelation during the Tribulation Age.

Comments on Verse 23

Now this seems very impressive. These professors present quite a résumé. What they claimed to have done is nothing to sneeze at. Wouldn't you think that Jesus would be impressed? They would be quite an addition to His ministry team!

Jesus declares with unbridled truthfulness, "I never knew you," which means Jesus never had a relationship with them. The lack of confessing with their mouth and believing in their heart made them religious zealots—lost religious zealots.

Christ desires a relationship, not a contractual agreement. If that is not sudden heartbreak and ear-piercing communication, He says, "Depart from me, you who practice lawlessness." Jesus views professors' religious practice as lawlessness. The word "lawlessness" means sin, which is any deviation from God's standards. It is willful defiance acting in direct opposition of the law (1 John 3:4). Stated differently, they spoke for God and interpreted for God things He never said. There ministry begat what they are, namely professors who practice sin in the name of Jesus.

Additional Insights on "That Day"
Let's pretend you are at church, and I am preaching this message. In the front of the church there is a casket. There is no body in it. It is closed. But it is a visual aid for these three verses. Jesus said "on that day" He would say to the professors, "I never knew you, depart from me you who practice lawlessness (sin)."

What happens when a professor dies? What will they experience? Hebrews 9:27 tells us that they have an appointment with judgment. This judgment is where they will appear before God's righteous throne to see if they will get into the Kingdom of Heaven. Luke 16:19–31 reminds us that there are no second changes. Once death has taken place, the professor cannot recant, return, relive, or have others intercede through prayers, lighting of candles, or baptisms for the dead. And the place of temporary confinement is a foretaste of an eternal place of judgment.

Revelation 20:11–15 reminds us of several things. There is a book called the Lamb's Book of Life. There are books that record the professor's life. The sentence of death is based on the Lamb's Book of Life. The degree of punishment is based on the books. No one can escape. Both great and small will appear.

The second death awaits professors because they said, "Lord, Lord" intellectually and emotionally, but never spiritually. They have never been heartbroken over their sin. They have never spoken from a poverty of spirit. They have never identified with the penitent thief on the cross who deserved punishment. They have never identified with the pleading heart of the publican who asked God to cover him in the blood.

The body is laid in the casket and returns to dust as God foretold in Genesis. Either the soul lives on forever in Heaven because of a biblical confession of faith and repentance marked by a subsequent life of change, or in Hell because of a profession and a life that bears no resemblance to biblical conversation.

Whether we die or live, everyone has an appointment with God. Will He find you as a confessor and speak the words every sinner longs to hear: "Well done good and faithful servant, enter the joy of your Lord"? Or will you be cast into eternal damnation by the "I never knew you, depart from me you who practice lawlessness."

No one has assurances of tomorrow. But you can be sure today and face tomorrow confidently knowing entrance into the Kingdom of Heaven is secure because you are doing the will of your Father in Heaven.

If I Don't Have Sex, He'll Dump Me!
A Battle Plan for Teens for Sexual Purity

This may be a strange chapter to include. However, as you read through this chapter, it is a necessary chapter for parents, teens, youth workers, and the local church to take an inventory on how they are doing with sexual purity. This chapter may help right the slowly sinking ship of a teen's life or a home life. This chapter may readjust the compass of a young person in order to renew their desire for purity and holiness by navigating along biblical principles. Before we begin, here are some suggestions on how to use this chapter.

I strongly encourage both the parent and the teen sit down and read this chapter together. Take notes. Make a list of all of the guidelines offered. Work together to evaluate the strengths of your teen's sexual purity decisions. Identify where the enemy has been or may breech your teen's sexual purity front lines. Re-enforce those areas. My prayer is that the collection of thoughts and the combined efforts in presenting this material will strengthen your teen's commitment to honor God, parents, and the body God has given him/her until marriage. Youth workers could use this as part of the teen curriculum with parental permission and church approval. I exhort teens to use this for their own personal Bible study.

The sexual revolution was a substantial change in sexual morality and sexual behavior throughout the Western culture in the late 1960s and early 1970s. And, this radical movement still has lingering effects today.

In 1999, the website www.beliefnet.com ran an article by Lauren F. Winner in which she stated that many young, unmarried Christians are sexually active and the rest of the church better get used to it.

A recent George Barna poll found that 36% of self-proclaimed born-again Christians approve of cohabitation, and 39% said indulging in sexual fantasies is morally acceptable.

The likelihood of teenagers having intercourse increases steadily with age; however, about 1 in 5 young people do not have intercourse while teenagers. Therefore 4 in 5 are sexually active.

Most young people begin having sex in their mid-to-late teens, about eight years before they marry; more than half of seventeen-year-olds have had intercourse.

- 93% of teenage women report that their first intercourse was voluntary.
- 37% of non-Christians said that they do not favor the idea of making it illegal to distribute movies or magazines that contain sexually explicit or pornographic pictures. (1997).
- 19% of Christians said that whether or not it is acceptable to see pornographic videos or pictures is a matter of taste, not morality (1997).

An attempt to unify evangelicals around a battle plan for sexual purity is noble but lacking. Evangelicals have established Purity Day, Purity Pledges, and the 1,000 Man Purity Campaign.

In May 2002, a group of biblical scholars called the Counsel on Biblical Sexual Ethics sought to develop a Bible-based statement on sexual purity. It became known as the Colorado Statement on Biblical Sexual Morality. I have printed this lengthy statement below. We applaud the common effort of so many, but without the direct understanding by the parent, teen, youth worker, and church, it may well fall on deaf ears.

> God intends sex to be a source of satisfaction, honor, and delight to those who enjoy it within the parameters of the moral standards He has established. Biblically speaking, human sexuality is both a *gift* and a *responsibility*. At creation, the gift of sex was among those things God declared to be "very good" (Gen. 1:31). What's more, the sexual relationship is invested with a profound significance in that it brings together a man and a woman within the context of the shared image of God (Gen. 1:27). Because sex is God's idea, and because it touches the image of God in human life, it is very important that the holiness of sexual behavior be diligently preserved. In fact, sexual behavior is moral only when it is holy (Eph. 1:4; 5:3; 1 Thess. 4:3–7; 1 Pet. 1:14–16).

A Battle Plan for Teens for Sexual Purity

Not only is sex good in itself; it is also given to serve good purposes. At creation, God made it very clear that sex functions in two ways: it generates "fruit" (Gen. 1:28); and it enables relational "union" (Gen. 2:24). In other words, sexuality does not exist merely for its own sake. Rather, sex fosters human nurturing, both through the union of husband and wife and also through the enrichment of society through the building of families and communities. God also made sex to reflect the mysterious spiritual relationship He will one day enjoy with all redeemed humanity following the wedding supper of the Lamb (Rev. 19:7, 9).

According to God's plan, sexual intimacy is the exclusive prerogative of husband and wife within the context of marriage. Sexual morality, on the other hand, is everyone's concern. It matters to single individuals, to families, and to society. Most of all, it matters to God.

Sex that honors God's guidelines and standards is pleasurable. He designed sexual activity to be physically enjoyable, emotionally satisfying, psychologically fulfilling, and spiritually meaningful because He delights in the joys and pleasures of His creatures (Song of Sol. 4:1–16). Men and women who honor God's standards for sexual behavior please Him as well as themselves (1 Cor. 6:20; also note analogy in Isa. 62:5).

But while sex is designed to be pleasing, not all sexual pleasure is ethical. Feelings are extremely unreliable as guides to the morality of sex. As a matter of fact, it is possible for sinful men and women to experience a form of physical enjoyment and degrees of emotional, psychological, and spiritual fulfillment even in sexual conduct that God considers abhorrent. For this reason, the Bible gives many solemn warnings against appealing to human passion or lust as the basis for our definition of moral sex (Rom. 1:24, 26; 13:13–14; 1 Thess. 4:5; 2 Tim. 2:22; 2 Pet. 3:3; 1 John 2:15–17; Jude 18). Our sex lives are moral only when conducted according to God's standards. When engaged in according to these guidelines, sexual activity is enriching, fulfilling, and eminently blessed.

We want to warn against deceptions that hinder or forestall this blessing of God upon our enjoyment of the wonderful gift of sex. We also want to help men and women understand God's good plan for sexual conduct, and thereby to realize all the joy, satisfaction and honor God offers to sexual creatures made in His image.

Based on our understanding of biblical teaching, we make the following declarations. We do not claim that these declarations cover everything the Bible says on sexual morality. But we do believe they highlight standards that are critical for our time.

1. **Desire and experience cannot be trusted as guidelines to the morality of sex** (Rom. 8:5–8; 13:14; 1 Cor. 2:14; 1 Thess. 4:3–5; 2 Tim. 2:22; James 1:14; 1 John 2:15–16; Jude 19). Instead, the morality of sex is defined by God's holiness (Lev. 20:7–21, 26; 1 Cor. 6:18–19; Eph. 1:4; 5:3; 1 Thess. 4:3–7; Heb. 13:4; 1 Pet. 1:15–16).

2. *Thus we affirm* that men and women are free to enjoy sex in any way that honors God's holiness. We affirm that God made sex to be physically enjoyable, emotionally satisfying, psychologically fulfilling, and spiritually meaningful, and that only sex that honors God's holiness can fully realize the complexity of His design at every level. We affirm that concepts of sexual morality founded upon anything other than God's holiness always pervert God's standards of sexual moral purity.

3. **God's standard is moral purity in every thought about sex, as well as in every act of sex.** Sexual purity can be violated even in thoughts that never proceed to outward acts (Job 31:1; Matt. 5:28; Phil. 4:8; James 1:14–15). Sex must never be used to oppress, wrong, or take advantage of anyone (1 Thess. 4:6). Rape, incest, sexual abuse, pedophilia, voyeurism, prostitution, and pornography always exploit and corrupt and must be condemned (Lev. 18:7–10; 19:29; 2 Sam. 13:1–22; Prov. 6:26; 23:27; Matt. 5:28; 1 Thess. 4:3–7; 1 Pet. 4:3; 2 Pet. 2:13–14).

4. *Thus we affirm* that God requires sexual moral purity in thought as well as in deed. We affirm that sexual desire must be disciplined to be moral. We affirm that thoughts of indulging sexual desire by outward acts of sexual sin are inward sins of lust. We deny that stimulating lust by images of sexual sin can be moral at any age or under any circumstances. We believe that no sexual act can be moral if driven by desires that run contrary to the best interests of another human being. We believe no sexual act can be moral that treats persons as impersonal objects of sexual lust. We reject the idea that thoughts about engaging in sexual sin are not immoral if not expressed in outward acts. We reject the idea that pedophilia, voyeurism, prostitution, or pornography can ever be justified.

5. **God's standards for sexual moral purity are meant to protect human happiness** (Prov. 5:18–19; 6:32–33; John 15:10–11), but sex is not an entitlement, nor is it needed for personal wholeness or emotional maturity. *Thus we affirm* that unmarried singles who abstain from sex can be whole, mature persons, as pleasing to God as persons who are faithful in marriage. We affirm that sexual celibacy is a worthy state for mature men and women (Matt. 19:12; 1 Cor. 7:1, 8; Rev. 14:4), and that lifelong celibacy can be a gift from God (1 Cor. 7:7). We affirm that freedom for service without obligations to spouse and children is a worthy advantage of the unmarried life (1 Cor. 7:32–35). We reject the idea that persons are not "whole" without sexual intercourse. We affirm that all persons, even unmarried teenagers, can rely on

God for strength to resist sexual temptation (1 Cor. 10:13). We deny that unmarried teenagers must have sex and cannot abstain from sex before marriage.

6. **God calls some to a life of marriage, others to lifelong celibacy, but His calling to either state is a divine gift worthy of honor and respect** (1 Cor. 7:36–38). No one is morally compromised by following God's call to either state, and no one can justify opposing a divine call to either state by denying the moral goodness of that state.

7. *Thus we affirm* that God is pleased with those He calls to serve Him through the loving expression of sexual intimacy in marriage. We also affirm God is pleased with those He calls to special witness and service through a life of celibacy apart from marriage. We reject the idea that God's Word ever represents the loving expression of sexual intimacy in marriage as morally compromised.

8. **Sexual behavior is moral only within the institution of heterosexual, monogamous marriage.** Marriage is secure only when established by an unconditional, covenantal commitment to lifelong fidelity (Gen. 2:24; Mal. 2:14–15; Matt. 19:4–6; Mark 10:6–8; 1 Cor. 7:39; Rom. 7:2; Eph. 5:31), and we should not separate what God has joined (Mal. 2:14–15; Matt. 19:6; Mark 10:9). Christians continue to debate whether there are a limited number of situations in which divorce is justifiable (Deut. 24:1–4; Matt. 19:9; 1 Cor. 7:15), but all agree that divorce is never God's ideal; lifelong commitment should always be the Christian's goal.

9. *Thus we affirm* that God established the moral definition of marriage, and that it should not be changed according to the dictates of culture, tradition, or personal preference. We deny that the morality of marriage is a matter of mere custom, or that it should be allowed to shift with the tide of cultural opinion or social practice. Furthermore, we affirm that God views marriage as an unconditional, covenantal relationship that joins sexual partners for life. We oppose the reduction of the moral obligations of marriage to a business contract. We do not believe that divorce for reasons of dissatisfaction, difficulty, or disappointment is morally justified.

10. **Marriage protects the transcendent significance of personal sexual intimacy.** Heterosexual union in marriage expresses the same sort of holy, exclusive, permanent, complex, selfless and complementary intimacy that will someday characterize the union of Christ with the redeemed and glorified Church (Eph. 5:28–33; 1 Cor. 6:12–20).

11. *Thus we affirm* that intimate sexual union in marriage is a reflection of the intimate moral and spiritual union Christ will someday enjoy with

the redeemed and glorified Church. We do not agree that the meaning and purpose of human sexuality can be defined on the basis of personal preference or opinion. We oppose the idea that sexual morality is simply a matter of culture, tradition, or individual aspiration.

12. **Sex in marriage should be an act of love and grace that transcends the petty sins of human selfishness, and should be set aside only when both partners agree to do so, and then only for a limited time of concentrated prayer** (1 Cor. 7:3–5).

13. *Thus we affirm* that sex in marriage should be enjoyed without selfishness. We do not believe that sex should be withheld as a way of controlling, punishing, or manipulating the behavior of a spouse. We reject the morality of any sexual act, even in marriage, that does not express love seasoned by grace. We believe no sexual act can be moral if it is driven by selfishness or ambition for power.

14. **Sex outside of marriage is never moral** (Exod. 20:14; Lev. 18:7–17, 20; Deut. 5:18; Matt. 19:9, 18; Mark 10:19; Luke 18:20; Rom. 13:9; 1 Cor. 6:13, 18; Gal. 5:19; Eph. 5:3; 1 Thess. 4:3; Heb. 13:4). This includes all forms of intimate sexual stimulation (such as foreplay and oral sex) that stir up sexual passion between unmarried partners (Matt. 5:27–28; 2 Tim. 2:22). Such behavior offends God (Rom. 1:24; 1 Thess. 4:8) and often causes physical and emotional pain and loss in this life (Prov. 5:3–14). Refusal to repent of sexual sin may indicate that a person has never entered into a saving relationship with Jesus Christ (Rom. 1:32; 1 Cor. 6:9–10; Eph. 5:3–5; Jude 13; Rev. 22:15).

15. *Thus we affirm* that God's blessing rests on sexual intimacy only when it occurs within the boundaries of marriage. We deny that sex outside of marriage is justified for any reason. We reject the idea that sexual intimacy outside of marriage can be moral if partners are honest, consenting, or sufficiently committed. We oppose the portrayal of sexual sin as a way of enhancing the popular appeal of entertainment. We reject the idea that sex between unmarried teenagers is acceptable if it is "safe." And we do not believe that churches should welcome into fellowship any person who willfully refuses to turn away from the sin of living in a sexual relationship outside of marriage.

16. **The Old and New Testaments uniformly condemn sexual contact between persons of the same sex** (Lev. 18:22; 20:13; Rom. 1:26–27; 1 Cor. 6:9; 1 Tim. 1:10); and God has decreed that no one can ever excuse homosexual behavior by blaming his or her Creator (Gen. 2:24; Rom. 1:24–25).

17. *Thus we affirm* that moral sex is always heterosexual in nature. We affirm that God gives strength to His people when they ask Him for

help in resisting immoral sexual desires, including desires for homosexual sex. We affirm that God has perfect knowledge concerning human sexual biology and made no mistake in prohibiting homosexual sex without qualification or exception. We deny the claim that science can justify the morality of homosexual behavior. We reject the idea that homosexual attraction is a gift from God (James 1:13). We deny the idea that homosexual relationships are as valid as heterosexual relationships. We do not agree with those who claim that it is sinful to make moral judgments that favor heterosexual behavior over homosexual behavior.

18. **The moral corruption of sexual sin can be fully forgiven through repentance and faith in Christ's atoning work** (1 Cor. 6:9–11; 1 John 1:9), but physical and psychological scars caused by sexual sin cannot always be erased in this life.

19. *Thus we affirm* that God fully forgives all who repent of sexual sin. We believe that relationships broken by sexual sin can be restored through genuine repentance and faith. We deny that there is any sort of sexual sin God cannot forgive. We oppose the idea that victims of sexual infidelity or abuse should never forgive those who have sinned against them.

20. **Christians must grieve with and help those who suffer hardship caused by sexual immorality, even when it is caused by their own acts of sin** (Rom. 12:15; Luke 19:10). But we must give aid in ways that do not deny moral responsibility for sexual behavior (John 8:11).

Thus we affirm that God calls Christians to love all who suffer social isolation, poverty, illness, or the burdens of unplanned pregnancy and single parenting, whether or not it was caused by their own sexual sin. We believe Christ set an example of loving ministry to those who suffer from the results of their own acts of sin. We reject the idea that our obligation to alleviate human suffering is valid only if such help is "deserved."

Someone has said you cannot legislate morality. I believe this to be true. A young person must stand alone against sexual immorality. Accountability encourages and strengthens, but this battle is individualized and personal. Therefore, it must be fought on those terms. One person's moral code of conduct is not necessary going to work for someone else.

The medical, psychological, and religious communities continue to prop open Pandora's box with their "safe sex" federally funded programs, reinterpretation of Scriptures, and secularized understanding of purity. Can we point a teen, especially a Christian teen and their Christian parents, to any clear call to develop a battle plan for sexual purity? Absolutely.

God, the Creator of all life, has issued a clarion call. In our lustful, selfish desires, we cannot hear His voice over the din of antagonistic, skeptical and mocking voices. Let's reconsider the Creator's voice and hear what He has to say.

The Commander's Call

The Bible is very thorough about sexual immorality or sexual impurity. It is replete with relevant Scriptures that address this practice as a sin. It not only speaks to the action but to the attitude of the heart that generates action. It is unnecessary to list scores of verses, texts, and passages to illustrate this point. Thus, I have selected nine passages, which are clear and are indisputable regarding what the Creator God has spoken. A brief explanation is given. The explanation is not intended to be an exposition.

1 Corinthians 5:1-2

> It is actually reported that there is immorality among you, and immorality of such a kind as does not exist even among the Gentiles, that someone has his father's wife. You have become arrogant and have not mourned instead, so that the one who had done this deed would be removed from your midst.

Paul was shocked that these Corinthian saints were approving a type of immorality that even the Greeks and Romans abhorred—a son was sleeping with his stepmother. The view the church took, Paul characterizes as arrogant. If you were to read further, Paul implements church discipline on the offender. Paul expected the church at Corinth to be sexually pure because God ordained it. A postscript: "The Church is not a building but individuals."

1 Corinthians 6:13

> Food is for the stomach and the stomach is for food, but God will do away with both of them. Yet the body is not for immorality, but for the Lord, and the Lord is for the body.

Paul writes that God created the body for fellowship with Himself in holiness and purity. God did not create the body for immorality. Immorality is focused on self. This was never God's intention. Our bodies belong to Him, for Him.

1 Corinthians 6:18

> Flee immorality. Every other sin that a man commits is outside the body, but the immoral man sins against his own body.

Here is a clear command. When confronted with the temptation of sexual impurity, we are commanded to flee; that means run away. Do what Joseph did and flee. Immorality is a sin against the body. The body was made by God and for God.

2 Corinthians 12:21

> I am afraid that when I come again my God may humiliate me before you, and I may mourn over many of those who have sinned in the past and not repented of the impurity, immorality, and sensuality, which they have practiced.

Immorality is called a sin. It is listed with impurity and sensuality—sexual sins. Sexual impurity requires repentance, not tolerance or permissiveness.

Ephesians 5:3

> But immorality or any impurity or greed must not even be named among you, as is proper among saints.

Paul writing to the saints at Ephesus reminds them that sexual impurity is not to be named among them. Each saint was responsible to remain free from accusation of sexual impurity. They were to abstain from any appearance of evil in this area. They were to be free from accusation from the pagan and fellow saints. Why? As an individual, his/her conduct affected the whole.

Colossians 3:5

> Therefore, consider the members of your earthly body as dead to immorality, impurity, passion, evil desire, and greed, which amount to idolatry.

Immorality was a practice from my former unregenerate life. These saints were to view such habits as dead, unresponsive, and buried. Like burying someone in the cemetery, all future contact and communication cease.

1 Thessalonians 4:3

> For this is the will of God, your sanctification; that is, that you abstain from sexual immorality.

What is God's will about sexual immorality? That every saint abstains from it. *This is God's will.* Clear, precise, and not open to interpretation. God's will is God's best.

Revelations 2:14

> But I have a few things against you, because you have there some who hold the teaching of Balaam, who kept teaching Balak to put a stumbling block before the sons of Israel, to eat things sacrificed to idols and to commit acts of immorality.

John writing to the Church at Pergamum rebukes those who are tolerating false teaching that promotes acts of immorality condemned and punished by God earlier in the Old Testament. John calls this a sin and warns the church of certain punishment if they do not deal with it.

Revelations 2:20–21

> But I have *this* against you, that you tolerate the woman Jezebel, who calls herself a prophetess, and she teaches and leads My bond-servants

> astray so that they commit acts of immorality and eat things sacrificed to idols. I gave her time to repent, and she does not want to repent of her immorality.

John rebukes the Church at Thyatria for the same thing—a false teacher called Jezebel whose teaching promotes acts of immorality. John calls this a sin and warns the church of certain punishment if they do not deal with it.

I'm sure other Bible passages have come to mind that clearly address the Creator's message of sexual fidelity and purity. But the point is God has spoken. Even if it were a single verse, His Word is sure, certain, absolute, and demands obedience from those who claim to be redeemed by His Son's blood. Here we have nine verses.

So it is certain and clear that our Creator, Redeemer, Savior, and Lord demands we walk in holiness, in purity, and blamelessly before Him in the area of sexual purity.

Since God has called us and we have a desire to obey Him because we love Him, then desire needs a plan. Desire is my best efforts, which are highly prone to failure. Desire plus a biblical plan is God's energy, resources, and enablement to succeed.

The following are guidelines, areas to examine, in establishing a battle plan for teens for sexual purity.

Developing a Personal Battle Plan for Sexual Purity

For the balance of this chapter, I will offer guidelines on how a teen can develop a battle plan for sexual purity. As with any guidelines, these must be individualized and personalized. No guideline that finds its foundation in the Holy Word of God is open for discussion, only creative implementation. These guidelines are not necessarily in any order. Giving attention to each one individually, as part of the whole, can guide your teen to a battle plan that works.

Study and establish your theology about the opposite sex relationship. Which concept will govern your relationships with the opposite sex? Dating, courtship, or betrothal?

Dating, I believe, is a relatively new concept. I believe we can trace its inception back to the WWII where many family values changed. Generally speaking, dating, by definition, is a boy and a girl attending a function alone. The philosophy behind dating is for the young person to develop social skills and to find out what they like and dislike in the opposite sex. I picture it like standing in a grocery store in the potato chip aisle. There are mesquite flavored, sour cream and chives, cheddar cheese, and dill flavors to name a few. In order to find my favorite, I must taste them all. I believe a glaring problem with this approach to the opposite sex is the devastation upon the human heart. Dating intensifies the relationship and pushes it to levels for which human emotions are not prepared. It breeds isolation. The breakups, for a variety of reasons, are emotionally devastating. The breakup can promote bitterness, revenge, stalking, and threats of suicide. Joshua Harris wrote an article for NANC entitled, "Seven Highly Defective Habits of Dating." You should secure this article.

Courtship is the process of determining if a person is suitable for marriage. Unlike dating, which is for self-gratification, courtship has a longer view in mind, a larger picture. Courtship is looking at the inner qualities that would make for a lifelong companion. Courtship has a more mature outlook on relationships. A teen is not physically, mentally, emotionally, or vocationally prepared for the lifetime responsibilities of marriage.

Betrothal is the arrangement of marriage for a boy and girl by the parents. This practice is still prevalent in many Middle Eastern countries. The children have no say in the matter. The arrangement is made very early in their lives. It usually involves a dowry. This practice stems from the Old Testament.

Understand your purpose and motivation for spending time with this person. Ask yourself these questions.

- Am I being selfish and looking for this person to fill some emotional need? What are my expectations?
- Am I a servant wanting to build this person up in his/her walk with the Lord? What am I willing to contribute?
- Can I foresee that when we say goodnight we both will be stronger in the Lord because of the investment of this time?

Recognize the difference between infatuation, lust, and love. Infatuation is the expression of emotions passionately and foolishly. It means an irrational fixation with someone or something. It is generally based on externals such as looks, fashion, prestige, position, or power. It is temporary and fickle. Lust is the desire to have someone or someone. It is self-gratification. It is a must that compromises. It is an over-powering strong emotion that leads to violation of laws and regulations for your protection. For the saint, it is rebellion toward God's patterns for purity. Love is a God-given choice to give one's self fully, completely, without reservations to another for his/her spiritual welfare. Love is described in 1 Corinthians 13. When a teen says they love someone, what they are feeling usually falls short of 1 Corinthians 13 and the model of our Lord. John reminds us that we are not to love in word only, but in deeds.

If you are involved emotionally in a relationship and cannot distinguish between infatuation, lust, and love, seek out the counsel of someone who knows you and can be trusted, and ask him or her to counsel you.

Seek the counsel of your parents and submit to their authority. A teen is under the authority of his or her parent. Some dispute when this authority ends. Some say it ends when they are legally of age. Others advocate that they are under authority until they are wed. Nevertheless, while a teen, you should seek the counsel of your parents about any opposite-sex relationship. Parents strive for the best for you. They have years of previous experience in this area and probably have made the mistakes they want to help you avoid. Obeying your parents is obeying the Lord.

Avoid one-on-one time. Temptation lurks in this area. Steer clear of places or activities that promote isolation: watching television in the basement of your parent's home; listening to music in your bedroom; drive-in movies or dark theaters; sitting in a car at night. This is unnecessary exposure to physical temptation. Enjoy the company of the other person in groups. Isolation dating often promotes falsehood. We want the other person to like us, so we are often not real. We pretend and put our best foot forward. This breeds what is known as a "green house environment." Relationships are quick blooming under the pressure of isolation. A better way to get to know a person is observing them interact with others. You might not know a person has a bad temper until it is too late and he strikes you. But you may spot his temper when he strikes out in the ninth, losing the game for his team. Or how he responds to criticism by others, or if he has to be the center of attention by boisterous speech or obnoxious behavior.

Honor your parents by being honest and open with them after each contact with the opposite sex. Tell them what you did with the time, what the other person was like, what you liked or disliked. Allow your parents to be a sounding board for you.

Stay away from evangelistic relationships. This type of relationship is dangerous. It generally doesn't work out. A female shares her faith. A young man seems interested because he likes her. He attends youth group, church, and social activities. There may be impure motivation by the young man. If one person shares their faith with the opposite sex, and there seems to be an interest in the things of the Lord, then find a same-sex person to complete the salvation presentation and be available to disciple.

Steer clear of counseling relationships. My comments would be the same as above. This is infatuation that leads to hero-worship because the other person saved someone's life from a pathway of sin and shame.

Determine and communicate clear physical contact boundaries. Is hand holding sinful? Is hugging sinful? What about a kiss? Doesn't the

Bible instruct us to give each other a "holy" kiss? Several thoughts occur to me here. Why do I want to hold the other person's hand? Why do I want to hug them? Why do I want to kiss them? What benefit am I seeking? Remember that one thing can lead to another. The old Lay's potato chip commercial, "You can't just eat one," may be appropriate. Here I am holding hands. Let's face it, after a while your hand gets sweaty! Now we want to put a hand around her shoulder. We draw her in closer. We feel her body. One thing leads to another.

Remember how guys are wired? Sight, smell, and touch. Lingering physical contact is a stimulant. Determine why you would want to offer this or receive it.

Maintain your relationships with family and friends. If you find yourself preoccupied with someone at the expense of your relationships with family and friends, the relationship is not healthy. If the person you are spending time with whines, complains, or get angry that you are not spending enough time with him/her, the relationship is becoming poisoned. If the person you are spending time becomes angry because you did not tell him/her your plans, who you were spending time with, where you were going, or that you went somewhere without him/her, the relationship is possessive.

Continue to fulfill all your responsibilities. Often there is a tendency to spend so much time with the other person that you neglect your responsibilities. For example, a college student may neglect his/her studies, miss homework assignments, fail quizzes, tests, or courses, and even find themselves on academic probation because he or she is spending so much time with someone. Or a teen can neglect household chores, make bogus promises of doing them later, or do them sloppily in order to spend time with a person.

Stay focused on God's will for your life right now. As a teen, if the Lord tarries, you have all the time in the world. You really do. God wants you to finish high school. He wants you to do your best. He may want you to go to college. He may want you to enter into a vocational career. He may want you to do a short-term mission trip. Even as a teen, you can have a good sense of God's will. Know what it is for right now and follow it. Do not allow another relationship to cause you to disobey God.

Avoid friends whose sexual purity standards are less than yours are. Bad company corrupts good morals. Proverbs tells us to avoid the fool, mocker, and scoffer. You become like those with whom you associate. Proverbs tells us we become wiser when we hang with wise people. Evaluate your friends. Do they have the same moral standards as you? If they mock or scoff at your sexual purity standards, they have a deliberate intention to bring you down. They will seek to put you in compromising situations. Why? Your light is exposing their darkness. They must do something about it. For them, it often becomes a game.

Dress modestly and appropriately. Modesty means propriety, that which is appropriate. It means unpretentious. Avoiding calling attention to yourself. Dress styles today are designed to flatter the Jenny Craig body. It is meant to highlight certain elements of the body: legs, stomach, or breasts. Dress that highlights your body becomes a temptation to the opposite sex. You should never highlight your body to be attractive. Your beauty comes from your relationship to Christ.

Pledge that you will not develop a relationship with an unbeliever. Many do not understand the difference between friendship and acquaintance. An acquaintance is a relationship based on common generalities. Students are often acquaintances because they are in the same math class. Friendship is based on equality, spiritual equality as Paul writes about in 2 Corinthians 6. Friendship is based on fellowship around the things of the Lord. This understanding of friendship is illustrated between David and Jonathan. The values and beliefs of the unbeliever are usually in stark contrast to a believer.

Pledge that you will not pursue a relationship with a weaker Christian of the opposite sex. You might be surprised by this. If the weaker Christian is a male, and we are working along the lines of courtship, the male is called to be the spiritual leader in the relationship. Pursuing a relationship with on OJT (On the Job Training) is not healthy. Generally, emotions ignore the lack of spirituality of the male. A mythological hope develops that over time he will mature and be a stronger Christian than the female. If God's hand is in the courtship, time is not a problem to worry. God brings together those He has foreordained to be one.

When with the opposite sex, remember he/she is first and foremost your brother or sister in the Lord. Would I replicate activities with this person with someone from my small group? We forget that the person I am spending time with is a fellow saint. If I allow him/her to touch my genitals, would I behave that way with another saint? We are to build each other up, not use each other.

Keep the Lord at the center of the relationship through beginning and ending prayer and stimulating biblical communication. You want to know the inner qualities of this person. You want to know what God is doing in his or her life. Here you have all this time, so during some portion of that time you should speak of spiritual matters.

Don't develop your battle plan asking, "How far is too far?" This is not sexual purity but immoral tolerance. Paul tells the Corinthians that it is not good for a man to touch a woman.

Recognize your weaknesses with the opposite sex. Satan appealed to Eve's intellect and emotions when he told her that by disobeying God she would be wise like God. Flattery is a manipulative tool to secure some lust. "Flattery" means excessive, insincere praise. It is like eating too much sugar and getting an artificial high. If you believe the insincere praise, you could then make a serious moral mistake.

Know what your eyes tells your brain. Avoid sexual terminology such as "fox," "babe," "hunk," or "hot." The eye sees and sends messages to the brain. Those messages can influence your behavior. I hear teens say (and this might be outdated), "She's a fox," or "He's a real hunk," or "What a babe!" or "She's really hot." These are derogatory terms. They are reserved for animals. They are expressions of animalistic feelings. Train your eye to see a person's tenderness, compassion, truthfulness, integrity, honesty, gentleness, kindness, wisdom. Then the message to the brain will be he/she is a growing, sincere brother in the Lord I would like to get to know.

Thank God for His perfect creation of your body. Avoid comparing yourself with others, or stimulating self-critical thoughts by looking at teen or glamour magazines. Psalm 139 tells you that you are fearfully and wonderfully made. God made you perfectly. You are His masterpiece. When you look at others, magazines, or the like, it tends to create an atmosphere of comparison. "If only I had curly hair, straight hair, smaller ears, if only I were taller, slimmer," etc. Often these feelings of dissatisfaction are created by what you are viewing. Accept how you look, and cultivate the inner beauty of a godly young person.

The battle plan for sexual purity also involves your private life no one sees but God. Our medical, religious, and psychological communicates have emphasized he acceptability of masturbation. They say it is a natural part of youth and growing up; that because God has made us sensual beings, He also has granted us the privilege of self-gratification. But the Bible presents a different viewpoint. Because this is a sin, it often erodes diligence in keeping oneself pure and holy before the Lord. If you are involved with this, you may want to seek counsel to find lasting solutions to stop this practice and enjoy the fruits of your battle plan.

Examine all media forms you expose yourself to (music, DVDs, videos, movies, books, magazines). The ratings assigned to the media are constantly being fudged. More and more latitude is being taken by the media industry to stretch the lines for acceptable immorality. Recognize those songs, artists, authors, and actors that participate in promoting a twisted form of moral purity. Avoid such forms of media. Get rid of any forms you may have collected in the past.

Control your thought life to avoid fantasizing. When I feel lonely, rejected, jealous that everyone else has someone, I can fantasize about what I see. I can look at him/her and allow my mind to think about what it would be like to spend time with him/her, what it might feel like to kiss him/her, or my mind and emotions can take me even further. Fantasizing is a form of discontent and dissatisfaction with God over your present situation. Be careful how long you think about such matters.

Practice modesty in your nonverbal communication, such as how you walk, look, make eye contact, or smile. Immodesty in these areas is known as flirting. You do not have to compete for the attention of the opposite sex. This type of behavior may be rooted in jealousy or lust. It can influence you to do or say things that are not pleasing to the Lord. If you have to do something to get the attention of another, don't waste your effort. It is apparent he/she is not interested. Allow God to draw attention to your inner beauty.

I will not become involved with clubs or attend certain events to look at or for the opposite sex. Many young people go to events or join clubs to "scope" out the "hotties." This motivation is lustful and self-indulgent. Remember as a Christian teen, you are to be motivated by the love of Christ (Paul uses the phrase "constrained by the love of Christ") to serve others in love. Be brutally honest with each event or invitation. Why do you want to go?

I will commit myself to daily Bible study. How can a young person keep himself or herself pure? By living life according to the Word. This means you must interact daily with the living and loving God by reading His love letter to you. Set a time and place. Pick a book of the Bible to read. Have pen and paper nearby. Take notes. Oftentimes the best notes are in the form of questions. This will stimulate day long thinking and meditation. Record commandments to obey, promises to claim, or sins to avoid.

I will commit myself to daily prayer. Prayer is your opportunity to talk to God. He wants to hear from you. He wants to know your struggles, desires, hopes, aspirations, fears, concerns, and worries. When you pray, you are telling God you desperately need Him. You are confessing to God that He alone can help you. You are recognizing that you need someone greater than yourself.

I will remind myself that my Lord and Savior is my true source of fulfillment and joy. When you become so preoccupied with someone else, you may be setting yourself up for bitter disappointment. Let's remind ourselves that no human being can be to us everything that God already is. No human being can always be there for you, completely understand you, have all the answers, and always show compassion and empathy. Human beings can be selfish. Your Lord and Savior is the constant, steady, and unmovable source of joy and fulfillment.

I will be busy serving the Lord and using my spiritual gifts, talents, and abilities. As a Christian teen, your first priority in life is to serve the Lord. Paul reminds the singles at Corinth that they have a greater advantage and opportunity to serve than when someone gets involved with a relationship. As a Christian teen, life-building and character-developing traits are learned through using spiritual gifts, talents, and abilities. Many a teen has found lifelong direction by serving God instead of investing inordinate amounts of time with another. In fact, we may be robbing the other person of the same benefits God wants to show them.

I will maintain a proper view of God, myself, sin, and my battle plan for sexual purity. When our emotions gain strength because of the time we spend with someone else, it is often the case that we lose the proper view of God, self, and sin, and we are prone to compromise our battle plan for sexual purity. It is a simple matter. Imagine a type of scale that has two bowls, one on either side. When we put more time, energy, and resources into the human bowl, it outweighs the other bowl, creating an imbalance. It is not a matter of balancing the human with the divine, but always having the emphasis in the divine bowl.

When I think I like someone or someone expresses interest in me, I will not keep secrets from my parents. I will share that information believing that my parents have my best interests at heart. When the heart grows fond of someone else, many teens develop a secretive and evasive relationship with his or her parents. Somewhere along the line, friends, the "person" or others tell horror stories of how their parents "broke them up." By all means, *don't tell your parents anything about him or her!* Young person, again, your parents possess a greater wisdom. You may be the youngest, and they have been around the block with your older siblings. They themselves worked through this type of thing at a personal level. Godly parents want to guide and remind. They are like the coaches at the Summer Olympics. The athlete must do the routine. But afterwards, the coach points things out for the purpose of helping the athlete to improve.

I will ask my parents to hold me accountable to this battle plan and be open to any questions they may ask me. Wow—this may be tough. Plans, as a rule, need accountability. When an executive officer of a firm asks one of his employees to develop a plan for marketing a new product, the executive will approve the plan and then monitor its progress. Likewise, when you develop your battle plan for sexual purity, let your parents know (if you haven't developed it together), so they can help you stay with the plan. It will usually come through their asking you questions. Avoid the feelings of being treated like a child or them controlling you. They want you to succeed and have great joy when you finally stand before God, the preacher, them, and the congregation, presenting yourself in all purity to your mate.

I will avoid every appearance of evil. Stay away from people, places or things that you have been taught or have come to know have the appearance of evil. For example, entering an establishment for a soft drink that you know sells pornographic materials or hanging with friends who run with a loose, drug, or alcohol crowd.

I will make no provisions for the flesh in words or deeds. Monitor your speech and words. Avoid words with double meanings, slang that carries sexual innuendo, symbols, or logos, evil media viewing or music selection.

I will daily pray for my protection from evil and the evil one. We talked about prayer. Here we are following the Lord's instruction on prayer to the disciples: "And deliver us from the evil one." Sometimes the devil and his demons enjoy hearing you pray about your moral purity. They won't bother you because you pray in generalizations. What rattles their cage is when you pray against them and in specifics. Pray about specific areas of temptation, people, places, and things.

I will avoid places of temptation. First, know what those places are. Take different routes home if need be. Tell your friends you can't go to them. It may be a simple movie, arcade, or mall, but you have discovered it is a stimulant to you sexually. Steer clear of such places.

I will cut off all relationships that are a source of temptation to me. Let's pretend you went to the dentist with a toothache. The dentist quickly agreed you have a bad tooth and it should come out. He writes you a prescription for the pain and tells you to go home. You may feel better in a couple of hours, but if he does nothing about the decaying tooth, you'd find another dentist! Likewise, it is often impossible to control others and their beliefs and values. You must control it by removing them.

I will memorize specific Scriptures for this area of temptation. When you hide God's Word in your heart, the Holy Spirit uses this powerful tool, bringing it to your mind. When acted upon, you avoid sinning. Everyone can memorize. It may be a challenge at first because your mind is lazy. But you can do it. It's a matter of beginning. Maybe find another young person with the same battle plan and memorize verses together.

I will install a filter on my computer and allow my parents full access for accountability. A prominent area to erode sexual purity is the Internet. This is especially true with high-speed Internet connections. We want to have the fastest connections. We want to click the mouse and instantly surf the Web. However, that means that you also receive unwanted emails known as pop-ups. We experienced this. Within the first twenty-four hours of using one provider, anytime we were logged on, pornographic messages, pictures, and advertising appeared—unwanted. You must select a good and proven filter. Protect your mind by installing such filters. Let your parents see your Internet history.

I will not be involved in any conversations that have sexual overtones. Slang, names, terms, and jokes can stimulate sexual fantasy and lead to compromising your battle plan for sexual purity. Shun friends who will not respect your plan. Turn off media that insults your battle plan. Take control. Be in control.

The Outcome of Perseverance

Develop your battle plan and work your battle plan. Don't expect instant "I am now free from sexually impure thoughts and temptations." Sexual freedom is like our American freedom. There was a price. It must always be guarded. We must be alert. Declare no amnesty! Take no prisoners!

I'm So Confused. Whom Can I Trust?
Be Careful to Whom You Listen

When we face a difficult decision, we often ask others what they would do if they were in the same situation. When we have health issues, we consult a doctor who may send us to a specialist. When we are experiencing financial concerns, we talk with a banker, tax consultant, accountant, or financial advisor. Buying a home? We check with friends, realtors, lenders, or real estate magazines. What about trying to select a college? We may talk with parents, fellow graduates, alumni of a particular college, or leaf through a deluge of college catalogs. Considering a major purchase, we would do comparison shopping, on-line research, or check out the latest copy of *Consumer Magazine*.

How do we know what they are saying is worth listening to? How do we determine if they are providing information for our best interests? How do we determine if we should listen to them? Can we blame them if their advice is bad? Do I have any personal responsibility in seeking guidance?

This chapter provides seven guidelines to help us discern to whom we should listen. If you begin to use these seven guidelines, it will promote your ability to hear from God, as He may use others in your life from time to time, and to know with confidence outside counsel is truly God's counsel.

Historical Backdrop
Solomon is dead. We read in 1 Kings 11:41–43:

> Now the rest of the acts of Solomon and whatever he did, and his wisdom, are they not written in the book of the acts of Solomon? Thus, the time that Solomon reigned in Jerusalem over all Israel was forty years. And Solomon slept with his fathers and was buried in the city of his father David, and his son Rehoboam reigned in his place.

How does the Bible describe the closing years of Solomon's life? Solomon loved many foreign women (11:1). Solomon was a polygamist. In fact, Solomon had 700 wives and 300 female concubines in a harem for his sexual pleasure. Many of these wives were from Egypt, and Moabite, Ammonite, Edomite, Sidonian, and Hittite women (11:1). God warned Solomon concerning this practice. God told Solomon, "You shall not associate with them, nor shall they associate with you, for they will surely turn your heart away after their gods" (11:2). Did Solomon heed the Lord? No. In fact, Solomon held fast to these loves (11:2).

God's Word is always true. Indeed, because of Solomon clinging to these loves, his heart was turn to idolatry for the sake of his wives. We read, "His wives turned his heart away after other gods; and his heart was not wholly devoted to the Lord his God, as the heart of David his father had been. For Solomon went after Ashtoreth the goddess of the Sidonians and after Milcom the detestable idol of the Ammonites" (11:4).

Solomon's heart was distracted. Solomon did what was evil in the sight of the Lord. Solomon built a high place for Chemosh, the detestable idol of Moab. The Scripture says thus also he did for all his foreign wives who burned incense and sacrificed to their gods (11:8).

Solomon in his early career gave counsel that glorified God and benefited those he ruled. Proverbs shows this wisdom. He was not always self-seeking. Only when his heart became distracted did his idols of selfishness drive him to use people instead of serving people.

Solomon violated God's basic commands for a king. Solomon collected gold, horses, and women. Here's what the Law says in Deuteronomy:

> Moreover, he shall not multiply horses for himself, nor shall he cause the people to return to Egypt to multiply horses, since the Lord has said to you, "You shall never again return that way. He shall not multiply wives for himself, or else his heart will turn away; nor shall he greatly increase silver and gold for himself" (Deut. 17:16–17).

In fact, the following references record the increasing interest in horses and chariots as a display of Solomon's military strength (1 Kings 4:26; 10:25, 28). It is interesting to observe that the collection of horses began with his father David (2 Sam. 8:4).

Be Careful to Whom You Listen

Solomon's pursuit of life, searching for purpose and fulfillment are recorded in the book of Ecclesiastes. It is a book of futility, vanity, and emptiness as Solomon pursues one venture, hobby, and craft after another. The word vanity is used sixteen times in this fatalistic book. Twenty-seven times Solomon employs the phrase "under the sun" to represent the emptiness of his pursuits. When all was said and done, the elusive pleasure from the thing pursued is empty. Such things did not produce the anticipated results Solomon sought. Twice he used the phrase "I set my mind"; a determined and resolute mental framework to achieve the goal that he determined would bring him peace and happiness.

Solomon had external problems with Hadad (Edom) and Rezon (Aram). We read in 1 Kings 11:14, 23:

> Then the Lord raised up an adversary to Solomon, Hadad the Edomite; he was of the royal line in Edom. Then the Lord raised up an adversary to Solomon, Hadad the Edomite; he was of the royal line in Edom.

Solomon experienced internal problems. Because of Solomon's self-centered rulership, God raised up a prophet to speak to Jeroboam. Jeroboam was part of the forced laborers who suffered under Solomon. Jeroboam was appointed sovereign over ten of the tribes of Israel. Solomon's son, Rehoboam, would be sovereign over two. Israel would be divided. The nation would undergo a terrible disunification.

> It came about at that time, when Jeroboam went out of Jerusalem that the prophet Ahijah the Shilonite found him on the road. Now Ahijah had clothed himself with a new cloak; and both of them were alone in the field. Then Ahijah took hold of the new cloak, which was on him, and tore it into twelve pieces. He said to Jeroboam, "Take for yourself ten pieces; for thus says the Lord, the God of Israel, 'Behold, I will tear the kingdom out of the hand of Solomon and give you ten tribes (but he will have one tribe, for the sake of My servant David and for the sake of Jerusalem, the city which I have chosen from all the tribes of Israel), because they have forsaken Me, and have worshiped Ashtoreth the goddess of the Sidonians, Chemosh the god of Moab, and Milcom the god of the sons of Ammon; and they have not walked in My ways, doing what is right in My sight and *observing* My

statutes and My ordinances, as his father David did. Nevertheless I will not take the whole kingdom out of his hand, but I will make him ruler all the days of his life, for the sake of My servant David whom I chose, who observed My commandments and My statutes; but I will take the kingdom from his son's hand and give it to you, even ten tribes. But to his son I will give one tribe that My servant David may have a lamp always before Me in Jerusalem, the city where I have chosen for Myself to put My name. I will take you, and you shall reign over whatever you desire, and you shall be king over Israel. Then it will be, that if you listen to all that I command you and walk in My ways, and do what is right in My sight by observing My statutes and My commandments, as My servant David did, then I will be with you and build you an enduring house as I built for David, and I will give Israel to you. Thus I will afflict the descendants of David for this, but not always.'" Solomon sought therefore to put Jeroboam to death; but Jeroboam arose and fled to Egypt to Shishak king of Egypt, and he was in Egypt until the death of Solomon (1 Kings 11:29–40).

Rehoboam witnessed all of his father's dealings. He observed his father's type of monarchy. He heard of the citizens of Israel grumbling and complaining over his father's lavish, abominable lifestyle. He was left having to pick up the pieces of a wicked reign of Solomon. Jeroboam and the disgruntled hid themselves. According to Prov. 28:12, "When the righteous triumph, there is great glory, but when the wicked rise, men hide themselves." So, how should someone exercise care when asking for advice? How can we discern to whom we should listen? There are several principles that we can conclude from the study of Rehoboam.

First Principle: Clearly identify the problem (12:4, 9)
Many times, it is difficult to know what the problem is. Our emotions cloud our judgment. Well meaning friends or family members tell us what they think we want to hear. Oftentimes, we get stuck in the mire of secondary issues missing the primary issue. We become side tracked.

We must believe that all problems are based on facts that can be verified. Jeroboam told Rehoboam that Solomon's yoke was hard (11:4, 9–10). Solomon's expectations were unreasonable. His wants and desires were selfish, and he used people to achieve his own personal goals. His foreign wives turned his heart away from God. Jeroboam clearly identified the problem. And by clearly identifying the problem, solutions that would produce better labor relationships and still fulfill kingly goals could have been reached. Jeroboam extends himself and says, "Therefore lighten the hard service of your father and his heavy yoke which he put on us, and we will serve you" (1 Kings 12:4).

Second Principle: Take time to consult counsel (12:5)
Rehoboam's only wise act recorded in this life-shattering event was to take time to consult with others. He tells Jeroboam and the assembly to leave and return in three days.

We live in a breakneck, fast-paced world telling us we need to make instant, snap, immediate decisions. We need to come to a decision right now! We are offered extraordinary deals, but we must act now! Don't take time to think. Opportunity is knocking and might not ever come this way again. Go with the flow!

But biblical history tells us that rash decisions are harmful. "The plans of the diligent lead surely to advantage, but everyone who is hasty comes surely to poverty" (Prov. 21:15). Cain acted hastily and murdered his brother. Balaam acted rashly accepting a bribe to curse Israel as a means to a quick and easy buck. David, when cheated by Nabal, reacted with a murderous heart until Abigail interceded.

By taking time to consult, we will avoid jumping to conclusions (Prov. 18:13). We will have the opportunity to gather all the facts (Prov. 18:17).

Third Principle: Seek counsel from sources who are knowledgeable (12:6, 9)
Multiple counselors were a common Old Testament practice for secular and sacred kings. David used numerous counselors, as did Nebuchadnezzar. Kings knew the tendency to have "yes men" as advisors. Multiple counselors, unless they corroborated together, could insure at least one would speak the truth. The Bible itself encourages the use of multitude counselors.

> Where there is no guidance the people fall, but in abundance of counselors, there is victory (Prov. 11:14).

> Without consultation, plans are frustrated, but with many counselors, they succeed (Prov. 15:22).
>
> For by wise guidance you will wage war, and in abundance of counselors, there is victory (Prov. 24:6).

Rehoboam consulted with the elders who had served his father Solomon while he was still alive and consulted with the younger men who grew up with him and served him.

What would be the advantages of the older counsel? They were closest to the situation with firsthand knowledge. They would be able to take the entire "Solomonic" problem into view. They had a broad grasp. They understood the historical development. If Rehoboam accepted the older men's counsel, it appealed to biblical concept of servanthood. Rehoboam would have displayed a gentler approach and conveyed his sincere desire to seek unification.

What would be the disadvantage of the older counsel? Age. They were too old to adjust to the changing times. They might have the perception of not understanding Jeroboam and his demands. Their counsel may be irrelevant. They could be accused of being out of touch with the times. They may continue the same tainted perception from the Solomonic régime. Like many older people, their mind is made up.

Then what would be the advantage of the younger counsel? Rehoboam would have friends, peers, and an alliance. They would be supportive of preconceived ideas. They could breathe energy and vitality to support Rehoboam's new administration. They possessed the strength to carry out his plans. Their viewpoint on people was they were obsolete or expendable. Jeroboam and his band of the disenfranchised were an intrusion to their personal agenda or they should rather be tools for personal achievement. Relationships hinder the goal.

What would be the disadvantage of the younger counsel? Some might view them as assertive, bold, and brash. They could be charged with being manipulative and their tactics viewed as intimidation. Because they were young, they only saw one dimension of the problem—"lighten our yokes." Their counsel would be viewed as divisive, not unifying. They might be charged with having a hidden agenda of self-seeking and promotion. Perhaps they would not be honest with Rehoboam fearing they might be discharged and lose their elite position. Although not written yet, they would violate Prov. 27:6: "Faithful are the wounds of a friend."

Fourth Principle: Be honest, open and teachable when seeking counsel (12:8)

Rehoboam decides to listen to and heed the counsel of those with whom he grew up. Undoubtedly, he, like Absalom, spent countless hours in discussion with these friends discussing the woes of the world, his father's rash and illogical decisions, and how, if Rehoboam were king, he would unify Israel. Perhaps he even made promises to them, if king, about how he would appoint them into powerful positions in the new kingdom. For Rehoboam knew he would be king someday simply by right of succession. Rehoboam failed to avoid the pitfall of seeking counsel until he heard what he wants to hear. His mind was made up, his agenda clear in his own mind, and those elders who advised his father would stand in opposition. So Rehoboam mustered together a coalition of like-minded self-centered men to support and carry out his policies.

Fifth Principle: Filter all counsel through your grid of biblical discernment (12:7, 10–11)

Rehoboam knew his father's rule violated God's ordinances. The older councilmen knew Solomon's reign near the end of his life was a direct violation of God's Word. If Solomon's reign were truly pure and biblical, the eldersd would have counseled Rehoboam to maintain a straight and steady course. Instead, they advised Rehoboam saying, "If you will be a servant to this people today, and will serve them and grant them their petition, and speak good words to them, then they will be your servants forever" (1 Kings 12:7).

Evidently, the younger advisors told Rehoboam,

> "Lighten the yoke which your father put on us." The young men who grew up with him spoke to him, saying, "Thus you shall say to this people who spoke to you, saying, 'Your father made our yoke heavy, now you make it lighter for us!' But you shall speak to

> them, 'My little finger is thicker than my father's loins! Whereas my father loaded you with a heavy yoke, I will add to your yoke; my father disciplined you with whips, but I will discipline you with scorpions.'"

We all have two filtering systems: human reasoning or biblical discernment. We can attempt to think things through using our finite wisdom and understanding. We can try extremely hard to separate our sinful, selfish desires from a truly biblical decision. But apart from wise counsel, we will fail, just like Rehoboam. Read the following verses to see the difference in discerning counsel through a biblical lens.

> Trust in the Lord with all your heart and do not lean on your own understanding. In all your ways acknowledge Him, and He will make your paths straight (Prov. 3:5–6).

> How blessed is the man who does not walk in the counsel of the wicked, nor stand in the path of sinners, nor sit in the seat of scoffers! but his delight is in the law of the Lord, and in His law he meditates day and night (Ps. 1:1–2).

> Your testimonies also are my delight; they are my counselors (Ps. 119:24).

Sixth Principle: Be prepared to live with your decision (12:12–14)
We often fail to realize that every decision produces results. Somehow, we think that the choice is separate from the results; that consequences are not connected with the decisions we made. Negative results may be derived from godless decisions (outside of God's will) or godly decisions (carnal or godless reacting to God's will).

Rehoboam followed through with advice given by his peers. He spoke to Jeroboam as his young advisors instructed him. He acted, and there was a reaction. Rehoboam acted harshly. He spoke callously. When Jeroboam and the people heard him, each departed to their tents realizing that Rehoboam's decision excluded them from an inheritance in David. History tells us that they later relocated to the North in Israel and established a rival worship system to prevent people from returning to the Temple in Jerusalem.

Galatians reminds us that what you sow you will reap. If the decision is based on God's Word, it is not a wrong decision just because people don't like the decision or you. Biblical decisions may be made, and carnal or godless people may oppose. Nevertheless, the decision is not wrong. Those who oppose a biblical decision or direction are more concerned about the opinions of others than the commendation of God. You can have the favor of men now or the favor of God later.

Seventh Principle: The sovereignty of God is involved in all of your decisions (12:15)
Whether the decision is godly or ungodly, God permits it. At times, ungodly decisions are used by God to affirm His revelation or to work out an aspect of His will. This is where God can take all things and work them out for good. We read in the text that God used these events to fulfill His prophecy spoken through Ahijah to Jeroboam.

However, it does not mean that we can discard the biblical principles of decision-making and wise counsel and cast out presumptuous fate onto the sovereignty of God.

Here are some practical questions to ask yourself when you are considering to whom you should listen:

- Whom will the counsel glorify? Self or God?
- Whom will the counsel benefit? Self or others?
- What will the counsel do? Unite or divide?
- On what is the counsel based? Service or power?

I'm Not Sure This Is What God Wants Me to Do
Second Guessing God

Have you ever "second-guessed" God? I mean, you believe a truth from His Word, and then you begin to wonder if that is what it really means. *Did I walk away with the right understanding?* You're strong for a while, and then circumstances beat you up, friends question you, and others just look at you funny. Some are jealous, and others are suspicious or angry with you. What seemed like a "no-brainer" suddenly becomes extremely difficult and uncomfortable. You begin to wonder. There are two ways to respond.

We can respond like David who experienced these feelings in 1 Sam. 23:2–4 and went back to God for clarification. Or we can react like Jonah who experienced these feelings and ran away from God.

Let's look at the story line found in 1 Kings 13. In this fascinating story, we are told of a young prophet who was commissioned to address Jeroboam for his wickedness, evil, and idolatry. The young prophet's denunciation was so powerful that it enraged Jeroboam to the point of his attempting murder. God intervened, and Jeroboam was compelled to entreat this nameless prophet to beseech God to reverse the physical judgment of his dried-up hand. The young prophet was instructed by God to return home a different way. His journey was interrupted by the resident prophet who deceived him by asking him to dine and stay. Because of this deviance from God's orders, when the young prophet resumed his journey, he was met by lions that killed him.

Lessons to Learn
Lesson Number One: The Word of God is fundamental in knowing the will of God.
It is important that we note that the phrase "the Word of the Lord" is used six times in this short chapter (13:1, 2, 3, 5, 9, and 17). The Hebrew word used is *dabar*, which means to arrange, signifying that the Word of God is orderly and reliable. The Bible is divinely inspired, but divinely arranged in thoughts, intentions, purposes. The will of

the Author is presented in an orderly fashion and is utterly reliable. One can unmistakably know God's will. Regardless of the questions or doubts, God's will can be understood. Despite everything pointing you in another direction, you can comprehend God's direction.

Unlike human wisdom that comes through education, this wisdom is limited by the instructor. Unlike human wisdom that comes through experience, this wisdom is limited by subjectivism. Unlike human wisdom that comes through experts, this wisdom is limited to present scientific data available. No other wisdom has stood the test of time, disbelief of humanity, skepticism of the doubters, and irreverence of the scoffers. God's Word reveals God's will. The Bible is central to knowing God's will. Without the knowledge of the Word of God, one removes something of which it transcends, is relevant and timeless, and is applicable to all people at all times in every situation and geographic area. The Bible is absolute.

This young prophet was provided a valuable lesson. As he began his ministry, it came about because of the Word of God. The Word of God gave him His message. The Word of God gave him his authority to approach the regal realm. The Word of God provided him discernment. The Word of God offered protection if he listened and heeded.

Like the prophet, we must not attempt to do, to act, or to move in ministry or life apart from the Word of God. Such presumptuous acting could be likened to a resident doctor who avails himself of a delicate surgical operation. There would be great harm that could ensue because the young doctor failed to abide by standard operating procedures. The saint places himself or herself in harm's way when he or she runs ahead, lags behind, or deliberately disobeys the Word of the Lord.

Lesson Number 2: The will of God is not always easy

> Now behold, there came a man of God from Judah to Bethel by the word of the Lord, while Jeroboam was standing by the altar to burn incense. He cried against the altar by the word of the Lord, and said, "O altar, altar, thus says the Lord, 'Behold, a son shall be born to the house of David, Josiah by name; and on you he shall sacrifice the priests of the high places who burn

> incense on you, and human bones shall be burned on you.'" Then he gave a sign the same day, saying, "This is the sign which the Lord has spoken, 'Behold, the altar shall be split apart and the ashes which are on it shall be poured out'" (13:1–3).

This is not a message that will endear you to the king's heart. This is not a message that will thrust you into the most wanted preacher's circuit. The message given by the Word of the Lord is an unpopular message. The content of this message is punishment. The message is personal. God is expressing His disfavor with Jeroboam. God is going to punish Jeroboam.

Imagine you are this young prophet. We know little else of this prophet other than what is recorded in this brief chapter. Imagine the difficulty of this task. What an overwhelming first assignment! But he would not be the first or the last to undertake such a huge endeavor of potential, unpleasant consequences. Noah was a preacher of righteousness for 120 years and only had eight converts. None were his neighbors. No political, sports, or Nobel Prize winners got into the ark. Think about Nathan confronting a sinful king. David had a temper. But you find Nathan the prophet pointing his stubby little finger in David's face and pronouncing, "You are the man." Or Ananias receiving the Word of the Lord to go and restore the eyesight of the one who was converted on the road to Damacus. What about Jonah? He received the Word of the Lord to preach to those who enslaved his people. And Esther received the Word of the Lord through prayer and fasting to appear before a king and reveal her identity to save her people from extermination. How hard it must have been for Ruth to leave her homeland and be faithful to her mother-in-law. And of course, Jesus endured the cross.

Somewhere in modern Christendom, the notion that the will of God is easy, good, feels right, is void of hardship, and the like has captivated both preacher and congregant. "Anything that is biblically right and hard must not be the will of God" becomes a prevalent ideology. Not only does the Bible discredit such a fairytale lie, but our forefathers in the faith endured great persecution and were smack dab in the middle of God's will. And I can bear witness to the truth that God's will is not always easy.

But it is in the midst of God's will, which is difficult and hard to understand, where the heart's praise, adoration, and trust are most evident. I can trust God's will. God's will is not for my comfort, but for His glory and my development of character and love.

Lesson Number 3: The will of God is certain and sure.

> Now when the king heard the saying of the man of God, which he cried against the altar in Bethel, Jeroboam stretched out his hand from the altar, saying, "Seize him." But his hand, which he stretched out against him, dried up, so that he could not draw it back to himself. The altar also was split apart and the ashes were poured out from the altar, according to the sign which the man of God had given by the word of the Lord (13:4–5).

Many people do not want to hear the Word of the Lord. Even if they hear the Word of the Lord, they balk, hesitate, lag behind, or refuse to do the will of God. Some get worried about doing the will of God, some barter with God, and still others get angry.

Jeroboam was angry at the Word of the Lord. He ordered others to apprehend the young prophet with the intention of killing him. His message infuriated Jeroboam. An old adage says, "Don't kill the messenger, he is just delivering the message." Jeroboam did not like the message and could not change the message; therefore, he reasoned that killing the messenger would change or remove the message.

God brings to pass what He has revealed. No one or nothing can prevent the will of God from taking place. The omnipotence of God insures the fulfillment of the will of God and assures us of the presence and power of God. What God commissioned the young prophet to do, He also enabled the prophet to perform. The will of God is sure and certain.

Lesson Number 4: Knowing the will of God supplies determination and destination.

> "For so it was commanded me by the word of the Lord, saying, 'You shall eat no bread, nor drink water, nor return by the way which you came.'" He said, "I cannot return with you, nor go with you, nor will I eat bread or drink water with you in this place. For a command came to me by the

word of the Lord, 'You shall eat no bread, nor drink water there; do not return by going the way which you came'" (13:9, 16–17).

At the first signs of opposition, verbatim assert the will of God. Here Jeroboam seeks to manipulate the young prophet with what appears to be an innocent offer of food and refreshment. But God already instructed the young prophet not to go with him, nor eat with him, or drink water in that place. In fact, this unnamed prophet was to return home by another way. We can renew our determination to the will of God by reciting the will of God, verbatim—word for word.

Why does opposition occur? Opposition may be due to your obedience viewed as threatening to expose another's sin. This was Jeroboam's response. His wickedness had been exposed by the truthful message of the prophet. Opposition may be due to someone's jealousy. Later in the story line, we read of the older prophet that tickled the ears of Jeroboam, but may have been estranged by the King. The older prophet was jealous of the stir the young prophet caused in the palace and town.

What kept Noah going for 120 years? How did Joseph survive being sold as a slave, tricked, deceived, and falsely accused? What aided Daniel as he served as an indentured vassal to three world empires? On what did our Lord anchor His life and ministry? Against all odds, despite any circumstance, and no matter what others say, the people of God who hear the Word of the Lord find renewed strength. Their determination to be obedient rises to new levels to meet the opposition.

Lesson Number 5: God reveals His will, and any changes to that will, to the person appointed to carry out His will.

> He said to him, "I also am a prophet like you, and an angel spoke to me by the word of the Lord, saying, 'Bring him back with you to your house, that he may eat bread and drink water.'" But he lied to him (3:18).

What is it about this situation that would cause God to change His mind? Did the young prophet hear again the Word of the Lord? Did God change His mind and forget to tell the young prophet? What was so different about this situation that God would choose to speak to the older prophet a message that seemingly is contrary to the original message given?

Has God spoken to you through His Word as He did earlier? It is highly unlikely that God will use another to tell you what He wants you to do. If God originally spoke to you, why would God speak through another? God will not tell you to marry a young woman via a friend. I was told of two people who were instructed that it was God's will for them to get married. The one telling them was a trusted friend in a Christian ministry. But God had not spoken to neither one of them about marriage, let alone to one another. Sadly, marital conflict occurred and a subsequent divorce.

God may use other's input for one of three purposes. First, confirming God's will. You know what God wants you to do. A spiritually mature person may affirm the Spirit's leading in your life. Second, correcting your abandonment of God's will. In sharing with this trusted spiritual mature person, he or she may be used by God to expose your misunderstanding or manipulation of Scriptures to avoid carrying out the will of God. For example, a young woman wants desperately to be married. Her biological clock is ticking. She knows that God does not want her to be alone. She believes she is called to be someone's helpmate. So, you probe and realize that she wants to marry an unbeliever. This is not God's will, and you must correct her. And finally, instructing you on God's will in general roles and patterns. You mistakenly do not understand God's will regarding general roles for your life such as a song, daughter, wife, husband, employee, employer, member of a local church, citizen of a government, or servant. You may not have been taught or taught erroneously about biblical patterns for your life in such areas as sexual purity, financial management, stewardship, and relationships.

Listen carefully. No one can tell you what God's will is. If others are telling you what God wants you to do, it must be based on an attitude or behavior that is not lining up with the Word of God. No one can say to you, "God spoke to me last night and He wants you to ..." That is soothsaying. God loves you so much He will provide for you the

Word of the Lord, and if in His sovereign foreknowledge, the plans for your life are further manifested—additional information needs to be conveyed—He will tell you, for He alone knows. Any outside input is for the sole purpose, as stated earlier, to confirm, correct, or instruct.

Lesson Number 6: Idolized-submission usually leads to misunderstanding God's will.

> So he went back with him, and ate bread in his house and drank water. Now it came about, as they were sitting down at the table, that the word of the Lord came to the prophet who had brought him back; and he cried to the man of God who came from Judah, saying, "Thus says the Lord, 'Because you have disobeyed the command of the Lord, and have not observed the commandment which the Lord your God commanded you, but have returned and eaten bread and drunk water in the place of which He said to you, "Eat no bread and drink no water"; your body shall not come to the grave of your fathers.'" It came about after he had eaten bread and after he had drunk, that he saddled the donkey for him, for the prophet whom he had brought back (3:19–23).

The younger prophet allows spiritual reasoning and past illumination to be clouded. Perhaps he was impressed by age, status, and position of this older prophet. What the younger prophet failed to recognize was what the old prophet pointed to as his source of truth. It was not the Word of the Lord. The old prophet's source was a message from an angel. The old prophet was equating the message of this angel with the Word of the Lord. He cited a supplemental supernatural declaration as his basis for truth, which changed the young prophet's intentions.

Now God did use angels in the past to convey His will. The previous angelic revelation was thirty-four years prior when angel of death punished David for taking the census. Prior to that was fifty-four years before when an angel appeared to Manoah with birth of Samson.

We are prone to appreciation and respect for a gifted preacher. We are often guilty of idolizing them. We take what they say as gospel. They are so much closer to God than we are. If what they are telling us were not the Word of the Lord, surely God would stop them from speaking. Yet, a cursory reading of Isaiah and Jeremiah records the lament of Jehovah, when false prophets spoke words that did not come from Him. Even Jesus in the Sermon on the Mount warned His disciples of false prophets. But why wouldn't God halt their speech? Then man would not have free will. Man would not turn to God to know the Truth. Man would ignore the relationship to the Holy Spirit who makes all things clear.

Everything I hear must be strained through the filter of God's Word. Everything. Whether it is from our favorite radio preacher, strain it through the filter of God's Word. The latest book? Strain it through the filter of God's Word. The newest seminar? Strain it through the filter of God's Word. A guest speaker? Strain it through the filter of God's Word. Everything. We are required to test the spirits (1 John 4:1). We can do this because of the residential work of the Holy Spirit (1 John 4:4). The Spirit of God is our teacher (1 John 2:20).

Lesson Number 7: There are inevitable consequences when we fail to stay in God's will until He speaks again in His Word.

      a. For ourselves
         i. Losses on a variety of levels

What are the inevitable consequences when we fail to stay in God's will? Consider the losses Jeroboam and those in this story suffered. First, Jeroboam lost the opportunity to repent and return to God's program. He simply sent the young prophet off. He saw and experienced firsthand the power of God to judge and restore. Did he repent? No.

Second, the old prophet was reinstated into the favor of Jeroboam but he continued to experience the disfavor of God because he remained a false prophet. Third, the old prophet's sons witnessed the corrupted model of spiritual leadership in their father. Fourth, a nation was misled deeper into sin and further away from God until they were captured by Assyria and exiled.

If we ignore, make light of, redefine, or disobey the Word of the Lord given to us, we will suffer on a variety of fronts. It would take a book to expound on the variety of fronts a saint can suffer. God is not bound to get our attention in one certain way. He knows which way is more potent to capture our attention to return to hearing and doing the will of the Lord. The bottom line can be taken from a message given by Jonathan Edwards, "Sinners in the Hands of an Angry God."

Doug Oldham was criticized for a trite saying, but it told a biblically accurate truth with which we can conclude this chapter. "If God said it, and I believe it, that settles it for me." Martin Luther uttered a similar concept from a more theological viewpoint at the Diet of Worms, "Unless I am persuaded by the Scriptures, I will not, I cannot recant. I take my stand and can do no other. God help me."

Dear God, Please ...

Be Careful What You Ask For

Let's begin this chapter with a parable. It is called the parable of King Midas.

King Midas was a very kind man who ruled his kingdom fairly, but he was not one to think very deeply about what he said. One day, while walking in his garden, he saw an elderly satyr asleep in the flowers. Taking pity on the old fellow, King Midas let him go without punishment. When the god Dionysus heard about it, he rewarded King Midas by granting him one wish. *The king thought for only a second,* and then said, "I wish for everything I touch to turn to gold." And so it was.

The beautiful flowers in his garden turned toward the sun for light, but when Midas approached and touched them, they stood rigid and gold. The king grew hungry and thin, for each time he tried to eat, he found that his meal had turned to gold. His lovely daughter, at his loving touch, turned hard and fast to gold. His water, his bed, his clothes, his friends, and eventually the whole palace were gold.

King Midas saw that soon his whole kingdom would turn to gold unless he did something right away. He asked Dionysus to turn everything back to the way it had been and take back his golden touch. Because the king was ashamed and very sad, Dionysus took pity on him and granted his request. Instantly, King Midas was poorer that he had been, but richer, he felt, in the things that really count.

There are modern day examples of people longing for something. They desire and crave a certain thing, but they do not consider the consequences of their coveting. Some examples are a teen who desperately craves acceptance. Or a young woman who is discontent with her singleness and yearns to be married at any cost. Or a young athlete who so badly wants a pro contract he bulks up on steroids.

I believe we can develop at least three Midas Touch Questions to help us be careful in what we ask for. Question number one: Am I ruled by wrong motives? (Js. 4:3). Question number two: Am I motivated by selfish desires? (Js. 4:3). Finally, question number three: Will this result in imbalanced priorities or tensions in family roles? (Ps. 127:1–2; 1 Cor. 14:40).

Before we examine 1 Samuel, chapters 8 and 12, to discover some vital lessons from the nation of Israel, let's explore the backdrop. In 1 Samuel 8, the children of Israel are discontent. A major reason for their dissatisfaction with God is they wanted a king who would judge them like all the other nations (8:5). They wanted to fit in. They wanted someone they could see, touch, and speak before them. The Israelites longed for a human leader to follow into battle.

In 1 Samuel 12, Samuel reminds the children of Israel who had brought them out of Egyptian slavery and who had fought for them to take possession of the land. It was Jehovah, unseen but omnipotent. God showed His displeasure with them when they sought after a king to be like the surrounding nations. God sent thunder and rain down upon them. They realized they had added a great sin by asking for this evil thing, but Samuel assures them that God is a forgiving God and urges them to continue following the Lord. In spite of what they sought after, as sinful and egregious as it was, if the children followed the Lord wholeheartedly, then God would even lead their king. But if they continued in their wicked ways, they and their king would be swept away (12:20–25).

What lessons can we learn from this portion of Scripture? Paul reminds us of the value of the Old Testament. He writes that these things, Old Testament stories and figures, were recorded so we might not crave the same evil things (1 Cor. 10:6, 11).

Lesson #1: We must identify our true motivation when asking God for anything (8:1–5).
The children of Israel claimed they wanted to be like the nations that surrounded them. I believe they saw the corruption in these nations. They imagined that if a king ruled them, it might be better than Samuel's son who did not walk in Samuel's way. They were ruled by fear (8:5). They imagined a harmful situation. If Samuel's sons became

successors, they would not be able to control the outcome. If they had a king before them, they thought they would be able to control the outcome.

The children of Israel was the only nation whose God was represented by a box. The Ark of the Covenant was four feet long by four feet wide by four feet tall, carried on poles by priests. How embarrassing! In fact, they were not permitted to take the Ark of the Covenant into battle for all the other nations brought the symbols of their gods into battle for good luck. The children of Israel were controlled by conformity (8:5). They wanted to fit in very badly. They felt like outcasts and wanted the other nation's acceptance. They were tired of standing out, for no other nation's government was like theirs.

The children of Israel were image conscious (8:20). No other nation operated like Israel. Who went before them into battle? Had they forgotten who it was that fought their battles? It was not a monarch. Yet they had this preconceived idea that they were inferior. Having a king would put them on par with the other nations. They would be equals because they could parade around their king. Or, erect signs announcing their territory of *King So & So, sovereign ruler of Israel.*

What is the evidence of spiritual decline? The evidence is when we want to imitate evil and reject good. 3 John, verse 11, says, "Beloved, do not imitate what is evil, but what is good. The one who does good is of God; the one who does evil has not seen God."

Lesson #2: We must recognize that certain prayers may reject God and erect an idol in our hearts (8:7–8).
Idolatry was clear in Bible times. It was bowing down before an image made of wood or stone. It was offering a sacrifice, animal or human, on an altar. Idols had specific names such as Baal, Molech, Chemosh, Asherah, Yam, and Mot.

God knew of the idolatry in the nation's life. God comforted Samuel. Israel was not rejecting Samuel, but God Himself. Ever since the days of Egypt, they found ways to forsake Jehovah. This cry for a monarch, a king to go before them, was a prayer of idolatry. God said so in verse 8.

Today's concept of Christian idolatry has been sophisticated and marginalized. How can a saint's prayer reveal an idol? Their longing for a Christian husband. Their craving for a spouse. Their passion for a more affluent lifestyle. Their thirst for more social status. Their yearning for more "things." Their desire for a certain position or title. The telltale sign that these prayers are ones of idolatry is how the person responds if their prayer is not granted. If God says, "No!" Christ says we should be content with food and clothing. Christ also says that the greatest need we have, or prayer we should be offering, is a deeper relationship and fellowship with Him. Paul said it this way, "That I may know Him" (Phil. 3:10).

We fail to see that our motivation challenges the sovereign rule of God in our lives with such prayers. The sovereign rule of God means three things. First, the sovereignty of God means His complete control. In God's universe, nothing is haphazard. Absolutely nothing takes our Lord by surprise. Second, the sovereignty of God means His infinite wisdom. He knows what is best for us. He is omniscient. He knows every detail of every situation. What we cannot control or recognize, what our prayers often fail to take into consideration, God accounts for the missing pieces. Third, the sovereignty of God means His perfect love. This perfect love is for our welfare. A child might want to fill up on sweets and subsequently be doubled over with a painful stomach ache. However, a wise parent who so dearly loves the child will not grant the child's pleadings. Likewise, our Heavenly Father loves us so much, although we tend to ask out of selfish desires, He knows that granting our request could yield much greater harm. He loves us immensely that His "no" is just as loving as His "yes" and "not right now" answers.

Lesson #3: We must sense God's warnings before He listens to us (8:10–22).
God warns us before He answers us! Read the warnings God gives to the nation of Israel.

> So Samuel spoke all the words of the Lord to the people who had asked of him a king. He said, "This will be the procedure of the king who will reign over you: he will take your sons and place them for himself in his chariots and among his horsemen and they will run before his chariots. He will appoint for himself commanders of thousands and of fifties, and some to do his plowing and to reap his harvest and to make his weapons of war and equipment for his chariots. He will also take your daughters for perfumers and cooks and bakers. He will take the best of your fields and your vineyards and your olive groves and give them to his servants. He will take a tenth of your seed and of your vineyards and give to his officers and to his servants. He will also take your male servants and your female servants and your best young men and your donkeys and use them for his work. He will take a tenth of your flocks, and you yourselves will become his servants. Then you will cry out in that day because of your king whom you have chosen for yourselves, but the Lord will not answer you in that day." Nevertheless, the people refused to listen to the voice of Samuel, and they said, "No, but there shall be a king over us, that we also may be like all the nations, that our king may judge us and go out before us and fight our battles." Now after Samuel had heard all the words of the people, he repeated them in the Lord'S hearing. The Lord said to Samuel, "Listen to their voice and appoint them a king." So Samuel said to the men of Israel, "Go every man to his city."

The phrase "he will take" occurs six times. God warns Israel about the answer to this prayer. Look at the downside of this prayer. If this prayer is answered, what will their life be like? The king will take your sons and place them in the military. Some of your sons will end up farming his land, forging weapons, and equipping his chariots. The king will take your daughters to make perfume, to perform the duty of a cook or baker. The king will take the best of your fields and vineyards and give them to his servants. He will force you to tithe off your produce, which will be given to his officers and to his servants. He will take your male and female servants, the strongest most virile males and your livestock to use for his work. He will force you to tithe off of your flocks and force you to become indentured to him.

In spite of this clear warning, nevertheless the people refused to listen to the voice of Samuel. They wanted to be like other nations around them.

Have you ever prayed so hard and long, and your prayer was granted, but the outcome was not anything like you expected? Answering your prayer may take away from family relationships (8:11, 13). Your time is not your own. How often have I seen child-centered homes instead of Christ-centered homes. The parents of these homes are jumping through hoops to make their children happy while disregarding the consequences of those actions. Do these things promote family unity or do they destroy the hard-fought family structure?

Idolatrous prayers take away other divine blessings (8:14–15). Our wives cease from being the fruitful vine, and our children are not becoming olive plants (Ps. 128:3). The precious and pure commodities of peace and joy give way to increased arguments and discord. You can hear someone say, "This is not what I expected when I prayed for this!"

Idolatrous prayers take away other resources (8:16–17). Often church attendance wanes because of exhaustion and fatigue. "It is the only day that I can relax." Prayer, Bible reading, or small groups vanish. Idolatrous praying takes away your freedom.

> Then you will cry out in that day because of your king whom you have chosen for yourselves, but the Lord will not answer you in that day (8:18).

I have become a slave to my prayer request. I am driven because of this prayer being answered. The text says that I will cry out to the Lord, I will want to renounce this idolatrous prayer, but God will not answer me. God will not relieve the consequences of that idolatrous prayer but will help you learn from that type of prayer, provided you do not turn aside from following the Lord, but serve the Lord with all of your heart (1 Sam. 12:20).

So what happened? How did they respond to this warning? They refused to listen to God, but God listened to them and granted their request for a king. The results of this prayer are more negative than positive. A careful study of the listing of kings in 1 and 2 Chronicles produces no righteous king, no king after the heart of David—only kings after the wickedness of Jeroboam and Manasseh. You have a few more good kings in 1 and 2 Kings.

Lesson #4: There is hope if I've been praying this way.

> Then all the people said to Samuel, "Pray for your servants to the Lord your God, so that we may not die, for we have added to all our sins this evil by asking for ourselves a king." Samuel said to the people, "Do not fear. You have committed all this evil, yet do not turn aside from following the Lord, but serve the Lord with all your heart. You must not turn aside, for then you would go after futile things which can not profit or deliver, because they are futile. For the Lord will not abandon His people on account of His great name, because the Lord has been pleased to make you a people for Himself. Moreover, as for me, far be it from me that I should sin against the Lord by ceasing to pray for you; but I will instruct you in the good and right way. Only fear the Lord and serve Him in truth with all your heart; for consider what great things He has done for you. But if you still do wickedly, both you and your king will be swept away" (1 Sam. 12:19–25).

If I have been praying the way described from these passages, if I can see I have an idolatrous prayer life, what should I do? Do what Samuel instructed the nation of Israel to do. First, repent of the prayer as evil (19, 20). Second, return to serving God with a whole heart (20, 24). Third, remember the great things God has done (24). Finally, receive prayer and instruction from godly counsel (23).

Fearfully and Wonderfully Made

Helping Caregivers Care for Crack Cocaine Babies

Why have I taken the time to write a chapter on the topic of "crack babies"?

He was being escorted against his will from his classroom to the director's office, screaming and cursing as he went. When he entered the director's office, he continued his tirade of yelling and vulgarity. He kicked her desk and pounded on the chair that held him captive. He was in the director's office because he struck one classmate and was bullying others. He was out of control, but this was his reputation. An after-school program at the local YMCA was where he was encountering such opposition.

His mother—single, affluent, and well educated—had adopted this troubled child. She shared with several staff members that her adopted son was a crack baby. His biological mother had used crack cocaine during her pregnancy. His behavior, attitude, and actions were the product of his mother's careless, unloving, and irresponsible actions. He couldn't help himself.

This ten-year-old little boy acted the same way at home. The mother did not know how to handle his outbursts, temper tantrums, and aggressive behavior. She had resorted to placating him, and expected the YMCA to follow suit.

After months of striking other students, intimidating others, a parental uprising, and in sheer exasperation by the management, he was banned from the program forever.

The mother believed that her son's behavior was a direct result of damage at birth because of the cocaine use of his mother during pregnancy. He was not responsible for his behavior because he had experienced fetal insult or damage. Expectations were nearly non-existent. His mother permitted him to do what he did because of the way she had come to view him.

My wife witnessed all of this for weeks. She came to me and asked me about crack babies, as his adoptive mother referred to the him. Frankly, I did not have many answers. I did some preliminary research but due to distractions of operating a counseling and training center, this "free-time project" got put on the back burner. After I heard the child was banned, it moved further down the list of "things to do."

But I am compelled, for some reason, to explore this topic, to do research, and consider how a biblical counselor would help a parent or adoptive parent whose child was labeled as a crack baby.

This chapter may be a bit laborious. In part, this will be attributed to studying numerous medical and psychological studies, findings, and reports to understand if there are fetal affects on a baby when a mother uses crack cocaine during pregnancy.

We will need to first observe and document the behavior of babies born from cocaine users. How did the frenzy of crack babies and their hopeless lifespan develop? Has the data changed? Should we expect the same perspective for the nearly 45,000 babies born each year from mothers using crack cocaine during pregnancy?

We will briefly look at the new statistic developing in Iowa. This crisis is meth babies, the newer version of crack babies. Similar things are being said about these young lives. Additionally, we will draw some conclusions and spend time discussing practical ways to work with parents, caregivers, and teachers who are committed to raising and influencing these young lives.

How would a mother's use of cocaine affect the fetus? What is the physiological process? When a mother ingests cocaine during pregnancy, the drug passes through the placenta, enters the baby's bloodstream, and passes through the fetal brain barrier, according to a study published in *JAMA*, May 26 issue. Some studies haven't found an association between cocaine and deficits in cognitive development, while others have.

218

According to *News Briefs*, September-October 1997, doctors believe that a mother's use of cocaine during pregnancy can affect the fetus by allowing the drug to cross the placenta and distress the fetus' brain by causing blood vessels to constrict, which would hinder the supply of oxygen and nutrients to the fetus.

Tracing a child's problems to prenatal exposure to crack cocaine is extremely difficult. For one thing, drug tests at birth indicate only whether the baby and mother have drugs in their bodies at the time of delivery. The tests don't reveal whether the mother used drugs early in the pregnancy, when risk to the fetus's developing nervous system occurs.

Some research indicates that alcohol has more damaging effects through crossing the placenta than cocaine. Dr. Ira Chasnoff was quoted as saying that the placenta provides better protection than society, referring to the draconian laws of arresting cocaine-using mothers and removing their newborns to foster care.

Historical development of crack babies: Where and when did it all start?
Crack hit the streets in 1984, and the press had run more than 1,000 stories about it by 1987. Many news outlets focused on the plight of the so-called crack babies. The handwringing over these children started in September 1985 when the media obtained Dr. Ira Chasnoff's *New England Journal of Medicine* article suggesting prenatal cocaine exposure could cause devastating effects on infants.

However, Chasnoff warned that the report needed more research, as only twenty-three cocaine-using women participated in his study. What did Dr. Chasnoff observe, which was published in the *New English Journal of Medicine*, to start this media frenzy? Dr. Chasnoff observed that the twenty-three newborns who were subjected to crack cocaine during pregnancy were less interactive and moodier than non-cocaine babies. He became widely quoted and fawned over in the press—*Rolling Stone* called him "positively Zen-like"—and he became known as the authority on what happens to babies whose mothers use cocaine.

The press had a field day. Remember that President Reagan was a significant promoter of the war against drugs. Here were "poster children"—products of cocaine-using women to keep the ire of the common man stirred up and to solicit from Congress more federal funding for the war on drugs.

Within days of the first story, CBS found a social worker who claimed that a one-month old crack-exposed baby she was treating would grow up to have an IQ perhaps of 50 and be barely able to dress herself.

Despite very little reliable medical documentation on the effects of cocaine on newborns and young children, the media had already concluded that crack babies were prematurely born, brain-damaged, unlovable, unteachable, unreclaimable, and even unadoptable. The media portrayed crack babies as children incapable of positive learning experiences and condemned to a joyless childhood.

If a child was exposed to drugs in the womb, people now assumed the worst. A June 1990 federal report explained that would-be adoptive parents were reluctant to take on crack babies because of their potential long-term problems.

Leake and Watts, a large foster care agency in New York City, still refers drug-exposed babies and their foster parents to a special program where, even if a child seems just fine, he is closely watched.

Columnist Charles Krauthammer for the *Washington Post* wrote, "Crack babies were doomed to a life of certain suffering, or probable deviance, or permanent inferiority."

The media created hysteria. The public braced for the day when these biological underclass would cripple our schools, fill our jails, and drain our social programs.

In the midst of the drug war hysteria, crack babies became an emblem of the havoc drugs wreak and a pretext for draconian drug laws. Hospitals began secretly testing pregnant women for cocaine, jailing them, and taking their children. Tens of thousands of kids were swept into foster care.

This mania infiltrated the presidential race, where candidate Ross Perot called these babies permanently and genetically damaged when he said in the first presidential debate "again and again and again, the mother disappears in three days and the child becomes a ward of the state because he's permanently and genetically damaged."

All of this occurred in the mid and late 1980s and stem from one man's empirical observations. Was it scientific? Was it medicine? Would time later reveal it was myth? Myth or Medicine?

Myth #1: Crack babies have significantly lower IQ scores.
Research paid for by the National Institute on Drug Abuse (NIDA) and the Albert Einstein Medical Center in Philadelphia concludes, "We were unable to detect any difference in Performance, Verbal or Full Scale IQ scores between cocaine-exposed and control children at age four years."

A recent study appearing in the February issue of the journal *Pediatrics* concluded that standard psychological testing revealed no significant differences in overall intellectual performance between the two groups of newborns (cocaine-addicted mothers and healthy mothers).

In the May 26, 2004, Vol. 291, No. 20 of the *Journal of the American Medical Association* (*JAMA*) researchers, after testing 415 infants, wrote in their conclusion: prenatal cocaine exposure was not associated with lower full-scale, verbal or IQ scores.

Two years after Dr. Ira Chasnoff's initial observations were recorded in the *New England Medical Journal*, he was quoted as saying that their cognitive development is normal when you control for the environment and other factors.

But there is strong evidence that indicates that crack cocaine babies are slightly behind from the normal age-based IQ standards. Researchers found that poor children tracked to 4.5 years of age performed poorly on cognitive tests compared to other children, whether or not the poor children had been exposed to cocaine prenatally. Of course, even if the cocaine babies did slightly worse on the tests, the most harmful effects to children from cocaine-using mothers could be due to the variety of other disadvantages the children experienced. Children of such mothers were more likely to live in poverty, to be victims of abuse and neglect, and to be inadequately nourished and to suffer other health problems according to the *Journal of Developmental and Behavioral Pediatrics*, 20:418–424, 1999.

Claire Coles has a collection of horror stories about children growing up neglected, especially by cocaine addicts. One crack kid who couldn't concentrate in class was in fact hungry. A five-year-old sister was raising another poorly developed crack baby.

Serena Gordon reports in her article "Prenatal Cocaine Exposure Has Lingering Cognitive Effects" the results of a study published in the May 26 issue of *Journal of the American Medical Association* that 400 children (190 cocaine-exposed and 186 not) were assessed at six, twelve, and twenty-four months. When they were four years old, they were tested using the Wechsler Preschool and Primary Scale of Intelligence—Revised. Along with IQ scores, this test also provides information on arithmetic, vocabulary, verbal comprehension, object assembly, block design, and picture completion skills. None of the researchers administering the tests knew which children had been exposed to cocaine *in utero*. The researchers found overall IQ scores were not significantly different between cocaine-exposed children and non-exposed youngsters.

The National Association of Prenatal Addiction Research and Education in Chicago tracked a group of 300 children born exposed to crack for almost seven years. The NAPARE's researchers concluded that the IQ scores of children exposed to crack were the same as children who were not exposed.

Myth #2: Crack babies have increased birth defects.
Katharine Greider writes in a Jud-Aug 1995 article that Claire Coles, a developmental psychologist at Emory University School of Medicine

in Atlanta, had graduate students watching infants for hours at a time. She concluded that you could not distinguish the cocaine-exposed babies from the other babies. Nancy Day, an epidemiologist at the University Of Pittsburgh School of Medicine, stood up at a conference six years ago and admitted she thought the impairments researchers were observing were not caused by cocaine. Unlike fetal alcohol syndrome, which can cause birth defects, cocaine is not associated with any pattern of defects.

In a JAMA article (March 28, 2001), a group of doctors critically reviewed outcomes in early children after prenatal cocaine exposure in five domains: physical growth, cognition, language skills, motor skills and behavior, attention affect, and neurophysiology. Their conclusion: Among children aged six years or younger, there is no convincing evidence that prenatal cocaine exposure is associated with developmental toxic effects.

Marylou Behnke, associated professor of pediatrics at the University of Florida led a new study to expose the many myths associated with crack babies. According to Behnke's findings, presented at the joint annual meeting of the American Pediatric Society and the Society for Pediatric Research, more than seventy-five percent of all babies studied had no major abnormalities at all—the same as a group who were not exposed to cocaine *in utero*. According to Deborah Franks, associate professor of pediatrics at the Boston University School of Medicine, the study's methodology is sound and it confirms that cocaine is not a major cause of structural birth defects.

In Chicago, March 27, 2001 (*Reuters*), a report in JAMA found no consistent association between prenatal cocaine exposure and the children's physical growth of development. Motor skill deficiencies linked to cocaine exposure usually disappeared after age seven months, adding that more research was needed on the drugs neurological effects.

In another JAMA report, March 28, 2001, Deborah Franks and a group of researchers concluded that crack cocaine exposure *in utero* has not been demonstrated to affect physical growth; it does not appear to independently affect development scores in the first six years.

Kandall Stephen, one time consultant for a New York state senator, wrote that what the media is presenting (1991) are interviews with "experts" in a patchwork quilt of untested assumptions, individual impressions, and anecdotal experiences that crack babies are tiny brained and incapable of learning. He further writes a poignant statement that since science may influence or even determine public policy, bad science may lead to bad public policy.

In an article, "Is There Evidence of a Cocaine Teratogenic Epidemic?" authors Martin, Khoury, Cordero, and Walters conclude that among the general population there has been no detectable increase in birth defects that may be associated with cocaine use during pregnancy (1992).

A sociology student inquired of a website why crack babies are so screwed up. The columnist responded to the myth saying, "No direct link was ever drawn between mother's use of cocaine and fetal damage. This was just hypothesized—crack is so bad that it must permanently damage fetuses. The original alarmist projections that crack babies were permanently damaged proved unfounded." In a follow-up just two years after the identification of crack babies, Dr. Ira Chasnoff found that their average developmental functioning level is normal. Remember, he was the one whose article in the *New England Journal of Medicine* touched off the crack baby turmoil. Chasnoff himself would state that the "smarts of crack babies are normal."

Claire Coles, a clinical psychologist at Emory University in Atlanta, who has studied crack kids, says there is no evidence of genetic damage, nothing like what was originally supposed. Cocaine itself has not proved to be any more damaging than any other drug used by pregnant women.

<u>Myth #3: Crack babies have decreased attentiveness and emotional expressivity.</u>
Brown University conducted a study in which Beata Napiorkowski wrote her conclusions in the July issue of the *Journal of Pediatrics* that cocaine-exposed infants were more jittery, had more muscle tension, and were harder to move because they were stiff. These babies also

displayed patterns of both excitability and lethargy, appeared to be more stressed, and failed to follow certain stimuli such as a rattle or bell compared to non-exposed infants. These conclusions were from observing fifty-seven babies one and two days old.

One research group said that newborn behavior does not predict what a child will be like at age three, six, or twelve. A 1992 commentary in the *JAMA* decried a rush to judgment about long-term effects of cocaine, concluding that the evidence was far too slim and fragmented to allow any clear predictions about the effects of intrauterine exposure to cocaine on the course and outcome of child growth and development.

Myth #4: Crack babies are hopeless and a burden on society.
In a *New York Times Magazine* piece entitled, "It's Drugs, Stupid," Joseph Califano Jr., a former Secretary of Health, Education and Welfare, wrote that crack babies can cost $1 million apiece to bring to adulthood, and suggested that the children of addicted welfare mothers who refuse treatment be put in orphanages or foster care.

In an article in the *Obstetrics and Gynecology* journal, doctors conclude the lack of quality of prenatal care is associated with undesirable effects often attributed to cocaine exposure: premature, low birth weight and fetal or infant death.

In a lecture given at Seminars in Perinatology, the lecturer said that provisions for quality prenatal care to heavy cocaine users (with or without drug treatment) has been shown to significantly improve fetal health and development.

Invest a fraction of the perceived monies that Califano suggests it takes to raise a crack baby in alternative programs to provide nurturing environments, and witness the dramatic results.

Myth #5: Crack babies are unteachable and out of control.
"Much of the early thinking on cocaine's effects on neurological development grew more out of anecdotal reports than scientific studies" reports the *Washington Post*. In the mid-1980s when the reporting of

the crack epidemic was at its zenith, doctors and researchers warned that crack babies might suffer from severe learning and behavioral problems. The crack baby epidemic became a powerful symbol as the nation marched forward in the war against drugs, the *Post* reported. Everybody bought the story of the crack baby, and that just snowballed and took on a life of its own, said Donald Hutchings, an expert on the toxic effects of drugs on fetal development at a New York State Psychiatric Institute.

In "Growth Development and Behavior in Early Childhood Following Prenatal Cocaine Exposure," *JAMA*, Frank writes that the idea that these children are uniquely unteachable or somehow out of control is simply not supported by data. The authors noted that developmental problems could be explained in whole or part by other factors including prenatal exposure to tobacco, marijuana, or alcohol and the quality of the child's environment.

In the 1994 *Journal of Early Intervention*, an article entitled "Prenatally Exposed to Cocaine: Does the Label Matter?" the authors write that presented with children randomly labeled prenatally cocaine-exposed and normal, childcare professionals ranked the performance of the prenatally cocaine-exposed children below that of normal despite actual performance.

Mary Bettis Walter, Ph.D. submitted an article to *The American School Board Journal* (1994) in which she wrote, "Even if we know certain children are so-called crack babies, we cannot automatically blame any problems they might experience in school solely on their exposure to drugs in the womb. Children who grow up with drug-abusing parents often live in a chaotic environment that puts them at risk of developing all sorts of problems: learning difficulties, hyperactivity, even tendencies to violence."

Antwaun Garcia was a shy boy whose tattered clothes reeked. Everyone knew his father peddled drugs and his mother smoked rock, so they called him a crack baby. It started in fourth grade when his teacher asked him to read aloud. Antwaun stammered, and then went silent. "He can't read because he's a crack baby," jeered a classmate. In the cafeteria that day, no one would sit near him. The kids pointed and chanted, "Crack baby, crack baby, crack baby." After that the taunting never stopped. Unable to take it, Antwaun quit school and started hanging out at a local drug dealer's apartment, where at age nine he learned to cut cocaine and scoop it into little glass vials. Antwaun finally returned to school and began learning to read a year later, after he was plucked from his parent's home and placed in foster care. Now twenty, he's studying journalism at LaGuardia Community College in New York and writing for a magazine called *Represent*.

Daniel was—is—what some would call a crack baby. When Janine, a forty-two-year-old African American volunteer at a Manhattan public hospital, first laid eyes on him in the boarder-baby nursery, he was tiny and asymmetrical. At four months old, he looked like a newborn. Janine started visiting Daniel every day. When he reached ten months, she brought him home with her and formally adopted him. Today, greeting a visitor at the door of his mother's comfortable home in an unassuming neighborhood in southern Westchester, he is a fine boy of four, slender but average height with shinning eyes.

Although Janine learned not to look for failure in Daniel, others dwelled on his drug exposure. The first school she took him to for enrollment saw a black adopted child and asked, "Is he drug-exposed?" Janine claimed she didn't know. The second school, a preschool special education program, proved more problematic. This school knew of Daniel's prenatal drug exposure and wrote evaluations detailing it, explains Janine. Everything was related to this history. At two, he could count up to twenty. He was beginning to learn how to count in Spanish by the time he was three. He knew his alphabet. But the school reports were horrifying. The school virtually described a different student, like he wasn't the same child. According to them, he couldn't repeat two numbers consecutively, couldn't turn the pages of a book, and he couldn't hold a pair of scissors. There was nothing this child could do. It was because the school knew and formed a prejudice, claims Katharine Greider, a freelance writer based in New York.

<u>The new crack baby phobia today</u>—Meth Babies
Columnist E.R. Shipp called on *New York Daily News* readers to consider the damage the crack baby myth has done. There was an urgent

plea to avoid rushing to judgment on the growing reports of babies being born to mothers who use methamphetamines. A number of recent "meth baby" stories echo the early crack baby cover. A July *American Press* article cautioned that an epidemic of meth-exposed children in Iowa is stunting infant growth, damaging infantile brains, and leaving these children predisposed to delinquency. In May, one FOX News station warned that meth babies could make the crack baby look like a walk in the nursery.

Specific Counseling Issues

Environment
What the medical and psychological communities mean by "environment" is the home life in which the child is being raised.

Deborah Franks of the University of Boston wrote, "The other thing that became quite clear was the quality of the children's environment has a much stronger effect on the children's outcome than the prenatal exposure."

Barry Lester, professor of pediatrics and psychiatry wrote, "These are fragile, vulnerable babies. With proper childrearing, they will do just fine."

One study wrote, "While crack-exposes babies may develop more slowly than others, many experts say they often appear to grow out of early problems if they receive proper care as infants and toddlers. Many believe their prognosis is as good as children born drug-free if they get early intervention."

Dr. Ira Chasnoff stated, "Environment may play a more key role than drug exposure in the womb."

Referring to a study of IQ capacity of crack babies, he wrote, "Those children who were exposed to cocaine but raised in foster or adoptive care had higher IQ scores than cocaine-exposed kids who were raised by their biological mothers. Researchers found their full scale IQ scores were one point higher than those of non-exposed children."

Dr. Harley Ginsberg, medical director of the Neonatal Intensive Care Unit at Ochsner Clinic Foundation Hospital in New Orleans, writes, "The home environment appears to be a major determining factor."

Preconceived ideas
Over twenty years later, the preconceived ideas of crack babies fostered by the media in the 1980s seem to linger like the smell of smoke after a forest fire.

One of the largest adoption agencies in New York City still refers potential adoptive parents to attend a workshop where they will be informed about the challenges of raising a crack baby.

The stigmatism remains prevalent in our culture today, like the mother in the opening of this chapter who blamed her adoptive son's behavior on being a crack baby, or the study in which caregivers' knowing that one child was a crack baby and another was not ranked the behavior and learning of the crack baby lower because of their knowledge and preconceived ideas. It is not unlike the stigmatism of children labeled as ADD or ADHD in the educational system.

In the *Pediatrics Journal* (1998), Dr. Fonda Davis Eyler summarized the article by saying, "We think [crack babies] are going to do poorly, we don't expect for them to do well, so we don't push for that."

What should be our perspective on a crack baby? They are fearfully and wonderfully made. "I will give thanks to You, for I am fearfully and wonderfully made" (Ps. 139:14). They are the objects of God's compassion. "Just as a father has compassion on *his* children, so the Lord has compassion on those who fear Him" (Ps. 103:13). They are a gift from the Lord. "Behold, children are a gift of the Lord, the fruit of the womb is a reward" (Ps. 127:2). They have greater potential for service to God as we train them. "Your wife shall be like a fruitful vine within your house, your children like olive plants around your table" (Ps 128:3). We are to give good gifts to these children.

> If you then, being evil, know how to give good gifts to your children, how much more will your Father who is in heaven give what is good to those who ask Him! (Matt. 7:11).

We must recognize their hearts are tender and teachable to truth.

> Truly I say to you, unless you are converted and become like children, you will not enter the kingdom of heaven (Matt. 18:3).

Eyler notes that the very act of naming a child a crack baby can, in itself, bring about great harm. She believes all stigmatizing labels can be a self-fulfilling prophecy.

Fear of the unknown
If a child were exposed to drugs in the womb, people now assumed the worst. A June 1990 federal report explained that would-be adoptive parents were reluctant to take on crack babies because of their potential long-term problems. Teachers, too, were aghast to learn as the 1990s began that they could soon expect the crack babies in kindergarten. The arrival of those first afflicted youngsters would mark the beginning of a struggle that will leave your resources depleted and your compassion tested warned an article in *The American School Board Journal*. It was estimated that the cost to New York taxpayers for special care for first and second grade crack babies could total $2 billon dollars over fifteen years. Harlem Hospital researchers estimated that the cost of caring for crack babies costs the country $500 million a year.

We need to remember that pediatricians were being asked to predict the future of hundreds of thousands of diverse drug-exposed infants who may face multiplicity of high risk factors. This was unreasonable and unscientific.

But as one article wrote, "But the day never came. Crack babies, it turns out, were a media myth, not a medical reality."

The initial observations of crack babies were wrong. One study admitted they observed babies that were one or two days old. Chasnoff's observations were in a hospital nursery. How could someone predict long-term effects with empirical data?

Between the junk science data and the feeding frenzy of the media, fear was sown.

Why would accepting and raising a crack baby be more challenging than raising a child with a permanent and perhaps deteriorating disability? Since God is truly the Author of all life, and since He is truly Sovereign over all life (and births and quality of births), and if He so moves and directs someone to adopt such a child, why would we fear that what is needed on a daily basis would be withheld from those caring for the child? Romans 8 reminds us, "If God is for us, who is against us? He who did not spare His own Son, but delivered Him over for us all, how will He not also with Him freely give us all things?" (8:31b–32).

Fear usually has no substance. It attempts to make problems larger than they are. Fear endeavors to place God and all of His resources in its shadow. Fear propagates a message that I am inadequate to deal with a situation. I do not have the resources. I am not equipped. If I chose to do this thing, no one will be there to help me when things become difficult. Such fear is groundless. Fifty-seven times the Bible commands me not to fear. Forty-six times, I am commanded not to be afraid.

The data, the studies, the findings point to the probability of a crack baby living a normal and productive life. The childhood outbursts of anger, disobedience, and selfishness can be attributed to the child being born from the lineage of Adam. The child received a sin nature, the flesh, the old man, the Adamic nature.

Every parent works through the fear of raising his or her child. My wife would say we have a one in four chance of one of our children going off the deep end. That's true. Why? Free will. Resistance to instruction and training. A number of reasons, but generally all within the child, not outside the child.

It's no different with a crack baby. Because there is no evidence for fetal damage, the child can potentially act in alliance with the sin nature. So how can biblical counselors alleviate the fears of caregivers? Refocus them on the goal of raising this child. The goal of raising any child, "special" or "normal," is for the child to accept Christ as Lord and Savior, become a disciple, and serve God with all of their heart, mind, soul, and strength. We cannot expect from the child what we do not believe and have not communicated.

Sinful tolerance
If we permit or ignore the behavior of a crack baby, we have chosen a form of eclecticism. We have resurrected Freud, Skinner, and Rogers. We will blame the child's parents for irresponsible physical restraint. We will blame the environment. We will say that the child needs to draw deep within himself to effect change.

Can a crack baby control behavior? Take time to study a crack baby. Can the child play alone? With other peers? Is the child able to concentrate on television or a game cube? Does the child make decisions that reflect cognitive ability coupled with a personal motivation? And we could ask several other questions. Enough to suffice. If you can answer yes to any of these questions, it is a strong indicator that the child has selective memory and choice.

How would you account for this? One major observation would be repercussions. Under certain circumstances, the child recognizes that misbehavior will have significant repercussions. They can range from a punishment, to shunning, shame, or embarrassment. In other situation, the child knows that the repercussions are tolerable and manageable. The caregiver, teacher, or adoptive parent will yell, scream, threaten, or take something away. To the child, no real significant repercussions that would motivate change.

We can help by instructing the caregiver the words of Jesus about the seriousness of sin. Jesus said:

> If your hand or your foot causes you to stumble, cut it off and throw it from you; it is better for you to enter life crippled or lame, than to have two hands or two feet and be cast into the eternal fire. If your eye causes you to stumble, pluck it out and throw it from you. It is better for you to enter life with one eye, than to have two eyes and be cast into the fiery hell (Matt. 18:9, 10).

This passage seems strange. What does Jesus want us to know? He tells us that we should remove the offense quickly, thoroughly, and immediately. There is an eternal perspective that demands serious consideration. If we do not deal with sin quickly, thoroughly, and immediately, it will affect our eternal standing before God in the sense of loss of rewards and shame.

We should be careful listeners to the speech. When there are lies, these falsehoods must be identified and removed from the heart, mind, and vocabulary of the child. "Remove the false way from me and graciously grant me Your law" (Ps 119:29).

The foolishness of the child must be corrected. It is bound up in his/her heart. The Bible says, "Foolishness is bound up in the heart of a child; the rod of discipline will remove it far from him" (Prov. 22:15).

Leaven is a picture of sin in the Bible. Here Paul instructs the importance of truthfulness and honesty that are foundational for good healthy relationships: "Your boasting is not good. Do you not know that a little leaven leavens the whole lump of dough? Clean out the old leaven so that you may be a new lump, just as you are in fact unleavened. For Christ our Passover also has been sacrificed. Therefore, let us celebrate the feast, not with old leaven, nor with the leaven of malice and wickedness, but with the unleavened bread of sincerity and truth" (1 Corinthians 5:6–8).

Our goal is to raise the child to accept Christ as Lord and Savior (must deal with the sin issue), become a disciple (must deal with the sin issue), and serve God with all of their heart, mind, soul and strength (must deal with the sin issue).

Instruction
Instruction is the means of training a child to become a productive responsible citizen. What should a caregiver or adoptive parent teach? The child should be taught right from wrong. The child should be taught proper standards and values. The child should be taught how to love and serve others. The child should be taught how to make wise decisions. The child should be taught discipline, integrity, honesty, dependability, and truthfulness. The child should be taught respect for

authority. The child should be taught how to respond to hardships, unfairness, and mistreatment.

The source of instruction is crucial. Many self-proclaimed sources promise a product they cannot fulfill. The source of instruction is crucial. The reasoning of men will fail. The philosophies or our current age will be unsuccessful. The traditions of old will disappoint. Only the Bible provides a universal absolute standard for instruction that is cross-culturally relevant, applicable to all circumstances, can be understood at any age or educational level, and makes sense.

Discipline
When we think of the word "discipline," our minds usually picture punishment. People will quote, "Spare the rod and spoil the child."

Discipline is a two-sided coin. Yes, on the one side is the concept of punishment, whatever form it takes in your mind. For some it is corporeal while for others it seems to be the prevalent practice of grounding. But if this is the only side of discipline applied, the probability of raising a rebellious son or daughter is increased. Punishment without instruction is dangerous and not biblical (Eph. 6:4)

The other concept of discipline is training. Consider the following verses:

> Behold, how happy is the man whom God reproves, so do not despise the discipline of the Almighty (Job 5:17).

> My son, do not reject the discipline of the Lord or loathe His reproof, or whom the Lord loves He reproves, even as a father *corrects* the son in whom he delights (Prov. 3:11–12).

> For the commandment is a lamp and the teaching is light; and reproofs for discipline are the way of life (Prov. 6:23).

> Listen to counsel and accept discipline, that you may be wise the rest of your days (Prov. 19:20).

> Apply your heart to discipline and your ears to words of knowledge (Prov. 23:12).

> But have nothing to do with worldly fables fit only for old women. On the other hand, discipline yourself for the purpose of godliness; for bodily discipline is only of little profit, but godliness is profitable for all things, since it holds promise for the present life and also for the life to come (1 Tim. 4:7–8).

Discipline is what an athlete must be to compete and win. One of the things that always impress me when watching either the Winter or Summer Olympics is the athlete's discipline. Consider the 100-yard dash, usually run in under ten seconds! The discipline of training, of routine, the sameness day after day to complete and hopefully win. Four years of training for one race lasting about ten seconds! Discipline. For such discipline, the athlete must be thoroughly convinced for the prize, the outcome.

Deuteronomy reminds us that we are to recognize the teachable moments and seize every one. That's discipline. We are to establish a standard that no matter what, no matter what circumstances, what is taught as sinful is always sinful. If lying is sinful, then it is sinful for a four-year-old and for a sixteen-year-old. This is discipline God's way. Consistency.

What is the outcome for caregivers of these children? The joy of seeing achieving, productive, God-fearing men and women who beat the medical and psychological odds of predicted failure and doom. The lost, tattered, useless, and throwaways leading normal healthy lives. This reminds me of brothers who rejected another brother and yet when in trouble pleaded for his help. That man was Jephthah.

Goals
Webster defines the word "goal" as "the objective toward which an endeavor is directed." It's where we are going!

In a recent abstinence recording, one author commented, "We should expect more virtue from our teens and they should expect more godly counsel from us." That's a goal.

Dr. Fonda Davis Eyler wrote, "We think [crack babies] are going to do poorly, we don't expect for them to do well, so we don't push for that." Expectations for crack babies live in the shadow of what the "experts" predicted without scientific or medical support. This cloud still lingers over many who care for these children.

As counselors, we need to work with the caregivers on establishing goals for the child. Goals must be age appropriate, measurable, reasonable, and attainable. Goals must be evaluated regularly to insure progress. Goals are not rigid but flexible. Some goals may be too high and should be modified so the child/parent is not frustrated at the lack of progress. Goals should be written. They should be based on foreknowledge of the child's developmental needs physically, emotionally, mentally, socially and spiritually. Goals should have a timeframe for accomplishment. Goals should have an incentive and reward when it is achieved. Goals have obstacles, like hurdles to the runner. These must be anticipated. Forethought must be given to what those hindrances might be. Then plans to overcome those hindrances must be available if the hindrance arises. Don't be caught flatfooted. Goals are really desired by the child. They help them become more confident in daily expectations. When progress is made, it is an opportunity for the caregiver to praise and encourage. Children enjoy the sense of accomplishment, endurance, and their rewards.

If you know of someone who is raising a crack baby either through adoption or assuming custody of a family member's child, maybe you want to pass along this chapter to him or her. Maybe you need to hang onto it and allow its truths to purge any misconceptions you have come to embrace about crack babies. Maybe repetitive listening will increase your confidence and resolve that these children are made in the image of God, have a sin nature that accounts for their behavior, need Christ as Lord and Savior, and need to become little disciples to grow in grace and knowledge of the Lord Jesus Christ. Reject the myths. Embrace the truth. Stay in the ring for the glory of God and the sake of these precious little ones.

It Seems I Can't Remember Anything Anymore

Dementia: Understanding Dementia and Counseling Those Who Provide Care

My wife's mother is well into her eighties. Had her husband lived, he, too, would have been in his eighties. If my parents were still living, they would have been in their eighties.

Five to eight percent of people over the age of sixty-five have some form of dementia. That translates to 1 in 15 people. The number doubles every five years over age sixty-five.

An estimated 2 million people in the United States suffer from severe dementia and another 1–5 million people experience mild to moderate dementia.

The prevalence of dementia has increased over the past few decades, either because of greater awareness, more accurate diagnosis, or increased longevity is creating a larger population of elderly, which is the age group most commonly affected.

Carol Watkins, MD, says 15–20% of people over age seventy-five suffer from dementia, while another 25–50% over the age of eighty-five have dementia. That translates to one out of every three people according to the American Geriatrics Educational Organization.

Bonnie M. French claims that 7.9% of all Canadians sixty-five years and older meet the criteria for the clinical diagnoses of dementia (Canadian Study on Health and Aging, 1994). Alzheimer's disease is the major cause of dementia, accounting for 64% of all dementias in Canada for persons sixty-five and older and 75% of all dementias for persons eighty-five plus.

Defining Dementia
According to the Northern County Psychiatric Association, dementia is the loss of mental abilities. Dr. Mavis Evans, a consultant psychiatrist in Old Age at the Clatterbridge Hospital in Wirral, UK, dementia can

be considered as a global impairment of intelligence, memory, and personality.

One health encyclopedia defines dementia has a term referring to a group of symptoms involving progressive impairment of all aspects of brain function.

The American Geriatrics Society defines dementia as a condition of declining mental abilities, especially memory.

We can conclude that this is a truly medical condition. This will be verified in just a moment. Dementia can be summarized as follows: loss, impairment, progressive in nature, declining. A person's mental capacity is diminished; a person's memory is affected. There is a change in the person's personality. There is deterioration of a person's brain function.

Types of Dementia
In a general overview, some dementia is reversible and can be cured partially or completely with treatment. Then there is irreversible dementia caused by an incurable condition.

There are approximately 870 different types of dementia. Some specific types of dementias are degenerative dementia such as Alzheimer's disease or Pick's disease caused by the progressive loss of nerve cells. Vascular dementia is caused by a series of small strokes. Anoxia dementia is from cardiac arrest. Traumatic dementia is from injuries to the body such as a head injury. Infectious dementia is from infections such as AIDS, and toxic dementia is from drug or alcohol abuse.

Symptoms of Dementia
I'm going to provide a list of symptoms cited in numerous sources on dementia.

- Progressive memory loss
- Inability to concentrate
- Decrease in problem solving skills and judgment capabilities

- Severe confusion
- Delusions or hallucination
- Altered sensation or perception of reality
- Impaired recognition of familiar objects or persons
- Altered sleep patterns such as insomnia or the need for increased sleep
- Impaired motor function such as the inability to dress oneself, gait changes, inappropriate movements
- Disorientation with regards to a person, place, or time or the inability to interpret environment cues
- Specific disorders of problem solving or learning such as the inability to generalize, loss of abstract thinking, calculating abilities, or inability to learn
- Short-term memory problems (can't remember new things) or long-term memory problems (can remember the past)
- Inability to comprehend speech, to read, to write, to form words, to name objects, poor enunciation, inappropriate speech, inability to repeat a phrase
- Personality changes such as irritability, poor temper control, anxiety, depression, indecisiveness, self-centeredness, inflexibility, withdrawal from social interaction, inability to function or interact in social or personal situations, decreased ability to care for oneself

Causes of Dementia

One neurology resource listed the following causes: untreated infectious and metabolic disease, substance abuse, a brain tumor, cardiovascular disease (hypertension), a head injury, kidney failure, liver disease, thyroid disease, and vitamin deficiencies, such as B12, folic acid, and B1 (thiamine).

The American Geriatrics Society includes depression and AIDS, also mentioning stroke and loss of nerve cells

Testing for Dementia
How do we know it is not just the natural part of aging? I found an interesting chart that helps to differentiate between aging and dementia.

Typical aging is characterized by

- Independence in daily activities preserved
- Complains of memory loss but able to provide considerable detail regarding incidents of forgetfulness
- More concerned about alleged forgetfulness than are close family members
- Recent memory for important events, affairs; conversations not impaired
- Occasional word-finding difficulty
- Does not get lost in familiar territory, may have to pause momentarily to remember way
- Able to operate common appliances even if unwilling to learn how to operate new devices
- Maintains prior level of interpersonal social skills
- Normal performance on mental status examinations, taking education and culture into account

Warning signs of dementia

- Person becomes critically dependent on others for key independent living activities
- May complain of memory problems only if specifically asked; unable to recall instances where memory loss was noticed
- Close family members much more concerned about incidents of memory loss than person
- Notable decline in memory for recent events and ability to converse

- Frequent word finding pauses and substitutions
- Gets lost in familiar territory while walking or driving; may take hours to eventually return home
- Becomes unable to operate common appliances; unable to learn to operate even simple new appliances
- Exhibits loss of interest in social activities, exhibits socially inappropriate behaviors
- Abnormal performance on mental status examination not accounted for by education or cultural factors.

Collateral information from caregiver or family member is essential to verify historical events, if obtained from the patient. Some questions to ask are:

- What is the most distressing problem?
- Are the cognitive or behavioral changes of recent onset or have they been developing over a period of months or years?
- Have there been changes in patient activities of daily living and instrumental activities of daily living?
- Has there been a change in patient social function or role?
- What chronic medical conditions exist?
- What is the patient's level of alertness?
- Has the patient had problems driving (citations, crashes, near misses, getting lost, or behavioral problems while driving)?

The person's medical history should be reviewed. Many commonly used medications can be responsible for cognitive changes, therefore careful review of medication usage is essential, including prescriptions and nonprescription drugs. This should include over-the-counter medications, herbal remedies, and nutritional supplements.

Specific medical tests are advised. They are:

- Serum electrolytes
- Blood chemistry
- Serum calcium
- Glucose test
- Thyroid stimulating hormone
- Thyroid function tests
- Liver function tests
- Blood ammonia levels
- B12 level
- Drug, alcohol levels
- Urinalysis
- Blood gas analysis
- EEG
- Head CT
- MRI of head
- CSF (cerebrospinal fluid) analysis

Treatment for Dementia
I was surprised by my research that little treatment options were given. Depending on the age when dementia is diagnosed often determines the treatment options, which overall are slim.

The older the person is when diagnosed, the perspective appears to be to make the person as comfortable as possible. The family member or caregiver should probably begin looking at social services or long-term residential facilities. Some medications such as antidementia and psychotropic drugs are administered. New studies fostered by the pharmaceutical industry often experiment on mice with new drugs attempting to draw some applicable parallels.

One article suggested improvements could be achieved through physical, emotional, and mental activation. They suggested seeking the help of a physiotherapist (for the body) and/or ergotherapists (for the environment)

Another article suggested that if it is in the early states to train the thinking and memory functions of the person, but cautions this should be done with great care so the patient is not always reminded of his/her diminishing mental abilities. This seems to replace the former popular approach of reality orientation training.

As with numerous other diseases, there is no cure for the illness but medication can improve disease symptoms.

Prognosis for Dementia
Glenn Brynes, Ph.D. and MD, wrote, "Depending on the cause of dementia, the course may vary. In some cases, the time between first obvious symptoms, through gradual loss of cognitive abilities, to death ranges from seven to ten years. Vascular dementia, which usually results from the blockage of small blood vessels in the brain, often has a more erratic course, at times with stepwise exacerbation that parallels the destruction of different parts of the brain."

Counseling those who provide care
Personal issues
<u>Physical</u>
Most articles on dementia include comments on how important it is for the caregiver to take care of himself or herself. Caring for a person with dementia, depending on the progression of the dementia, is physically draining.

The caregiver should rest when the patient is resting. Housework should be limited in scope. If necessary, hire someone to do the cleaning, laundry, and even meal preparation. This would divide basic responsibilities and ease the physical burden of those tasks. Many social service agencies can provide these services either as part of the patient's health insurance or under Medicare or other state assistance.

The caregiver should attempt to find something physically attractive that would maintain the strength of the body as well as provide enjoyment. Walking, jogging, a stair stepper, tread mill, or walking the stairs in the house. The exercise one gets from caring for someone with dementia is not the same. Whatever profit may be derived may also be quickly lost because of the emotional and mental strain of caring for a dementia person. A physical workout will increase the heart rate, get the blood circulating, strengthen breathing, clear the mind, and often is refreshing. It can provide a clearer perspective on that which the caregiver is involved.

<u>Mental</u>
"As a man thinks, so is he," Proverbs reminds us. I was recently channel surfing and stopped at a sporting event called extreme running. It went beyond a marathon or a triathlon. These people were involved with a race over the course of twenty-four hours straight. It was so intense that they had to run on the white line on the shoulder of the road so their shoes would not melt from the asphalt. One athlete interviewed was asked why he punished his body so. In commenting, one thing that he said was that the pain involved is won or lost in the mind. It was a mental game.

I would image it would be so easy to succumb to the mental barrage each time the person with dementia would soil themselves, or act aggressively, or become frustrated that they are unable to communicate what they want, or any number of things they might do. Thoughts of:

- "Why am I doing this?"
- "It's my husband's parent, not mine."
- "Isn't it time we consider a nursing home?"
- "Just because I am a stay at home mom and the other siblings work, why can't they come over and spell me for a few hours?"
- "When they do come over, no one really sees Mom as she really is. It seems like she waits until they leave and she starts."

These thoughts, and others, can lodge themselves into the mind of the caregiver, and they can lose perspective, lose focus. When you lose focus, you are more prone to question why you are doing what you are doing.

One way of regaining focus might be to remind yourself of Christ's Word when commending the tribulation saints by saying that what they did, they did for Him because they did it to the least of them. When the tribulation saints cared for the Jews during the period of anti-Semitism, they were ministering to Christ. This is what He means. And when a caregiver provides to the best of their ability, they are serving Christ. When you think of all the people in the New Testament who served Christ, they did so with joy out of a deep sense of personal gratitude for being a benefactor of His intervention, grace, and mercy.

Emotional
Only one article in my research alluded to the need to be on the alert for parent abuse. Unaccounted bruising, broken bones, falls, or extreme loss of weight may be signs of abuse by the caregiver.

Now, I think we can say that we might know how this could occur. But knowing how it could occur does not mean the lack of self-control should be condoned or justified.

The physical and mental strain, the loss of social contact often for the caregiver, the spiritual depletion because of the time demands can influence emotional responses. Those responses usually are anger, rage, wrath, or at times fear, worry, or anxiety. The latter can lead to depression in the life of the caregiver. The former can lead to bodily harm for the person with dementia.

What should a caregiver do to control these emotions? How should they deal with such strong feelings?

Prayer—turning to God immediately when the sense of overwhelming feelings begins to rise inside. Pouring your heart to God about being overwhelmed.

Make a phone call to someone trusted to express your frustration at that very moment. At times, the emotion can magnify the problem. An objective observer could provide clarity and creative insight on how to handle the situation gracefully

Provided your leaving would not place the patient in harm's way, take your Bible, go outside, and spend time with God. He invites you to come and reason together and for those who are weary and heavy laden to come to Him and find rest.

Understand what the biblical replacement is for the emotion. Quickly recognize the warning signs of the sinful emotion and more quickly remind yourself and practice the biblical replacement.

Share with another family member or other caregiver that you need a break. Explain to them how you are becoming easily agitated over the care of this person. Plan on how you can gain renewed perspective emotionally by removing yourself from the situation for an hour or longer if possible.

If these sinful emotions persist, seek counseling. Some core issues may need to be addressed and perhaps some hard decisions that have been avoided need now to be made.

<u>Social</u>
Anyone caring for someone with dementia must have designated times of relief in order for him or her to:

- Go out for a cup of coffee with a close friend
- Go to dinner with the mate or family
- Go bowling
- Go to a church function
- Attend a movie
- Attend an overnight or weekend getaway with their mate
- Attend Bible study

- Attend Sunday school or church
- To go shopping simply to go shopping, not for some specific need for the person with dementia

Different people (without demanding problems), different scenery, and a different routine and schedule is refreshing. Under normal circumstances, usually everyone takes a vacation from the rat race to recharge and refresh. How much more important for those who are caregivers, whether family or professionals.

Spiritual
If caregivers are a born-again Christians, it will be vitally important for them to feed off the Living Word for their day-to-day strength.

Psalm 119 contains some precious nuggets for strength while being a caregiver. "I will meditate on Your precepts and regard Your ways" (119:15). There may be times where you are confused as to how to best help this loved one or just your own personal need for fortitude in acting biblical toward the loved one who insists you are a stranger trying to harm them. Meditation on His Word will show you the way to respond. Verse 24 states, "Your testimonies also are my delight; they are my counselors."

"Take away reproach and contempt from me, for I observe Your testimonies" (119:22). At times other family members, the patient's close friends, or others may question your motivations. God's Word gives assurance to a clean and clear conscience.

When fatigue and exhaustion try to take over, verse 25 reminds the caregiver, "My soul cleaves to the dust; revive me according to Your word."

When your heart breaks over the degeneration of one so strong, verse 28 records, "My soul weeps because of grief; strengthen me according to Your word."

When you wonder about all you may be missing, the huge investment of time, energy and resources, and your feelings give way to questions, remember, "Turn away my eyes from looking at vanity, and revive me in Your ways" (119:37).

And the list of verses, not only from Psalm 119, but also from other passages, becomes verses of daily, and even moment to moment, revival for your soul and spirit.

Caregivers must be people of prayer. They must realize that the inner strength to minister in such times is undergirded through fervent prayer and intercession. Verses on prayer should be memorized or written on construction paper and posted throughout the home for a constant visual reminder to turn to prayer. In such times, no amount of human effort can replace the need for supporting prayer.

Caregivers should surround themselves with mature saints who know the Word and who know how to pray. What a comfort and sense of strength for the caregiver. Solicit seven or more men and women to uphold the caregiver in prayer. Assign them each a specific day of the week. Furnish specific prayer requests. Tell them of answers to their prayers.

The caregiver's church must become involved. Most dementia patients are older as the data shows. Probably most are widows or widowers. Timothy provides clear instruction as to the care of our parents. However, the church as the guardian and shepherd of the soul of the caregiver and the person with dementia must take an active role. Regular times of visiting, many times for the sake of the caregiver to comprehend fully the daily pressure of such demanding care, will help the church grasp the task at hand. Meals, cards, flowers, helpful biblical literature, church bulletins, message tapes, and more are just some simple ways for the institution of the church to be involved.

Memorization would be an added resource. Hiding God's Word in the caregiver's heart will provide ready access to liberating, comforting, and encouraging truth.

If appropriate, times of fasting, whether it be for one meal or half a day, can help. Fasting could provide deeper spiritual insight on victoriously handling the person with dementia.

Legal issues
There may be the need to have a lawyer draw up certain documents that will help facilitate the care of someone with dementia. These documents should be drafted with the best interests of the one with dementia and allow the caregiver to operate more efficiently to accomplish the goal of the patient's best interests.

Healthcare Directive is a document that allows you to designate a person to make healthcare decisions for you if you are unable to do so. It also allows you to state your wishes regarding the withholding or withdrawal of life-sustaining procedures under certain circumstances.

Codicil to Will is a document used to change one or more provisions of a will as an alternative to creating a new will.

Do Not Resuscitate Guide provides information about pre-hospital do not resuscitate programs. DNR programs authorize emergency responders to withhold certain medical treatment such as cardiopulmonary resuscitation.

Power of Attorney authorizes another person or organization to act on your behalf in a variety of financial and legal issues.

Living Trust is used to create a trust to manage a person's assets during his or her lifetime. It provides for payments of income to that person and distributes the remaining assets of the trust upon his or her death.

Living Will description is the same as Healthcare Directive.

Organ Donation Form allows you to state your intent to donate organs or tissues. You may also instruct that your donation be used for such purposes as transplantation, education, or research.

Will is a document that states your wishes as to the distribution of your estate at the time of your death.

Medical issues

Incontinences
Can be a sudden onset often with a worsening of confusion and is often a sign of a urinary tract infection or constipation. It may have a physical cause such as atonic bladder, stress incontinence, or prostatic hypertrophy with overflow. This may be controlled by using incontinence pads and establishing regular and more frequent toileting routines.

Fecal incontinence
This is usually caused from constipation, overflow, or diarrhea. It may become impossible for a caregiver to look after the patient at home. Diapering may help.

Constipation
This often is a common problem in the elderly. It can be minimized by a good diet, plenty of fluids and whenever possible exercise. Mild aperients may be needed.

Malnutrition
One would think under a caregiver or even in a residential facility, that someone with dementia could not become malnourished. The quantity eaten tends to become smaller, so it is important that quality goes up. Contributing factors may be poor fitting dentures (or lack of them), the presence of a sweet tooth, convenience foods (less messy when she can feed herself sandwiches); these can lead to a poorly balanced diet. Such dietary practice means the lack of protein and vitamins and iron.

Food intolerance is also common because of decreased gastric motility and slower emptying time. Rich or fatty foods may cause stomach upsets or diarrhea. Seek advice from a dietician. Prescription for food supplements may be required.

Intercurrent illness

Infections, especially chest infections, tend to cause rapid worsening of confusion, sometimes to the extent of an acute or chronic confusional state. Antibiotic treatments usually produce dramatic results. Other illnesses, malignancy, osteoporosis, and cardiovascular and cerebrovascular disease are frequently seen in a population of this age group. Treatment should be given as appropriate. In the later stages of a dementia, invasive investigations should not be considered unless the pathology found will be treated.

Financial issues

The total annual cost for treatment of dementia is estimated at $100 billion dollars, which include costs of medical, long-term care, home care, and loss of productivity as reported by the American Geriatrics Foundation.

The state of Michigan issued a report indicating the average cost to care for one individual with dementia per year is $25,000. Depending on the severity, it could be as low as $18,400 and as high as $36,000 per person per year.

If you factor in "direct medical costs," you add another $6,000 annually. If there are medical claims due to a fall, you can add another $19,400 in medical and therapeutic treatment.

If the demented person attends an adult day care center three times per week, this may add to the total expenses by $6,552 (average $38 per day plus $4 transportation fee).

Medicare claims it will pay up to 80% of justified submitted bills. However, over the years they have been extremely rigid in the areas of physical, occupational or speech therapy, as well as psychiatric labels where dementia is a secondary diagnosis.

The average cost of nursing home facilities is $22,000 nationally. In Alaska, the cost is nearly tripled, while in some other southern states the cost may be cut in half. A private room nationally is $70,080 per year, or $192 per day according to a MetLife Market Survey. Based on these figures, most residents will be poor in three months, and approximately three-quarters will be broke within a year. This means moving to a state facility or services provided at what the state, Medicare, or health insurance will cover. This may translate into services that are less than desirable to the family. It is wise to inquire if the amount quoted from the facility (i.e., $3,000) covers everything. Many nursing homes have a basic rate, and such things as laundry, ironing, incontinence care, spooning feeding, cost of incontinence pads, tissues, and hand and skin lotions are additional charges, as are doctors, pharmacy, and surgical supplies.

The above figures are fairly current. It would be nearly accurate to say that the cost of health care will increase from year to year, and the possibility of healthcare benefits may decrease each year. The above figures do not include the cost of home care providers, social workers, special nursing staff, or permanent nursing facilities cost.

It is more economical to care for someone with dementia at home than at a nursing home. There may come a time when serious, thoughtful, and prayerful consideration may need to be given to such assistance.

Caregiving issues
Memory problems and disorientation
Too often, the caregiver will argue with the dementia sufferer, correcting their mistakes and sometimes becoming angry himself or herself. The caregiver should be advised on the pathogenesis of dementia symptoms and behavior. This information may help the caregiver come to terms with the implications and dementia's responses.

Aggression
Aggression is more likely in a demented patient as disinhibition develops. It tends to be situational, usually in response to confrontation or fear. Example: an elderly woman wishes to leave the house to collect her children from school. Being pulled away from the door or told she must not go out leads to frustration and anger, culminating in an

aggressive or tearful outburst. Look beyond the aggression. Talking through the reality that her children are now grown up may be beneficial, or distract into other activities.

Sleep disturbance
The elderly need less sleep but more rest than in their youth. The rest is best obtained in a comfortable chair, perhaps with simple activities or talking over shared memories used for stimulation of the brain. At night a comfortable bed and quiet environment is needed; a night light may reduce disorientation as the patient can recognize familiar surroundings when awakened. Some may recommend sedation. This may be unproductive, especially if the thought is to administer stronger and stronger doses so the caregiver can rest. This is counterproductive. Why? The sedation will continue into the following day, increasing confusion and risk of falls, generally making the patient harder to look after.

Wandering and falling
Safety and degree of acceptable risk needs to be assessed for each individual, and changes with time. Some exercise is important for general health, prevention of pressure sores, and aid to sleeping. Advise should be sought about small items of furniture, loose rugs, trailing wires, etc., that could pose a bodily harm.

An alarm system on entry doors can prove helpful to alert the caregiver than the person with dementia is attempting to leave the home and may be in possible harm.

Sometimes falls occur because of the patient's posture or ill-fitting shoes. Painful feet lead to unsteadiness.

Communication difficulties
Decrease in visual acuity is universal with age. Seeing an optician would prove helpful. Deafness is also common. Waxing causing mechanical obstruction may need appropriate treatment or a hearing aid may be necessary. Use of pictorial charts to express basic needs often helps.

Psychotic features

Mislaying and forgetting where possessions should be can lead to accusations of theft against the caregivers or others. This can be upsetting and stressful to both the patient and the caregiver. To the best of the caregiver's ability, insure that you know where everything should be. Observing what is most used and important and where the patient seems to locate it readily can reduce this paranoia. Often if the accusations persist, the medical community recommends antidelusional medication, most commonly sulpiride, or thioridazine.

Failure to recognize family members or familiar surroundings

As the confusion worsens, the demented person may remember their husband or daughter as they were 20–30 years earlier, and misidentify a son as a husband or refuse to accept that the caregiver is not a stranger. They may no longer be familiar with their surroundings, continually trying to "go home."

Knowing that the disease will only worsen, it may be wise to walk the patient regularly through the home, pointing to pictures, memorabilia, or items associated with family members. This may reduce or slow the failure to recognize family members or familiar surroundings.

When and how to select a nursing home

There may be a number of factors that should be considered when thinking about placing a loved one in a nursing or residential facility.

A recent survey by John Hancock (1996) provided the top ten reasons why people are in nursing homes. The number one reason was dementia or Alzheimers (36%)

An excellent website I found on how to select a nursing home is www.efmoody.com/longterm/nursinghome/html. The value of this site, and particular this lengthy article (eighteen pages), is its providing outstanding things to look for at the nursing home, as well as pointed questions to ask in a number of areas. Check it out, print it, file it for ministry use, and distribute to those who find themselves at this point in the care giving for a loved one with dementia.

Perhaps we need to gently remind ourselves of a biblical premise, namely God expects that both the church and family care for aging parents. Consider these verses:

> Honor widows who are widows indeed; but if any widow has children or grandchildren, they must first learn to practice piety in regard to their own family and to make some return to their parents; for this is acceptable in the sight of God. Now she who is a widow indeed and who has been left alone has fixed her hope on God and continues in entreaties and prayers night and day. But she who gives herself to wanton pleasure is dead even while she lives. Prescribe these things as well, so that they may be above reproach. But if no one provides for his own, and especially for those of his household, he has denied the faith and is worse than an unbeliever (1 Tim. 5:3–8).

> Now at this time while the disciples were increasing in number, a complaint arose on the part of the Hellenistic Jews against the native Hebrews, because their widows were being overlooked in the daily serving of food (Acts 6:1).

The divine system God instituted in the nation of Israel's life is known as the kinsman redeemer. This is vividly portrayed in the book of Ruth. Bereft of her husband and two sons, Naomi returns to her hometown. The life of a widow was seemingly destitution and often prostitution. To prevent this, God instituted the kinsman redeemer concept whereby the immediate next of kin was responsible to take the widow into his home and care for her. If she had no children, he was obligated to raise up children so the family inheritance would remain for the family and that the family name would not be extinguished.

In 2 Samuel, we see David's willingness to provide permanent and total care for an eighty-year-old man who sustained him when David fled from his son Absalom. We read:

> Now Barzillai the Gileadite had come down from Rogelim; and he went on to the Jordan with the king to escort him over the Jordan. Now Barzillai was very old, being eighty years old; and he had sustained the king while he stayed at Mahanaim, for he was a very great man. The king said to Barzillai, "You cross over with me and I will sustain you in Jerusalem with me." But Barzillai said to the king, "How long have I yet to live, that I should go up with the king to Jerusalem? I am now eighty years old. Can I distinguish between good and bad? Or can your servant taste what I eat or what I drink?

Or can I hear anymore the voice of singing men and women? Why then should your servant be an added burden to my lord the king? Your servant would merely cross over the Jordan with the king. Why should the king compensate me with this reward? Please let your servant return, that I may die in my own city near the grave of my father and my mother. However, here is your servant Chimham, let him cross over with my lord the king, and do for him what is good in your sight." The king answered, "Chimham shall cross over with me, and I will do for him what is good in your sight; and whatever you require of me, I will do for you." All the people crossed over the Jordan and the king crossed too. The king then kissed Barzillai and blessed him, and he returned to his place (2 Sam. 19:31–39).

These are just some passages that support the premise that aging parents should be cared for by their children and children's children.

Now someone may say that this begs the question because dementia is not a normal part of aging. And carefully I ask, "Why isn't it considered the normal part of aging?" How is it any different from other aging problems such as blindness, deafness, dialysis, stroke, or heart attack and its after effects such as paralysis? I could mention many other diseases that require the same, if not perhaps more, time, energy, and resources in the care of that person.

And in such cases as above, like the progressive degeneration associated with dementia, the ability to provide adequate and safe care becomes the issue. If the statistics are true, that somewhere between 7–10 years death occurs for dementia patients, there are significant cost factors. Not even considering the financial costs (which we have already discussed), but the physical, emotional, mental, social and spiritual costs. If the caregiver is the sole provider, even with relief provided daily or weekly by a social agency or someone else (mate, older children, neighbor, church member), the toll is great. As the disease progresses, there may be certain tasks that create embarrassment for both the person with dementia and the caregiver, such as personal hygiene duties. It may be that the safety of the patient is in question as the caregiver finds it difficult to provide safety because of the person's aggressive behavior or constant wandering (many times occurring at night). Therefore, we have health issues for the caregiver also.

So there are a number of considerations that must be weighed prayerfully and carefully in deciding when to begin considering long-term facilities for the person with dementia. This decision is highly personal, can be emotionally charged, but with great integrity must be approached with a spiritual lens to examine the data.

May I relate a true story to illustrate the importance of examining the data through a biblical lens that can check the caregiver's own motivations? Art was a member of my first church. Early on as his pastor, I received a call that his wife suddenly died. They had no children. He had a sister, brother-in-law, nieces, and nephews through their union. Art had been a piano mover. He was a large framed man with a huge neck. Looking at him from behind, you could image from the size of his neck the Incredible Hulk. For the next year, I met with Art for lunch, each Wednesday. He had two favorite restaurants he liked. It became a joke as to what we would order. He orders either the baked apple pancakes or the fish of the day. I ordered veal cutlets with extra gravy. During that year, Art showed signs of decline. He permitted me to drive. When you watched him walk it looked at times he would fall, but he never did. He read a chapter from Proverbs each day, five from Psalms, and a chapter in Romans.

During that year, Art committed to memory over seventy-five verses. One day he called me at the office. He was crying. He told me that his sister was going to place him in a residential facility. I called her to find out her reasoning. After church, Art would drive to meet her and his brother-in-law for Sunday brunch. It was always at the same place—Fountain Blue, a very fancy restaurant. She told me that he was becoming an embarrassment. He would dribble on his clothes, spill bread crumbs in his lap, and when he went to the men's room, he often returned smelling like urine. I knew that. I had experienced that for the past several months of our luncheon appointments. I encouraged her to reconsider. Art was devastated. I was a bit too bold, but I told her that in my opinion if Art were placed in a residential facility, he would quit living and die within a year. He did, to the day.

I am not about to minimize the demanding task of caring for the elderly, especially if they have a debilitating disease. But we must be extremely careful about our motivations. Here are some questions to ask yourself:

- Is there a genuine health issue I no longer can care for?
- If I had a break, would my perspective change and would my strength be renewed?
- Would securing the services of a social agency for specific tasks ease my burden where I could continue providing care?
- Is the person with dementia acting out more? Could it be that they are feeding off my own anger and frustration towards them?
- If I were asked to make a list of reasons for placing this person in a residential facility, what would those reasons be? If I were to ask a trusted advisor to look at my list, would more eyes that are objective be able to find solutions I cannot because I am to close?

Suggested ways to begin the journey of caring for someone with dementia

Recognizing the possible early warning signs of dementia may help facilitate a smoother transition for both the patient and caregiver. Once a certain diagnosis is made, then consider beginning to work on the following suggestions (besides what has already been discussed).

Develop a picture book with common items used in the course of a day they can point to when communication declines. The picture book should contain basic pictures of tissues, water, lotion, various favorite items of food or snacks, pen/pencils, telephone, newspaper, magazines, bathroom, chair, television, radio, etc. The patient can point to items their mind still recognizes but their speech cannot express.

Because we know that one of the characteristics of dementia is failure to recognize loved ones, a large photo album should be constructed. The album should contain pictures of the spouse, children, brothers and sisters, extended family members, close neighbors, special events such as weddings, baby dedications, birthday parties, and holiday events. These often remove the confusion and bewilderment by having familiar things in their surroundings. With technology today, still photographs can be digitized and placed on DVDs. Like a screensaver, this could be played on a television in the patient's room.

In the early stages of the diagnosis, sit down with the patient with a cassette tape recorder and have them record their memories. Such events may be their childhood memories, insights on their parents (grandparents of their children), their own engagement, and marriage, the birth of their children, anniversaries, birthdays, vacations, or special holidays.

Make available favorite music of the patient. This can make the person comfortable and remove rising frustrations of feeling as if they need to "go home" or being in a "strange place." Another media idea would be to play the patient's favorite movies either on video or DVD.

Most medical agencies, social services agencies, and geriatric organizations are reporting that senior citizens are living on an average 15–19 years longer than before. With greater longevity for our aging loved ones, there is a greater possibility they will contract some degree of dementia. Being forearmed and staying abreast of the various kinds of dementia can better equip us to help those caregivers at the prospect of this overwhelming ministry of loving, compassionate, and kind service.

Bashful, Doc, Dopey, Grumpy, Happy, Sleepy, Sneezy

Helping Someone Who Grumbles

Let's begin this chapter with a humorous story. A man decided to join a monastery and one of the rules of the group was that you were only allowed to speak two words every ten years. At the end of ten years he said, "Bad food!" Ten more years went by and he said, "Hard bed!" Finally, on his thirtieth anniversary with the brothers, he thundered, "I quit!" And the priest in charge responded, "You might as well. All you do is grumble anyway."

CULTURED GRUMBLING
Americans are known for their grumbling by other countries. Grumbling is often re-titled "free speech" or "self-expression." Child psychologists advise against inhibiting the self-expression of a child because of long-term effects. Exasperated parents ignore or tune-out the grumbling of their children. The following poem accurately portrays America's grumbling epidemic.

>In country, town, or city, some people can be found
>Who spend their lives a grumblin' at everything around.
>They grumble, grumble, grumble no matter what we say.
>For these are chronic grumblers;
>They grumble night and day.
>They grumble when it's rainin'
>They grumble when it's dry;
>And if a little chilly, they
>Grumble and they sigh.
>And when they go out shoppin'
>And see the price is high,
>They grumble, grumble, grumble,
>They'll grumble 'til they die.
>They grumble at the preacher;
>They grumble at his prayer;
>They grumble at the offering
>They grumble everywhere.

They stay away from meetin'
Because it's hot or cold
Or when it looks like rainin';
A headache or a cold.

Isn't it true? The grass is always greener in the next lawn, and the traffic always moves faster in the next lane.

Because we are so accustomed to grumbling, when someone doesn't they are an anomaly. The problem is not them, it is us. As Pogo said, "We have met the enemy and it is us!" If the enemy is truly us, then the only source of hope we can turn to is the Word of God. God loves us so much He painstakingly and graphically describes grumbling, and just as lovingly and pointedly records solutions for grumbling.

DEFINING GRUMBLING

The same basic cognate is used even with other tenses like "grumbling," "grumbler," "grumbled," regardless if the cognate is singular or plural.

"Grumbling" is a derivative from German language meaning to enrage. Webster defines grumbling as "unintelligible sound in the throat, to growl, to mutter or murmur, to complain in a peevish or surly way reflecting the attitude of self." The result of grumbling is discontent.

The Hebrew affirms the definition of murmur, complain, and growl. The etiology from other reference books from the Hebrew, Greek, and Aramaic etiology of words does not list any specific explanation of the word, like love, joy, hatred, and anger. I conclude that humanity knows all too well the meaning of grumbling.

USAGE

The word grumble is used twenty-one times in the Old Testament and eleven times in the New Testament. The ratio between the Old Testament and the New Testament is 2:1. All OT references to grumbling are found in two selections of the Pentateuch, Exodus, and Numbers with the exception of one recording in Psalms.

How to Recognize Grumbling
Again, we need to examine the backdrop of the book of Exodus. God delivered Israel with ten marvelous plagues that decimated every Egyptian god. They then were miraculously delivered from the pursuing Egyptians by crossing the Red Sea. Before Israel's eyes, they witnessed the drowning of Pharaoh's army.

RECOGNIZING GRUMBLING FROM EXODUS
Grumbling is usually based on an immediate perceived or felt need (15:22). Israel grumbled that there was no water. They were thirsty in the hot, arid desert. Later they grumbled because they were hungry. There was no food to eat. Again, they would grumble that they would rather have remained in Egypt to die. They did not see any means of rescue from the pursuing Egypt army.

Grumblers are seldom patient (15:22). The Israelites traveled three days and found no water. The water they did find was bitter and not fit for drinking. Israel did not leave Egypt without water. They knew the journey would be long. Yes, they expected to find water along the way. They were descendents of Abraham, Isaac, and Jacob, bedouins who knew how to travel in such harsh climates and conditions. They had water. The issue was, from their perspective, that they did not have enough water. Grumblers are consumed with self-interest and hoard. They are dominated by fear.

Grumbling is generally directed against authority figures (15:24). People who grumble do so to anyone who will give them the time of day. But people who grumble seem to delight in grumbling against authority figures. People who grumble run in packs. The more grumblers you have grumbling against authority figures, perhaps the more power is displayed to get what you want. The text says, "So the people [plural] grumbled at Moses." Moses was the object of their outburst. It was all Moses' fault for them not having enough water.

Grumblers can readily and easily point out problems, but rarely offer biblical solutions (15:24). When you read this text, as well as others in the Bible, people who grumble find it easy to point out the obvious. They can clearly see what the problem is. "We do not have water. We do not have anything to eat. It is too hot. It is too cold. This is taking too long." However, rarely do grumblers offer any concrete solutions. They are problem oriented, not solution oriented. They say to another, "Here is the problem. You fix it."

Grumblers seldom express gratitude for meeting their needs. It becomes a rights issue to them. Do you see anywhere in this text, or for that matter, other texts on grumblers' words of appreciation? "Thank you Moses for taking care of us. Thank you for looking to the Lord to meet our needs. Moses, what great sweet water you found for us." No. Because their need was met, to the grumbler it was a matter of, "What else should you have done? Let me die of hunger or thirst! Your meeting my needs is my entitlement. You should have done so. You don't need to be thanked for doing what you did."

When faced with the slightest difficulties, grumblers want to return to the past because they believe the past was better than the present or future (16:3). Listen to the grumblers' cries. "Would we have died in Egypt." "We sat by pots of meat." "You will kill this whole assembly with hunger." But grumblers fail to see the past reality objectively. Did they really sit by pots of meat? According to Exodus 1:13, they were subject to rigorous labor. In 1:14, their lives were bitter with hard labor. In 3:7, only God sees the affliction of His people; the Egyptians didn't. In 3:7, only God sees their sufferings under the Egyptian taskmasters. In 5:9, again they are enslaved to heavy labor. And in 5:13, they are given no leniency in making bricks. They now had to get their own straw and they were expected to keep the same quota.

Grumblers fail to see how circumstances are leading them to a clearer understanding of God and themselves (16:3). Remember that God instructed Moses to return to the mount where he was commissioned. Returning would be a sign of God's power to deliver. Israel's travels led to Sinai. They would soon be at the Mountain of God. Here they would learn who God is and what God demands. They would also learn who they were and how they should respond to God and each other. When people grumble, they lose sight of what is up ahead, for they only can see the obstacles in front of them.

God hears all grumbling. All grumbling is against the great I AM (16:7–8). Moses was able to separate himself from the attacks of his brethren. Moses tells them that the Lord hears their grumbling and that what they are doing is actually grumbling against the Lord. To grumble against Moses and Aaron is nothing. Israel was grumbling against the I AM, the name given to Moses to identify who it was that would deliver them. I AM is eternal, Almighty, dynamic and active self-existence and Israel's Redeemer. What foolishness for them to fail to recognize that God is not their servant, at their beck and call, but they are the redeemed and now slaves of Jehovah.

A man sat down to supper with his family, saying grace, thanking God for the food, for the hands, which prepared it, and for the source of all life. But during the meal, he complained about the freshness of the bread, the bitterness of the coffee, and the sharpness of the cheese. His young daughter questioned him, "Dad, do you think God heard the grace today?" He answered confidently, "Of course." Then she asked, "And do you think God heard what you said about the coffee, the cheese, and the bread?" Not so confidently, he answered, "Why, yes, I believe so." The little girl concluded, "Then which do you think God believed, Dad?"

Grumblers usually are cowards. They are strong in a group, even stirring up individuals to form a group, but rarely will one stand face-to-face against God and grumble (16:9). Grumbling is like eczema. The more you itch (grumble) the more it spreads. Both drive a person crazy. Both can lead to severe health and spiritual complications. Both are serious conditions. God calls the nation to Himself to address the problem for all who listened to these grumblers and especially those who joined in were rebels.

It is not uncommon for a grumbler to return to the same complaint (17:3). When grumblers return to the same complaint, they usually will add details to reinforce their complaint. Consider the exaggerations added in the following verses. In 15:24, "What shall we drink?" In 17:3, "You brought us up ..." They charged Moses with trying to "kill us ..., to kill our children ..., to kill our livestock with thirst."

RECOGNIZING GRUMBLING FROM NUMBERS

If a grumbler is never confronted, he grows in boldness and grumbles against God (14:3). The redeemed people tell God it would have been better to die in Egypt, or to die in wilderness. But by God, bringing them into "this land" to die by the sword is terribly wrong. How could He have not foreseen this? How could He have done this? They have exchanged places with God. God is no longer the potter. Israel is the potter, and they want to fashion Jehovah into the type of God they think is best for them.

There is such a thing as a "chronic grumbler" (14:22). The Lord said "all the men who have seen My glory and My signs which I performed in Egypt and in the wilderness, yet have put Me to the test these ten times." I'm not sure if "ten times" refers to the plagues or another ten different times Israel balked at the leading and wisdom of their Deliverer. These people find something to grumble about. No matter what good may be in the blessing of God's provision, they are able to find something to grumble about. Like the Pharisees who always grumbled when Christ performed miracles.

God labels grumbling as "evil" (14:27). The Hebrew word used for evil is *ra*. It means ruin or breaking up. It is a picture of destruction. The idea is that what God has made is ruined by sin. It comes to mean trouble that such ruin causes. It can be pictured as a life-dominating sin, corrupt lifestyle, fraudulent patterns, dishonest routines, and crooked manners of living. Grumblers destroy the blessings of God. Their grumbling overshadows the gracious intervention of God.

Grumblers can exhaust the patience of God and bring upon themselves inevitable judgment (14:29–35).

> "Your corpses will fall in this wilderness, even all your numbered men, according to your complete number from twenty years old and upward, who have grumbled against Me. Surely you shall not come into the land in which I swore to settle you, except Caleb the son of Jephunneh and Joshua the son of Nun. Your children, however, whom you said would become a prey—I will bring them in, and they will know the land which you have rejected. But as for you, your corpses will fall in this wilderness. Your sons shall be shepherds for forty years in the wilderness, and they will suffer

for your unfaithfulness, until your corpses lie in the wilderness. According to the number of days which you spied out the land, forty days, for every day you shall bear your guilt a year, even forty years, and you will know My opposition. I, the Lord, have spoken, surely this I will do to all this evil congregation who are gathered together against Me. In this wilderness they shall be destroyed, and there they will die."

Grumblers live on the horns of a dilemma: they lose God's blessings and are forced to watch God bless others (14:29–35). Under these circumstances, the grumbler will quickly develop bitterness and hardness of soul.

Unrepentant grumblers usually come up with their own plans to circumvent divine consequences (14:40). Grumblers want to avoid the consequences of their grumbling. Often they will verbally agree to God's plan. They are like the little child who is told to sit down, but remains standing up on the inside. If a grumbler is permitted to participate in God's plan apart from confession and repentance, and if the outcome is not what they anticipated or there is a snag, they will return with an additional zeal to their grumbling.

God views grumblers as turning away from Himself (14:43). Until grumbling is replaced by loving submission, God opposes the grumbler. James reminds us that God opposes the proud. A grumbler is a proud person and God will stand before the grumble to oppose.

Grumbling is a form of pride (14:43).

Grumblers attempt to support their complains by enlisting others and propping themselves up with respected people.

Grumblers challenge authority not for responsibility, but for privileges (16:3). These brash Israelites come to Moses accusing him of hogging all the glory, honor, and prestige. They get to stand out before the people. They lead. They are esteemed. They have privilege. Grumblers attempt to compare themselves as equal. When they should be followers, they want to be leaders. They fail to endure the pain to enjoy the gain. They want position without persecution. They want honor without homage.

Grumblers usually have a list of past complaints that blame others, avoid personal responsibility, and culpability (16:13–14). Again, Moses is the culprit. He removed them from the posh life of milk and honey (Egypt) to this wilderness. They had nothing to do with their existence. They made no decisions. They were not living with consequences from their choices or the choices of their ancestors. Again, their impatience is noted. They are sojourning to the Promised Land. Their grumbling, in fact, is causing the delay and in fact a forty-year detour.

Grumblers are often second-generation grumblers (16:41). Those who approached Moses were descendants of Korah, Dathan, and Abiram. They were second generation grumblers. They observed, witnessed, and probably sat around the dining room table and listened to their tribal leaders grumble. They learned a behavior. Postscript: It can be unlearned!

How to Help Someone Who Grumbles
Prayer
If you are the one being grumbled against, begin with prayer. Pray for personal wisdom and insight.

> Then Moses led Israel from the Red Sea, and they went out into the wilderness of Shur; and they went three days in the wilderness and found no water (Exodus 15:22). So Moses cried out to the Lord, saying, "What shall I do to this people? A little more and they will stone me" (Exodus 17:4).

Use intercessory prayer. Do not allow fatigue and weariness to stop you from standing in the gap for the grumbler. "But on the next day all the congregation of the sons of Israel grumbled against Moses and Aaron, saying, 'You are the ones who have caused the death of the Lord's people.'"

Why pray for those who are attacking you? Do not lose your belief in the mercy of God. Remember your own journey of grace. Love for God's people.

Allow God to vindicate you.

> Is it not enough that you have brought us up out of a land flowing with milk and honey to have us die in the wilderness, but you would also lord it over us? Indeed, you have not brought us into a land flowing with milk and honey, nor have you given us an inheritance of fields and vineyards. Would you put out the eyes of these men? We will not come up! (Numbers 16:13–14).

I do not read anywhere in the chronicles of Moses' life and ministry as the leader of Israel of him grumbling himself. He cried out to God, but Moses then stood toe to toe with Korah or others and defended himself. He never vindicated himself. He allowed the Lord to do so and remained faithful in doing God's will and carrying out God's program. Moses allowed God to vindicate his character. We need to allow God to vindicate our character (1 Peter 2:23).

Cultivate Patience (Exodus 16:4)
The nation was hungry. They wanted food now. They expected Moses to be able to feed millions of people plus livestock instantaneously. Moses learned to wait on God for His voice on what to do. It would have been easy for Moses to use his own wisdom. "Hey everyone. Let's start getting some sage brush and whatever you can find and we can make a wilderness stew." When your direction is not clear on what to do, do not allow the vocalizations of grumblers pressure you into stepping out in your own wisdom to solve their problem. Self-wisdom is disastrous (James 3:14–16).

Don't Be Afraid to Rebuke
The grumblers failed to understand they were testing God. (17:2). Why didn't Moses go further with them? Why didn't he attempt to cajole them? Pacify them? Why? You can't deal with a fool. Proverbs 26:4 says, "Do not answer a fool according to his folly, or you will also be like him." Proverbs 19:19 adds, "A man of great anger will bear the penalty, for if you rescue him, you will only have to do it again.

Did they not realize they are failing to see God's provisions? (16:12; 17:5; Rom. 2:4).

Display Godly Sorrow before Them (Numbers 14:5)
Moses and Aaron fell on their faces in the presence of all the assembly of the congregation of the sons of Israel. How heartbreaking for Moses and Aaron. Yet it appears that only two within the congregation understood the grief grumbling was causing—Joshua and Caleb. Throughout the pages of Scripture, we see such men as Ezra, Nehemiah, Jesus, and Paul weeping and pleading for people and their wicked ways. Grumbling is a sin like any other sin.

Believe God Will Raise up Advocates (Numbers 14:6–9)
How brave and courageous were Joshua and Caleb. They refused to blend in. They refused to go with the flow. They swam against the current. They swam upstream. They stood up and testified again about the goodness of the Land. They reminded the people what God promised to do. They exhorted the people not to rebel. They spoke with confidence that God was with them and already had begun to make the hearts of the inhabitants melt.

How refreshing for Moses and Aaron. A leader who is often grumbled against gets discouraged. They become exhausted standing up for what is right. They often feel like they are the only ones. They can develop an Elijah syndrome. Moses and Aaron welcomed voices of truth from another corner. Allow God to raise peers up against the grumblers on your behalf.

Teach Discernment
How do we help others avoid those who grumble? (16:24–27).

> Then Moses arose and went to Dathan and Abiram, with the elders of Israel following him, and he spoke to the congregation, saying, "Depart now from the tents of these wicked men, and touch nothing that belongs to them, or you will be swept away in all their sin." So they got back from around the dwellings of Korah, Dathan and Abiram; and Dathan and Abiram came out and stood at the doorway of their tents, along with their wives and their sons and their little ones.

Warn them to stay away from such influences. Why? Because they will be less likely to pick up the grumblers' way. They do not want to be labeled as a grumbler by association. Neither do they want to experience the grumbler's condemnation.

Provide Incentives to Stop Grumbling
When grumblers repent and fully obey, God brings them into greater joy and blessing. God guided His people to Elim (Exodus 15:27). There were seventy date palms and twelve springs. There was immediate and sufficient supply to refresh them from their journey and to prepare them for their journey. Here God proved again His faithfulness and complete care for them. They could leave Elim in faith and confidence that God would see them through all hardships and bring them safely to the Promised Land.

Fail, Phail, Flop

Helping Those Who Feel They Are Failures

I used to enjoy watching the old TV sitcom *The Jeffersons*. The theme song started out with, "Moving on up to the East side." Mr. Jefferson worked hard in his dry cleaning business. He did seem to get ahead. Wheezy, his wife, was content with where they lived, but George could not accept it. One day, they made it big. So big, they moved to the upper east side of New York in a fancy high rise. All the accommodations—a doorman, cab service, and living with the rich and famous. George considered himself successful.

What determines success or failure? "Rick, I thought you were going to talk about helping someone who feels like they are a failure." I am, but you cannot talk about failure apart from success. One encompasses the other. How do people reach the conclusion if they are failures or successes?

I know a young married man who owned several companies. He had an affluent accounting firm, several Internet businesses, and a computer company. Yet, he didn't feel like he was successful. Is he a success, and if so by what measurement? And if he is truly a failure, what does he point to or would you point to?

Others determine failure by what they still have not attained or feel they should attain or deserve to attain. They have a mental and emotional check list.

- We keep up with the Joneses.
- Then we move up the rung to the Pedmonts.
- One more rung to the Wrigleys.
- Above them would be Jordans.
- Above that would be the Rockefellers.
- At the top of the heap? Perhaps Bill Gates.

Every major metropolis has its symbols of failure or success. A mark of success is where someone lives. For Chicago, it could be the affluent suburbs like Naperville, Oak Brook, Barrington, South Barrington, or even downtown in the Loop.

We are told that success is based on "dressing for success." Motivation tapes tell you that success is a mental framework. To be success, you must "think like a winner."

Before we begin, let me offer some preliminary thoughts. Success and failure are not nouns, they are verbs. Each requires some sort of personal involvement. Today, people define success and failure using nouns. Success is related to people, places, or things.

I can always find someone more successful than myself. When asked how much was enough, Rockefeller said, "Just a little bit more." I can always find something more fulfilling. I can always find some place more challenging or exciting.

When success or failure is kept as a verb, it is the actor (myself) acting on something that determines success or failure. For the Christian, he or she acts upon the Word of God.

The standard by which people measure success may not always be the Bible. When another inferior standard is used or when success seems to elude their grasp, many people feel like a failure. Failure always attacks one's character. When a setback occurs, often you can hear a demoralizing perspective. However, one must accept that there is a difference between failing and being a failure.

Failing is an everyday part of life. Failing is inevitable. Someone who thinks they will not fail is deceived. They are not living in a real world, but a fantasy world. Failing can happen to anyone, any time, over anything. Failing is not the end of the world.

Failure, I think, is different. Failure is a thought process that leads to resignation. Someone who considers himself a failure stops trying. They give up. They quit. We will all fail, but we do not have to accept another's evaluations of our actions or our own self-evaluations labeling us as a failure.

Today, those who are viewed as successful find little solace in their achievements. Their success does not carry them through all phases of their lives and through all circumstances. The attainment or achievement often leaves them empty and desiring more. The standards by which successful people judge themselves often are no longer satisfying. Like Solomon, they yearn for more by pursuing new ventures. Like Rockefeller, they want just a little bit more.

Both failure and success affect human personality and, for some, reflect their understanding of self-esteem. Failure or success becomes personal. These two options become identities of people who are driven by either success or failure. It often leads to arrogance or despondency. Success or failure is not a matter of perspective or feelings, but the issues of knowledge and measurement. Consider the following summary thus far of our understanding of success and failure.

- At the heart of success is obedience.
- At the heart of failure is disobedience.
- The knowledge of success or failure is derived from the Word of God.
- Success or failure is measured, not by man, but by God Himself.

There is one passage I often use when counseling someone struggling with success or failure. There is power in this one passage. It is Joshua 1:1–9.

What is the historical context of this passage? Israel is on the brink of entering the Promised Land. For the previous forty years, they have been wandering because of their disobedience at Kadesh-barnea. Because of their rebellion, they failed to enter the Land of Promise and enjoy the victory of God by faith and obedience. Moses has died, and Joshua is the successor. This new generation is not battle tested. They have fought very little during their wanderings. They are familiar with the wanderings, but have not had a taste of war, blood, and battle.

What does God tell Joshua to motivate and encourage him to deal with the failures of the past and prepare for the successes of the future? God reiterates His covenant to the people (v. 2). God repeats He has already given the land to his covenant people (v. 3). God says again the breadth and depth, the scope, the boundaries of the land (v. 4). God asserts His power to provide and protect, and His presence to guide and direct during each battle; battles that humanly could result in defeat and viewing life as a failure (v. 5).

Now God issues a series of commands that you can use to help someone deal with failure and gain a biblical perspective on success.

Failure is banished and success enthroned when I am strong and courageous to carry out God's will (v. 6). Fear keeps failure alive in a person's life. Fear keeps the one who has failed living in the past. Fear removes the hope of the future.

Courage and strength come from knowing and doing all God's commands. There is a diligence and meticulousness in adhering to God's Word. Parts of God's Word are not optional or left to viewer discretion. All aspects, no matter how simple or difficult, are to be performed with great speed and care.

There is to be a simple but diligent singleness of focus, a determination to stay a steady course, a singleness of heart, mind, and soul that blocks out all distractions, clamoring voices, traditions of men, false reasoning, and human philosophies. The potential for success is every saint's reality. Notice the specifics of success are in direct keeping with God's Word—the boundaries of the land and inhabitants of the land.

Our success is first and foremost a clear conscience whereby we can say, with the Apostle Paul, "My conscience is clear." We can say confidently that at this point in our lives, we are reflecting the patterns of God in all areas about which God is teaching us.

How should Joshua avoid failure and insure success is further amplified in verse 8. Successful people allow the book of the law to address all issues in their lives and that they meet. The book of the law proceeds from their mouths. They speak God's Word to each and every situation. Their speech is biblical. They apply the Word of God in their conversations. What comes forth from the mouth must first reside in the heart. The mouth speaks from the meditations of the heart. A successful person meditates, thinks about, dwells upon, considers, ruminates, and invests time to focus on the law of God. The mouth draws from the wellspring of the heart; a reservoir of truth, clean, pure, refreshing.

This meditation always enables clarity of direction and sensitivity to avoiding that which distracts, draws away, busies us into the tyranny of the urgent. The formula results in success as worded in certain terms of a promise—you will have success.

Applying God's Truth
If you believe you are a failure, ask yourself the following questions.

1. Am I basing my failure on comparing myself to others? My peers?
2. Am I pursuing a selfish ambition that excludes God, or at best, have I informed God of my plans?
3. What sin is the Holy Spirit revealing in my life as I study the Word of God?
4. Then, repent, confess and turn from that sin.

If you believe you are successful, ask yourself the following questions.

1. On what basis would others say I am successful? My Christian character and conduct, or what I have achieved and accumulated of this world's goods?
2. Can the degree of my success be improved? In what specific areas of my life have I turned to the right or the left?

3. Am I really having success "wherever I go"?

4. Could I improve my standing of success, by disciplining my speech to reflect thoughts that are more biblical, expression and words? Are there specific areas of conversation that I need to address with others or myself with the book of the law?

5. If this is a weak area, how much time do I devote to the reflection, thinking about, considering, meditating on God's Word so my mouth has something to draw from in my heart?

Failure is a matter of disobedience. Success is a matter of obedience. The manifestation of success is always left with and to God. A successful person will always be a growing Christian and a spiritual giant. Anything else is additional mercies of a loving God during this temporary journey called life.

I Never Saw It Coming

The Warning Signs of Temptation

Alexander struggled with temptation. This young boy was saving his pennies, nickels, and quarters for that special Sammy Sosa baseball bat. One evening his mother overheard him pray this prayer. "Lord, help me save my pennies, nickels, and quarters for that special Sammy Sosa baseball bat, and Lord please keep the ice cream truck from coming down my street!"

Temptation is like the candy jar sitting on the secretary's desk or on the coffee table in your home. You walk by and see the contents of the candy jar. What lies inside is one of your favorite treats—chocolate-covered almonds. So you have one and continue with your tasks. But then you begin to find reasons to return to the scene of the candy heist and help yourself to more.

Temptation is like the junk mail you receive. It is designed to be colorful, to be eye appealing, and to present something you just can't live without. Temptation is an RSVP to sin's invitation. Temptation is negative and designed to mar your character.

Here are some biblical facts about temptation.

1. Every saint is tempted. Just because we are born again doesn't mean the flesh has been removed. We will be tempted by the world, flesh, and the devil. Which leads us to our next thought.

2. Temptation is not a sin. Temptation is the invitation to sin. It is a solicitation to commit evil. I can receive an invitation but I can decline. Someone may solicit me to do something wicked, but I can decline. Solomon exhorts his sons not to consent when a sinner entices them (Prov. 1:10). Jesus was tempted yet without sin, and we are commanded to imitate Jesus.

3. Every sinner is tempted. We wrongly think that only saints are tempted. This is erroneous. Unbelievers, the unregenerate, and the sinner have the Adamic nature and are tempted.

4. Every saint can resist temptation. The saint is able to oppose temptation's solicitation consistently. When a saint succumbs to temptation, it is by choice. The saint does not rely upon self-determination or sheer will power. The saint is endowed with a personal trainer. The precious Holy Spirit indwells each believer and provides complete awareness of the tempter and temptation and readiness to resist and remain holy unto the Lord.

5. Not every sinner can resist temptation. The sinner must rely upon self-determination, will power, and a belief that what they are being lured into doing is actually wrong. Most sinners live by their feelings, or forms of relativism, or situational ethic and morés. The consistency to withstand temptation is inconsistent.

6. I see six warning signs that can help the saint arrest temptation before it results in sinful actions. These warning signs are found in James 1:13–15.

Warning Sign #1: When I feel God is unfair or unloving
Do you remember the old comedy that starred Flip Wilson? Do you remember his famous line? "The devil made me do it!" When I feel that God is being unfair or unloving about a situation in which I find myself, I tend to blame to others, my circumstances, or even God Himself for my sinful response.

A saint cannot blame God, because it is contrary to His nature. God is holy. Therefore, He cannot be tempted, cannot be invited to think evil, and cannot be solicited to devise evil. Because of the nature of God's holiness, I can trust God. He never has a moral lapse. He never lies to me. He never has inappropriate actions.

Neither can we blame God, because it is contrary to His character. He never tempts anyone nor ever asks me to do evil. God's character is love. God's love is never harmful. His love is never manipulative. His love is never selfish. I need to evaluate all feelings by the facts of God's proactive love, grace, and mercy.

Warning Sign #2: When I am drawn away from God-ordained authority
Temptation is always individual; it is not a corporate or group event. We see the individuality of temptation when James uses the phrase "carried away." The Greek means to be drawn out, to drag away, lure, to capture, or remove from safety.

How is a believer drawn out? It may occur when a question is raised to create doubt about the person, character, or nature of God. The serpent raised an eyebrow and a question that caused doubt in Eve about the goodness of God. She was tempted to believe that God was withholding something good from her and Adam.

Second, an unbelievable statement may draw me away. Usually, when someone utters an unbelievable statement, you can take it as such—it's unbelievable. The basis for its truthfulness is the person's experience or on the testimony of another. If it is based on truth, then it is truth that is exaggerated or misrepresented.

Third, I may be drawn away because of another's testimony. How can anyone discredit another's testimony? If you did suspect another's testimony, you would be calling that person a liar. Their testimony is a sure as truth. Sometimes, for some people, it is more sure than the truth.

Fourth, I may be drawn away because of peer pressure. If I long for the acceptance and approval of my peers, I will often buy into what they say lock, stock, and barrel. This is how young people often get involved with smoking, drinking, and illicit sex. Others slur them, and they collapse.

From what is the believer being drawn away? Believers are drawn away from five God-given authorities. Those authorities are government, employers, husbands, the church, and parents.

The other word in this verse is "enticed." Entice is a colorful Greek word that provides keen insight. The word is used to illustrate an angler or hunter's ploy to draw out the prey. The intention of the sportsman is to deceive the animal into believing that what it is looking at is real. I have friends who hunt in the winter. They dress up in camouflage pants, coats, hats, and gloves. They bring along handcrafted wooden "callers," Which make sounds like the animal they are hoping to snare—deer sounds, squirrel sounds, and an array of many more.

The angler may use live bait or artificial bait. They cast the bait into the stream, and "dance" it across the bottom or near the top of the water. By using this jerking hand motion or slowing reeling the bait in, they are trying to convince the fish that it is real because it is moving. They even have "fish spray" that can be applied to make the bait seem more real and convincing.

Some time ago, a scientific magazine published an article concerning a certain species of alligator. Being lazy beasts, they seldom hunt for their dinner but just wait for their unwary victims to come to them. They lie near the bank with open mouths, acting as if they are dead. Soon flies begin to light on their moist tongues, and several other insects gather. This crowd attracts bigger game. A lizard will crawl up to the alligator to feed on the bugs; then a frog joins the party. Presently a whole menagerie is there; then there is a sudden "earthquake"—wham!—the giant jaws come together and the party is over! Here's the lesson: don't be lured away from your net of safety (authority).

When I am tempted, I must surrender my will in obedience to God. I must ask myself, "Would all of my God-given authorities encourage me in this? Have I asked God if there is hidden harm in this decision?"

Warning Sign #3: When I have a strong desire for self-gratification contrary to the Word of God.

What is lust? The Greek word is *epithumia*. It means a passionate longing for the forbidden, to crave, and to desire. We can see a number of pictures of lust in the Bible. In Genesis 3, Eve longed to be like God, knowing good from evil. The Bible tells us that she saw that the tree was good for food, and that it was a delight to the eyes, and that the tree was desirable to make one wise (3:6). Yet, her Creator used

Adam, her husband, to warn her because she told the serpent verbatim God's warning.

Another example of longing for the forbidden is King David. His lustful desires and catastrophic personal downfall is recorded in Second Samuel 11–12. Lust follows a pattern. David saw (11:2), inquired (11:3), and took (11:4). David already had numerous wives. David was in the wrong place at the wrong time. He should have been bivouacked with his troops when kings go out to war (11:1).

1 John 2:16 provides the pattern of lust. It follows the lust of the flesh, eyes, pride of life.

Have you ever experienced the "bait n' switch" sales tactics? You receive a circular in the mail advertising a product for a certain price. When you get to the store, that product is no longer available, but another similar product is at a higher price. This is called "bait n' switch"." Temptation is like that. Temptation seeks to entice us, bait the hook, and switch the product. It is never that it appears to be.

What is lust's goal in the believer's life? One of lust's goal is to deceive (Eph. 4:22).

> In reference to your former manner of life, you lay aside the old self, which is being corrupted in accordance with the lusts of deceit.

Another goal of lust is to enslave (Titus 3:3).

> For we also once were foolish ourselves, disobedient, deceived, enslaved to various lusts and pleasures, spending our life in malice and envy, hateful, hating one another.

Lust wants to rule over me (1 Peter 1:14).

> As obedient children, do not be conformed to the former lusts, which were yours in your ignorance

Besides wanting to rule over me, lust desires to lead me around (2 Tim. 3:6).

For among them are those who enter into households and captivate weak women weighed down with sins, led on by various impulses.

I need to affirm the will of God as good, perfect, and acceptable instead of seeking to fulfill my self-gratification that is contrary to the Word of God.

Warning Sign #4: When I allow the desire to dominate my thought life

James uses the birth analogy to provide further spiritual insight to the temptation cycle. James likens temptation to the physical conception between a man and a woman. Certain conditions must be right for physical conception to occur.

Likewise, spiritual conception needs the right conditions. Those conditions are the person's thought life and a fertile mind.

When does spiritual fertility often take place? This conception (deception) can take place when I am tired as with Elijah who thought he was the only one serving God. This conception between our thought life and receptive mind can take place after a great disappointment. I can have high expectations but the outcome does not match what I hoped. This conception can take place when I experience a wide range of emotions like fear, anger, or worry. In fact, under any circumstance, people can abandon control of their thinking and allow a thought to dominate their mind along with a predisposition to blame God for the outcome.

I need to take every speculation and every lofty thing raised up against the knowledge of God into obedience to Christ (2 Cor. 10:4–5). This is a fascinating verse. The verse says the longer we think about a sinful thought the more we will tend to believe its lie. The word speculation is *logismos*. It means reasoning or thought. It involves a reckoning or computation. It means reasoning or thinking that is hostile toward Christian thought resulting in passing judgment. The Greek word for lofty thought is *hupsoma*. It means to elevate as in a bulwark, rampart, or barrier. The longer someone thinks that God is unkind, unfair, or unloving, the more that person will draw the conclusion. Someone can present biblical truth, but the person has dwelled so long on the lie that he or she cannot move past his or her own barrier to believe the truth.

We are flirting with temptation when we allow a desire to dominate our thought life. This warning sign is a call to check what we are allowing our minds to spend so much time on. The wrong thoughts can move us beyond temptation to sin.

Warning Sign #5: When I develop ways to act out the temptation because I am not guarding my mind
The medical and scientific communities debate when a life begins. For the Christian, physical conception, even though small, shows that life is present. Spiritual birth is the serious consideration of an action. The birth of sin is seldom a quick action. Like physical birth requiring nine months for maturation, the course of action is determined by the mind. It is not acted upon, but the course is set in motion and nearly irreversible.

An example would be Jezebel, who considered how to get Naboth's inheritance for her wicked husband, Ahab. Ahab solicited Naboth to sell his inheritance. Evidently, it was just outside of Ahab's bedroom, close to the castle. Naboth knew the law and refused to sell it. Jezebel entered their bedroom and observed Ahab with his face toward the wall, like a little child pouting because he was unable to fulfill his selfish desires. Jezebel told her husband not to concern himself about his selfish desire, for she would remedy the situation. She conspired with other wicked people to falsely accuse Naboth and then to sentence him to death.

I need to repent for sin that resides in my heart. Although no one can see my heart, God sees and demands that I confess and repent (Matt. 5:21, 27, 31, 33, 38).

Warning Sign #6: When I reject and substitute God's divine pattern by acting on the temptation
Unless the Lord returns before people die, their physical birth guarantees they will die. The moment the child leaves the mother's womb, death begins.

The spiritual birth of sin results in death. For the believer, the death represents broken fellowship with God. A true believer cannot lose salvation. But the spiritual intimacy is damaged. The once pure openness has melted. You remember when Adam and Eve broke fellowship with God by sinning, they *hid* themselves. You also remember when Jonah broke fellowship with God by deciding Jonah's will would supercede God's clear revelation, he tried to *hide* from God. The psalmist in 139 cries out, "Where can I flee from Your presence?" When I reject and substitute God's divine pattern by acting on the temptation, I break fellowship with God. Broken fellowship is the result of rejecting God's divine pattern and substituting your own human pattern.

Consider an airport. You have to pass through a security system. A device is used to detect metal objects and subsequently sound an alarm. One airport I traveled through had a three-sided cubical where each passenger was sprayed with a mist. I later discovered the purpose was to discover if a person was attempting to bring biological substances onboard an airplane for terrorist purposes. A standard metal-detection device scans you and permits advancement to your destination. Cleared for takeoff! You have passed the test. No warning signals alert the security officer of anything wrong.

Likewise, the Holy Spirit inspired James to record these warning signs so when we encounter various trials or temptations, we will be able to guard the purity of our walk before Him who chose us, redeemed us, and desires intimate fellowship so He will use us for His glory and kingdom.

I Can't Seem to Lick This Problem

Fifteen Biblical Ways to Tame Temptation

Have you noticed how assembly kit instructions are changing? The assembly kit now comes with instructions in multiple languages, large detailed pictures, and a list of tools necessary to complete the task successfully. You don't have to necessarily read, just be able to understand the meaning of the pictures to successfully assemble and enjoy your product.

We have a spiritual instruction book to tame temptation. It is always relevant and timely. It crosses all language barriers. It is ageless and timeless. It describes the victory of our Lord in the wilderness showing fifteen tools that can be used to tame temptation. Christ's tools are so powerful that He Himself taught the disciples the secret to taming temptation. Remember no one was with Him during the temptation. What are these tools?

This chapter will be brief, listing the tools with a brief explanation. Other fine works by endowed scholars have written well on this significant section of the Bible. Let's us begin.

1. **Expect temptation when you commit yourself to the work, word or will of God (3:15 baptism of Jesus)**
Baptism means identification. In 1 Corinthians 10, Paul writes that the children of Israel were baptized under Moses. The Gospel of John records the baptism of John. In fact, when Paul was in Ephesus, he found disciples who were baptized in the name of John, which was a preparatory baptism to seek and believe on Christ. Paul writes in Romans 6 about being baptized into Christ. So the word means "to identify with."

When a saint purposes, resolves, and commits to truth, the enemy will not let your commitment slide. The tempters of the saint will challenge your commitment.

Perhaps take some time and read Nehemiah 4–6. Nehemiah returned to rebuild the walls. In these chapters, Sanballat, Tobiah, and Gesham attacked his resolve in a variety of ways. They mocked, intimidated, and wrote inflammatory letters to the king that Nehemiah was only rebuilding the walls as an act of rebellion.

Today when we resolve to do the will of God, the enemies of our spiritual walk will use things like discouragement, criticism, mockery, and character assassination. Be alert. Be aware. Avoid spiritual naïveté. A commitment to spiritual things invites the attacks of the world, flesh, and the devil.

2. Expect temptation when you are experiencing the favor of God (3:17 well-pleased)

The favor of God comes when we are obedient. God was well pleased with His Son. His Son was resolved to do the will of His Father. He proclaimed that He came to do what was written in the scrolls. He asserted His meat was the meat of His father. The evidence of His obedience was complete surrender to the Father's wishes regardless of people's responses, results, or opposition from the religious leaders.

What are some evidences of obedience for the believer's life? What would the favor of the God look like in the saint's life? Some would tell you that it would be health, wealth, and prosperity. Only good things come from God, for God is the giver of all good gifts. If God's favor is truly only good, without problems, rejection, and opposition, then some of God's most choice servants did not have God's favor. God's favor is not linked to how your life is going. You may be in some terrible straits, but if you are obedient, trusting God, living at peace with all men as much as is possible, counting on the joy of the Lord which is your strength, then you will and do have the favor of God. It may not *feel* like it, but God's favor is nothing about feelings.

Solomon was a very wealthy man. You can try to determine his assets by reading portions of 2 Kings and the book of Ecclesiastes. One would say he certainly must have had God's favor. But Solomon was filled with pride, compliancy, and arrogance. Because of his disobedience, God withdrew His favor. Solomon directly rebelled against God's laws, and a careful reading of Ecclesiastes shows how miserable he was. All of his possessions were his way of pursuing meaning and purpose. He did not have God's favor because Solomon was living in sin.

3. Expect temptation when you are Spirit led (4:1)

Why is this? The Spirit leads us in ways contradictory to our natural inclinations and the broad pathways of worldly destruction. There was nothing wrong with Jesus going into the wilderness. There was nothing wrong with the amount of time Jesus spent in the wilderness. Both the location, purpose, and length of time are fraught with meaning, but the temptation could have taken place by the Sea of Galilee, or the inner city of Jerusalem, or the outskirts of Capernaum with the same results. He was tempted in all points but without sin.

Perhaps you are led to home school. There is nothing wrong if you are convinced that the Lord is leading you to educate your children this way. There is nothing wrong with looking for employment that does not require you to work on Sundays. There is nothing wrong with responding to a short-term mission's trip.

When you believe you are Spirit led, your confidence will rest in the Word of God. It cannot be some feeling or emotion. You cannot base your decision on a group consensus or the popular Christian fad of the moment. Because when temptation comes, those gnawing questions arise, and those questions of doubt are raised by outsiders or within yourself, it is only the Word of God that will strengthen your resolve, "This is the will of God."

4. Anticipate new spiritual blessings when you tame temptation (4:2 forty days)

Some scholars attempt to assign meaning to every number of the Bible. This is dangerous. However, there are certain numbers that have meaning to them. The number three represent the Trinity. The number six represents man. The number seven represents perfection. And the number forty represents something new is about to take place.

Here are some examples for the number forty, representing something new is about to take place.

- Noah: it rained forty days and forty nights
- The children of Israel ate manna for forty years before they entered the Promised Land when the rain of manna stopped
- Moses was on Mt. Sinai forty days receiving the law, a new way of approaching God
- It took forty days to spy out the land before entering it
- Eli ruled forty years before a new form of government arose
- Saul, David, and Solomon each ruled forty years, each bringing something new to the monarchy
- Goliath boasted forty days before David took him down
- Elijah's journey was forty days before God introduced Elisha onto the prophetic scene
- The message of destruction to Nineveh was forty days but God relented as they repented

When temptation arrives at my door and knocks, as I deal with that temptation, anticipate a new spiritual blessing of growth, maturity, and modeling before others how to live victorious.

5. **Know your greatest area of vulnerability (4:2 hunger)**

After a spiritual victory, guard your greatest area of weakness. For Jesus, it was hunger. Imagine what the human body would feel like after withholding food from it for forty days. Imagine the emotional and mental state of someone not having eaten for forty days.

Solomon's great area of vulnerability was sensuality. He defiled the gift of wisdom by his sensuality. David's great grace was nearly defiled by his anger. Saul's victory was married by self-willed, pride and blame shifting (1 Sam. 11, 13–15).

We can become prideful after a great victory. We can boast in the arm of the flesh. "Hey, see what I did!" The reason we were victorious in taming temptation was not because we were so cunning. It was not because we were so strong. It was not because we were so intellectually superior to our opponent. Our victory came through the Lord and the use of His Word. After a great victory, know your greatest area of vulnerability.

6. Understand that your position in Christ does not grant you special privileges to sin (4:3 if you are the Son of God)

Two out of the three temptations, Satan begins by mocking the claim of Christ to be deity. Satan says, "If you are the Son of God, then…" Because Christ was God, He should not be hungry. He should be able to take common stones and make bread for Himself. As the Son of God He deserves this. It is not right that the Son of God be famished. He has a real legitimate need. And You have the power to meet that need. Go ahead. Meeting this real human need is not wrong.

Because we are God's child, we should not contract cancer, have a rebellious child, lose our jobs after thirty-one years, or lay our children in the grave because of a drunk driver. We should be immune to the harsh realities of life. Or if we have the means to bypass life's difficulties, our position as a child of God should afford us the opportunity to do so. If we have to sin to avoid temptation to circumvent life's problems, we fail to comprehend our position in Christ. Our position in Christ does not grant us a special dispensation to sin and "get out of jail free" card.

7. Allow God to meet real legitimate needs (4:3 turn stones to bread)

I tipped my hand to this concept under number 6. We cannot meet legitimate needs illegitimately. Jesus had a legitimate need. He was hungry. Had He turned those stones into bread, He would have violated the nature of those stones. Stones are not designed to eat. Stones are inedible.

When we fail to allow God to meet real legitimate needs, we will violate another portion of God's Word. For example, we have a need for housing but we lie on the application about the number of occupants.

We need money so we gamble or we work two jobs, abandoning our role as wife/mother or husband/father.

Many Christians run ahead of God. They preempt God's gracious intervention. They take matters into their own hands. Their need becomes so overwhelming they allow a real need to crowd out a real God.

8. Live by the principles of the Word of God (4:4, 7, 11 It is written)

The Word of God has unique and special characteristics that no other forms of literature, past, present, or future, will possess. The nature of the Word of God is immutable (unchanging), inspired (God-breathed), infallible (incapable of error), inerrant, trustworthy, and truthful.

God provided the Law to govern all of Israel's life. God wrote out precisely how the Jews were to live socially, civilly, and religiously. There was not an area that God did not specifically express to His redeemed how He wanted them to live. Moses and Aaron received God's clear instructions. Those who helped Moses rule were aware of God's preciseness. Later, the priests would remind the people of God's exact words.

The saint must live by the principles of God's Word. Three times Jesus renounces the devil's temptation by saying, "It is written." We knew in full the Word of God. We have the Spirit to guide and teach us. We can find God's principles regarding speech, money, child raising, entertainment, purchases, friends, feelings, thought-life, time, vocation, relationships, dating, loneliness, and knowing God's will. No aspect of life is left to our finite reasoning because we are commanded not to lean on our own understanding (Prov. 3:5).

9. Know how to use the awesome power of God's Word (4:4 live by every word *rehma*, not *logos*)

Man is to live by every word (*rhema*) that proceeds out of the mouth of God. *Rhema* means the exact, precise, and specific word of God. In each temptation, Christ quotes specifically from the Book of Deuteronomy, chapters 6 and 8. Christ did not throw out a concept. He quoted Scriptures that were an exact and appropriate defense for the temptation. When He was tempted to turn stones to bread to eat, Jesus points to the words of life from His father. When He was tempted to test God's protection, and even Satan used Scripture (out of context), Jesus quoted Scriptures that addressed the heart the temptation, and that was not to test God presumptuously. When Jesus was tempted by the riches of the world, Christ used Scriptures that spoke of only worshipping God.

Precise, exact, and appropriate Scripture must be used to cause Satan to flee from you. Correct use of the Word will help you resist the devil. If you examine Ephesians 6, you will see that the sword of the Spirit is the Word of God. You will also observe that this text is referring to wrestling with the underworld powers—unseen forces, principalities, and powers. We are given a full suit of armor. The offensive weapon is the sword. This sword is the small dagger the foot solders wore into battle. It was used for hand-to-hand combat. It was a battle of a close encounter. At this point in the battle, a soldier could not try and pull out of his sheath the long Darth Vader sword! There was no room to raise a shield. It was toe to toe, dagger to dagger. One small error would be fatal. Likewise, the saint must know the Word to use it accurately. I can resist using the preciseness of the two-edge sword. Here is where proper memorization can be most valuable.

10. Guard against embracing cultural beliefs (4:5 pinnacle of temple)

There was a rabbinical belief that Messiah would leap from the highest point on Temple and be unharmed, establishing His deity. Because Jesus had not performed according to cultural belief, He could not be the Messiah.

There is enormous cultural embrace by Christians today. We see it in marriage, homosexuality (gay parade), alcohol, psychological labels, disorders, addictions, diseases, and compulsions. What culture deems acceptable is not the standard to determine what is right and truthful. Cultural determination and subsequent acceptance simply translates into peer pressure. It the "majority rule" syndrome. The majority in the Bible was never right. Just because many are traveling on the broad pathway only means they are headed for destruction. Cultural beliefs will never be able to bow low enough to enter through the narrow gate.

11. Accurately interpret the Scriptures (4:6 misquotation of Ps. 91:11–12)

We do not want to over magnify the power and presence of Satan, but neither do we want to be ignorant of his devices. Paul reminds us that one of the benefits of clothing ourselves with the full armor of God is to be able to stand firm by recognizing the schemes of the devil. Schemes is *methodeia* in the Greek. You see the word "method." One of Satan's methods to tempt us is to change Scriptures. Satan knows Scriptures. Satan leaves important parts out. When Satan quoted Psalm 91, he left out "to guard you in all your ways." Using parts of Scriptures can make what is being said acceptable to God and therefore license for the saint to act.

A saint needs to study to show himself approved. This laborious tasks leads to proper interpretation. The saint must invest time into study. One cannot study devotional ding-dongs and expect to become spiritual. The saint must study the Scriptures, not books about the Book. The saint must set aside time to reflect and meditate on the Word (2 Tim. 2:15).

12. Learn contentment by recounting the faithfulness of God (4:7 not test God)

Israel was notorious for testing God. They were not long out of Egypt until they tested God for water in wilderness. God just provided manna. Their memories should have remembered the previous miracles of crossing Red Sea and the ten plagues. They were discontent and grumbling, not satisfied, critical, and complaining. It seemed like nothing satisfied them.

When God proves Himself, because He is immutable, you don't have to keep testing Him. His faithfulness to you is fact. You can trust Him in every new situation.

13. Remember the transitory nature of life (4:8 kingdoms of the world)

Imagine the kingdoms Christ saw. Kingdoms past (Assyrian 248 years; Babylon 65 years; Medo-Persia 206 years; Greek 11 years; Egypt 123 years; Rome 200 years), and kingdoms future (U.S., USSR, Britain, Japan, China, India, European Union). But those kingdoms past, like these kingdoms future, are fleeting. They are temporary until someone overthrows them.

If we adapt a divine perspective on this life, it is temporary. One day could be as long as one thousand years, and one thousand years could be as short as one day. Job came to understand the transient nature of life. In a very short time, Job lost everything through robbery, hail, lightening storms, war, tornados, and hurricane.

If we worship things that by nature are short-lived, we will become disillusioned, bitter, and angry. What human being would not have jumped at the chance of having all the kingdoms of the world and their glory? What power. What prestige! What emptiness. What vain hopes placed wrongly in an empty cistern. Jesus knows what is eternal. It is the worship of His Father.

14. Pursue eternal, life-changing goals (4:10 worship and serve God only)

It is not what God does for us that demands our worship, but that God is. Our life goal is to know Him (Phil. 3:10). Paul, in this chapter that summaries his life, lays out his lineage, his pedigree, and then his resume. Paul, after his conversion, came to understand how vain and empty these things were. What he thought constituted life was meaningless compared to knowing Christ. For so many years he lived in the earthly and now. He did not have an eye on the future. He thought his den full of degrees, letters of accolades, and newspaper clippings would give him meaning and purpose in life. But as Paul attests, after finding Christ, he took all those things and counted them as rubbish or dung. They held no more allurement. Their deception was recognized. True value in life is eternal.

The life-changing goal for any believer is to pursue the will of God. I John 2:17 reminds us "the world passes away with its lusts, but the one who does the will of God lives forever." What other pursuits should a saint strive for? Read Paul's words written to young pastor Timothy.

> But flee from these things, you man of God, and <u>pursue</u> righteousness, godliness, faith, love, perseverance and gentleness.
>
> Now flee from youthful lusts and <u>pursue</u> righteousness, faith, love, and peace, with those who call on the Lord from a pure heart.

These, and many others you find in the Bible, are the only goals worth pursuing, for they are eternal.

15. A single victory moves you to the next level of spiritual challenge (4:11 Satan left for a more opportune time)

With each temptation the saint encounters and when that temptation is tamed, that victory often moves us to the next level in our spiritual walk. Paul reminds us we are to move from faith to faith to faith (Rom. 1:17). Peter tells us:

> like newborn babies, long for the pure milk of the word, so that by it you may <u>grow</u> in respect to salvation (1 Peter 2:2) and again but <u>grow</u> in the grace and knowledge of our Lord and Savior Jesus Christ. To Him be the glory, both now and to the day of eternity. Amen (2 Peter 3:18).

Jesus was attack by the Pharisees, Sadducees, Herodians, and even Peter. With each attack, truth was displayed and Christ moved closer to doing the will of God in His substitutionary atonement for mankind's sin.

The New Testament Church experienced attacks from the outside and from the inside. Each temptation met and each victory secured means spiritual maturity, a new challenge, and the advancement of Christ's Kingdom. Like the "seats" in tennis—each opponent defeated raises you in the ranks. It is possible for a virtual unknown to take Wimbledon!

I have trouble knowing where I leave my tools while I am involved in a project. I get so wrapped up and preoccupied, trying to concentrate and stay focused, that I forget where I laid the tape measure, screw driver, or hammer. That's why they invented tool belts.

We have a spiritual tool belt. It is the Word of God that helps keep safe and secure these fifteen biblical tools to tame temptation. Wear the belt, and use the tools!

My Family Doesn't Know How to Do Anything without Fighting
Developing Unity in Our Relationships

In one of my favorite Peanuts cartoons, Lucy demands that Linus change TV channels and then threatens him with her fist if he doesn't.

> "What makes you think you can walk right in here and take over?" asks Linus. "These five fingers," says Lucy. "Individually they're nothing but when I curl them together like this into a single unit, they form a weapon that is terrible to behold."
>
> "Which channel do you want?" asks Linus. Turning away, he looks at his fingers and says, "Why can't you guys get organized like that?"

Have you ever experienced a great time with another couple and walk away thinking to yourself, "Why can't my husband be loving and attentive like hers?" Or you have a game night with another family, and you ask your spouse, "Why don't our kids behave that way? I mean they were volunteering to clear the table!" Have you thought, "Why can't my family get organized like that?"

There may be some reasons why. There may be unresolved conflict within the family structure. One family member may be anger or bitter toward another. There may be a lack of trust, unforgiveness, or resentment. It could be the fact of differences of opinions, philosophies, beliefs, or values. Family unity is destroyed by self and sin.

In these brief verses, we will see Paul's concern about developing unity in our relationships.

Paul reminds us about the call to unity (v. 1).
Paul begins this section of Ephesians applying what he has written about in chapters 1–3. Paul presents practical theology. In light of what you have read or heard, here is what you do with it. This is what your theology should look like in everyday life. This is very typical of Paul's writing. He follows doctrinal instruction with practical teaching.

It reminds us that the practice of Christianity is only as strong as the person's theology.

He therefore connects what has been written in chapters 1–3. Paul says, "Stop and remember what God has done for you." What has God done for us Paul records in the first three chapters of Ephesians. I have made a partial list for you in bullet form.

- Chose you 1:4
- Predestined you 1:5
- Adopted you 1:5
- Redeemed you 1:7
- Forgave you 1:7
- Lavishes the riches of His grace on you 1:8
- Made known the mystery of His will 1:9
- Given you an inheritance 1:11
- Sealed you 1:13
- Loved you 2:4
- Made you alive 2:5
- Gave us peace 2:14
- Calls us fellow citizens 2:19
- Apart of God's household 2:19
- We have boldness 3:12
- We have access 3:12

In light of all that God has done for us, Paul begs and pleas with us to decide to live out what we have come to know emotionally and intellectually. Stated differently, "Walk the talk!" Paul entreats these saints to show the proof of the pudding. Put the rubber to the road. "Where's the beef?" as the old Wendy's commercial advertised. Put some motion in the ocean. If you don't, you come precariously close to being the man in James that says to the hungry and naked person, "Go, be

Developing Unity in Our Relationships

warmed and be filled." Or worse, the demons who believe that God is one, but that does not alter their eternal destination (Js. 2:14–19).

Paul knows it's tough to live the Christian life, but talk is cheap. Paul cites his own circumstances (a prisoner of the Lord) to remind us that our circumstances do not grant a special dispensation of disobedience. Living the Christian life is not *optional*, it is *mandatory*! Paul is not asking these saints do anything that he has not done, is not doing now, or would not be willing to doing the future. He was a prisoner for doing, not mere talking.

Paul says we are to walk in such a way as to represent before others what we claim verbally. Paul calls us ambassadors in 2 Corinthians. Exactly what is our calling? We are called saints (1:1), sons (1:5), and His workmanship (2:10).

We are required to walk a certain way. "Walk" represents a lifestyle, behavior, conduct of life. We are to walk in the good works He has prepared for us (2:10), not to walk as Gentiles (4:17), not to walk in the futility of our mind (4:17), to walk in love (5:2), to walk in light (5:8), and to walk carefully (5:15). He also says we are to walk consistently (4:1.)

We are to walk in a manner worthy of the calling to which you have been called. The word picture here is one that represents balanced scales. Someone would order a pound of meat in the marketplace. The vendor would place a one pound weight on one side of a pair of scales. On the other tray, he would begin to add the meat until the scales were leveled. Likewise, Paul exhorts these saints to be balanced in their Christianity. Talk must never outweigh their walk; and walk must never outweigh their talk.

If Christianity were the "silent" faith, that would mean our actions must speaker louder than our words. God reminds us that unity focuses on the goodness, grace, and mercy of God. Disunity focuses on self-absorbed and self-centered people. Because I am called an ambassador, I am mandated to represent the one who sends me regardless of how I feel or what I think. Unity is not about me.

What are the attributes of unity? (4:2–3)
Paul lists several characteristics of unity that will help develop intimate and Christ-like relationships.

The first Paul lists is humility. The Greek word means lowliness of mind or self-abasement. I understand that there was no Greek or Roman word for humility in their culture. The Greeks and Romans loathed the word. Anyone who was humbled was weak and inferior. He was not a man. One way of understanding humility is by how we think about others in light of ourselves. Do we think we are better because we have a degree and someone has a diploma? Do we think we are superior because we live in a suburb while someone lives in the inner city? Do we believe we are above another because we have two cars and they take public transportation wherever they go? Humility is a mindset. The opposite of humility is pride. Pride also has a mindset. Consider the thought life of the Pharisees. In Matthew 9:3, the Pharisees thought they were better than those who flocked around Jesus, the tax collectors and sinners. In Luke 6:8, the Pharisees were more concerned about a tradition than seeing a fellow Jew healed and restored to Jewish life by having his withered hand healed. In Luke 7:39, Simon's attitude toward the town harlot spoke only of pride. He considered himself more holy and clean than Jesus.

What are some marks of humility? There will be confession of sin, servant-hood, submission to authority, and peace.

The second characteristic of unity is gentleness. The word means a disposition, meekness, not timidity, cowardice, or weakness. Warren Wiersbe defined gentleness or meekness as power under control. James likens the power of the tongue to that of an unbridled horse or a ship without a rudder. The power of a horse without a bridle cannot be utilized. A boat without a rudder loses direction. Likewise, a saint without gentleness is powerless and lacks direction.

We see several examples of gentleness in the Bible. The first that comes to mind is how David dealt with Saul. On two separate occasions, David could have become king. All he had to do was kill Saul. It seemed like God provided an opportunity to do so. But David refrained because he remembers that you should not touch the Lord's anointed (1 Sam. 24 and 26). He had the power, but he was gentle. He could have, but he didn't.

When Christ was in the garden and a regiment came to arrest Him, He had the power to escape or simply take them out. Unlike Peter who drew a concealed sword, Christ acted in gentleness trusting the will of the Father.

Gentleness is the opposite of vengeance or revenge. It does not take matters into its own hand. Gentleness is willing to be misunderstood without convincing the other person how wrong they are. Gentleness does not have to defend its reputation.

What are the marks of gentleness? Some are self-control, willingness to do God's will, and most often in how we speak and use wisdom.

The third characteristic of unity is patience. The word means forbearance and slowness in avenging wrong. Abraham waited a century before he saw the promises of God fulfilled to him. Noah patiently preached righteousness and builds the Ark for 120 years. He did not give up because of people's ridicule, hardened hearts, or ignorance. Js. 5:10 refers to farmers who patiently wait for the early and late rains. Now in all of these examples, it dawns on me that patience has to know when only God can do something about the situation. Abraham could do nothing about the miraculous conception of Sarah. They tried before usurping God's timing and it was a disaster. Noah couldn't bring on the rains any earlier or prevented them from coming. The farmer is at the mercy of the Creator of Heaven and Earth for the nourishing rains, the right amounts and at the right time.

The opposite of patience is anger.

The marks of patience are trusting in the sovereignty of God and remaining focused on the will of God.

The fourth characteristic of unity is tolerance. We are commanded to show tolerance for one another in love. The word "tolerance" means "endurance, steadfastness, or putting up with." When Paul became exasperated with John Mark, Barnabas exhibited patience by taking John Mark under his wing. Later Paul would say that John Mark was profitable for the ministry. Why? Someone—Barnabas—was tolerant with him. Tolerance is marked by covering things under love with attempts to help the person mature and grow.

The opposite of tolerance is prejudice, preconceptions, narrow-mindedness, or presumptuousness. This is what Paul displayed when he refused to consider taking John Mark on the second missionary trip. Paul presumed that John Mark would desert them again as he did before.

Perhaps a summary would be appropriate here in our discussion.

- Unity is disrupted when I replace humility with pride.
- Unity is disturbed when I trade gentleness with revenge
- Unity is interrupted when I exchange patience with anger
- Unity is lost when I substitute tolerance with prejudice

When there is disunity in our homes, we need to identify the attribute that we have replaced with sinful behavior. Paul reminds us of the effort it will take to walk the talk when he uses the word "diligence." It means labor, hard working, effort, and perseverance. It carries the idea of not being left behind.

Paul displays this diligence when writing to his yokefellow in Philippians 4 and again to Philemon. Paul wants the yokefellow to be diligent in his efforts to bring unity between Euodia and Syntyche. Paul urges Philemon to be diligent to avoid the culture practices regarding a runaway slave who was a thief. Resist this mentality; be diligent to receive Onesimus back, more than a slave but as a brother in the Lord.

Several years ago, I took a group of teens white water rafting in West Virginia. I had never been before. I am skilled in the water, but this would be a new challenge for me. The girls were in one raft, and the boys and me in the other. The second day is where the real challenge raised its head. We were navigating Class 3s, 4s and one Class 5 rapid. After traversing what appeared to be a rough riding Class 3, our guide yelled at us. We got stuck against a boulder in the river. It could have been dangerous. When we got stuck, most of us stopped paddling and expected the guide to move us safely from the boulder and danger. Sitting on top of quiet water, she ripped us big time. "Keep paddling until I tell you to stop," she screamed. "We need to work together as a team!"

I learned a valuable lesson that sunny morning. When it comes to unity in relationships, there are no riders. Everyone's ores are in the water!

What is the basis for unity? (4:4–6)

The basis of Christian unity is outside of me and those with whom I seek to live in harmony. Paul summarizes the basis of unity in a sevenfold doxology with the prefix of "one."

- One body: Each living under the authority of Jesus Christ, the Cornerstone.
- One Spirit: Each utilizing divine power, not human reasoning or resources.
- One hope: Each being found faithful until the Lord's soon return.
- One Lord: Each focusing on no one else save our resurrected living Lord.
- One faith: Each consulting and staying true to the only absolute and objective source of doctrine pertaining to matters of life.
- One baptism: Each counting ourselves dead to sin and alive to Jesus Christ though our identification with Christ's death, burial, and resurrection.
- One God and Father: Each living as if God Father of all, who is over all and through all and in all.

Let's conclude this chapter by providing three guiding questions to guard unity.

1. How can I use my present circumstances to promote unity in my relationships?
2. What attribute is most needed to promote unity in my relationships?
3. Which "one-factor" will restore unity in my relationships?

What Kind of Person Am I? What Kind of Person Should I Be?
My Heart—Christ's Home or Time Share?

My Heart Christ's Home is a book written by Robert Boyd Munger and Andrea Jorgenson. The basic theme of the book is posed in a question: "Would Christ be welcomed in your home?" They develop a picture of rooms of a home within the human heart. Is Christ welcome to go into every room of my heart? The basement, attic, garage, living room, bedrooms, or family room? Would Christ feel uncomfortable because of books, videos, DVDs, or magazines?

Time shares are living units that can be purchased and then used throughout the year on a reservation basis. If you buy into a certain time-share company, you then have access to wherever their time shares are located. You could vacation in California, Tennessee, Texas, or Hawaii. Many saints have a time-share mentality with reference to their relationship to Christ. Within a spiritual calendar year, they might have a season of real fellowship through Bible study and prayer. Then return to the normalcy and stress of daily living and never return to Bible study and prayer. This may linger for a number of months. Then a crisis occurs, and they return to their "spiritual time share." And the cycle repeats itself.

Paul writes 1 Corinthians to address certain problems church members brought to his attention. One problem Paul addresses is the spiritual condition of the worshipper in the church.

The passage before us is similar to Christ's parabolic teaching to the disciples about the spiritual condition of people that they would encounter as they spread the Gospel message (parable of the sower and the seed).

The spiritual condition of men and women in any congregation is of vital importance to the shepherds for several reasons. First, knowing the spiritual condition will determine relationships. Am I an evangelist, mentor, disciple-maker, or admonisher to this person? Second, knowing the spiritual condition will determine ministry concentrations. Is it best that I lead a mentoring or discipleship group, participate in small groups, or do counseling? Third, knowing the spiritual condition will determine the scope of service opportunities. Should I be a Sunday school teacher, Awana worker, deacon, or elder?

The spiritual conditions Paul writes about are the natural man, the spiritual man, the fleshly man and the babe or new believer.

The Natural Man (2:14)
How does Paul describe the natural man? What are some of the characteristics of a natural man? The natural man does not accept the things of the Spirit of God. He considers spiritual things foolishness (1:18, 21). He does not have the ability to understand spiritual things. The book of Romans describes the natural man as one who suppresses the truth, does not honor God, does not give thanks, uses worldly wisdom, is an idol worshippers, is given to sinful practices, is self-righteous, and is hypocritical by pointing to what they do (Rom. 1:18–32).

What does the natural man need? The natural man needs salvation. The natural man needs to cut his ties with human reasoning, works-righteousness, and pride. The natural man can be compared to the first soil Jesus speaks of in Matthew 13. The good seed is broadcasted on this soil, which is hard. It is the footpath around the field that the laborers used to come and go. It is trodden down. The soil is impenetrable. The generously sown seed simply lies on top of this unbreakable earth. Jesus comments that the birds will come along for a free meal because the seed is unable to break through the soil and germinate.

In Romans 10:9–10, Paul states clearly what the natural man needs to do.

> But what does it say? *"The word is near you, in your mouth and in your heart"*—that is, the word of faith which we are preaching, that if you confess with your mouth Jesus as Lord,

and believe in your heart that God raised Him from the dead, you will be saved.

The Spiritual Man (2:15)
The second person Paul describes is the spiritual man. What are the characteristics of a spiritual man? First, the spiritual man appraises all things. The Greek word is *anakrino*, which means to examine or to examine repeatedly. This kind of examination could be compared to what a forensic scientist does.

There are now several *Crime Scene Investigators* (*CSI*) television programs airing during any given week. *CSI Miami* and *CSI New York* are the latest additions to the *CSI* family. The goal of the program is to show how crime scene investigation helps solve crime. The team investigates, asks questions, calls into account, looks at the crime from every angle, tests, measures, analyzes, and repeats it all over again if a crime scene investigator gets stumped.

This is the first characteristic of a spiritual man. He or she is not spoon fed the milk of the word. He or she knows how to dine off the sumptuous lean meat of the Bible. They ask questions, they look at the text from every angle, they test the spirits, they measure themselves by the word they study, they analyze, they harmonize, and they internalize.

The second characteristic of a spiritual man is no one appraises him. It is the same Greek word *anakrino*. He or she does not find himself in a spiritual position whereby another has to point a sinful attitude or action out to them. The Spirit is truly leading them so they do not fulfill the lusts of the flesh. The Spirit teaches them so they can walk in the Spirit. When someone lives a life of self-appraisal, no one can find fault with him or her. Three people in the Bible who lived such a life were Job (1:1), Elizabeth and Zacharias (Luke 1:6). It is recorded of them that they walked blamelessly before the Lord. Their neighbors, friends, and near or extended relatives could not find fault with them as to breaking one of God's Laws. Paul reminds us that before observing communion, a spiritual exercise for every saint is to examine himself so he may judge the body rightly (1 Cor. 11:28–29).

A third characteristic of a spiritual man is he or she possesses and uses the mind of Christ. Because regeneration has occurred, the saint has a new capacity to think biblically. This new way of seeing life is possible on a daily basis because the saint's mind is renewed (Rom. 12:2; Eph. 4:23; 2 Cor. 4:16; Col. 3:10).

How does the spiritual man stay spiritual? The spiritual man can be likened to the fourth soil Jesus speaks about in Matthew 13. The fourth soil represents the heart that receives the seed (Word) and bears appropriate fruit. It is the heart that is quick to listen, slow to speak, and slow to anger (Js. 1:19–20).

The spiritual man strives to abide in fellowship with Christ. The spiritual man realizes that in and of himself, he cannot do anything that is profitable for the Kingdom or will turn the head of God in his favor. This abiding Jesus speaks of in John 15:5 is controlled by the spiritual man. Jesus always longs for intimate fellowship with His redeemed. When the spiritual man is utterly transparent in his relationship to Christ, Christ is most welcomed in the man's life. Christ is always present in the believer's life. But, if you please, Christ is crowded and finds possessions and events as competitors.

To prevent competitors, the spiritual man lives in James 1:25.

> But one who *looks* intently at the perfect law, the law of liberty, and *abides* by it, not having become a *forgetful* hearer but an *effectual* doer, this man will be blessed in what he does.

Notice the words I italicized. The spiritual man *looks* intently at the perfect law of liberty. This means the spiritual man stoops to a thing in order to look at it. When my children were growing up, I often would bend my knees so I could see the whites of their eyes as I spoke with them. When I did so, I had their undivided attention. The spiritual man looks into the perfect law of liberty so he is not distracted by anything or anyone else.

The spiritual man *abides*, which means to remain beside, to stay close to, or to continue to always be close and near. Nothing can pull him away from this exercise to cultivate his intimacy with his Savior. The spiritual man is not *forgetful* about what he sees or hears. In fact, he works very hard at retaining and performing biblical truth. He is an *effectual* doer. The word means strenuous labors or efforts, tirelessly and consistently practicing what he sees. He avoids being a hearer only.

The spiritual man can and often does sin. I do not want you to think that someone can attain a stature of spirituality and never sin. A spiritual man can sin in both omission and commission. When temptation lures or sin wins a temporary battle, the spiritual man follows 1 John 1:7. As he is walking with the Spirit, when temptation knocks on his heart's door or when sin momentarily wins a battle, the spiritual man has developed a sensitivity to walking in the light to maintain fellowship with others and God. Unlike the next two people, the flesh and babe, the spiritual man's conscience is sensitized to the very whisper of the Holy Spirit. He hears and does.

The Fleshly Man (3:1, 3)
The word "flesh" is used two ways in the Bible. The term is used to describe an unbeliever, as are such terms as old man, natural man, and Adamic nature. It is also used to describe an unrepentant believer practicing sin. Such is the case here by the term "brethren." What sins has Paul already written about that are the results of living by means of the flesh? Partiality, adultery, lawsuits, legalism and licensure, and disorderly table manners.

What are the characteristics of a fleshly man? There is the presence of jealousy. Jealousy is the evil desire to want something God has not given. There is the presence of strife. Fleshly saints are quarrelsome, argumentative, and contentious. Paul describes them as walking like mere men. Fleshly saints have returned to their former spiritual condition revealed by the way they act. Suppose a man gets marvelously saved. Prior to regeneration, he had a severe temper. After conversion, this man begins to grow. His temper is driven out by love, gentleness, and service to others. But one day, a situation occurs and his temper returns. Has he lost his salvation? No necessary, but he chose to give in to the old man who still resides within him.

Fleshly men draw from unbiblical source of wisdom (Js. 3:14–16). When this happens, unbiblical sources of wisdom lead to behavior that is undistinguishable from the world (Gal. 5:19–21). Sometimes it is most difficult to distinguish between the actions of a sinner and a fleshly saint. For the fleshly man, at the heart of the matter is selfishness.

What does a fleshly man need? The fleshly man needs pruning (John 15:2). The pruning of a fleshly man can help him become a spiritual man. The Spirit of God uses the Word of God to reveal an area of life that is displeasing to God within the fleshly man. The fleshly man must have a proper response to the *kergama*. Js. 1:19–20 is a warning to all Christians that when we hear the Word of God we must be quick to hear, slow to speak, and slow to anger. Oftentimes, the fleshly man is slow to hear, quick to speak, and quick to anger. The fleshly man must become a doer of the word and not just a hearer (Js. 1:22). The fleshly man can become distracted, like the first man looking in the mirror, and forget what he should do. For the fleshly man to grow in becoming a spiritual man, he needs to be under the leadership of the Spirit so eliminate the deeds of the flesh and produce the fruit of the Spirit.

The Babe 3:1–2
What are the characteristics of a babe or a new believer? The Greek word means infant, little child, minor, not of full age. A babe or new believer is single-minded, unskilled, and untaught. Babes desire milk to drink. Their senses are not developed to take in solid food. Their spiritual appetite needs expanding and developing.

Like an infant, spiritual babes require continuous attention, care, and nurturing. They are very dependent upon others. They are often messy. They get into trouble because they are learning. They have a desire to learn and grow, but some of their ways to grow are more harmful than helpful. They need to be spoon fed, and they frequently cause interruptions.

What does a babe need to develop into a spiritual person? Referring again to the parable of the sower and the seed, the babe or new believer can be likened to the second soil. This soil receives the word and grows up quickly. But when pressures of life come, they do not know how to use their faith properly and they wither. I Peter 2:2 reminds those caring for these new believers to help them cultivate their spiritual appetite. Before conversion, they fed on the philosophies of the world, they dined on their emotional responses to life and disappointments, and Satan set a banquet of lies before them. The cravings for such delicacies are not easily removed. The palate has been seasoned for the standby spiritual food, and the new spiritual food is foreign, isn't easy to swallow, and at times is unsavory. But we need to help them to taste and see that the Lord is good.

In Acts 2:42, new believers need to devote themselves to some new spiritual exercises. They must join in the teaching, fellowship, communion, and prayer of their brothers and sisters in the faith. They must understand that this new spiritual journey has a singular goal and that goal is for them to be made into a disciple (Matt. 28:19–20). This discipleship process is designed to be a sweet partnership between an older man and a younger man according to Titus 2:1–2. We see the sweetness of this between Barnabas with John Mark, Moses with Joshua, and Paul with Timothy, Silas, and Luke, to name a few.

Visualize for a moment, four chairs in front of you. Each chair is labeled as follows: natural man, spiritual man, fleshly man, and babe. If I were to ask you to sit in the chair that best represents you right now, which one would it be?

It is easy to slide from chair to chair—spiritual to fleshly or fleshly to spiritual or babe to fleshly or fleshly to babe. From this chapter, do you acknowledge that you know you are the natural man? Has your heart been warmed? Do you want to change chairs? Then renounce your sin, believe on the Lord Jesus Christ as Savior and Lord, and commit yourself to becoming a follower of Christ. Find a local church that preaches the Word and that will help you grow. Tell someone of your new found Friend, Jesus.

If you were to sit in the chairs labeled babe or fleshly, God has outlined biblical action steps for you to take. Re-read those sections. Ask the Lord to help you change and grow. Find a local church that will provide instruction and counsel.

If you believe you are a spiritual man, Psalm 1 reminds you that you must be bearing fruit in each season of your life. This happens as you abide.

I Can't Handle Another "Let's Be Friends" Talk
Navigating the Landmines of a Breakup

We have all witnessed it. Many of us have firsthand experience with it. The hot tears streaming down our cheeks or the intense introspective questioning. The irrational statements such as "I just can't live without him or her," or the despair, despondency, and depression. The near emotional immobilization by calling in sick to work or the disappearing act from religious and social communities. The despondency conveyed by our body language, the myopic vision of futility in just living life today, and the monologue conversations with whoever will listen as we search for the reason why the relationship ended like it did.

This lifestyle may continue for weeks or months depending on the mental, emotional, and spiritual condition of the person. Loved ones will attempt to provide guidance, small group leaders will offer counsel and prayer, and even the pastor may suggest resources to help heal the broken heart. In some cases, all of these wonderful resources lie dormant because the wounded person only wants to know why the relationship ended and what he or she can do differently to restore the relationship.

We see these people in the marketplace; they are our co-workers. We see them in church; they are our sisters and brothers in Christ. We see them in small groups, discipleship classes, and mentoring relationships.

What can we do to help our single friends who are agonizing over a breakup? What counsel can we offer to them without sounding trite? Are there lessons God desires the singles to learn who is involved in a breakup? Is there evidence of God's sovereign protection preventing deeper wounds and hurts? How can we help the single make sense of it all?

In this chapter, it is my intention to address several fundamental areas. First, what are the common reasons for breakups? Second, what are the typical responses to a breakup? This chapter is designed to help singles. But there are three types of singles according to Barna research group. There are those who have never been married, those who are divorced, and those who are widowed. This material is targeted for those who have never been married. The principles, however, can be applied to the other two categories.

Reasons for breakups
Immaturity
No one is perfectly mature in every aspect of life. We all have areas that are under construction and development. What I am referring to is a specific area of immaturity that handicaps the relationship. This level of immaturity is a warning sign of a serious character flaw.

For example, one person in the relationship is always easily offended. The partner innocently says something and the other takes it as a putdown. It can progress to the point that the one partner is unable to be him- or herself for fear of offending the other. Silence is perceived as being upset, and honest, open communication is viewed as insensitive to the need of being accepted for who they are.

Or, one person is spontaneous. This is seen in his or her spending patterns. If they want something or want to give something to the other, he or she purchases the item without forethought as to the cost, how he or she will pay for it, or what steps will be required for the mounting indebtedness and its future impact. "I want to be pleased or to please you," is the motto of life. So, immaturity is a reason why many couples break up.

Incompatibility
The word means mutually exclusive or antagonistic qualities or things. It means not in harmony or agreement. Initially, the strong differences are fun. They are the spark that keeps the relationship interesting. They say opposites attract, we must fit into that mold. The compatibility is the extreme differences. But at the heart of what keeps such people together, until the breakup, is more than likely physical attraction or the sense of competition.

But as time marches on, these strong differences become points of contention. They slowly mount inner irritations and frustrations. They lead to arguments. Sorrow may be part of the process to mend the fragile relationship, but the wounds are deep and the healing is superficial, like applying a Band-Aid. Eventually, communication is strained. Each wonders what they see in each other. The relationship breaks up. Hindsight wants to blame the other person for being stubborn and viewing other's opinions as a personal threat to his or her personhood.

Uncommon denominator
This is lack of deeper interests in life. They both have some common interests. They may like bowling, hiking, or going to sci-fi movies. But beyond that, one may have a strong community activist interest, while the other believes in not interfering with the course of human events. Or one is deeply religious and serves actively in his or her church, while the other was raised in a nominal denomination that is more social than spiritual.

The deep fabric of life shaping events is no more profound than the compatibility of Star War fans and Star Trek fans. There is no common denominator.

Lack of mutual direction in life
Often this is honestly dealt with much too far into the relationship. One is pursuing her law degree. The other is pursuing his degree as a medical doctor. His expectations are a little house in the suburbs with a picket fence and 2.6 children with a stay-at-home wife and mother. Her expectations are marriage, no kids, and involvement with representing and fighting for inner city families who are forsaken and abused by the system.

She wants to live by her work; he wants to live in the quiet and safe suburbs. He wants children, she doesn't. If he gets a partnership in another city, he is willing to relocate the family. She cannot leave her clients.

Noncommittal
How long is long enough before the woman can expect a marriage proposal? How long is too long for a relationship without commitment?

A proposal should not come until there is as complete knowledge of the other person as humanly possible. Depending on age (older), it could be around six months. For younger couples, it may be wise to have at least a year.

However, there have been known to be cases where a couple has dated for literally years. One or the other is content with the relationship and doesn't want any pressure about marriage. Things are going well. "Why rock the boat with talking of marriage? We both are enjoying this season of our life." But in reality, one wants desperately to be married. Family, friends, and the culture are applying pressure on one or the other. "Why hasn't he proposed yet? Is there something wrong with him?"

Sometimes what is the hindrance is a commitment to care for an aging parent. Marriage would sidetrack him or her from keeping this commitment. A parent may take precedence over the proposal. Hence, one or the other issues an ultimatum. The other does not meet the ultimatum, and the relationship ends. Then, there are thoughts of why I invested so much time into him or her. I feel like I have wasted half of my life in this relationship. What do I have to show for it—a stuffed teddy bear!

Control issues
Someone's thoughts, words, and actions must always be the same as the other. Differences of thoughts or feelings are viewed as threatening to the relationship. One person struggles with security in the relationship because he or she views the differences as a sign of waning affection.

Another form of control is jealousy. One person must always know at all times exactly what is happening in the life of the other. Phone calls, who he or she spoke to and for how long and why; why it took him or her so long to get home; why he or she did not tell the other he or she was going out afterwards with friends—and who those friends were, what they did, and when he or she got home.

Control issues suffocate a relationship. It places unnecessary strain on the relationship. It is stifling. It can be likened to living in a burning building where there is no flame, only daily breathing of noxious smoke. It chokes the life out of any relationship.

Forms of substance abuse
We will primarily refer to alcohol or drugs. My comments will be general enough to include both. First, one should understand that each partner is an individual who enters into a relationship with, hopefully, uncompromising values, and beliefs. Therefore, both should determine what their tolerance policy is on alcohol or drugs.

Substance dependency leads to other behavioral problems that have an effect on the relationship. It may result in physical abuse, certain forms of violent behavior, verbal abuse, manipulation, and solicitation to unlawful acts. Substance abuse is a form of escape or avoidance. It is the symptom of deeper character blemishes that require substantial counseling.

Too often in counseling, I hear a spouse lament the woes of living with a substance abuser. Yet during such times of investigation, it is revealed that he or she recognized this pattern or willfully chose to overlook the defect.

Emotional instability
Again, no one is perfectly stable with his or her emotions. We are looking at extremes or repetitive emotional problems.

Because I am biblical counselor, my position toward emotional problems is considered narrow, but I consider it biblical. I could enter into a lengthy teaching in this area, but I hope the following comments will be sufficient.

Unless the medical community can specifically identify the cause of the emotional imbalance, one should consider the behavior as an expression of a broken relationship with God and his or her fellow man.

Couples break up, and rightfully so, should break up if one or the other displays anger to manipulate the other. Or the anger is such that it instills fear for the other's safety. Or if the anger is directed at other people or things. His or her anger is destructive and harmful.

Or, if he or she is petrified by worry, fear, or anxiety. He or she can perform basic level living (going to work), but will avoid socialization, church functions or family functions. He or she may have been hospitalized and might be on antipsychotic or antidepressant medications.

This relationship should be evaluated carefully, for it can be extremely demanding of time, resources, and effort.

Parental disapproval
Should parents have input about whom their child sees? Especially if they are in their twenties? When does parental authority cease? Each single within their parental structure must grapple with those difficult questions.

However, the issue at hand is if the parents disapprove of the one they are dating. This can be a source of break ups. Parents have a level of maturity and age about them because of living life. They themselves probably have experienced similar relational challenges. Perhaps you are a younger sibling, and they have already navigated these waters with an older sibling. Maybe it is because you are knowingly violating a family value you have been taught.

Most parents who disapprove do so in an effort to direct their child to God's best. Although you may feel they are picky or controlling your life, in reality they sense you are settling with someone inferior; you have lowered your sights.

Peer pressure disapproval
Sometimes friends are more objective about the relationship than you are. They have nothing to gain or lose by telling you the truth about him or her. They only want your best. They are demonstrating great friendship qualities.

They might point out some serious defects that in your starstruck, moonlight eyes you are overlooking. The little things you now laugh at will eventually become gigantic irritations that often are irreconcilable.

Following counsel
Some relational breakups are the result of seeking out counseling from someone you trust. You are candidly honest. The person carefully listens to the pros and cons of the relationship, noting your concerns. Based on the preliminary data you share, they offer you their insights as to what you should do.

As a counselor, couples thinking about engagement come to me wanting pre-engagement counsel. Each share their concerns and the problems they are facing. They share their feelings and what they are attracted to in the other person. And after some time of asking questions and probing for answers, I have recommended that at the present time it would be unwise for them to continue pursuing the relationship.

I can remember one young man who was devastated by such counsel. But he followed counsel, sought personal help in areas noted as serious character flaws, demonstrated great change and progress in serving the Lord, and he and the young lady were later (about one year or so) married and doing well. Following counsel may result in a breakup.

Major character flaw
Anger. Anger is destructive. Listen to these two illustrations.

> During World War II, the U.S. submarine Tang surfaced under the cover of darkness to fire upon a large Japanese convoy off the coast of China. Since previous raids had left the American vessel with only eight torpedoes, the accuracy of every shot was absolutely essential. The first seven missiles were right on target; but when the eighth was launched, it suddenly deviated and headed right back at their own ship. The emergency alarm to submerge rang out, but it was too late. Within a matter of seconds, the U.S. sub received a direct hit and sank almost instantly.

> I have heard that if a rattlesnake is cornered, it can become so frenzied that it will accidentally bite itself with its deadly fangs. In the same way, when a person harbors hatred and resentment in his heart, the poison of his own malice often hurts him.

What are some telltale signs of a person who is dominated by anger? Muscular tension (possibly clenched fists and/or jaws, facial grimaces, other muscular tension). Feelings of frustration, irritation, agitation, and/or annoyance. Ruminating on angry thoughts, which may include distorted thoughts about the other person and his/her intentions. Other tell-tale signs are:

1. Pacing around
2. Name-calling, making insulting remarks
3. Inordinate amount of time to calm down
4. Inordinate amount of time to receive counsel
5. Denial of being angry
6. Smoothing over the explosive episode with platitudes

This character flaw can result in a spouse becoming a batterer. Recognize the signs and thank God for showing you the way of escape.

A spendthrift person simply loves to spend money. Often it is on someone else he or she wants to impress. At other times, the focus of spending may be selfishness or staying in step with an elite crowd in which he or she desires to be a part.

This type of person may be communicating several things. First, they are insecure. They compensate by purchasing things for others to secure the person's favor, or they purchase for themselves so they can fit in. Second, they are self-centered. They believe they should be noticed and the center of someone else's universe, so they spend to impress. Third, they want to feel good about themselves. New things create a certain feeling for them, a feeling of joy fueled by the compliments of others. They forget about their inadequacies temporarily. But it will always be newer, better, and more of to maintain the illusiveness of this good feeling.

In a possessive situation, one person is compelled to know everything that the other person is doing. He or she wants to know who the other spoke with, for how long, about what, and why the person even talked with another. One wants to know when the other goes out, where he or she is going, with whom, why he or she is going, and why the other was not invited.

There is an increase in phone calls, a decrease in spending time with family and friends, a decline in old familiar enjoyable activities because he or she doesn't like them, increased emails and text messaging, endless and often unenjoyable time spent together doing little to promote the relationship into deeper maturity but resulting in fighting and making up.

Sometimes there is guilt over levels of premarital sex. Each single person knows how far he or she will go in the physical relationship. But each single may or may not have established how to hold the line in their mind.

Some singles have been raised in an evangelical home where open discussion about the relationship between a man and a woman has been taught, while other singles have been raised in overly permissive homes.

When two singles become an item, these differences are often noticed quickly. One equates levels of the physical dimension with love and acceptance. The other understands the pursuit of the physical as lust and a warning sign to guard themselves.

A single that compromises his or her higher moral code will experience guilt. Initially, the guilt can be overpowered by justifications or rationalizations such as, "It only happened once," "It won't happen again," or, "We didn't go all the way!"

When he or she initiates any sexual advances, God is revealing the hidden, lustful character of him or her. You are spiritually unyoked. Flee immorality!

Sometimes there are unrealistic expectations. An expectation is something hoped for. It is something looked for. It is an eye on the future. It means a probably occurrence, considered likely to happen.

Unrealistic expectations are just that. They are not possible to achieve without bending the other person. He or she is not capable of performing in a certain way. He or she wants the other to be like someone else. There is a comparison. "If you were only like my father," or, "My mother always did this. I don't know why you can't!"

Unrealistic expectations ignore the God-given talents, skills and abilities God gave to the other, reject the other, and seek to remold that person into the image of the one with the expectations.

You can spot this by listening carefully to the comments expressed such as, "If you would just … then I would know you love me," "If you wouldn't do this or that, then I would know that I am important to you." Unrealistic expectations are rooted in conditional love.

Sometimes a partner is discontent. "I am not satisfied with my station in life. I am resentful that I am still single, without someone, and everybody I know as someone, is engaged, or married." The words also include the idea of grievance. "I am basically unhappy with God. He is displeasing me right now. I should be married by now. My biological clock is ticking. I am getting past my prime."

You may be discontent because you think God did you a disservice when He created you. If you only had this, or if you did not have that, then you could attract others to you. You may be discontent because you feel God has forgotten you. Somehow He has lost you on His radar of relationships.

It may be unrelated areas of discontent, such as work, church, family, or friends that compound the problem of being single or recovering from a breakup.

Typical Responses
Disbelief
The thought and feeling that "this can't be happening to me!" The bewilderment of attempting to sort through all the events leading to the breakup and searching for some explanation. A sidebar: Many breakups are rooted in falsehood. The reason for the breakup is not

truthful in an effort to prevent further hurt to the other person or to avoid personal attacks by the other person.

Mate hopping
This may take place because the identity of one person was so intertwined with the other he or she feels absolutely lost without someone to be with. Some call this "rebounding" and more often than not this creates complicating problems. Emotional and rational stability are not clear and concise. Mate hopping can also happen in the attempt to make the former person jealous that he or she moved on with life so quickly. It is a manipulative attempt at revenge.

Hatred toward the person and his or her friends
"How dare they dump me," she says in anger. And the war of words, gossip, slander, and rude behavior begins. One struggles to be civil with the other. When with friends, the person who was left behind finds comfort and solace in rehearsing all the bad points of the relationship, declaring he or she is glad that it is over. The one comes to believe that his or her friends contributed to or were the cause of the breakup. The ripple effects of hatred and bitterness stretch far and wide, often leaving a wake of unnecessary destruction.

Anger
This is self-explanatory: anger towards him or her, his or her friends, or his or her family. The anger is evident by the person's words, tone, and nonverbal body language. Hardened facial lines become etched on his or her face. The friendliness disappears and is replaced with scowls.

Fear
There may be a combination of things creating an atmosphere of fear in the person's life. Fear of not being loved by someone, especially that someone who just ended the relationship. Fear that something is wrong with me. Fear that I am getting older. Fear that I will never get married. Fear that if I get married I will be too old to have children. Fear that others know of the breakup, and imagining what they might know. Fear that he or she has painted me in a bad light. Fear of embarrassment in meeting his or her family and friends. Fear that

I have to see him or her at small group, or he or she continues to be a co-worker. Fear.

Manipulation
Tears. Hot, steamy tears that stain my pillowcase at night. Emotional and often uncontrollable weeping during the breakup or subsequent conversations. This type of behavior may raise concerns for the one who initiated the breakup over the welfare of the other. So much so that he or she may recant and resume the relationship.

Promises
"It's just not working out" is not sufficient for the one hearing those words. The prying begins. The onslaught of questions, probing to discover the real reason for the breakup. Constant inquiring. Snooping by inquisition of others. This is an attempt to find reunion by making promises of change. "I know I have a temper, I see it now thanks to you. I promise I will get help for this. I don't want to lose you!" Or, "I can change that, I really can. Please give me a chance. If you really love me, you will give me a chance."

Threats
"I have never loved anyone like you before. I don't think I can go on without you. I need you." This could be allusion to self-destructive thoughts or direct statements of suicidal ideology. Sometimes the threats are meant to disgrace or expose the other person. He or she has something on the other that if revealed could be very damaging.

Stalking
Any of the above mentioned responses can take a serious mental or emotion leap resulting in stalking. Stalking is where people will not accept a breakup and uses much of their time, energy, and resources to restore the relationship. At first, it might be showering the person with gifts or cards. When this fails, then threats, vandalism of personal property, sudden appearances and the like occur. In extreme cases, people become so intimidated they file a police report and take out an order of protection. In very extreme cases, some result in the murder of the person or murder-suicide situation.

Introspective analysis
"What's wrong with me?" "What did I do?" "What did he or she really expect?" "Maybe if I ..."

Heart Issues

Discontent

The Bible only uses the word "discontented" once. It is with reference to what type of men surrounded David when he was a refugee. The idea is some of these men were unhappy with the actions of King Saul and the conditions created by his actions and policies.

We all know people who are discontent and believe that if they find "Mr. Right," life would be fulfilling. It may be young women who are discontent with their father's household rules. It may be feeling like a fifth wheel when he or she is around paired-off friends. It may be dissatisfaction with some physical appearance. Then someone comes along who accepts him or her as they are, but one means it only as a friendship, the other as a love relationship.

Discontent, for the believer, is a rejection of God's handiwork and sovereignty. It is a belief, ignited by feelings, that somehow God is not paying attention to his or her needs. It is a feeling that God has forgotten him or her.

Impatience

Impatience is a desire out of control. It is a longing without restraint, a passion for something or someone that disregards and defies logical and common sense.

Impatience often acts from emotions or contaminated reason. It rearranges the available facts to fit its presuppositions. Impatience justifies its course of action when challenged. It points to circumstances. "I know he is not saved yet, but with time I know I can love him to the Lord." "No, you're right. She does have some flaws, but I'm no prize either. We can grow out of them together." "Yes, he drinks, but only occasionally. He has promised me he is not going to drink anymore. I love him, so I must believe him." "Okay, she lost her temper once. But she was provoked. She knows it's wrong. It's under control and it won't happen again." "I don't think there is anyone out there who meets my criteria. I think I need to lower my standards. Mr. Sir Lancelot doesn't exist. Besides, I'm not getting any younger."

Church, peer, or societal expectations
Biological clock ticking. Often this is a heart issue, though not verbalized. The medical community declares that there is a prime age for bearing children. After that age, the risk factors of birth defects rise. So women nearing the prime child bearing years may be more eager for male relationships and the prospects of a marriage proposal, making serious compromises in their standards to be married and have children. No doubt, the risks rise after a certain age for child bearing. But, this fear comes from an over-generalization. Many studies show that women are having children later in life without any birth risks.

Should be married by now
Bless grandma's pea-pickin' heart, the well meaning Sunday school teacher, or Aunt Veranda! Just because they were married at seventeen and had six kids in annual succession does not mean this is a pattern to be duplicated by every young women in the family!

"You are so lovely. Why hasn't some young man snatched you up?" "Because it is evidently not God's will for me to be snatched up right now!" The pressure of well meaning friends and family members can be too much.

"Are you gay?" This is blatant, but inferred by some. If you are not married by a certain age, maybe something is wrong with you. "You do like boys, don't you, Sue?" There is nothing wrong with being single. There is nothing wrong with waiting for God to fill your non-negotiable character quality list. We have discount quantity grocery stores, such as Aldi's, Sam's, and Costco. Don't shop at these stores for a life's mate!

Not knowing or accepting God's will
Many times when I am counseling a woman who is bemoaning her singleness or recent breakup, I ask her, "How do you know God wants you to be married?" Most often she replies, "I don't want to be alone

for the rest of my life." "I feel God wants me to be married." "He says, 'It is not good for a man to be alone.'"

"I" is often the problem. A preconceived idea was planted and grows with each relationship and is cultivated by each circumstance. He or she has not studied the Word of God to determine the will of God.

The Bible speaks of those who are not married. Some are not married by choice, some are not married by dedication to divine service, and some are not married because of God's timing. But what is Paul's instruction to the single? Paul admonishes them to be active in the Lord's work. They have such unique opportunities that those who are married do not have. They are not distracted by marriage. Therefore, instead of looking and searching for a relationship, look and search for ways to serve the Lord.

Redirected anger
Wanting to leave the house—escapism. I have alluded to this earlier. But it bears repeating. The heartbreak of a young person who feels the only way to escape the unbearable rules and regulations of his or her home is to find a relationship and get married. He or she is so angry with a parent he or she pursues headlong this destructive course of action. It is my belief that the parents should approve any opposite sex relationship, and the parents must bless any marriage proposals.

Misconceptions about marriage
"Marriage will bring me ultimate happiness. Marriage will remove all the woes, evils, and hardships of life. My problems at work, home, and school will disappear if I only get married. We will be like Cinderella and Prince Charming." Marriage brings joy, not happiness. With joy, comes sorrow. Marriage is both. It is not a utopia of myth and wuffle dust!

"Marriage will fulfill my every wish and desire." These are unrealistic expectations. No one person can completely and consistently fill another's wishes and desires. This is humanly impossible. Why? Because we are prone to selfishness. He and she have feet of clay. Disappointments -are part of growing healthy relationships. There is only one who can fulfill every wish and desire. That person is Christ Jesus.

"Marriage eliminates my current problems." I knew one women who came to see me. She was engaged to be married. Her church was concerned about the relationship. Her parents were encouraging the marriage. She was emotionally unstable. She was losing her reputation as a good worker. She did not show up for work. She did not call in. She told me she was getting married soon, so her lack of performance was okay. Her husband was a professional and would make good money. She could just stay home and the pressures of co-worker relationships would cease.

"Now is the best time for me to be married. After all, I think I am ready." Many of the previous heart issues discussed would contribute to this way of thinking.

To fit in
"All my friends are getting married." "All of my friends 'have someone.'" "I hate going to parties or church social functions because everyone but me is paired off."

Not to disappoint the parents
Well meaning parents can be unknowingly cruel. They want their son or daughter to be happy. They think being happy means getting married. They want their son or daughter to get married so the parents can have grandchildren. Young people should not get involved with in a relationship for the purpose of getting married to provide grandchildren to their parents.

Self-worth (loser without)
This person's identity is wrapped up in the other's person's approval of them. "The existence of a relationship with the opposite sex establishes my worth and value because someone likes me, wants to hang out with me, takes me places, spends money on me, calls me, and says he or she loves me." The heartbreak comes when these things stop because the relationship has ceased.

Responding to what God is doing
Knowing and accepting His will for your life right now!
But what is God's will? God's will for you right now is whatever you do. Whether you eat or drink, do all for the glory of God. God's will is for you to glorify Him in everything.

What is God's will? For you to obey Him, to do what you know to be right, just, and holy before Him right now! James says that to him who knows to do good and does not to it, to him it is sin.

What is God's will? For you to prove you are His disciple by bearing much fruit (John 15:8). What is God's will? For you to bring forth the fruits of the Spirit (Gal. 5:22–23). What is God's will? For you to exercise wisdom from above, not below (James 4). What is God's will? For you to redeem the time for the days are evil (Eph. 5). What is God's will? "And this is the will of God, even your sanctification that you abstain for sexual immorality." What is the will of God? That you visit the widows and orphans in their distress, you control your tongue, and you remain unstained by the world (James 1).

Frequently in relationships, biblical injunctions like the ones cited above fall by the wayside because the relationship turns inward and becomes exclusive, not outward, upward, and inclusive.

Sometimes God must interrupt a relationship because it is becoming too parasitic. The God of sovereignty and human relationships is excluded. So God rearranges the relationship to make it perfectly clear who must be first and foremost. This is similar to how God tested Abraham to see if Abraham still loved God more than the gift—Isaac.

"How should I respond to this breakup?" Go back, re-familiarize yourself with the will of God, and resume performing it right now.

Loving God instead of being angry with God.
Do you believe that God loves you? Do you believe His love for you is pure? Do you believe that God's love for you is without malice,

hatred, or harm? Do you believe that God's every thought and intention of His heart are focused upon you for your best?

Then rein in your feelings of anger and chose to believe God loves you through this breakup. The only ulterior motive God has which motivates His every action is your holiness before Him. His love for you wants to protect you from becoming contaminated by the world.

Often a father's love is viewed as harmful, cruel, and uncaring. Children view their parent's "no"s as restrictive and insensitive. But over time, the child grows to be a teen and then an adult, and he or she now understand that "no"s issued were out of love and for his or her welfare. It was not always easy to accept or welcomed, but it was for his or her good.

Trusting God rather than fighting God
We fight when we don't get what we think we deserve. I remember vividly fighting with God. I was in a relationship, and it was disintegrating quickly. We were engaged to be married. Many did not approve of the union. But we were pressing forward. Then it ended. She went to work that morning. I stayed in the apartment to pack and leave for out of state. I clearly remember arguing, crying, pleading, and fighting with God to restore this sinful union. He did not, and I am so thankful He didn't. I was not trusting God. Once I began to trust God, to walk in His ways, and to acknowledge Him in everything, He gave me what I truly needed. Her name is Carolyn, my bride of thirty years, a faithful, honest companion.

When you start trusting God, an overwhelming sense of His peace floods your soul, and one day you will be surprised by joy, as C.S. Lewis writes.

What lessons is God trying to teach you?
God's actions are not random. They are deliberate and purposeful. Each divine decision has meaning and direction. If we are angry at God and fighting with Him, we may miss the important lessons He has designed to be revealed to us.

What lessons is God trying to teach you? Did you neglect personal spiritual disciplines because of this relationship? Did you isolate yourself from others? Were you careless in your responsibilities? Did you compromise your standard of purity? Was there something about this relationship that troubled your conscience but you ignored it? Did this other person become an idol in your life? Did your life revolve around him or her? Did you act like an old married couple, fighting and arguing only to makeup? How did this relationship make you a stronger Christian? How did the relationship spur you on to good works? Did you find yourself praying or repenting?

In what way is God trying to protect you from some danger you cannot see or you chose to ignore and deny?

When God does something that we perceive as negative, we must affirm that God sees something we cannot see. This is His way of protecting us.

We might not be able to recognize it because we are too emotionally involved. We might not be able to observe it because we are in denial. We hope that what we are seeing will go away and not be a problem.

But the believer understands that God is omniscient. He is all knowing. He knows the actual and the possible. He is able to look into the human heart and know it like no one else. He tries and tests the human heart's motivation.

God's "no"s are just as good as His "yes"s and "wait"s. We should rejoice that what we cannot see, and what we perceive as hurtful, are God's hidden blessings revealed. Time will reveal the joy of trusting, loving, and obeying God. What I saw as good, God saw as destructive and removed it from my childish and selfish desires.

In what ways has this relationship changed your God-ward focus to being earthbound?

One of the refrains in the book of Ecclesiastes is "under the sun," and "vanity of vanities." Here is a king, given a great spiritual gift, and he uses it in the pursuit of pleasure and satisfaction. He was earthbound. Just read the book and record all the earthly activities he engaged in seeking happiness, a happiness already given to him by Jehovah.

Here is a practical exercise. Make a list of everything you were involved with that was Godward prior to meeting him or her. Now, with all honesty and integrity, cross off all Godward focus that this relationship replaced. For example: Prayer and Bible study daily from 5:15—6:00 a.m. Crossed off because I couldn't get up because I was too tired from the date the evening before. Meeting with small group replaced by spending time with him or her. That was the only time during the week he or she was available. Unable to meet consistently with my accountability partner because I used that time to talk to him or her.

Since God is sovereign, can you see His sovereign intervention in this breakup? One other thought I might add to this area is, "How many opportunities did God present to you to end this relationship, but you didn't?" I think breakups become more difficult and painful because we finally realize we should have obeyed God much earlier.

Learning that waiting on God is difficult but will ultimately bring out the best rewards.
Do you remember as a child your parents or older siblings talking about Christmas, and how excited you became? If you were like me, you probably had a difficult time comprehending time. You may have thought that Christmas was tomorrow. Later, as you became older, you realized that it was still several weeks off.

God promised Noah that He was going to send a flood to destroy the wickedness of humanity. Noah was commanded to build an Ark, which he did for 120 years. He also preached that length of time God's impending doom and righteousness. Only Noah's wife, his three sons and their wives, and Noah himself enter the safety of the Ark.

God showed Joseph his prominent role through two specific dreams. Yet Joseph was envied by his brothers, sold to the Midianites, then to the Egyptians, imprisoned under false charges before God exalted him as promised.

David was anointed king before his brothers during the reign of King Saul. It would be years before David ascended to the throne.

Abraham and Sarah were promised a child to continue their lineage and the covenant of God. It would be twenty-five years before Isaac was born, and they would be eligible for social security!

Consider the following Scriptures:

> For Your salvation I wait, O Lord (Gen. 49:18).
>
> Indeed, none of those who wait for You will be ashamed; those who deal treacherously without cause will be ashamed (Ps. 25:3).
>
> Let integrity and uprightness preserve me, for I wait for You (Ps. 25:21).
>
> And now, Lord, for what do I wait? My hope is in You (Ps. 39:7).
>
> I wait for the Lord, my soul does wait, and in His word do I hope (Ps. 130:5).
>
> Yet those who wait for the Lord will gain new strength; they will mount up with wings like eagles, they will run and not get tired, they will walk and not become weary (Isa. 40:31).
>
> The Lord is good to those who wait for Him, to the person who seeks Him (Lam. 3:25).
>
> Therefore, return to your God, observe kindness and justice, and wait for your God continually (Hos 12:6).
>
> But as for me, I will watch expectantly for the Lord; I will wait for the God of my salvation. My God will hear me (Mic. 7:7).

Practical life application

1. How do I deal with my feelings?
2. How do I deal with my loneliness?

3. How do I deal with my anger and bitterness?
4. What if I am not convinced we should be apart?
5. What if there really was something I did, that if I corrected, we could get back together?
6. Here is an acronym that answers each of those questions:
    a. F.A.I.T.H.
    b. How do I deal with my feelings? **Focus**. Instead of focusing on how you feel, focus on what God requires of you. Looking to Jesus the author and finisher of your faith. Focus on what He has done for you, and what He wants from you.
    c. What if I am not convinced we should be apart? **Accept**. Accept that you have finite wisdom. Accept you are related to God who is infinite in wisdom. Accept that God's every thought and intention of His heart is for your wellbeing. Accept this decision as the will of God, which is good, perfect, and acceptable.
    d. How do I deal with my loneliness? **Involvement**. Loneliness can isolate you. Loneliness only sees how miserable you are. Loneliness is introspective. Loneliness is a decision not to serve. I deal with my loneliness by returning to involvement. It may be returning to Bible study, small group, accountability group, church, or social activities with friends. Involvement is reaching out to others and not having to be reached out to.
    e. How do I deal with my anger and bitterness? **Trade**. When I use the word "trade," consider the implications of exchange, or put off and put on. I must trade my anger for peace and my bitterness for joy. This is an act of my will. I must choose to do this as often as these feelings or thoughts encroach upon my living for Jesus.
    f. What if there were something that if I fixed, we could get back together again? **Humility**. If you have a character flaw that result in the breakup, then your motivation to address

it must be to please God, not to get the him or her back. Humility recognizes that we need the help of our divine Savior to address an area of our lives that is displeasing to Him and harmful to relationships. By His grace, I submit willingly to the Spirit's refinement so I can serve God more effectively.

7. So as practically as I can, faith is the solution as an acronym for dealing with the realities of life after a breakup. Without minimizing faith, it is part of the divine trio in Corinthians (faith, hope, and love). Faith is essential to please God. My Christian life illustrates a growing faith as described by Paul—faith to faith to faith.

I know how the heart feels when a relationship ends. I have experienced the hurt, pain, and tears. Everything I have said in this chapter, I know firsthand. But what I know more, and what I trust more, and what I choose more is to trust, obey, and follow my loving Savior who cares immensely for me, whose every action is for my best and whom I can trust.

Okay, God, I've Got a Few Questions I'd Like to Ask You

Asking God the Tough Questions in Life

When I was a child, there use to be a commercial on advertising Morton Salt. Its slogan was, "When It Rains, It Pours!" People feel that way when they are having a bad day. One illustration I ran across said, "You know it's going to be a bad day when …

- … You wake up face down on the pavement."
- … You see a *60 Minutes* news team waiting in your office."
- … Your birthday cake collapses from the weight of the candles."
- … You turn on the news and they're showing emergency routes out of the city."
- … Your twin sister forgets your birthday."
- … You wake up to discover that your waterbed broke, and then you realized you don't have a waterbed."
- … Your horn goes off accidentally and remains stuck as you follow a group of Hell's Angels on the freeway."

On a more serious note, there are times in your life when you feel like things are never going to change. Like:

- When a substance abuser breaks another promise.
- When there is continual refusal by a spouse to join in seeking marital intervention.
- When there is prolonged opposition by in-laws over your decision about alternative schooling.
- When a teen's rebellion and disrespect has intensified over the past four years.
- When another voicemail message says, "Thank you for your interest, but we have filled the position."

- When there is growing frustration and sense of isolation as one family member cares for an aging parent alone.
- When your boss is a real jerk and you're in a deadend job—you can't move up and you can't move out because you are at that age of life.

These, and many more real life situations, raise some tough questions we'd like to ask God or even to fellow Christians, but we're afraid to ask. We've been told that such rhetoric is unholy, offensive, and challenging an Almighty God! Questions like:

1. How much longer will this go on? When will it be over?
2. Does God really care? Where is God?
3. Why doesn't it work? I mean, what the preacher keeps preaching about? It's not working for me!
4. Will my situation really change? Will it be any better? Is there really hope? Is there really a light at the end of the tunnel, and it's not the express train from downtown Chicago to Lombard, Illinois?

Let's consider some preliminary observations from Psalm 13. David is the author. We are unable to pinpoint the exact occasion of his affliction. It is reasonable to conclude that it was when David was a refugee from Saul. Notice the intensity of the affliction as noted in the phrase "How long."

This psalm can be broken into a three-fold outline:

1. David's perspective, verses 1–2
2. David's petition, verses 3–4
3. David's praise, verses 5–6

The first question David asks is, "How Long, O Lord?" This question can be rephrased, "How much longer will this go on? I can't take much more!"

This issue is time. The phrase "how long" recorded fifty-four times. It is recorded of God speaking to man. It is recorded of man addressing God.

Because the issue is time and because we are finite, we grow impatient. Time becomes a measurement of activity and productivity. When time passes with no apparent change to our situation or circumstances, we grow impatient. What we fail to remember is God is in charge of all time (His sovereignty) and God is outside of time (transcendent).

We are a society that unable to deal with time. This is evident by the following expectations.

- Guaranteed ten-minute oil changes
- Microwave meals
- Minute Maid Rice
- One-hour photo developing
- Express checkout lines
- Speed Pass at Mobil
- I-Pass on most toll ways
- One-hour dry cleaning
- Priceline.com for airline shopping
- Peapod for online grocery shopping delivery

Revelation 6:10 tells us that God is outside of time. The passing of time means that God is accomplishing His purposes and His will.

> And they cried out with a loud voice, saying, "How long, O Lord, holy and true, will You refrain from judging and avenging our blood on those who dwell on the earth?"

2 Peter 3:8–9 tells us that not one of God's promises will fail or be broken. Time cannot lull God to sleep or into complacency when it

comes to His Word. In fact, the passing of time shows God's immeasurable patience.

> But do not let this one fact escape your notice, beloved, that with the Lord one day is like a thousand years, and a thousand years like one day. The Lord is not slow about His promise, as some count slowness, but is patient toward you, not wishing for any to perish but for all to come to repentance.

Galatians 4:4 reminds us that God acted in the right, exact, precise time sending His Son forth—400 years after the close of the Old Testament.

> But when the fullness of the time came, God sent forth His Son, born of a woman, born under the Law.

The passing of time and what appears to be a changeless situation may lend itself to accusing God of forgetting you. A true Christian believer will not, cannot, and must not entertain the thought that God has forgotten. God remembered Noah after forty days of rain. God remembered Rachel after Leah had given birth to four sons. God remembered Israel after 430 years of captivity. God remembered His promise of the Messiah after 400 years of silence. God does not forget.

Isaiah 49:15 tells us:

> Can a woman forget her nursing child
> And have no compassion on the son of her womb?
> Even these may forget, but I will not forget you.

Hebrews 6:10 reminds us:

> For God is not unjust so as to forget your work and the love which you have shown toward His name, in having ministered and in still ministering to the saints.

We need to develop patience. You have the essential of patience if you claim to be a Christian. It's part of the fruit of the spirit.

Psalm 40:1 tells us to wait patiently.

> I waited patiently for the Lord;
> And He inclined to me and heard my cry.

Isaiah 26:8 tells us to wait eagerly.

> Indeed, while following the way of Your judgments, O Lord,
> We have waited for You eagerly;
> Your name, even Your memory, is the desire of our souls.

The second question David asks is, "How long will you hide your face from me? If we were to rephrase this question, it may read, "Where is God? I don't feel God's presence." The issue is feelings.

I traced the concept of God hiding His face. It seems you can categorize this phase two ways.

First, God's face seems hidden when we are suffering.

> Why do You hide Your face
> And consider me Your enemy? (Job 13:24).

> Why do You hide Your face
> And forget our affliction and our oppression? (Ps. 44:24).

> And do not hide Your face from Your servant,
> For I am in distress; answer me quickly (Ps. 69:17).

> Do not hide Your face from me in the day of my distress;
> Incline Your ear to me;
> In the day when I call answer me quickly (Ps. 102:2).

When we feel overwhelmed by our circumstances, when we feel there is no way out, when we feel like the problem is never going to be resolved, when we cannot feel God in our problems, we conclude that God is hiding His face from us. He has turned His back on us. He has left and abandoned us.

Second, God's face is hidden when we live in willful sin.

> Hide Your face from my sins
> And blot out all my iniquities (Ps. 51:9).

God cannot look on sin. He is holy. That is why our Savior uttered those ear piercing words, "My God, my God, why hast thou forsaken me?" God hides His face from us so we are not consumed by His holiness. This is broken fellowship. It is when, like the publican, we plead the propitiation, the application of His blood, that God looks at us through the blood of His Son. This is restoration through confession and repentance.

Feelings must stand on the theological premise that God is with us. The saint lives in the presence of God. Consider the promises of God's presence in the following verses.

> Do not fear, for I am with you;
> Do not anxiously look about you, for I am your God.
> I will strengthen you, surely I will help you,
> Surely I will uphold you with My righteous right hand (Isa. 41:10).

> When you pass through the waters, I will be with you;
> And through the rivers, they will not overflow you.
> When you walk through the fire, you will not be scorched,
> Nor will the flame burn you (Isa. 43:2).

> But Zion said, "The Lord has forsaken me,
> And the Lord has forgotten me.
> Can a woman forget her nursing child
> And have no compassion on the son of her womb?
> Even these may forget, but I will not forget you.
> Behold, I have inscribed you on the palms of My hands;
> Your walls are continually before Me" (Isa. 49:14–16).

The presence of God is a fact, not a feeling. It is essential, not an emotion. You see, God was forsaken as our substitute, so that we might not ever be forsaken as His child!

The third question David asks is, "How long shall I take counsel in my soul?" If we were to rephrase this, it may read, ""Why doesn't it work? It just doesn't make any difference if I do what is right or if I don't do what is right!" The issue is Christian perseverance.

Perseverance is the outworking of trust. It is the 6" double "H" principle: Head to heart! It is what every saint needs to work through, moving what we know to our heart or the motivation for living.

In Luke 8:15, Dr. Luke reminds us that fruitfulness comes only when perseverance is prevalent. "But the seed in the good soil, these are the ones who have heard the word in an honest and good heart, and hold it fast, and bear fruit with perseverance."

Romans 5:3 instructs us that perseverance is part of the cycle that enables God's Word to effectively work in my situation because it proves my character and results in hope. And not only this, but we also exult in our tribulations, knowing that tribulation brings about perseverance. And Romans 15:4 states that with what was written before and through the encouragement of the Scriptures and perseverance, we might have hope and perseverance, proven character—and with proven character, hope.

Noah persevered 120 years in building the Ark under extreme difficult times. Abraham waited twenty-five years for God to fulfill His promise. Job suffered intensely for one year, losing everything but one servant and his wife. Joseph languished in prison for thirteen years before God moved, but was found faithful. Daniel spent a lifetime serving three world empires, but always persevered and never lost hope. When people tell me that God's Word doesn't work, I usually respond that they have not worked God's Word. I then ask them:

1. Are you doing it God's way?
2. Are you diluting God's counsel with human reasoning (Prov. 3:5–6) or ungodly counsel (Ps. 1:1)
3. Are you doing it consistently? (Jos. 1:8)
4. Exactly how many times have you done it?
5. How long what you done it?

The fourth question David asks is, "How long will my enemy be exalted over me?" Rephrased it might read, "Nothing's going to change! The situation is hopeless." The issue is faith.

1 John 5:4 teaches us that the extent of experiencing daily victory is directly proportionate to your level of faith.

> For whatever is born of God overcomes the world; and this is the victory that has overcome the world—our faith.

Did you know that the Gospels reveal three levels of faith? There is no faith (Mk. 4:40), little faith (Matt. 6:30, 8:26, 14:31, 16:8; Luke 12:28) and great faith (Matt. 8:10; Luke 7:9).

In 1 Corinthians 15:57, Paul writes we already have the victory in Christ Jesus. John 16:33 says that the world cannot remove this victory from you and we can take encouragement and strength that Christ is victor over the world. Romans 8:37 states that we are overwhelmingly conquerors, and Proverbs 21:31 records that God alone provides the victory to His people.

You may feel right now you are losing, and it very well may be that you are, but you have only lost a battle, not the war!

Next, let's examine David's petition. The psalmist anticipates God to answer him. God is not afraid of our tough questions. It is not blasphemous to ask God such pointed questions. It is not insolent. But note the psalmist is not asking "why." The psalmist is asking for enlightenment. He's at the breaking point.

Enlightenment is a glimpse of illumination that shores up hope. It is the flicker of light that shines enough so we can get a glimpse of what God is up to. Ezra 9:8 says, "But now for a brief moment grace has been shown from the Lord our God, to leave us an escaped remnant and to give us a peg in His holy place, that our God may enlighten our eyes and grant us a little reviving in our bondage."

Our prayer may be along these lines: "Lord, grant me understanding so I can see clearly and remain focused in the middle of these cruel circumstances, and that I may be alert to the entrapments of my emotions, and that I may discern the right pathway to maintain a steady forward course toward the goal."

The psalmist believed that without such resources, he felt his enemy would prevail. He believed his enemy would kill him. If this happened, then his enemy would have won. No one observing such difficult times would know of any difference a personal relationship with God made.

Satan rejoiced over the closed and sealed tomb with the dead corpse of Jesus in it, but his mockery was put to shame and humiliation in three days. People will mock your life because it is patterned after what you believe.

David rises to the heights of praise as he closes this psalm. David says he has trusted in God. Notice the past tense. This is not for salvation. This trust is rooted in his relationship to Jehovah. David then says he has trusted. What is the object of David's past trust? It is God's loyal love. The Hebrew word is *hesed*. David says his heart shall rejoice. The object is God's salvation. He has confidence that God will deliver. His God will rescue. David does not allow his countenance to be downcast.

> Why are you in despair, O my soul?
> And why have you become disturbed within me?
> Hope in God, for I shall again praise Him
> For the help of His presence (Ps. 42:5).

> Why are you in despair, O my soul?
> And why have you become disturbed within me?
> Hope in God, for I shall yet praise Him,
> The help of my countenance and my God (Ps. 42:11).

> Vindicate me, O God, and plead my case against an ungodly nation;
> O deliver me from the deceitful and unjust man! (Ps. 43:1).

David says he will sing. His song of praise is God's faithful activity. David knows that God is immutable.

David could refresh himself in his present circumstances by reflecting on God's past performance, which helped David to refocus in the present and take the next step toward the future because God is immutable.

Let's summarize this chapter with for statements. First, it's not okay for you to wallow in self-pity, despair, and anguish. Second, it's okay to ask God tough questions. Third, it's okay to expect God to answer. Fourth, it's okay to look for understanding and encouragement.

In addition, in your presence circumstances, you chose to praise God, which will strengthen your patience, control your feelings, increase your perseverance, and deepen your relationship with God.

I Can't Handle One More Thing on My Plate!
Stripping Stress of Its Destructive Power: Biblical Life Skills for Stress Management

In 1997, *Reader's Digest* reported in their Book of Facts that the number of aspirin taken by Americans each year was 33,000,000,000.

The *Harvest Business Review* in the same year reported that the percentage of medical office visits made for stress-related symptoms was 60–90%.

In the same year, Fuller Institute of Church Growth reported on pastoral stress.

- 40% of pastors surveyed reported a major clash with a church member at least once a month.
- 50% felt ill-suited to face the rigors of the pastorate.
- 70% had a lower self-image than when they first began ministry.
- 80% said that ministry had influenced their family negatively.
- And 90% felt inadequately trained for ministry.

I hear people say,

- "If one more thing is added to my plate, I'll just scream!"
- "I don't think I can handle one more problem!"
- "I need a vacation from my job. It creates so much stress for me."
- "I'm so stressed right now!"
- "I just feel I can't cope anymore!"

There are some basic axioms about stress of which we should remind ourselves. First, everyone has stress. Second, everyone must deal with stress. Third, even the ones who say they don't get stress but create stress must deal with stress. Fourth, stress is part of everyday life. Fifth, there is no escaping it.

Sixth, each day has some type of stress.

- Waiting in traffic and you are fifteen minutes late
- Caught by another long slow moving freight train
- Sitting in a doctor's office or waiting at the dentist office
- A traffic ticket
- A jammed copy machine while others are waiting
- Slow dial up modem connections for Internet
- An insufficient funds notice
- A headache or toothache
- A sick child or aging parent
- Inconsiderate neighbors with their loud music
- Walking home late at night in a changing neighborhood
- An angry person on the other end of the telephone line
- Loss of job or measure of health
- Selling or buying a home
- Geographic move
- A promotion or being passed over for someone younger with a college degree
- Paying for two children in college
- Home repairs and who to trust, contact, believe
- A poor job performance review

And the list goes on and on. I know you could add a hundred others without blinking an eye.

Seventh, stress is inevitable. Eighth, stress can be external and internal.

The question is not whether our lives will be touched by stress, but what we do when stress does touch our lives? Sometimes we develop a romantic perception of Bible characters, as if their lives were stress free. That somehow, if we only lived back in "those days," when you could hear directly from God and life was simpler, stress would not be a problem.

I challenge you right now to make a list of twenty-five Bible characters. Then think carefully about their lives, and you will see each had stress. Adam and Eve, Cain, Noah, Abraham, Sarah, Moses, Joshua, Samuel, David, Solomon, the kings and prophets; Jesus, the disciples, Paul, Timothy and the Apostle John. They all had to deal with stress. That's the key. How does God want me to deal with stress?

We should begin by defining stress. The American Heart Association defines stress as your body's response to change. They say that stress is an individual thing. What may cause stress for one person may not bother someone else. The National Agricultural Safety Database defines stress as your reaction to something you consider a challenge or a threat.

The National Mental Health Association says that stress is hard to define because it means different things to different people. But they say that it is clear that most stress is a negative feeling rather than a positive feeling.

In an article by Steven L. Burns, MD, "Unbearable Stress," he defines stress as follows: "To your body, stress is synonymous with change. Anything that causes change in your daily routine is stressful. Anything that causes change in your body health is stressful. And imagined changes are just as stressful as real changes."

The Website Mind Tools—Introduction to Stress Management defines stress as anything that stimulates you and increases your level of alertness.

Georgia Reproductive Special defines stress as the wear and tear our bodies experience as we adjust to our continually changing environment; it has physical and emotional effects on us and can creative positive or negative feelings.

The insurance company Aetna's website, InteliHealth, defines stress as the feeling you get when you try to balance the ever-growing demands of work with the never-ending needs of family. Stress occurs when you perceive outside demands as being greater than your emotional resources.

What are some conclusions we can draw from these sources? Stress involves change. Stress is viewed as negative. Stress is a stimulant. Stress is a response to our environment. Stress is related to perceived or actual imbalance. Stress is a response to demands.

Are there different types of stress? I was amazed to discover there are different types of stress, or different levels of stress. The most common form of stress is called acute stress. It comes from demands and pressures of the recent past and anticipated demands and pressures of the near future. Usually acute stress doesn't have enough time to do the extensive damage associated with long-term stress. The most common symptoms include muscular problems (tension headaches and back pain), emotional distress (anger, irritability, anxiety, depression), stomach ailments (bowel problems, heartburn, acid stomach, diarrhea), and transient issues such a elevated high blood pressure, rapid heartbeat, heart palpitations, dizziness, and migraine headaches.

Then you have episodic acute stress (EAS). EAS is anyone who suffers from acute stress frequently. These people are always in a rush, but always late. They take on too much. They have too many irons in the fire. They are type "A" personalities, with an excessive competitive drive, are aggressive, are impatient, and live in the tyranny of the urgent. Often they are worrywarts seeing disaster around every corner. Many times this lifestyle is so ingrained and habitual that they see nothing wrong with the way they conduct their lives. They can be fiercely resistant to change. Those with EAS experience tension headaches, migraines, hypertension, chest pain, and heart disease.

Then there is chronic stress (CS). CS is the grinding stress that wears people away day after day, year after year. It destroys bodies, minds, and lives. It is a stress of never-ending troubles. There is no hope because they see no solutions. They never see a way out of a miserable situation. The worse aspect of CS is that people get used to it. CS kills through suicide, violence, heart attacks, stroke, and perhaps even cancer. People wear down to a final fatal breakdown. Because the physical and mental resources are depleted through long term attrition, the symptoms are difficult to treat.

What are the suggested causes of stress? There are several major sources of stress. Survival stress may occur in cases where your survival or health is threatened, where you are put under pressure, or where you experience some unpleasant or challenging event. Here adrenaline is released in your body, and you experience all the symptoms of your body preparing for fight or flight.

Internally generated stress can come from anxious worrying about events beyond your control, from a tense, hurried approach to life, or from relationship problems caused by your own behavior. It can come from an addiction to and enjoyment of stress.

Environmental or job stress where you're living or working causes stress. It may come from noise, crowding, pollution, untidiness, dirt, or other distractions. Alternatively, stress can come from events from work.

Fatigue and overwork stress builds upon over a long period. This can occur when you try to achieve too much in too little time, or whend you are not using effective time management strategies.

Are there any harmful effects from stress? According to *United Press International*, February 17, 2005, as reported in Orlando, Florida, marital stress increases women's risk of heart disease and death as reported at the Second International Conference on Women's Heart Disease and Stroke.

In New York, *Reuters Health* reported on February 10, 2005, that stress within families may help trigger diabetes-related autoimmunity in infants as well as accelerate the progression of the disease in children who already have diabetes.

Stress can affect your digestive system. It is common to have a stomachache or diarrhea when you are stressed. This happens because stress hormones slow the release of stomach acid and the emptying of the stomach. The same hormones also stimulate the colon, which speeds the passage of its contents.

Stress can affect your immune system. Chronic stress tends to dampen your immune system, making you more susceptible to colds and other infections.

Stress can affect your nervous system. If you fail to manage stress properly, stress hormones produce persistent feelings of anxiety, helplessness, and impending doom.

Stress can affect your cardiovascular system. High levels of cortisol can raise your heart rate and increase your blood pressure and blood lipid levels. These are risk factors for both heart attacks and strokes.

Stress can worsen many skin conditions such as psoriasis, eczema, hives, and acne.

Stress can affect your relationships. Under stress, most people become so wrapped up in their own problems that they forget about everyone else. At the same time, they begin to take out their feelings on family members and friends.

Stress can affect your work. Over the long haul, stress will gradually wear you down. You will become physically weaker and begin to tire easily. At the same time, you will find it difficult to concentrate and will begin to make poor decisions. Your productivity decreases.

Stress can create more stress. Stress has a snowballing effect because of all the problems it causes in your health, family, and work. These new troubles in your life add to your stress level.

We have read what the "experts" are saying about stress. As a child of God, we have a different worldview. It is a biblical worldview. The Christian wants to know what God has to say about stress.

Can we define stress biblically? Psalm 55:3 states, "Because of the voice of the enemy, because of the pressure of the wicked; for they bring down trouble upon me and in anger they bear a grudge against me." The word "pressure" is the equivalent to stress. The Old Testament word means to totter, to be weigh down or crushed.

In 2 Corinthians 11:28, Paul writes, "Apart from such external things, there is the daily pressure on me of concern for all the churches." The Greek word for pressure is *epistasis*. *Stasis* means to stand and *epi* (the preposition) means upon. Paul is saying that he has the weight of superintending or giving attention to all the churches and their spiritual growth and what hinders that growth. The word can mean to set upon or to set up. Paul set up these churches, and they were set upon him for direction and guidance as fledging church plants.

Here is a working definition of stress that I will use for the remainder of this chapter. *Stress is the feeling I have toward situations that appear to be overwhelming in my judgment.* Let's key in on some words from this definition.

<u>Feeling</u> represents my emotions. Stress usually is viewed with bad feelings. Stress is viewed as undesirable and having no value. It is unwanted and meant to be avoided at all cost. Feelings of anger, despair, discouragement, anxiety, or worry are typical when you are stressed.

<u>Situations</u> mean what is surrounding me at that moment, an event of some sort. It could be an event that happened in the past that I return to think about such as the death of a life mate. It could be an event that I have to deal with right now such as the lack of finances because my mate did not have sufficient life insurance. It could be an event that is yet to come such as alternative housing because it is impossible to maintain the home or pay the taxes.

<u>Appear</u> means my perception. Conclusions are drawn on limited information. It is often an immediate and rash conclusion because it is fueled by feelings.

<u>Overwhelming</u> means unable to bear up underneath. A sense of unending pressure, lack of solution or resolution, even fatalistic.

<u>Judgment</u> means all of these things taken into consideration and making a decision. The decision is based on my feelings, the impossibility of the situation and a sense of despair so I am not able to recognize my resources.

To begin to strip stress of its destructive power, let's take some time and develop four essential theological principles. We must develop a right understanding of God. We must begin with the sovereignty of God. According to Jerry Bridges in his book *Trusting God*, the sovereignty of God is God being completely in control, infinite in wisdom, and perfect in love.

Let's use the following example. A man receives word that one of his grown children has been killed in a random act of violence. A few days later, his accountant calls him and tells him he has lost his fortune in the stock market. Where is God? Why did God allow this to happen?

To begin to process this stress biblically, this man must acknowledge the sovereignty of God. These events did not surprise God. In fact, if one could accept and understand, perhaps even God orchestrated such events. Whether or not He did is moot. He was completely in control. He was not caught by surprise. God's calling the shots. He's running the show. Either He's in full control or He's off His throne. He has purpose for this man in this stressful time. The man must accept that God is infinite in wisdom. God knows the beginning from the end. God knows the desired outcome of this stressful time. God factored in all the variables and constants to make this trial achieve His purposes in this man's life. Finally, the man must accept that God loves him. These events have been filtered through the loving hand of God. The harmful effects have been removed. God loves this man so much that He would not overwhelm this man with more than he could handle in God's strength.

This man was Job. Job had heard of God with his hearing ear but now he sees God with his seeing eye. Job grew immensely through these stressful events. He acknowledged the sovereignty of God. He wept and rejoiced in God. He struggled to comprehend but never drifted from the mooring that God is good all the time and all the time God is good. His steadfast faith and God's divine purposes restored all that Job lost and even more.

God governs the world, and we have only to do our duty wisely and leave the issue to him.

God is your Heavenly Father. We must come to embrace wholeheartedly that this is true. In the 1970s, it was taught that our concept of God as our father was in direct proportion to our understanding of our earthly fathers. This was psychology in the church. My earthly father abandoned me as a child in fourth grade. I never saw him again until I was twenty-one or twenty-two. Should I fear God's abandonment? No! He promises that He will not abandon us.

God is my heavenly Father period. He is not tainted by my human earthly patriarchal relationships. As my heavenly Father, He is above all of my circumstances. He has a very clear view of what is happening. His position gives me comfort. Like Moses who stationed himself on the hill above the battle Joshua and the Israelites fought so Joshua could see him and receive directives, so my Heavenly Father is seated high above in the heavenlies. His position is my assurance that what I cannot see or comprehend, He is already looking at and wants to direct me through that stressful time

He is my Heavenly Father. Father. I have a relationship with the creator of the Universe. I am related to this Omnipotent, Almighty, El Shaddai, Lord of Sabbaoth by faith in Jesus Christ. My Father does right by me. His best is for my benefit. As a child sits high atop of a playground slide, and is coaxed by his father to trust him and slide down—that his father will catch him—so it is with my Heavenly Father. He says, "You can trust Me. I will not deliberately allow anything into your life of a destructive nature. You may feel or think this stress will destroy you, but it will not. I have it under control. Slide on down."

We must also come to a right understanding of man. We understand a little about God in the midst of stress. We need to understand ourselves. We are finite and limited. We are restricted by time. We have limitations as to knowledge. Without full and complete knowledge, stress is viewed as negative and something we want quickly to go away. When stress is perceived or actually occurs, we intensify our efforts to maintain control. Stress creates a feeling of being out of control. When I feel I am out of control, I fear harmful results. As a Christian, I am never to be in control but dependent upon God—desperate for God because of who God is. I cannot control things, and even if I could the probable results of controlling things would be more harmful than I could anticipate. The great act of faith is when man decides that he is not God. Wouldn't it be a wise thing to turn to God immediately when stress rears its ugly head, acknowledging I have limited understanding of what is happening?

The second thing we need to know about ourselves is our resources are solely inadequate to handle any amount or level of stress. Because God is sovereign, everything in and around our lives is first spiritual in nature. When there is a car accident, there is a spiritual theme. When I lose my job, there is a spiritual theme. When I get a promotion, there is a spiritual theme. When things are delayed, there is a spiritual theme. But too often, we look at life from under the sun. We think that our education, experience, talents, and abilities can handle stress. I can use my earthly, fleshly, or demonic wisdom to deal with the stress. James tells us that the result will be selfish ambition, jealousy, disorder, and every evil thing. He goes on to say that this wisdom (way of handling life) is not from above. Therefore, the second thing I need to know about myself is that my resources are woefully superficial and unable to stand up against the stress of life. I need God, His Word, communion with Him through prayer, and the fellowship of the church and saints knowing that the weapons of our warfare are not of the flesh but divinely powerful for handling stress (tearing down fortresses).

We must come to a right understanding of salvation. So we have some truths about God and man. But we still remain powerful and dominated by stress because we possess no divine understanding. What do I mean? Let me illustrate. As my children were growing up, they would invite their friends over to play or for an overnight. There were certain basic rules when their friends came over. At times, after their friends left to go home and we sat around the dinner table, my children would complain that our rules seem to make play difficult for them with their friends. My children knew the rules. They understood what we expected from them. Did their friends? No, they lacked understanding why we did what we did. Why? They are not in my family. They are not related to me.

If someone going through stress does not have a right understanding of salvation, they are crippled for walking successfully through the valley of the shadow of stress. They will accuse God and resort to implementing a plan rooted in human reasoning and the traditions and philosophies of men. This leads to no divine empowerment.

Without a proper understanding of salvation, I am a stranger to the power of God. Paul reminds me in Ephesians 2 that I am walking according to the philosophies of this world. I am driven to live according to my lusts and desires. Let me illustrate it this way. Recently I was invited to Honduras for a speaking engagement. When I arrived at the airport, I knew I was in trouble. Everything was in Spanish. Everyone spoke Spanish. Everyone knew where they were going and what the signs said. I was a foreigner. I was not a citizen of that country. I couldn't even order at McDonalds because everything was in Spanish. I was powerless. I didn't even know if I was receiving the correct change back from the currency I rendered. That is how it is for someone who does not have a proper understanding of God, man, and salvation.

We must also come to a right understanding of walking in the Spirit. Paul raises a very interesting question to the saints in the Galatia territories in chapter 3 of the book of Galatians. Somewhere along the line, these dear saints reach the conclusion that holiness and purity in life is a performance issue. Paul asked them how they got saved—works or faith? Of course, the answer is faith. He then draws the conclusion. How were they to live the Christian life? Works or faith?

Most Christians struggle with this issue. Somewhere in our Christianity, we slide into the pit of performance. It is known as the "list." For example, did I read my Bible today? Did I pray? Did I pray long enough? Did I go to church? Am I serving in the church? Am I tithing? Am I tithing enough? Do I tithe on the gross or net? Should I go to this movie? Should I listen to this music? Is this dress acceptable? And the list goes on.

Yes, we should be concerned about these matters. They are matters of character and virtue. But the motivation is equally important, and may I suggest more important than the deed! Why do I read my Bible, pray, etc.? Should it not be that I am constrained by love? I have a debt of love I owe. Is it not because the life I live now I live by faith in the Son of God who loved me and gave Himself for me?

If I approach stress by performance, I will not manage it well. But if I approach stress by faith, motivated by love, it will always bring forth one of the fruits of the Spirit in my life as well as prepare me for the next stage of God's will for my life. It's a matter of motivation.

The theological remedy for stress is rest and peace. These are terms the Bible uses to provide hope to those living with stress. The first word God records which gives hope to the stressed is *rest*. Notice how rest is pictured and described in the Bible.

- God says I will give you rest—Ex. 33:14 (2 Samuel 7:11; Matthew 11:28)
- God says He gives you rest—Deuteronomy 12:10 (Joshua 1:13)
- God has given you rest—Joshua 22:4
- The Lord has given rest—Joshua 23:1
- God promises rest on every side—Joshua 21:44 (2 Samuel 7:1; 1 Kings 5:4; 1 Chronicles 22:18; 2 Chronicles 14:7; 2 Chronicles 15:15)

- The Bible says there is a complete rest—Exodus 31:15 (Exodus 34:21)
- The Bible says there is a solemn rest—Leviticus 16:31
- You must enter into His rest—Hebrews 4:1–12
- The Bible is equally frank and honest that there are those who found no rest—Jeremiah 45:3 (Lamentations 1:3)
- And there are those who find no rest—Deuteronomy 28:65

I hope you noticed that different tenses God used to encourage his stressed-out people. Rest is described in the past, present, and future. Rest is available. This divine rest is better than a twenty-four hour diner is!

I want to take a few moments and take another look at Matthew 11:28 and Hebrews 4, two essential passages that speak of rest for the weary and stressed.

In Matthew 11:28, 29, we observe the following. The first thing we notice about the text is the invitation, "Come." Invitations can be accepted or rejected. We can accept Christ's invitation to come to Him to find rest, no matter how ridiculous the means of finding rest may be to our way of thinking. Rest begins when we come. To accept the invitation means to come to the point of believing in such a way as to demonstrate our submission to His Lordship.

The invitation is given to those described as weary and heavy-laden. The two words encompass stress. Weary is the internal exhaustion of stress. Heavy-laden is the external exhaustion.

Rest is pictured as a yoke. The yoke was a hand carved, upside down "U" that was attached to a long pole. It was designed to unite the efforts of two animals in a common goal. The Bible strictly forbid the union of a donkey with an ox (Deut. 22:10). This law was for the protection of the weaker animal. The concept of "yoke" was used by Paul forbidding the union of a believer with an unbeliever (2 Cor. 6:14). It would be destructive.

A Bible dictionary suggests that Jesus, when He talks about the yoke, is not referring to the animals, but the yoke that was worn by a porter. When the load was humanly impossible, the yoke helped to support and transport the load.

Jesus describes His yoke as easy and light. Many view the biblical injunctions for handling life as unrealistic, out of touch, and impractical. This passage says that any other way of handling stress will only continue or increase the stress. For example, I am being considered for a promotion. It creates stress. Am I qualified? Will they think I am qualified? What if I muff the interview? I don't have a Master's degree. I begin to jockey for favor and recognition when I should allow the Lord to exalt me in due time as I continue to humbly serve my company as unto the Lord.

If Jesus' way is superior, how do I enter His yoke—to draw from His strength? He tells us. We are to take His yoke. We are to believe that any other way of handling stress remains harmful and destructive. Any other means will only mask the harmful effects. They will remain hidden from view only to rise again when other stress points occur. To take something means I must lay something down. I lay down the humanistic, materialistic, and hedonistic ways of handling stress for the gentle, light, and easy ways of our Lord.

Jesus also says that once we take His yoke, we enter into a discipleship relationship. We are to learn of Him. He is the Teacher, I am the student. The student doesn't challenge the teacher. The student understands the teacher has far superior answers. The student demonstrates an eagerness to learn. I remember teaching at a Christian college. I thoroughly enjoyed teaching the adult learners. They worked hard all day and sacrificially came to learn at night. They were eager to learn. I was asked to teach the full-time day students who took an evening class. That was the hardest class I ever taught. They were there because they couldn't get a day class. Some would openly challenge and dispute what was being taught displaying a contentious spirit. They were not learners.

Jesus expects me to learn, yield, and obey. This is what keeps me in His yoke. This relationship is my strength and power so I am not overwhelmed or hurt by the destructive forces of stress.

The text says that when I do this I will find rest and I will have rest. First is the promise of rest. This is the incentive. Can other stress management techniques promise complete rest? No! But Christ invites and offers. Then He promises when I follow through. Some Christians "try God" and when they do not experience the promised results, they blame God. "God failed me. I did what He said." Oh, really? We can get into another whole tape series on partial and full obedience. Had Joshua and the Israelites only walked around Jericho five days the walls would not have come down. If they had not blown the trumpets, the walls would not have come down. Get the point? God doesn't fail. We fail God. God's program always works. We don't work God's program!

In Hebrews 4:1–11, we observe the following. This passage is talking about rest. Perhaps we should stop and consider this word specifically, and not in general. Rest means a cessation of activity, from striving toward or against, to stop my laborious efforts. It means to cease from self-efforts. It means the end of trying to deal with stress through my feeble and fleshy works. It means freedom—freedom from easily being annoyed or bothered by things outside of my control. It also means stability, security, or fixed, unmovable.

My first observation is that there is a promise of rest. Rest is available. There is hope in finding rest, but there is a limitation and qualification for this rest. Failure to seize the moment by proper means results in falling short of the immense benefits rest provides. The writer appeals to the urgency and seriousness of this rest when he uses the word fear that is someone who would not enter this rest.

The writer refers to the days of Moses and Joshua. Like them, we have had good news preached to us. This good news of rest is both soteriological and sanctification. The good news preached to us first came by our Lord Jesus Christ and then was carried on by the Apostles. Moses and Joshua preached the good news of a land flowing with milk and honey, a land God promised to Abraham and reiterated to Isaac, Jacob and to Moses. But why was it that when you read in Judges the sons of Israel are not free? They are captives, because they failed to obey God in driving out the inhabitants of the land. The writer says they heard but did not unite what they heard with belief. When you do not believe, you will fail to act. When you fail to act, you will forfeit the divine blessings promised.

Those who did not enter the promised rest were disobedient. But the disobedient could not nullify the offer of rest to others who would choose to obey. The faith of Joshua and Caleb remained even when the other ten spies disbelieved. They were spared. But here in the text the urgency again to enter into this rest is set in a sphere of time: "today." Joshua's rest was temporarily enjoyed or forfeited by the obedience or lack thereof by the sons of Israel. God's rest, however, is permanent. He has provided it. It is always available. The common denominator is our obedience and faith.

We are reminded that to remain in God's rest is a matter of individual, personal diligence. Avoiding the snares and entrapments of stress and its destructive power in our lives is our choice. We believe or we do not believe. We act and remain, or we reject and lose. Failure to obey hinders full and complete rest on all sides. This is often observed in people's lives by their emotional highs and lows. Either they are up on Jesus and He is wonderful, glorious, or they are down on spiritual things, "they don't work" and "what's the use?"

We need to summarize from these two passages how to enter into God's rest to strip stress of its the destructive effects.

1. I must hear and receive God's invitation to "come." That means I must be humble and deal with my pride.
2. I must recognize that stress is trying to ruin my insides and outsides. Not only are there external pressures (deadlines, people's critical spirit, etc.) but internal reactions (fear, worry, anxiety).

3. I must acknowledge that His yoke is not harmful; His ways are superior to my contemplations of stress management.

4. I must believe that He is offering an authentic promise of rest only He can fulfill.

5. I must be willing to become the student, not the teacher. I must exchange my sinful pattern of thinking for His righteous, simple, and humble ways of dealing with stress.

6. I must act upon what I hear. I have to unite faith to my hearing. I must be a doer of the word, not merely a hearer only.

7. I must reject others' experiences and realize that though they did not find rest, I can. There experience only validates the truth they lived by sight and in disobedience.

8. I must understand that any other means of stripping stress of its destructive power is temporary. God's promise of rest is permanent, lasting in, through, and for all stresses of life. His principles are universal and timeless.

9. I must commit myself to working hard at keeping this rest. Although it has been provided and remains, I must be diligent to practice its principles (faith and obedience). I must control my emotions to changeless or changing circumstances and people by faith in and obedience to His Word—regardless.

10. Finally, how serious am I for this rest? As badly as I want the rest from stress, I must want the Author of rest more. A relationship with Him sustains this wonderful rest that exceeds all mental and emotional comprehension guarding my heart and mind in Him alone.

The second word God gives to the stressed is the word *peace*. What is the difference between rest and peace? I envision rest as external and peace as internal. We have spent a lot of time discussing rest and drawing some powerful entrance principles. Now let's look at the concept of peace.

The word "peace" is found 340 times in the New American Standard Bible. It is interesting to note it occurs numerous times in Leviticus with reference to the peace offering. It is one of the major subjects of the Psalms. I also find it interesting that it occurs most in the prophetic books, with particular mention in Isaiah. The gospel of Luke mentions it more than any other Gospel. Paul uses it frequently in the book of Romans.

A brief word study provides a greater understanding of this word. Like so many others we use, we are hard pressed to define them with precision. In the Classical Literature, peace is the antithesis to war. It was a condition resulting from a cessation of war. Peace is the state of law and order, which gives rise to the blessing of prosperity.

The Hebrew word is *šālóm* (shalom). It means the opposite of any disturbance in the communal wellbeing of the nation. In the widest sense, it includes health, prosperity, and a contentedness. It reflects in good relations between men and nations. It appears to be summed up in Numbers 6:24 and closely associated (peace) with the presence of Yahweh.

The Greek word is *eirēnē*. The New Testament is greatly influence by the Old Testament and the LXX (Septuagint). It means the opposite of war (Luke 14:32). It refers to external security (Acts 24:2). In 1 Corinthians 14:33, it carries the idea of opposite of disorder. And in Galatians 5:22, it means harmony with men. The biblical concept of peace is primarily that of wholeness.

Significant peace passages adding to our understanding of *how* to strip stress of its destructive power.

1. Deuteronomy 20:10—there are terms of peace.
2. Ezra 9:12—there is a type of peace to be avoided.
3. Psalm 29:11—the Lord promises peace (Ps. 85:8; Eze. 37:26).
4. Psalm 34:14—we are commanded to pursue peace.
5. Psalm 119:165—our love for the Lord gives us great peace.
6. Proverbs 3:2—yielding to parental counsel adds peace to my days.

7. Proverbs 16:7—even when opposed by people, God gives me peace.
8. Isaiah 26:3—a convinced and steadfast mind guards my peace.
9. Isaiah 32:17—doing the right thing insures peace.
10. Isaiah 54:10—God's promise of peace is unmovable.
11. Jeremiah 14:19—no peace comes apart from God and His ways (Jer. 8:15, 12:12).
12. Mark 5:34—faith is a prerequisite for peace (Lk. 7:50, 8:48; Rom. 5:1).
13. John 14:27—God's offer of peace is so totally different from the world's offer of peace.
14. Romans 8:6—what we set our mind on can bring peace or remove peace.
15. Romans 16:20—God has my stress under control.
16. Galatians 5:22—peace is solely the work of the Holy Spirit.
17. Philippians 4:7—biblical peace transcends all of our circumstances.
18. Colossians 3:15—I must allow peace to umpire my heart.
19. 1 Thessalonians 5:23—God's peace results in maturity and holiness.

What are some other tools for stripping stress of its destructive power? Diet can play a very important role. Almost any article on stress management points out the need for diet. What I take into my body for consumption may be a stimulant to stress or fuel present stress. High doses of caffeine or excessive fast-food dining do not provide the nutritional value required to maintain equilibrium.

Exercise is another important tool. Exercise is a good way to deal with stress because it is healthy way to relieve pent up energy and tension. It can protect the cardiovascular and immune systems from the consequences of stress.

Understanding who really is in control is important. Do I think I can do anything about my environment or circumstances? If I can, will I remain in God's biblical patterns or would sin be a result? Remember earlier in this series, as believers it is our responsibility to quickly and confidently affirm the sovereignty of God in all matters of life, especially the stressful ones. He is so loving and wise, instead of trying to change or escape, He will provide the way out so I can endure it (1 Cor.10:13).

Though all these ways may help with controlling stress, the Bible wants us to be able to function for the glory of God. Therefore, there are biblical ways to deal with sin.

We all must biblically deal with sin. Stress can be the result of unconfessed sin. David had a lot of stress in his life after committing adultery with Bathsheba. You can read about his stress in Psalm 32: 3, 4.

The Holy Spirit applies pressure in response to the Bible's holiness requirements. This pressure is known as guilt. When a saint ignores guilt, it only intensifies. Guilt is a divine resource. It has a good purpose. It is not relieved until God's child deals with the source of the guilt—sin. Now people have found all sorts of ways to avoid guilt. They deny it or run away from it. But funny thing about guilt—is it not external but internal? You can't run away from yourself or God (Psalm 139).

We all must biblically deal with conflicts. Conflicts, unresolved people problems are a source of stress, especially if you are married or a co-worker. I suppose you could quit your job, but you can't quit your marriage!

Why do people problems exist? I think the fundament root of people problems is pride. Pride to be right. Pride to guard some perceived right I might lose or I feel is being threatened. Pride to be superior or to lord it over another. Pride. I believe Jacob had stress with Esau. He was stressed when he fled for his life. And even though he lived hundreds of miles away, got married, had children, and God's hand of blessing was on his wives, family, and livestock, when he heard that Esau was coming to meet him, he stressed out. Ephesians 4 reminds us to deal quickly with broken relationships and not to allow the sun to go down on such affairs.

The Bible issued a command for a sabbatical rest. I use the word "sabbatical" as meaning a deliberate break. Pastors take study sabbatical or a break with a purpose. Because stress is part and parcel of daily life and it is inevitable, we must take a sabbatical. It may be a few minutes, several hours, or a weekend.

Every saint should do anticipatory planning. Some stress is caused by lack of planning. We work long hours, go home, drop into bed, get up, and repeat the process. Even when we plan, we often fail to work the plan. We become distracted or someone frustrates us, and we abandon the plan and think we if just freelance it, work faster, harder, and longer, we can catch up. How utterly bogus.

Anticipatory planning forces us to look at what we really need to do. It provides an opportunity to assess time and resources. Planning is really a safeguard against stress. One of my favorite sayings is "plan tomorrow the night before." Then my day has structure and I can enter it more confidently and boldly because I know what is required of my time limitations, my available resources, and me. I think it can also help me say "no" to those impetuous requests and avoid the tyranny of the urgent most of us slip into.

Do we have trusted friends who will offer biblical counsel to us in times of stress? A friend loves at all times, and a brother is born for adversity (Prov. 17:17). Faithful are the wounds of a friend (Prov. 17:26). Oil and perfume make the heart glad, so a man's counsel is sweet to his friend (Prov. 27:9).

At times we are so close to a situation, we cannot see those divine resources for stripping stress of its destructive power. We need someone objective, a trusted godly friend, to remind us, encourage us, or even rebuke us. Our thinking may be reflective of the man on the sea, tossed all about. We need a friend who can be objective and honest.

Remember the laws of communication. When we are stressed, we usually become short, curt, and abrasive in our speech. When we do this, most often we drive people away from us who want to help. They stand on the sidelines, afraid to get close for fear of losing a limb, figuratively speaking.

What are these laws of communication? **Be honest and open** with what you are feeling and what you perceive to be happening. Denying, exaggerating, lying, or misrepresenting the situation only complicates the matter and drives you further away from biblical solutions and hope. **Keep short accounts.** Take relationships seriously. Do your best to resolve matters in a timely fashion. There is nothing more important than righting a wronged relationship. Remember that unresolved people problems are stressors. **Attack the problem, not the person.** Stressed people often become aggressive. They think that by doing so they can regain control of a situation they feel is out of control. We need to redirect our time, energy, and emotions toward the problem and instruct and teach the person. Then, we'll get somewhere. If someone feels attacked, you and I both know how he or she will respond—defensively. Now we have a further complicating problem besides the original problem. **Act, avoid reaction.** Ephesians 4:31 and 32 clearly show the difference. Here is a practical assignment. Write Ephesians 4:31 on one side of an index card. Turn the card over and write Ephesians 4:32 on the other. Keep the card with you. When you feel stressed, pull the card out, and review the characteristics of someone who reacts and one who should act. Now make a choice and strip the stress of its destructive power.

During stress, we want to be served. We need to serve one another in love. Improper response to stress creates selfishness. We become focused on our problem and what it is doing to use. We must set the stress in a biblical context, reaffirm our rest and peace, and then siege every opportunity to love others. Imagine the stress our Lord was under. Yet He said He came to serve, not to be served.

I have developed a Stress Matrix. Perhaps it will help summarize this chapter. It is a step-by-step, workable, and practical way to process your stress in light of these biblical truths.

The Stress Matrix has five branches. Each branch specifically examines an area of the counselee's life. Carefully go through each branch to have the most effectiveness in helping them live victoriously.

External Stress

- Can I do anything about the stress without violating God's Word?
    - If I cannot, then I must examine the lives of Joseph, Daniel and Jesus to learn how they lived victoriously in the midst of very difficult times.
- Is this stress a result of sinful actions?
    - If it is, then I must comply with biblical confession and repentance.
- Is this stress the result of someone else under pressure that I am serving underneath?
    - Read and implement Luke 6, which lists the activities a Christian is commanded to perform when living under the stressful actions of an enemy.
- Am I assuming responsibility for a situation outside of my control?
    - Live under the authority of a good, gracious and loving God, affirming His sovereign control in which He desires to work out all things.
- Is this stress attributed to another's expectations or demands of me? Are these demands reasonable?
    - Remind yourself of the Christian's authority, biblical submission, the biblical appeal process (see Daniel and Esther) and choose whom you will serve.

Internal Stress

- Is this stress attributed to laziness or slothfulness?

- - o Plan out your day. Use a Time Scheduler for activities. Understand the purpose for living and work. Redeem the time for the days are evil.
  - Is this stress attributed to hidden or unconfessed sin?
    - o Repent, return, and repeat godly attitudes and actions.

Emotional Factors

- Am I angry or do I have unresolved conflicts with someone?
- Am I concerned about what someone may think of me?
- Am I worried about something?

Physical Factors

- What are my diet patterns?
- What are my sleep patterns?
- What are my exercise patterns
- Has there been a recent illness?
- Am I consuming to much artificial stimuli as a coping device? Has food or beverage become comfort food to me?

Spiritual Factors

- Am I in the Word daily?
- Am I praying daily?
- Am I accountable?
- Have I slacked off in Christian service?
- Who are my companions?

Using the matrix requires that you are honest. Remember the words of Jeremiah: "The heart is more deceitful than all else and is desperately sick; who can understand it?" You may need to ask a trusted friend, one who will speak the truth in love, to help you process your stress using the material from this chapter and this matrix.

Satan, You and Your Crew Have Been Served

The Power of Biblical Counseling: The Demoniac

She sat in my office, head down, non-communicative, no eye contact, and trembling. She related that she had been raped by a man and woman. She told us that she often found herself driving in Indiana, Wisconsin, and Michigan not knowing how this happened. She related several sexual assaults. She related how her brother repeatedly sexually molested her. After approximately fourteen to sixteen sessions, Josephine gave glory and praise to God, is living a healthy and spiritually active life, and publicly testifies to God's transforming power.

A couple came for counseling because the husband was experiencing panic attacks. He was fearful of losing his businesses. He was a believer. God blessed him abundantly financially. He was nearly paralyzed by his fears. About eight or nine months later, Mark had acknowledged the Lordship of Christ in his life. He was being mentored. Both he and his wife were growing in their roles as husband and wife, parents and communication. Mark is now assuming a full time position as pastor of families and discipleship in a new church plant.

What do these two case studies have in common? They both were given a psychological label. They both were prescribed medication. They both felt helpless and hopeless. They both were barely functional. They both knew there had to be better answers. They represent the demoniac's story. They represent hundreds of thousands of men and women who have not yet found superior answers because those redeemed by the Wonderful Counselor have diminished the superiority of the Bible by turning them away to the "experts."

Verse 1 sets the context. "They" refers to Jesus and the disciples. Jesus and the disciples crossed the Sea of Galilee after He gave His first discourse of the Sermon on the Mount. The Sea of Galilee is where the Lord called Peter and Andrew into ministry. It is where many healings took place. And from this story, it later became a later ministry to the ten cities known as Decapolis.

They came into the country of the Gerasenes. They had a major city of trade. The city was magnificently comprised of temples and huge buildings. There was a triumphal arch celebrating the visit of Emperor Hadrian. The amphitheater could seat 3,000 people.

In verses 2–6, we are introduced to the counselee. The counselee is a male. Please note where the man is living. He was living in the tombs (2). He had his dwelling among the tombs (3). This was his permanent abode. This is where he existed. This is what he came to expect. There was no hope of anything better.

We also read that an unclean spirit held him. This phraseology is used thirteen times in the Gospels (NASB). An unclean spirit means a demon, which gains control over a person's thoughts, actions, and emotions. It is a debilitating spirit. Debilitating spirits today are bitterness, anger, resentment, worry, anxiety, and fear—just to name a few.

The power of deliverance (truth setting a counselee free) must always start by identifying the problem as a sin issue, unless there is clear medical proof for an organic cause. Avoid redefining the problem with psychological reclassification labels.

Notice how the townspeople dealt with him. They had no ability to control him. They used chains to restrain him. They used shackles to reduce his movement, to confine or limit him. They did not want him returning to town. They did not want him disturbing the day-to-day routine. They did not want his presence because some people were afraid or annoyed at his antics.

What are modern day chains and shackles? Psychology tells us that people are victims, helpless, addicts, that they need medication or psychotherapy. They are given labels and prescribed medications. They will always be this way. Change is highly unlikely and improbable. They say they work towards acceptance not transformation. The result is isolation, just like the demoniac.

Note how their treatment added to the man's outward behavior. He was tormented night and day. He was experiencing *mental* problems.

He was screaming. He was having *emotional* problems. He was suicidal. He was having *physical* problems.

Now we must ask ourselves how could this situation develop and reach this level? Why did their repeated efforts to help failed? Their failure was due to misdiagnosing the problem. They merely looked at the behavior and reduced the options of help to controlling the behavior. Their failure was due to treatment options that only addressed the symptoms, to alleviate the symptoms so the man "fits" into society's morés. The same problems resurfaced, and they took extreme measures of removal, isolation, and an attempt to control at a distance. All involved adopted the mentality, "This is the way you will be for the rest of your life."

Methods that exclude God are ineffective in helping solve man's problems. Secular treatment options are a life sentence of despair and hopelessness. They produce years of psychotherapy, shock treatment, medication therapy, group sessions, and incarceration in mental facilities.

Now let's watch the Wonderful Counselor in action. Let's peek in on the counseling session as recorded in verses 7–13. First, note that this man is desperate for help. He runs to Jesus and bows down, an act of worship and humility. This man recognizes that he is in the presence of Someone greater than himself and others. Only Jesus, upright before him, has authority and power.

Note the conundrum in which the man finds himself in verse 6. Humanly, he is looking for help and needs hope. Spiritually, he is fearful and angry, hopeless and filled with despair. Notice the anguish of the man wanting to believe. But the fear of his behavior is all he has known. The actions of his friends, neighbors, and relatives have reinforced that the man's condition is hopeless.

Jesus determines that the man's problem is spiritual and took charge (v. 8). Jesus dealt with every spiritual issue. Jesus recognized that one sin leads to many. This man's problems are represented by the name of the demon being "legion." The way the townspeople dealt with this man was destructive in nature and void of genuine spiritual power.

The solutions were producing death and destruction (v. 10–13). But after counseling with Jesus, the change in this man's life was spectacular and astounding. The report reached the city of the failed solutions and the superior answers through the changed life of the man.

There are usually two results from people who see true biblical counseling take place. For the townspeople, it was fear. They wanted Jesus to leave. Why? Jesus was rocking the boat. The treatment plan didn't fit their concepts of mental health. They could not admit they were wrong—to do so would mean they had to change. This might result in personal and professional loss.

For the counselee, "the before and after" portraits speak for themselves. Before he was restless and agitated, but now he is sitting down. Before he was naked, but now he is clothed. Before he was irrational and emotionally unstable, but now he is in his right mind.

Paul writes in 2 Timothy 1:7, "For God has not given us a spirit of timidity, but of power and love and discipline." This transformed man on whom friends, neighbors, church, relatives, and society had given up, wanted to share his testimony of the power of Christ and the superior answers he found. Jesus gave him a new job description. He was to report about the great things that God did and God's mercy. Jesus would return to this area and have a powerful evangelistic ministry because of the obedience of this man. His cure was sure.

I think we either know someone or have heard of someone who displays unacceptable behavior such as bipolar, manic depression, ADD, or ADHD. We hear from the "experts" that this person has a chemical imbalance. We also hear that this person cannot help what is occurring. The only solution for the person is medication treatment (anti-anxiety or anti-depression), combined at times with cognitive therapy. But when pressed on how they reached this conclusion, neither the medical nor the psychological communities can produce the first shred of evidence. Their diagnosis is based on the person's thinking, feeling, and doing.

As Christians, we must—and are commanded to—believe and practice that the Bible has superior answers. Why? Who knows us better than the One who created us? God in His infinite wisdom included a real life story of a man crippled by sin, nearly destroyed by inferior counseling practices, but fully and completely delivered by a power encounter with the Son of the Living God.

Beloved, there is no hopeless situation or helpless person. If the Omnipotent God can rescue us from the horrors and torments of the deserved eternal state of Hell through the atoning work of His Son, what makes us believe He suddenly becomes impotent to rescue men and women, husbands and wives, moms and dads, families and marriages from the horrors and torments of sin?

Wildest Police Chases

The High Cost of Rebellion

Nothing in life is free. Have you ever heard someone make that statement? As a general axiom, the statement is true. The free items that are advertised do cost. The costs may vary, but there is a cost. For example, recent commercial advertising home sites in Hot Springs Village, Hot Springs, Arkansas, are sprinkled with the word "free": a free weekend including air flight, free meals, and a free luxury hotel suite for the weekend. So it doesn't cost anything, right? Wrong! It will cost you time and energy, listening to lengthy sales presentations, emotions to resist the pressure to buy something you can't afford, and returning home with a deed or exhausted from resisting the free trip. There is always a cost. Even our salvation involved a high cost. Salvation cost Christ his life! And rebellion is no different. It carries a *very* high cost. In our culture today, and often in our pulpits, the cost of sin is down played.

We down play sin by re-labeling it using the DSM 4. The person has a psychosis, a disease, an addiction, or is a victim. We downplay sin by replacing the standard we use to measure sin. It is not adultery, but consenting adults. It is an alternative lifestyles, not homosexuality. We downplay sin by allowing pop culture to determine moral right from wrong.

A story is told of a preacher who delivered a powerful sermon on the subject of sin. After the service, one of the church officers confronted the minister in his study and offered what he thought was some needed counsel. "Pastor," he said, "we don't want you to talk as openly as you do about man's guilt and corruption, because if our boys and girls hear you discussing that subject they will more easily become sinners. Call it a mistake, if you will, but do not speak so plainly about sin." The pastor removed a small bottle from a shelf behind his desk. Showing it to the man, he said, "You see this label? It says 'Strychnine,' and underneath in bold, red letters is the word 'poison.' What you are asking me to do would be like changing this label. Suppose I write over it 'Essence of Peppermint.' Someone who doesn't know the danger might use it and become very ill. The milder the label, the more dangerous the poison."

This chapter is designed to reintroduce what the Bible says about the *high costs of rebellion*. This chapter can be used for personal enrichment. Or, give this chapter to someone who is living in rebellion and blinded to the high stakes lurking around the corner. This chapter could rescue them from deep heartache. This is a great resource to be used in a small group Bible study for education and edification.

Before we begin, we must define terminology first. Disobedience can be translated using to two Greek words. First, *parakoe*, which means to hear amiss. It alludes to a misunderstanding or failure to comprehend. The second is *apeitheo*, which means disbelief, not allowing oneself to be persuaded.

Rebellion also has two major words. The first is *marah* meaning contentious. *Marah* could be construed as standing against human/divine authority, or simply put, refusal to comply. The second word is *pasha*, which means transgress. This is one of the Old Testament words for sin. It means a deliberate and with full knowledge violation of a law.

We will be using the word rebellion in the balance of this section. Rebellion may start with hearing amiss or a failure to be persuaded due to some human obstacle of disbelief. However, rebellion is an inward attitude of the heart that is observable through deliberate choices that violate known laws and regulations. Here is an example on how disobedience may lead to rebellion. "Bob, I noticed that you are not clocking in and out for lunch. Remember you are on your own for lunch. The company doesn't pay you for this time." This is failure to hear or be persuaded. Bob persists in not clocking in and out for lunch. He believes the company should pay for his lunch. Every other company he has worked for has paid for lunch time. He feels justified because he is an outstanding employee. That's rebellion.

Another example of disobedience that leads to rebellion. I arrange to pick up my friend at O'Hare airport. I tell him I will be waiting outside the American Airlines departure level. I park at the curb and remain in the car looking for my friend. A friendly police officer informs me

I cannot stand, sit, or park in this area. She points to a clear visible sign reiterating this information. I leave the area, use the airport loop to circle back around, and find another spot close to American Airlines arrival gate to wait for my friend. Another police officer taps on my window and wants to see my driver's license and proof of insurance. I get a ticket! Why? I was rebellious. Knowing the law and acknowledging the sign, I knew what was right but failed to do so mentally justifying my actions. By the way, this was an actual event I witnessed. No, it was not me! I hope these examples, in a small way, help you see the difference between the two concepts.

There is always a choice to rebel or to submit. God always gives us a choice. He is such a loving and holy God that He tells us up front what our options are. And the options are clear. They are non-negotiable. They are simple. God says, "You can obey Me or disobey Me." He reveals rewards for obedience to Himself and punishment if I choose to disobey Him.

No one can say, "I didn't know." God is not unfair. He does not have certain rules for some while others live by a different set of rules. Nor does God make up the rules as your relationship with Him develops.

Consider Deuteronomy 30:15, 19:

> See, I have set before you today life and prosperity, and death and adversity; I call heaven and earth to witness against you today, that I have set before you life and death, the blessing and the curse. So choose life in order that you may live, you and your descendants.

Or Jeremiah 21:8:

> You shall also say to this people, "Thus says the Lord, 'Behold, I set before you the way of life and the way of death.'"

My choice is made because I love Him or I love myself. I accept His rule in my life, or I want to rule my life. I believe He knows what is best for me, or I know what is best for me. I yield to His infinite wisdom, or I rely upon my own understanding. My choice is either loving submission or rebellion.

You see this concept clearly in the phrase God uses throughout Scripture. God says, "If you…" Here are some examples. Take a moment to open your Bible and read these verses: Leviticus 26:3–13 and 26:14–39; Deuteronomy 28:1–14 and 28:15–68; 1 Samuel 12:14 and 12:15; 1 Kings 9:4–5 and 9:6–9; and Galatians 6:7–8.

We should note God always lays out both options so that the one choosing can make an informed decision. God always rehearses what the rewards will be if a person chooses to obey and what the consequences will be if a person chooses to disobey. We have a choice. We can never say we did not know because God did not tell us.

What are some reasons for rebellion? Cain rebelled because he felt God was unfair in accepting his brother's offering and rejecting his. Abraham rebelled because his heart failed to cling to God's promises and he listened to the ungodly counsel of his wife. Lot rebelled because he wanted to be accepted by the "in crowd." Joshua rebelled because he relied upon his own wisdom influenced by what he saw when he looked at the Gibeonites. The twelve tribes of Israel rebelled because the task of ridding themselves of the "ites" took too much effort. Samson rebelled because he enjoyed the female attention he received. The rich young ruler rebelled because he thought the loss of selling everything was far greater than the perceived reward Jesus described. Demas rebelled because he loved this present world more than the world yet to come.

Everybody who rebelled in the Bible, if you could ask them, would explain why they rebelled. Their explanation reveals an idol. Knowing the idol will help you understand its propagating message. Identifying the message helps you remove the lie with liberating truth.

It is time we walk through the pages of Scripture to take a survey of the high cost of rebellion. Before examining Jonah's great cost of rebellion, the Bible in general addresses the high cost of rebellion. Here is what God says about the high cost of rebellion.

- Rebellion will be punished—2 Cor. 10:6
- Rebellion has a just penalty—Heb. 2:2

The High Cost of Rebellion

- A rebellious person will not have rest—Heb. 4:6
- Rebellious people are delivered into the hands of the oppressor—Neh. 9:27 and they will be abandoned to the hand of the enemy (v. 28)
- They may experience physical harm—1 Kings 13:26
- They will experience loss of divine blessings—2 Kings 18:20
- God will oppose them—2 Kings 24:1, Isa. 63:10
- They will face hard labor—Ps. 107:11—and no one will help them when they fall
- God turns away and permits horrific evil—Ezek. 5:6
- God pours out His wrath—Ezek. 20:8
- There will be captivity—Book of Judges and Daniel's prayer in Dan. 9
- They will be pursued by their enemies—Hosea 8:1
- There will be destruction—Hosea 7:13
- There may be death—Dt. 13:5
- They will experience guilt—Ps. 5:10—and the consequences of their own devices
- There will be poverty—Ps. 68:6
- Their rebellion will enslave them—Ps. 106:43

We will use Jonah to teach us the high cost of rebellion. As usual, we need some general background to understand the context. Jonah was a prophet. This means he was a servant of God in the declaration of God's revelation. He foretold God's heart, mind, and purposes. Jonah had previous prophetic ministries and would have been considered successful. Jonah was a prophet to Israel, the ten tribes to the North. Israel was under divine judgment for their idolatry. God was using the Assyrians to chastise them. The Assyrians were vicious warriors. They would lead their captives away with fish hooks in their lips and inflict other atrocities on their captives. This historical setting was where Jonah, who had known obedience and blessing, received his new ministry assignment.

I want to pose some introductory questions to consider. How did Jonah rebel? God specifically told Jonah where to go and what to say. God's instructions were crystal clear. There was no mistaking what God wanted Jonah to do. You see, this is God's only way of communicating. He is clear. There is no ambiguity when He speaks. His message is not open to interpretation (1:2).

What prompted Jonah's rebellion? It is apparent what prompted Jonah's rebellion. We read in 4:2 that Jonah had a long talk with God at the initial calling. He did not want to go because he knew if the Assyrians repented, God would relent. Jonah felt that the Assyrians needed to perish for their awful treatment of his brethren. Jonah was angry and prejudiced.

What are some of Jonah's high cost of rebellion? A high cost of rebellion is living in a world of deception (1:3). With clear instructions from God and a conversation with God that did not change God's mind, Jonah fled from the presence of the Lord.

Did Jonah honestly believe he could flee from the presence of the Lord? Had he torn from his Bible Psalm 139:7–12, which says:

> Where can I go from Your Spirit? Or where can I flee from Your presence? If I ascend to heaven, You are there; If I make my bed in Sheol, behold, You are there. If I take the wings of the dawn. If I dwell in the remotest part of the sea, even there Your hand will lead me, and Your right hand will lay hold of me. If I say, "Surely the darkness will overwhelm me, and the light around me will be night," even the darkness is not dark to You, and the night is as bright as the day. Darkness and light are alike to You.

People living in rebellion deceive themselves into believing that they can sin against the holiness of God and hide it from God. They embrace the lie that somehow God cannot see their actions. The dimly lit or darkened room where they fornicate blocks out God, or God doesn't know they are at some flop house doing drugs because He doesn't have an address!

Adam and Eve thought they could hide from their Creator when they deliberately sinned with full knowledge.

People think that if the rebellion is not discovered, then it has been hidden.

But the Bible says,

> For nothing is hidden, except to be revealed; nor has anything been secret, but that it would come to light (Mark 4:22).

> You have placed our iniquities before You, Our secret sins in the light of Your presence (Ps. 90:8).

> And there is no creature hidden from His sight, but all things are open and laid bare to the eyes of Him with whom we have to do (Heb. 4:13).

God will properly access all of our actions and even motivations. Paul writes, "Therefore do not go on passing judgment before the time, but wait until the Lord comes who will both bring to light the things hidden in the darkness and disclose the motives of men's hearts; and then each man's praise will come to him from God" (1 Cor. 4:5).

Finally, Galatians reminds us not to be deceived. What we sow, we will reap. Do you remember the sowing and reaping principles? If you sow to the flesh, you will reap of the flesh. If you sow corn, you get corn. You always reap in a different season. You always reap more than you sow.

A high cost of rebellion is to forsake liberating truth and allow circumstances to guide you (1:3). Jonah had clear instructions. He was to go to Nineveh. Because he chose to rebel, he headed for Joppa, where circumstances took over guiding him deeper into his rebellion. What were those circumstances? He found a ship going to Joppa. He happened to have the right fare to purchase a ticket. They just so happened to have one place left.

How could this be? How could Jonah reinterpret God's directives? How could Jonah do the exact opposite of what he clearly heard God say? First, Jonah was bitter and angry that God would tell him to go to these people who were so abusive to his kin and family. Second, Jonah thought he knew better than God did. These people did not need to hear a message of grace and forgiveness, but needed to experience retribution. Third, Jonah knew exactly how God would respond if the Ninevites repented. Jonah did not like God's will, so he decided to attempt to forestall God's will (4:2)

A young woman knowing that God demands moral purity fornicates believing that the man will commit to her in marriage.

A husband who knows that marriage is a sacred institution, but feels the lack of intimacy. So he decides to find solace with a co-worker through emails and luncheon appointments.

A college baseball star scouted by an NBA team knows that the use of steroids is legally and spiritually prohibited, but he also knows that he needs upper body strength for the long ball. He capitulates.

And the examples could continue. When rebellion finds a receptive heart, circumstances justify the sinful practice. The more one practices rebellion the further away they walk from liberating truth. Truth becomes the lie, and the lie is the truth.

A high cost of rebellion puts people and things in harm's way. The rebellion of Adam affected the entire human race according to Romans 5:12. The rebellion of Cain brought harm to Abel and shame to his parents. Abraham's rebellion has brought worldwide war between the Arabs and the Jews.

Rebellion always affects something or someone. According to 1:4, the ship was in danger of breaking up. Why? Jonah's rebellion and God's discipline. God sent a fierce storm on that sea that nearly broke the ship asunder. According to 1:5, Jonah's rebellion cost this freightliner its cargo and the sailors' lives came close to perishing (1:8, 10). They had to jettison the cargo to lighten the ship. They thought if they threw the freight overboard, it would lighten the ship so they could maneuver it during the storm.

Jonah did not consider the cost of his rebellion upon others. Usually, most rebellious people don't. They are not concerned about how their actions may affect others, only how they can benefit from their rebellion.

The young woman who is so desperate to marry that she marries an unbeliever, doesn't realize the pain and sorrow she inflicts upon her parents. The young man who does drugs fails to understand the financial and physical ruin that awaits his parents. The pastor or counselor who must watch and wait and be available to pick up the pieces of a shattered life because a counselee rebels against counsel given them as he/she is considering a dangerous action.

The rebellion of Achan put Israel in harm's way as they fought against Ai. Gideon's rebellion returns Israel to idol worship after his great victory over the Midianites. Lot's rebellion placed Abraham and his men in harm's way when they went to rescue him. The Roman centurion in charge of Paul's ship to Rome placed all the prisoners in harm's way because he did not like the port they had to stay at through winter. Rebellion has a high cost—especially for others!

A high cost of rebellion is self-delusion (1:6). Where do we find Jonah during the storm? Is Jonah on deck helping to bail water? Is he available to jettison the cargo? Is he assisting other sailors with the ship's rigging? Is he calling upon his God? No, Jonah is fast asleep in the bottom of the boat. He is completely numb to the storm or the plight of the sailors, or for that matter to his own probable plight. Jonah is sleeping.

How is it that Jonah could sleep during such a tumultuous storm? Jonah believed he was doing the right things. Jonah concluded that because he found a ship, he had the right amount for the fare, and the ship had a bunk available he must have misunderstood God's first directive. He had mentally convinced himself that he was able to sleep. This is delusion. He came to believe what he wanted to believe.

I found this interesting verse in Isaiah. The prophet records these words,

> You felt secure in your wickedness and said, "No one sees me," Your wisdom and your knowledge, they have deluded you; for you have said in your heart, "I am, and there is no one besides me" (Is. 47:10).

How does delusion work in a rebellious person's life? The person is exposed to a persuasive argument. The argument is always against a biblical principle or pattern. The argument may be external, say with another person, or internal, say with themselves in their mind. The Bible records "that no one will delude you with persuasive argument" (Col. 2:4).

These people are religious. They have knowledge of what the Word says but they find ways to avoid performing it. They use their knowledge as a cloak to cover up their sinful practices. James says,

> But prove yourselves doers of the word, and not merely hearers who delude themselves (1:22).

If a rebellious person continues to refute with the convicting work of the Holy Spirit, the delusion itself takes on a personality and philosophy so they reject plain truth believing what is false. "You shall surely not die!" the Bible says, "For this reason God will send upon them a deluding influence so that they will believe what is false" (2 Thess. 2:11). Throughout the Old Testament one of the accusations God has against the prophets, priests, and kings is they delude those under their authority with falsehood, speaking lies as though they were truth and coming from God.

Jeremiah 10:8 says,

> But they are altogether stupid and foolish in their discipline of delusion—their idol is wood!

I want to key in on the phrase "discipline of delusion." Those who are rebellious are not somehow mystically captured. They have not somehow lost their ability to know right from wrong. To be "disciplined of delusion" means they are actively practicing delusion and actively figuring ways to keep the falsehood before them, as well as others attempting to convince others they are right and to find continued strength to maintain their own facade.

The High Cost of Rebellion

The high cost may be that they will reach a point where they cannot recognize genuine truth and will live out their days in delusion. It might be recognized by such statements as, "Why did I wait so long to do something about this?" Or, "I am sorry for all the waste years. I know now what I refused to accept."

A high cost of rebellion is mocking God (1:9). "Mocking" means to treat with contempt or ridicule. It means to express scorn or to deride, to make fun of. Jonah mocked God. When asked a series of questions from the captain, who was shocked to find him sleeping, Jonah said:

> I am a Hebrew, and I fear the Lord God of heaven who made the sea and the dry land.

Jonah feared the Lord God of Heaven who made the sea and the dry land! The Hebrew word is *yare*, which means to stand in awe of, to acknowledge awesome acts of someone, or to inspire reverence or godly fear. Now I would conclude from this definition that if Jonah feared God of Heaven who made the sea and the dry land, Jonah would have been on a different ship heading to Nineveh.

Jonah mocked God. His mockery was evident. His actions mocked God. His speech beguiled. This is an intellectual ascent. There was a basic knowledge that idols did not make the world or control the world as Greek mythology taught. But Jonah was living life from theory, not reality. Reality is truthful and responds appropriately. Theory is just that—open to interpretation and equally open to acceptance or rejection.

The Bible says it is futile to mock God. Be not deceived, God is not mocked. The Bible says that it is a fool that mocks at sin. Proverbs 14:9 says, "Fools mock at sin."

What are some ways that a rebellious person mocks God? Arguing what the Word says; denying what the Word says; leading others astray from what the Word says; not practicing what the Word says.

A high cost of rebellion is increasing punishment if the rebellion is not repented of (1:11, 13). Verse 11 of chapter 1 says that after all of the sailors' efforts, the storm did not subside and they still had no control over the ship. It says that the sea was becoming increasingly stormy. This must have been an unusual storm for the sailors to do all that they did and still be terrified. Verse 13 says they continued to try to row out of the storm, but the sea was becoming even stormier against them.

I think the clearest picture of this principle is in Israel's life as a nation. After entering into the Promised Land, Joshua warns them they were unable to serve God because He was a jealous God and they were rebellious. When you read the book of Judges and interlace the prophets' predictions, you see the increasing punishment for rebellion.

- Israel lived in captivity to Cushan-rishathian, King of Mesopotamia, for eight years
- Then to Eglon, King of Moab, for eighteen years
- Then to Jabin, King of Canaan, for twenty years
- Then to Midian for seven years
- Then to the Philistines for forty years
- Then to the Babylonians for seventy years

A high cost of rebellion is increasing punishment if the rebellion is not repented of. Repeated fornication, abortions, sexually transmitted diseases, HIV, agonizing death. Drinking, detoxification centers, drinking, DUI, drivers license suspended, repeated job loss and hiring, unemployment, wife leaves with the children, liver damage, living in shelters, death. Ongoing rebellion leads to death by steps. If someone does not know why his or her life is taking the direction it is, it may well be directly attributable to the person's rebellion. In each of these examples, there is a downward spiral. That downward spiral becomes more severe as it plummets headlong to self-destruction and the destruction of precious human relationships.

The High Cost of Rebellion

A high cost of rebellion is probable personal endangerment (1:12, 15, 17; 2:3, 5, 6). The old adage says, "If you play with fire, you are going to get burned." Rebellion not only affects others, but the rebellious person runs the risk of personal injury and harm. Note the "personal injury and harm" passage the Spirit records from Jonah's lips.

> "Pick me up and throw me into the sea." So they picked up Jonah and threw him into the sea. And the Lord appointed a great fish to swallow Jonah. And Jonah was in the stomach of the fish three days and three nights. The current engulfed me and the breakers and billows passed over me [he is sinking]. Waters encompassed me to the point of death. The great deep engulfed me. Weeds were wrapped around my head. I descended to the roots of the mountains.

After the rebellion of Adam and Eve, it says, "And they died." The rebellious inhabitants of the world drowned. Samson had his eyes plucked out and he was chained to a mill stone like an animal because of his rebellion. The thieves on the cross died because of their rebellion. Judas suffered great harm because of his rebellion.

Now the probable harm to the rebellious person may take a variety of different forms. It may take the form of mental harm, such as the numerous unproven psychiatric labels assigned to people today. It may take the form of emotional harms, such as the numerous unproven DSM IV labels assigned to people today. It may take the form of financial problems, downsizing, overlooked for a promotion, being fired, or being underemployed. It may take the form of relationship problems, such as marital, separation, divorce, teen problems or in-laws and out-laws. It may take the form of health issues as diabetes, heart, ulcers, stroke, unexplained headaches, backaches, or a variety of other ailments.

What I am *not* suggesting is that every time something like one of the above occurs that the person is rebellious. That's like looking for a demon behind every rock or shrub. However, many of the physical ailments in the Old Testament and the Gospels were related to rebellion. It is wise to ask God to search your heart to see if there is any wicked way in you. It is an unmistaken truth that rebellion will in some way bring probable harm to the rebellious person.

A high cost of rebellion is joyless service. In chapter 3, Jonah is the most miserable evangelist ever recorded. After the fish story, his commission has not changed. He doesn't outwardly rebel. Perhaps he fears a "smaller" fish and a longer stay. The message has not changed. The location has not changed. His audience has not changed.

A sidebar: Oftentimes when someone rebels against the will of God, the rebellious person hopes or believes that the will of God will change. They will get a new assignment. When a soldier goes AWOL, is captured, stands trial, and completes his sentence, he is oftentimes returned to the unit from which he fled.

One would think that Jonah would be ecstatic that the ministry of the Word was having such a wide impact. From the king down to the common person, and even down to the animals, repentance was occurring with the hopes that Jonah's powerful God would also prove Himself merciful.

A rebellious person who is still involved with service/ministry is miserable and joyless. So how did Jonah respond to the workings of God and seeing the people repent? Jonah was displeased and angry (4:1). The very thing Jonah feared came about. Jonah pouted. Like the Pharisees, Jonah despised the goodness of God. He was self-absorbed and vindictive 4:2. Count the number of times Jonah used the personal pronoun "I" (four times). This conversation with God, as God's servant, is all about Jonah, not God nor the people rescued.

Jonah was hopeless, helpless, and fatalistic (4:3). Because he did not get his own way, he wanted to die. Life was not worth living. "What hope is there if I cannot have what I think is best?" Jonah was unresponsive to God and unteachable (4:4). God attempted to lead Jonah to right thinking. He asked Jonah if he had a good reason to be angry. What about God's grace, compassion, and abundant lovingkindness was provoking Jonah's anger? Were the results that upsetting to him? We see his unresponsiveness because he left not answering God a word. His silence was loud. His actions were even louder. He built himself a shelter and sat under it. Why? He was waiting to see if God were going to accept the repentance of these wicked, godless, and violent people!

Jonah lived in bitter isolation 4:5. The message Jonah preached was forty days and God would destroy the city. We read that the city was large and it took three days to walk its length. It was on day one that the people who heard repented. It was from those people that the news spread like wild fire. The entire city repented. This means that at the outside Jonah had this conversation with God at about day four, leaving him thirty-six days, over a month, to pout, brood, and wallow in his bitter spirit.

Jonah enjoyed God's benevolence but clung to his rebellion (4:6). God wanted Jonah to recognize that no matter how God responded to people who formerly rejected Him, living in rebellion, He was the same to Jonah with all the benefits. God grew a tree. Jonah enjoyed the tree, but clung to his bitterness. God appointed a worm that destroyed the tree. Jonah remained unchanged in his rebellion—tree or no tree.

How do we help someone avoid the high costs of rebellion? (4:10). First, establish biblical priorities. We have to help the rebellious person establish biblical priorities. It will begin with repentance. In the passages where God begins, "If you," you can read that when they repented or when they returned, God restored them. A rebellious person begins dealing with his/her rebellion by confession and repentance. When this divine purging takes place, then he/she can establish biblical priorities. The focus is on God, not themselves. A biblical priority is seeing all of life from God's point of view with a commitment to allow those patterns to mold and shape one's life for His honor and glory. Repentance helps to remove self patterns. This void must be filled with God's patterns. Removal of self is not enough. If biblical priorities do not fill the void created by repentance, another rebellious attitude or action will fill the empty space. Biblical priorities are firmly rooted in a person's life by perseverance, diligence, and discipline.

Second, people have to accept correction. A rebellious person must accept correction. He/she must be open to the correction from others. This will demonstrate a heart change from acting like a fool to acting like a wise person.

> The wise of heart *will receive commands*, but a babbling fool will be ruined (Prov. 10:8).
>
> Wise men *store up knowledge*, but with the mouth of the foolish, ruin is at hand (10:14).
>
> The way of a fool is right in his own eyes, but a wise man is he who *listens to counsel* (12:15).
>
> A wise son accepts his father's discipline, but a scoffer does not listen to rebuke (13:1).
>
> He who *walks with wise men will be wise*, but the companion of fools will suffer harm (13:20).

The rich young ruler was given wise counsel, but refused correction. He perished because of his rebellion.

Accepting correction implies brokenness. Accepting correction implies humility. Accepting correction means dealing with self, and pride. Accepting correction means I am not as smart as I think I am. Accepting correction means I acknowledge another wiser, more powerful than myself.

Third, a rebellious person must submit and repent. Jonah never did submit or repent. You may object that he did repent in chapter 2. But I propose to you that he did not. Had he fully and biblically repented, would he not have had a sweeter spirit in ministry, rejoicing at the repentance of his arch enemies, and would he not have stayed in the city instead of sitting on the hill waiting for its destruction? A rebellious person must submit to one who is in greater authority. A rebellious person must repent of his/her rebellion and all associated sins. There must be a demonstration of godly sorrow, not worldly sorrow. Dr. Stuart Scott does an excellent job in explaining the difference between worldly and godly sorrow from 2 Corinthians 7:9–11. You can secure this valuable teaching by ordering a NANC conference cassette tape entitled "Repentance or Penance" by Dr. Scott. Failure to deal with repentance allows rebellion to maintain a foothold in a person's life.

Fourth, the rebellious must demonstrate compassion. When rebellion is biblically dealt with, a new outlook on life begins to take place. Once hard, angry, and bitter eyes are now replaced with lovingkindness and compassion. I think of the Levite and Pharisee who "saw" the plight of a fellow Jew who had been beaten, robbed, and left for dead in the middle of the road between Jerusalem and Jericho. Each saw. But each man's heart was in rebellion simply performing his religious obligations. A dreaded Samaritan saw the plight of the beaten Jew, an enemy, but was moved with compassion to get involved and provide assistance. Read the story and note all the action verbs after the Samaritan saw and was filled with compassion. Compassion is a sign that rebellion is being changed. It may ebb and flow, depending on the depth of and length of rebellion in a person's life. But if someone remains entrenched in his/her rebellion, continuing to view people as Jonah did, the root has not been removed. That is why you continue to see the fruit. Rebellion can be like a dry, hard sponge—useless. It is not pliable and is unprofitable for anything. It is brittle. Compassion is the water that softens the brittle sponge, making it pliable and useable, fulfilling its purpose. Jonah's heart was so hard that even the idea of children who could have perished, let alone livestock, did not soften his heart.

The costs of rebellion are enormous. The price is high to live a rebellious life. It bothers me that the book of Jonah closes so abruptly. Jonah is on the outskirts of the city, sitting under a ramshackle lean-to, getting beaten by the east wind with God's words ringing in his ears, "Should I not have compassion on Nineveh, the great city in which there are more than 120,000 persons who do not know the difference between their right and left hand, as well as many animals?"

Wouldn't it be sweet and encouraging to have a verse 12: "And Jonah arose, returned to the great city of Nineveh and rejoiced over the gracious and compassionate God who is slow to anger and abundant in loving-kindness, and one who relents concerning calamity."

That, my friend, is a sign that rebellion has been crucified! Sometimes it is necessary to forewarn someone of the high costs of rebellion. It is a biblical and legitimate way to influence the thinking of a person given to considering a rebellious pathway. God uses this pattern.

There's Just Not Enough Time

Getting the Most out of Your Twenty-Four Hours: Biblical Life Skills for Time Management

Are you like thousands of other Americans who need more time? Have you ever said, thought, or felt the following?

- "If only I had more time!"
- "I need more time!"
- "If only I had twenty-five hours in a day!"
- "I don't know where the time goes!"
- "Time flies!"
- "I have so much to do and so little time!"
- "I don't have time for this [sickness, delays, viewing others as impeding your progress]!"
- I could complete by tasks if I just had a few more hours of time each week."

The Roman playwright, Seneca, said, "We are always complaining that our days are few and acting as though there would be no end of time."

H. Jackson Brown says, "Don't say you don't have enough time. You have exactly the same number of hours per day that were given to Helen Keller, Pasteur, Michelangelo, Mother Teresa, Leonardo da Vinci, Thomas Jefferson, and Albert Einstein."

Another has replied to the statement of timing flying by saying, "Yes, time flies, but you're the pilot!"

It is a true axiom. Everything requires time. It is the only true universal condition. All work takes place in time and uses up time. Yet most people take for granted this unique, irreplaceable, and necessary resource.

The Theology of Time

Time is limited. An old adage says, "Work expands to fill the time allotted." In other words, if I allow one hour to do a task that takes fifteen minutes, it will take one hour. Time is limited. No one has unlimited time. Even the richest person does not have unlimited time.

Exodus 20:9–10 reminds us, "Six days you shall labor and do all your work, but the seventh day is a Sabbath of the Lord your God; in it you shall not do any work." This verse is repeated eleven times in Exodus and Leviticus and nine times specifically in Exodus. God is telling His people time is limited.

Job speaks of the limitation man's time when the Spirit records, "Man, who is born of woman, is *short-lived* and full of turmoil. Like a flower, he comes forth and withers. *He also flees like a shadow and does not remain.* You also open your eyes on him and bring him into judgment with yourself. Who can make the clean out of the unclean? No one! *Since his days are determined, the number of his months is with you; and his limits you have set so that he cannot pass.*" (Italics for emphasis.)

Hebrews 9:27 tells us that there is a time in which man dies, there is a limitation to life expectancy and limitations for divine opportunities. Hebrews 3:7, 13, 15 says, "Therefore, just as the Holy Spirit says, 'Today if you hear His voice,' But encourage one another day after day, as long as it is still called 'Today,' so that none of you will be hardened by the deceitfulness of sin. While it is said, 'Today if you hear His voice,' Do not harden your hearts, as when they provoked Me." Time is limited. It has limitations. Man does not have an unlimited quantity of time.

The Lord already establishes the maximum number of productive years. "As for the days of our life, they contain seventy years, or if due to strength, eighty years, yet their pride is but labor and sorrow; for soon it is gone and we fly away. Your eyes have seen my unformed substance; and in your book were all written the days that were ordained for me, when as yet there was not one of them." Some people's productive years are thirty-five, and for others it may be eighty-eight. Not only does the Lord establish the length of our days but the productivity during those days.

Psalm 1 reminds us that we are to "yield its fruit in its season." This seems to indicate that with each season (decade of our life), our existence is for the productivity of God.

John 15 seems to support this by indicating different levels of fruit bearing from fruit, more fruit to most fruit. This means aging and maturity, living and working to the fullest in cooperation with the years established by the Lord.

Good King Hezekiah is a pitiful portrait of a man who failed to except the years established by the Lord. Because of his rejection of the Sovereignty of God, the last fifteen years of his life were unproductive and destructive. Take a moment and read 2 Kings 20. Hezekiah is mortally ill. He will die. He has been a great king, purging the nation from wickedness and idolatry. Yet at the revelation of going to Paradise, he weeps and mourns bitterly. God directs the prophet to return and tell Hezekiah that fifteen years will be added to his life. His productivity sharply declines. He shows to his future captors the great storehouse of riches. He allows idolatry to creep back into the nation's life. God knows best, and the days ordained for us to be productive for Him in the Kingdom are wisely and lovingly established.

We are commanded to count our days. Psalm 90:12 records, "So teach us to number our days that we may present to you a heart of wisdom."

From an advertisement in *TIME Magazine*, "My life is hectic! I'm running all day, meetings, phone calls, paperwork, and appointments. I push myself to the limit, fall into bed exhausted, and get up early the next morning to do it all again. My output is tremendous; I'm getting a lot done. But I get this feeling inside sometimes, 'So what? What are you doing that really counts?' I have to admit, I don't know."

What does our life mean? What are we doing on a daily basis to impact eternity through our lives, our thoughts, emotions, and actions? Do we really live appropriately in relation to 1 Cor. 10:31 that whatever we do it should be designed for the glory of God? How are we using each day wisely? For evangelism, discipleship, mentoring, fellowship, accountability, growth in holiness, so others are attracted to our Savior, Lord, Creator and Redeemer? Do we comprehend that time is short, fleeting, and passing quickly? That our sight should be on the eternal, not the temporal? Like Moses who sought a better city, and was a sojourner, we too need to leave the condominiums of life and return to the transient tents of eternal matters.

I once read a thought-provoking article entitled, "If You Are 35, You Have 500 Days to Live." Its thesis was that when you subtract the time spent sleeping (23 years), working (16 years), watching television (8 years), eating (6 years), travel (6 years), leisure (4.5 years), illness (4 years), dressing (2 years) and religion (1/2 year) you will have roughly the equivalent of only 500 days left to spend as you wish. How would you live then? No wonder the psalmist advised, "So teach us to number our days that we may apply our hearts to wisdom."

Time requires accountability. Imagine for a moment that some benefactor daily provided an allowance to you. You could spend it any way you wished. You would receive $1,440 per day. The only stipulation is what you did not spend you forfeited. You could not use it the following day.

Likewise, God gives us 24 hours per day, or 1,440 minutes per day, or 86,400 seconds per day. Each day consists of opportunities, challenges, problems, the past, present, and future. At the end of the day, if we were called into a strict accountability, what could we show for such a prized commodity?

The Gospel of Matthew tells stories of masters who entrusted to their slaves their possessions. The master expected the slaves to invest these possessions and return to him not just the principle, but interest as well. Each story tells of the slaves giving accountability.

Each story records the master's pleasure and reward or displeasure and disdain.

1 Corinthians 3 and 2 Corinthians 5 remind the believer that we will all appear before the Judgment Seat of Jesus Christ to give accountability for the deeds we have done in the flesh since becoming a Christian. It will include a judgment on our spending, talents, abilities, and it will include time management.

Without proper stewardship of time, our accomplishments will reflect "self" or "selfless." Richard Baxter, the great Puritan Reform preacher wrote, "Spend your time in nothing which you know must be repented of; in nothing on which you might not pray for the blessing of God; in nothing which you could not review with a quiet conscience on your dying bed; in nothing which you might not safely and properly be found doing if death should surprise you in the act."

Time is an entrusted gift by God. "We must work the works of Him who sent Me as long as it is day; night is coming when no one can work" (John 9:4). Soon in your hand will be placed a priceless gift. Look at it closely. There is no price stamped on it. It cannot be weighed, because no scale can balance its value. A king's ransom in comparison is as nothing, yet it is given to beggar and prince alike. The giver asks only that it be used wisely and well. This jewel, rare and unique, is not displayed in any shop window. It cannot be purchased, cannot be sold. No other treasure holds the possibilities this gift offers—none can surpass its golden splendor. Of all gifts, this is one of the most precious. It has been offered many times before; today, from the depths of a limitless love it will be given again. It will be left to you to find the golden thread running through it. Only with great care will the jewel retain its luster. Carelessness, ingratitude, and selfishness will tarnish the brilliance, break the unspoiled thread, and mar the perfection. Guard it closely, lest through weak fingers it slip from the hand. Look often at its faultless beauty. Accept it as it is offered from the heart of the giver. Consider it is the most treasured of possessions, for of all gifts it is by far the greatest. It is the gift of time.

I think that perhaps the greatest advancements for the Kingdom come through the wise use of our minutes—seizing the moment, capturing the opportunities, believing that God is entrusting to us *time*. Jesus recognized the windows of opportunity. They were not always convenient, were they? When He was tired and thirsty, He ministered to the woman at the well. When it was bedtime, Nicodemus came to see Him at midnight. When He was traveling to Jarius's house, a woman interrupted Him, but He took time to minister to her needs. He stopped to raise the only son of the widow of Nain. He took time to feed the multitudes that followed Him for three days.

Why did Jesus do this and why do we struggle, viewing people, at times, as interruptions? I think one reason is the people represent time and eternity. His investment of time in them would multiply for eternity. It is true, isn't it? There will always be "something" to do. You will never completely accomplish your to-do list. The list can wait. People can't. Lists can be revised and re-written. People live once, opportunities often only come once. People die. At the end of each day, who on your list can you check off as using time wisely to encourage them, edify them, pray with and for them, exhort or rebuke them, comfort them. The biblical commands of the "one another"s require time!

Time is unrecoverable. We discussed the concept of time from the parable of being given $1,440 a day to spend, and if it was not all spent, you would lose it. Time, unlike many other assets, cannot be saved, banked, or hidden from view to return to later to use.

Ecclesiastes speaks of a time for every season. There is a point in which time has passed, and you cannot go back to recover lost moments. A workaholic father cannot recover time in his child's life. He cannot go back and make it up. Time is lost forever.

Ephesians 5:16 tells you to make the most of your time, because the days are evil. There is a time for ministry, for capitalizing on the here and now, for not squandering the present on selfish idolatrous pleasure. God opens doors and windows, but He also closes them.

2 Timothy 4:3 teaches us that there will come a time when they will not endure sound doctrine; but *wanting* to have their ears tickled, they

will accumulate for themselves teachers in accordance to their own desires. There is a time for salvation and sanctification. If not seized, unsound doctrine and the philosophies of men will replace sound doctrine.

Hebrews 5:12 says, "For though by this time you ought to be teachers, you have need again for someone to teach you the elementary principles of the oracles of God, and you have come to need milk and not solid food." There is a time for spiritual maturity. But laziness and procrastination pin us to immaturity when we should be so much further along.

1 Peter 1:17 says, "And if you address as Father the One who impartially judges according to each one's work, conduct yourselves in fear during the time of your stay on earth." There is a time for judgment. When we understand that life is short, we conduct ourselves in the fear of the Lord knowing there is a time of judgment. We wisely select, choose, and participate in only those things that will benefit the Kingdom and glorify God.

Each day is made *by* the Lord *for* the Lord. A humorous story illustrates this premise.

> At long last, we have them! And in sufficient quantity so that you can have this for your very own. Please cut yours out and save it. Put it in a safe place. Try not to lose it. Or better yet, keep a few spares on hand. These *TUITs* have been hard to come by, especially the round ones. But now by special arrangement, you can have yours. We're happy because the need has been so great. Now that these are available, most of our problems about attendance, starting on time, and getting things done at church will be solved. We look for our attendance at services to double, now that everyone has his *round TUIT*. For you see, so many have said, "I'll get started in church just as soon as I can get a *round tuit*." Others have said, "I should come to the evening service, but I never seem to get a *round tuit*." Or, "I know that my Bible knowledge would increase if I came to class, but I never get a *round tuit*." Or, "I've been wanting to start singing in choir and I've been planning to begin tithing my income, but we've been so busy that we just haven't gotten a *round tuit*." Well, now that is all past! Everyone can have his own *round tuit*. If you meet someone who never gets a *round tuit*, give him one. Keep a good supply on hand. Great things are in store for us!

Psalm 118:24 tells us, "This is the day which the Lord has made, let us rejoice and be glad in it." The psalmist says that the Lord makes each day. The Lord grants the ability to continue breathing through the night, directs our bodies to open our eyes and to move our limbs, and sets us on our way. We are blessed by God to live in the day He has made. Because He is the author of the day in which we live, He possesses the right to direct our day and has the right to expect that the benefactor of His grace do what He requires with rejoicing and gladness, for the day is not about us or even for us, but about Him and for Him. Delay, procrastination, indifference, apathy, slothfulness, laziness, unconcern, hesitation, or vacillation renounces the time management principles that the day is from and for the Lord.

Everyone has the same amount of time. Arnold Bennett writes, "You wake up in the morning with twenty-four hours of the unmanufactured tissue of the universe of your life. It is yours. It is the most precious of possessions. No one can take it from you. It is unstealable. And no one receives either more or less."

We have all thought or said, "If only I had more time." I really don't think that more time is the answer. If we cannot utilize the time we have now properly, adding more time would only add more guilt because we would mismanage the additional time given.

Why is it we would make such a request? Perhaps one reason is the subject of this very study—we are not managing our time wisely. Secondly, we put off and put off. This is known as procrastination. We procrastinate because the task is too large, too great or we view it as too difficult. Or we think we have more time than what the task requires. We cram our schedules full of tasks, and then mis-prioritize those tasks. We major on the minors because they are easier to accomplish and bring a sense of immediate satisfaction. What was necessary was the harder, more complex task. But we failed to do it and then complain that we ran out of time or we wished we had another hour or two. Paul Tournier writes, "God gives me the gift of twenty-four hours a day; yet He is kind enough to accept in return the little time I give back to Him."

There are seasons for tasks appropriate to the event and time. Then God said, "Let there be lights in the expanse of the heavens to separate the day from the night, and let them be for signs and for seasons and for days and years" (Gen. 1:14).

Ecclesiastes 3 reminds us that there is an appointed time for everything. There is a time for every event under Heaven; a time to give birth and a time to die; a time to plant and a time to uproot what is planted; a time to kill and a time to heal; a time to tear down and a time to build up; a time to weep and a time to laugh; a time to mourn and a time to dance; a time to throw stones and a time to gather stones; a time to embrace and a time to shun embracing; a time to search and a time to give up as lost; a time to keep and a time to throw away; a time to tear apart and a time to sew together; a time to be silent and a time to speak; a time to love and a time to hate; a time for war and a time for peace.

I believe this concept speaks to the issue of priorities in relation to time. Many of us operate on the mentality of, "I deserve…" "I deserve to rest and relax. I have worked hard. I am tired." We postpone our responsibilities for temporary pleasure. The athlete doesn't get the gold metal until he has trained and won. The soldier doesn't get the Purple Heart until he has fought and won. The farmer doesn't get to taste the crops until he has plowed, sown, weeded, and harvested.

There is a time to relax. But there is a time to work. I would also suggest that this concept addresses the old adage that work expands to fit the time allotted. We should get into the practice of setting reasonable time for each task; otherwise, we run the danger of wasting time. For example: My to-do list for Saturday consists of mowing the lawn, washing the family car, and straightening up my tool room. To use time efficiently, to accomplish these tasks, and to be able to rest and relax with a clear to-do list, time should be assigned. Mowing the lawn will take me thirty minutes. Washing the family car will take me forty-five minutes. Straightening up my tool room will take me one and a half hours. With those timeframes in mind, I have set goals, I can work more efficiently and I can probably be done before noon on Saturday and have the rest of the day and evening to enjoy my family, favorite book, or sports event.

Take time to plan and prepare. Dawson Trotman, the founder and first president of The Navigators, once said, "The greatest time wasted is the time getting started." Work is 90% preparation and 10% perspiration. The loss of time is attributed to the lack of planning. Even when people plan, they somehow get distracted and don't work the plan.

Nehemiah 2:11–16 records Nehemiah's arrival in Jerusalem. It must have been overwhelming to see the rubble and desolation of his beloved city. It was equally difficult to fathom the destitution and poverty of the saints who lived in and around the once great city of David. Where would Nehemiah begin? How could he rally the troops to work on such a mammoth building project?

Tasks, whether large or small, are best accomplished when you make prepare and plan. Nehemiah did a midnight survey of the problem. He then spoke to the inhabitants about the plan. The plan promoted hope and they put their hand to the good work, had a mind to work, and accomplished the work in fifty-two days.

Some tasks are quite large. Even Nehemiah recognized that, and smaller assignments were made. It was not one man's responsibility, but wise delegation and assignment saw the wall rise out of the rubble and the gates burned with fire, rebuilt and re-hung. Plan the work; then work the plan.

When the Shepherd is in charge, the use of time becomes a perpetual blessing. Psalm 23:6 declares, "Surely goodness and lovingkindness will follow me all the days of my life, and I will dwell in the house of the Lord forever." Proverbs 3:2 states, "For length of days and years of life and peace they will add to you.

In the shepherd's psalm, many blessings are provided by the Shepherd for those who claim Him as the Lord. One such blessing is time. "All the days of my life" are marked by the Lord's goodness and lovingkindness following me. In the Hebrew, the phrase "will follow me" can be rightly understood as "chasing me" all the days of my life. Why? Because the Lord is my Shepherd. The Lord's acts of gracious benefit and His steadfast loyal love are constants in the sheep's life.

In Proverbs 3:2, this blessing comes as an encouragement from listening and obeying the instructions of authority. Here, it is the instructions of a father. Hearing and heeding the words of God insure the full length of days and a life filled with peace. My days will not be cut short because of foolishness or selfishness. My life will possess a quality of peace that is beyond human comprehension. When the Lord is in charge of my time, He only works out all things for my good and His glory.

Invite God to help you know your limitations. Psalm 39:4 says, ""Lord, make me to know my end and what is the extent of my days; let me know how transient I am." A little success often goes to our heads. We extend ourselves and embark on better and greater things. Young people often think they are invincible. Endless strength and energy. But here the psalmist asks God to remind him of his limitations. God is not concerned with the amount we do, but the quality in which we do anything. God is a God of excellence and He expects those who know and love Him to imitate Him. God is endless in energy and strength. We are not. He told His disciples after ministry to come apart for a while, and as Vance Havner added, "Or to come apart if they didn't."

Because God is omniscient and we are finite in wisdom, only He can tell us of what we are capable. He must be consulted regularly so we can accomplish with excellence all He has called us to do. Js. 4:13–17 reminds us that God must be consulted with the use of our time. There is nothing wrong with planning and preparing. However, when God is excluded, the author of time, we become selfish and sinful. At times, our plans are for self-promotion, motivated by greed. The plan may sound biblical, right, and true. But it doesn't ring true. There is a sour note. When we push God-ordained limitations, we become fatigued, tired, anxious, angry, and a very poor testimony to others. God's limitations are for our welfare and His glory. Accept them. Rest in them. Find rejuvenation to return to what He has called you to do.

Take time to evaluate and review so you can improve. Psalm 77:5 says, "I have considered the days of old, the years of long ago." Deuteronomy 32:7 records, "Remember the days of old, consider the years of all generations. Ask your father, and he will inform you."

History repeats itself because we do not learn from the past. We often ask our children, "Well, what did you learn from this experience?" We are hoping that experience and life were the better teachers.

How can we make improvements if we do not evaluate what we just did? How can we make necessary adjustments if we do not consider how a certain project went?

We will never know if we took too much time on a segment of a task and not enough time on another segment of the same task if we do not take time to evaluate.

The only one who does not need to evaluate is God Himself. Everything He does is good and very good. But we humans need to. Why? Because our drive, methods, and procedures may be tainted with self-promotion and gratification, when the saint is called to do everything for the honor and glory of God.

Wisdom adds and multiplies time. Proverbs 9:11 states, "For by me your days will be multiplied and years of life will be added to you." Proverbs 19:20 adds, "Listen to counsel and accept discipline that you may be wise the rest of your days." These two verses make reference to another who is more qualified in the area of time and how best to use it.

I can change the oil on my vehicle. I really can. I would pull the Jeep into the garage. I would purchase six quarts of oil and a new oil filter. I would hunt for the oil pan and oil wrench. I would stabilize the rear wheels, and perhaps jack up the front end slightly (I've gained weight recently). Then I would crawl under the Jeep, tug and pull on the oil filter (trying to remember clockwise or counter-clockwise), finally loosen the filter and dodge the oil splatters. Then I would tug and pull on the oil pan nut and hope that it does not fall into the oil pan and

I have to go fishing. I could replace the oil nut, filter, and then add oil. I would then start the car and let it run for a few minutes. I would shut the engine off and check the oil levels. I would then lower the car, remove the rear tire bracings. I would put the tools away, and try to figure out what to do with the old oil filter and oil. I figure I can change my oil in about sixty minutes. Or, I can go to Jiffy Lube and be in and out in about 15–20 minutes, oil changed, new filter, tire air pressure checked, exterior bulbs checked, and not have a drop of oil on me. They are the experts. I can do it, but I will waste time. They are trained to be efficient and because they are, I am with my time.

Wisdom is Jesus personified. I Corinthians 1:30 says that Jesus has been made unto us wisdom. Using wisdom (Jesus) guides me in avoiding the pitfalls of wasted time, resources, and energies. I can accomplish more because wisdom wants me to succeed for God's honor and glory. Proverbs speaks of wisdom as calling to me from the streets and marketplace. Wisdom knows completely and thoroughly. I do not. How foolish to believe I can be more efficient and even multiply my time apart from an utter dependence upon wisdom.

Time is short so invest it. Ephesians 5:16 declares, "Make the most of your time because the days are evil." As mentioned earlier we only have seventy years life span and perhaps ten additional years by God's grace. Time is an asset. We invest in time—period. One way or the other, we use time as a commodity. The dividends are determined by how we invest in time. We are forewarned in Ephesians the reason to invest wisely—because the days are evil. The twenty-four hours in each day are evil. Why? Because the god of this world rules in this realm. He is a murderer, a lair, and the accuser of the brethren. He comes to seek and destroy. But in his darkness, saints shine forth brightly as the noonday sun.

The more the saint invests in bold, righteous acts of love, we, for now, repel the full encompassing darkness that will take place once the Church is removed. The dividends of wisely investing in time are the equipping and maturing of the saints for the ongoing work of ministry. Someone has written, "Just a tiny little minute, only sixty seconds in it. Forced upon me. Can't refuse it. Didn't seek it, didn't choose it, I must suffer if I lose it; give account if I abuse it. Just a tiny little minute, but eternity is in it."

Time is a reflection of God's attribute of patience working out a special something in your life. I Peter 3:20 makes reference to the patient waiting of God during the wicked days of Noah. For 120 years, Noah was faithful to the commission of God to build the Ark. We also know that besides constructing the Ark, Noah was a preacher of righteousness. What was the result of Noah's efforts? Eight people enter the Ark and the rest drown.

Why didn't God just supernaturally have the Ark appear and write in the sky the impending doom because of humanity's wickedness, so more could enter the Ark? Why have Noah go through all that agonizing work of building and preaching to no avail but his own family members?

Here, instead of being busy using time, we are exhorted to wait on time. When things don't appear to be on track, things are moving slower than usual, and we find ourselves frustrated and perhaps even angry that what we think should have happened by now and it hasn't—time even in this respect involves God who is transcendent—not confined or limited by time.

This concept can be likened to the child who spotted a cocoon. His mother explained that inside the cocoon was a butterfly trying to get out. She went on to describe the brilliant colors that would be seen soon; the bright oranges and red, and the golden yellows with sharp black stripes. One day passed, then another. Now almost a week was approaching and no butterfly. So the child decided to help the butterfly out. He sneaked some scissors out of the house and quietly climbed the tree. He then carefully and gently began to cut open the side of the cocoon. But instead of releasing the beautiful butterfly, out came a liquid thick substance. The child jumped from the tree and ran to his mother crying. He couldn't wait, and in his attempts to help only made matters worse. Like many Christians, we struggle to wait for God's perfect timing. They jump in to help, but in the end only make matters worse.

The mismanagement of time brings certain ruin and destruction. Proverbs 24:30–33 is a very interesting passage. Solomon records, "I passed by the field of the sluggard and by the vineyard of the man lacking sense, and behold it was completely overgrown with thistles; its surface was covered with nettles, and its stone wall was broken down. When I saw, I reflected upon it; I looked and received instruction. A little sleep, a little slumber, a little folding of the hands to rest, then your poverty will come as a robber and your want like an armed man."

Procrastination, laziness, slothfulness, and indifference are the tools that cultivate ruin and destruction. All work involves time. To ignore time, to think we have more time than we need for a task, may well find the manager of the project burning the midnight oil to produce usually an inferior product.

What is equally sad is you and I observing this person, shaking our heads, commenting inside our hearts that would never happen to you or me. But reality is reality. We often find ourselves in the same situation. We saw, we committed, but we lacked follow through. We are no different.

There is an ancient story about three demons who were arguing over the best way to destroy the Christian mission in the world. The first demon says, "Let's tell all the Christians there is no Heaven. Take away the reward incentive and the mission will collapse." The second demon says, "Let's tell all the Christians there is no Hell. Take away the fear of punishment and the mission will collapse." The third demon says, "There is one better way. Let's tell all the Christians that there is no hurry" and all three immediately say, "That's it! All we have to do is tell them there's no hurry and the whole Christian enterprise will collapse."

What are some time management solutions? First, analyze. Analyze the time you are spending and determine if you are chasing after the wind or striving under the sun. How does this help build the Kingdom? Is it more self than serve? Who is really benefiting from this? Learn to say "no."

Second, do a personal inventory. Ask yourself, How does the use of my time reflect Kingdom living? Will it really matter in eternity? Do I get angry when my schedule is interrupted? By taking on a new assignment, will I reduce or eliminate time required to fulfill my present duties with excellence? This is known as robbing Peter to pay Paul. You may be good at everything, but excellent at nothing. Has God provided talents and skills for this new area? Can my spiritual gift be used in this new area? Do I have time to invest in a learning curve? Will my present time management allow me to learn how to do this new assignment well? Will I receive training or support for the new assignment? Am I accepting this new responsibility to avoid a biblical pattern? Am I accepting this new responsibility to avoid a difficult task? Am I accepting this new responsibility to gain someone's approval?

Third, Plan steps of correction. I need to measure my tasks in light of the time I have. I must be honest with myself—can I accomplish this within my present abilities? I must correct biblical imbalances in my life before I am successful with time management (Ps. 127:2). I must search the Scriptures to understand and implement biblical solutions. This is God training me in righteousness. I must recognize the sinful life choices that influence my present decision making. This is known as preconditioning. I must choose to serve God, not myself. I must continually ask myself what God wants me to become. Utilize a time log with a task section to plan your work.

Learn how to take larger projects and break them down in smaller achievable steps. Ask: "What should the finished project look like? What resources will I need to acquire? What logical steps do I need to follow? What comes first sequentially? Would it be wise to solicit help for any or the entire project? Can I gather information by talking with others, going to the library, etc.?"

Check your schedule before you assume new responsibilities. Remove distractions and remain focused. Estimate the time for each task to be accomplished. Set time frames for each task to help maintain a proper attitude and quality of work.

Learn to be liable to others for accountability. Always check with your immediate authority figure; i.e., husband, pastor, elder, or boss. Consult with godly, mature, trusted advisors. Regularly share with others where you are and what you intend to do. Ask them to check up on your progress periodically. Be open to their exhortations, rebukes, and encouragements.

Develop yardsticks to measure progress. Consult your to-do list. Consult your task log. Consult your authority figure. Consult your advisors. Take a mini-retreat to review. Step back from the daily routine to see the larger picture. Ask yourself, "What are some high points? What are some low points?" List four or five major accomplishments or changes. Ask others to list major changes and areas for continued improvement.

The "Time Manager and Responsibilities Reminder." Here are some practical suggestions.

1. Go on your computer. Using an 8 ½" x 11" sheet of paper in portrait and a table, create two columns and as many rows to encompass 6:00 a.m. through 10:00 p.m. in fifteen-minute increments.

2. For the next one or two weeks, daily keep a time log. Record everything you do in that specific fifteen-minute time slot. This may reveal some startling data that could help influence you to make significant changes in how you use your time.

3. Evaluate where you could have used your time more wisely. Consider if you allowed too much or too little for a required task.

4. Next, add to the upper right of the paper, another table consisting of only one column with fifteen rows. This is your task scheduler. You have five rows to schedule tasks for the morning, five for the afternoon, and five for the evening.

5. Record the night before your tasks. Determine when you will perform these tasks. Then assign an amount of time for each task. Schedule it in your time log.

6. Nightly evaluate the amount of time you scheduled, and how the task turned out. Was it done successfully? According to plan? Relatively free from stress and anger? Was there not enough time? What would you say was the reason for insufficient time to complete the task? Interruptions, distractions, or poor planning?

7. Make adjustments for future tasks using your time log and task scheduler.

It has been my prayer throughout the development of this chapter that the content and suggestions would be biblical, practical, and relevant. If any of this has been accomplished, it has been because of God's rich grace and mercy.

I have a bit of discouraging news for you as we close, however. Time is perpetual. We may grasp these principles now and make changes for the glory of God, but we must remain diligent and vigilant in guarding this priceless commodity as we seek to honor the One who bestows us with time. One day we will live with no time pressures, constraints, or restrictions. Until that time, may we use this time in His time.

I'm at My Wits' End!
What Can You Do When You Can't Do Any More?

"What can you do when you can't do any more" seems like a strange title, doesn't it? But stop and think about it. Haven't you ever experienced this in your life? Let's say you have applied for a job. You complete the application form. You attach your resume to the application. You either left that packet with the receptionist of Human Resources, or you mailed it, or you did all of this electronically through www.Monster.com. Then you adhere to the proper protocol, waited several days, and followed up with a phone call. You might play telephone tag with the interviewer, but you finally connect. An appointment for an interview is set. After a thirty-minute interview, he/she tells you that you seem to fit the qualifications. The company procedure is, after interviewing all the applicants, they narrow the field down for a second interview. They will be in touch. You wait … and wait … and then you are asked to come back for a second interview. You believe it went well. They tell you they will be making their decision by the end of May. It is only the beginning of April. You may begin to think, "What else can I do to let them know I really want this job," or "How can I market myself more? Should I send a follow up email? Maybe a fancy thank-you card or letter? A telephone call? Or would these actions show them I am anxious or desperate?"

We have all experienced doing everything we can and still find ourselves waiting and wondering what else we can do.

Presently, my wife and I are living in the middle of this title. We have at least four major fronts that are ripe for an answer from God. My wife and I have considered what else we could do. One area is selling our home. Well, we could lower the asking price, but there are some reasons why we can't do that. I could stand at an exit ramp on one of Chicago's major expressways holding a sign, "House for Sale—Must Sell Immediately. Cheap!" But I may get arrested or worse yet get hit by a vehicle. I could … You see, that's the problem. I could … "I could" eliminates the presence and sovereign operation of God. "I could" believes there is always something else that could be done, I just have not thought of it yet. "I could" pushes the sovereignty of God and elevates the probability of acting independent from God, which is sinful. If I have done everything I can do biblically, I cannot do anything more without sinning. "I could" leads me to "I shouldn't have"—regrets.

What are some things we shouldn't do?

Try harder. We become Avis saints. When someone tries harder, they believe they have not done enough. They feel they could have done more. Since things are not working out, they think, "What have I done wrong or what should I have done or what more can I do to bring about the results and the timing of those results?" They do a lot of rehearsing and rehashing, and perform dangerous microscopic surgery. When our motivation to try harder conflicts with nothing more can be done biblically, we will sin. We will violate one of God's ordained patterns. We will deepen the problem and lose significant blessings.

Manipulate. We attempt to control people. We try to influence circumstances. We use people to accomplish our own agenda. Whenever possible we work our desires into the picture. We maneuver people, places, and things toward our goals. We lie, deceive, exaggerate, or misrepresent the truth. We can to this by our words, facial expressions, and nonverbal cues. Our goal is the most important. The dictionary defines manipulation in the original as "back information." It means to manage or influence shrewdly or deviously; to falsify or tamper with for personal gain.

Display sinful emotions. Sinful emotions reveal the human heart. Anger, worry, bitterness, fear, anxiety, or vengeance are indicators of selfishness. We did not get the desired outcome so self takes the throne of our heart and shows its discontent. Sinful emotions pull back the curtain on an idol in our life. We want something so badly that it drives our thinking, feeling, and doing. Ezekiel 14 says that we firmly place the idol to live in our hearts (motivation) and it sets up a stumbling block before our eyes. Stated differently, we lose sight of God's direction and will for our lives, being steered away from the divine will not towards it, like magnets that either repel or attract.

Become restless and discontent. Because we believe we must do something and we are faced with the reality that we cannot without sinning, we experience restlessness and discontent. Life no longer satisfies. Our God-given joy and peace are robbed. We move from one thing to the next, like a fly that cannot land. William Law (1686–1761) writes, "All the wants which disturb human life, which make us uneasy to ourselves, quarrelsome with others, and unthankful to God, which weary us in vain labors and foolish anxieties, which carry us from project to project, from place to place in a poor pursuit of we don't know what, are the wants which neither God nor nature, nor reason hath subjected us to, but are solely infused into us by pride, envy, ambition, and covetousness."

Resign, quit God, and give up. This is near fatalism. God has failed us. "If He really cared, He would have seen to it that I received an answer in a timely fashion! Why should I spend time reading His Word to find out His heart, when He doesn't care about my needs? Why should I pray and express my innermost desires to Him for He is not listening because I have received no answers of my liking. Why should I attend church and fellowship with others whose only counsel to me in my complaint is to be patient?" God is working though you cannot see it.

There are three things we should do.

Work. We must work for the right reasons and from the right motives. Instead of working to manipulate a situation, I should be working so God is glorified. I must resume and assume my daily responsibilities to the honor and glory of God. If I am not working for the glory of God, I am most likely working for the honor of the world, flesh, and devil.

Let's consider this: When I have done everything I can, what does the Scriptures exhort me to do? "And lovingkindness is Yours, O Lord, for You recompense a man according to his work" (Ps. 62:12). There is blessing in staying focused on my responsibilities. When the heavens seem like brass and my prayers seem repetitive, rising each day to work and serve the Lord of the universe is an act of faith knowing that God sees that I desire to please Him by fulfilling what He has given me to do. He recompenses me according to my work or service.

"Let the favor of the Lord our God be upon us; and confirm for us the work of our hands; Yes, confirm the work of our hands" (Ps. 90:17). Here is a prayer lifted up in the morning and perhaps throughout the day asking for God's favor and that what I am working on for Him this day, He would confirm or bless. God's blessing confirms that what we are involved with He is pleased with, and this token of His favor encourages me to believe the larger picture that what only God can do will be fulfilled.

"For we hear that some among you are leading an undisciplined life, doing no work at all, but acting like busybodies" (2 Thess. 3:11). Failure to work will lead me into a life that is undisciplined, and I can end up as a busybody. An undisciplined life means I am not fulfilling my daily responsibilities. For example, a wife who feels she must do something more often neglects her responsibilities at home. Instead of finding joy and fulfillment from being obedient to Scriptural roles, I look for sympathy from others with whom I share my woes.

"Therefore, my beloved brethren, be steadfast, immovable, always abounding in the work of the Lord, knowing that your toil is not in vain in the Lord" (1 Cor. 15:58). These saints, having done everything they could, are commanded to continue to fulfill their daily tasks. They were to be steadfast, consistent, and reliable; they were to be immovable, solid; and they were to not only work but to abound in their work. Their motivation was their acts of service were unto the Lord who takes notice. They worked knowing God was working.

"For God is not unjust so as to forget your work and the love which you have shown toward His name, in having ministered and in still ministering to the saints" (Heb. 6:10). I have not done everything if I am not fulfilling my responsibilities. Here is a word of encouragement that while we are working at fulfilling our responsibilities, God sees. What God sees, He responds to.

Noah is an example of the work ethic. He was called by God to build an ark—an ark of destruction because of the wickedness of man. Noah and his three sons worked on that ark, and Noah was a preacher of righteousness. God was in charge of the timing of the flood. Noah was responsible for building the ark according to God's plans and warning the people of the impending doom. Noah did everything he could and when there was nothing more he could do, he kept doing the will of God, which was to build the ark and preach.

An old farmer who was about to die called his two sons to his bedside and said, "My boys, my farm and the fields are yours in equal shares. I leave you a little ready money but the bulk of my wealth is hidden somewhere in the ground, not more than eighteen inches from the surface. I regret that I've forgotten precisely where it lies." When the old man was dead and buried his two sons set to work to dig up every inch of ground in order to find the buried treasure. They failed to find it but as they'd gone to all the trouble of turning over the soil, they thought they might as well sow a crop, which they did, reaping a good harvest. In autumn, as soon as they had an opportunity they dug for the treasure again but with no better results. As their fields were turned over more thoroughly than any others in the neighborhood were, they reaped better harvests than anyone else did. Year after year their search continued. Only when they had grown much older and wiser did they realize what their father had meant. Real treasure comes because of hard work.

Failure to work (fulfill my responsibilities) will lead to a slothful life. Proverbs describes the slothful life: "How long will you lie down, O sluggard? When will you arise from your sleep?"

Worry about what more I can do produces weariness. People like this often sleep more than usual or what their bodies require. The soul of the sluggard craves and gets nothing, but the soul of the diligent is made fat. With all their worry, they still are no further ahead. Jesus says that worry cannot add one cubit to my height!

The sluggard buries his hand in the dish, but will not even bring it back to his mouth. The normal daily functions overwhelm people who become preoccupied with having to do more. The sluggard does not plow after the autumn, so he begs during the harvest and has nothing. They fail to realize the long-term consequences of their actions of worry and not working. The desire of the sluggard puts him to death, for his hands refuse to work. This fixation of "doing" for the wrong reasons deepens the feelings that God really doesn't care or take notice. The sluggard says, "There is a lion outside; I will be killed in the streets!" They know what they are doing is sinful, but they persist. The sluggard is wiser in his own eyes than seven men who can give a discreet answer. They reject the liberating truth of God's sovereignty, providential care. They know better than God Himself as revealed in His holy Word.

The second thing I can do is watch. This second thing we must do when we have done everything we can doesn't seem to fit with the concept of work. What we are watching for can improve or impede our work. Worry impedes our work, while watching improves our work. It becomes a matter of focus.

The word "watch" comes from the Old English that means to be awake. Webster goes on to define watch as to look or observe attentively or carefully; to look and wait expectantly; to stay awake at night while serving as a guard, sentinel, or watchman; to keep vigil; to keep a watchful eye.

What are we watching? When we have done everything we can and there is nothing left we can do without sinning, then we are watching for God's hand of movement and operation. David Mains use to have an exercise in his 50-Day Adventures called the God Hunt. His intention was to sharpen our focus in looking for God's hand of activity.

The Bible tells us that God never sleeps. He never slumbers. God is vigilant. He is alert. He is working whether we recognize it or not. An example is His infinite working during the Inter-testimental Period. God used the world empires of Babylon, Medo-Persian, Greece, and Rome to bring about the fullness of time when God sent forth His son to be born of a virgin. The majority of the Jews did not recognize His sovereign hand. Many became discouraged and lost hope. But there were a handful, like Simeon and Anna, who longed for and looked for Israel's blessed hope of consolation. With each baby that Simeon blessed he wondered if this were the hope of Israel. He was watching with great anticipation. God made a promise to Simeon that he would not die until he saw the promised child. This promise and his hope in that promise kept him watching daily. God has given us great and precious promises, which, when believed, help us remain watchful.

One of the problems with watching is we stopped working. The Thessalonians had this problem. They were watching for the rapture and stopped fulfilling their responsibilities. When this happened, they became a burden upon the other saints. Conversely, Nehemiah worked and set a watch.

Is it possible to watch for something and not see something? That seems like a funny question. God reminds Judah that He will do something new and asks if they will be aware of it (Isa. 43:19). It is a rhetorical question that can be answered "yes" or "no." I can be watching for God to do something and miss what God is doing. Often when we are looking for God's hand of intervention, we are carefully watching for the gigantic, the colossal, or the enormous answers. We are looking for mighty miracles. The broad strokes of God's miracle brush. When we do not see the gargantuan, we wonder if God really cares because we cannot see Him doing anything. Yet, because of the truth of Scriptures that God is always alert and working, we miss the tiny delicate brush strokes of His grace and mercy. I am on guard against discouragement and despair because I am looking with anticipation and eagerness for the fingerprint of God not the handprint! While we are waiting for the sale of our home, our municipality requires a building inspection. Our city is notorious for its inspectors. God showed Himself mighty on our behalf. The building inspector found only six minor violations that can be corrected in a matter of hours. Though we are still waiting for the house to sell, we saw God's fingerprint of blessing that fortified us.

I want to share three illustrations to this point. A little book, long out of print, called *Expectation Corner*, tells of a king who prepared a city for some of his poor subjects. Not far away he constructed a large storehouse where everything they needed would be supplied if they would only send him their requests. There was one condition, however: *they should constantly be on the lookout* for his messengers so that when they came with the gifts in answer to their urgent pleas, the petitioners *would always be found waiting and ready to receive them.* One faithless subject, not actually expecting to get what he requested, *never watched for delivery.* One day he was taken to the king's storehouse; and there, to his amazement, he saw scores of packages that had originally been made ready for him. The messengers had come to his door, but because *he was not looking for them,* the king's gifts never satisfied his needs. Sometimes God makes us wait for things, simply because we are so unbelieving and insipid in the way we ask for His heavenly favors. Many miss out on desired blessings because they close themselves in the gloomy chambers of doubt. (Italics added for emphasis.)

The second illustration is when Janice Gravely's husband Edmund died at the controls of his small plane while on the way to Statesboro, Georgia, from Rocky Mount-Wilson airport, North Carolina, Janice kept the plane aloft for two hours until it ran out of fuel. During this time, she sang hymns and prayed for help. As the plane crossed the South Carolina-North Carolina border, she radioed for help: "Help, help, won't someone help me? My pilot is unconscious. Won't somebody help me?" Authorities who picked up her distress signal were not able to reach her by radio during the flight because she kept changing channels. Jnaice finally made a rough landing and crawled for forty-five minutes to a farmhouse for help. How often God's people cry out for help to God, but switch channels before God's message comes through. They turn to other sources for help, looking for human help. When you cry out to God for His intervention, don't switch channels!

The third illustration is when a woman telephoned the manager of a large opera house and told him she had lost a valuable diamond pin the night before at the concert. The man asked her to hold the line. A search was made and the brooch was found; but when he got back to the phone, the woman had hung up. He waited for her to call again and even put a notice in the paper, but he heard nothing further. What a strange and foolish person, we say, but isn't this the way some of us pray? We tell the Lord all about our needs, but then fail to "hold the line." As a result, we miss the joy of answered prayer and the thrill and reward of a persistent faith.

Watching requires of me the following: perseverance, a steadfast adherence to a course of action, belief, or purpose, to persist; unswerving dedication (I often describe this word as "going power"); unstoppable belief with appropriate actions—this brings the concept of watching and working together; faith, the confidence, not necessarily based on logic, proof, or material evidence, a conviction I know is true because of the Person who told me (Christ). Obedience means to hear and to do; to yield and follow; to receive and to comply; to listen and to carry out.

A biblical example of a saint who did everything they could and now had to watch is Moses, who led Jacob's twelve sons out of Egyptian captivity after 430 years of servitude. God performed ten mighty miracles that immobilized the Egyptian gods. Pharaoh finally relented and urged them to leave. However, Moses and the children of Israel (some 2.5 million) came to their first challenge of faith. Before them was the mighty Red Sea. Behind them, the Egyptians pursed them to recapture them. On either side were a mountain range and a desert. The people complained. Moses prayed. God told them to stand still and see the salvation of the Lord. "Watch!" And, as Paul Harvey says, we know the rest of the story. When I have done everything I can biblically, I am found fulfilling my responsibilities. I must watch expectantly, eagerly, and with great anticipation. It might be today!

So when I have done everything I can, I work, I watch, and now I wait. Many people think of this word in its passive form. Some equate passivity with resignation and defeat. However, for the saint to wait on God means anticipation. Consider the following Scriptures. "Wait for the Lord; be strong and let your heart take courage; Yes, wait for the Lord" (Ps. 27:14). While waiting, I am to be strong and allow my heart to take courage. I am to ward off, resist, and fight against discouragement, despair, and defeat.

"Rest in the Lord and wait patiently for Him; do not fret because of him who prospers in his way, because of the man who carries out wicked schemes. Cease from anger and forsake wrath; do not fret; it leads only to evildoing" (Ps. 37:7–8). My waiting is with patience. Patience means a complete knowledge that God is in control, is effectively working, and will accomplish in His perfect timing what He has ordained for me. By waiting with this heartfelt attitude, I can cease from anger, forsake wrath, and avoid running ahead of God, which only results in evildoing (sinful actions).

"Wait for the Lord and keep His way, and He will exalt you to inherit the land; when the wicked are cut off, you will see it" (Ps. 37:34). While waiting, I am responsible to keep His way. I am to be obedient to His patterns for living holy before Him. When this becomes my spiritual act of worshipful living, then He will exalt me and I will see how He dealt with unrighteousness that opposed me.

"My soul, wait in silence for God only, for my hope is from Him. He only is my rock and my salvation, my stronghold; I shall not be shaken. On God my salvation and my glory rest; the rock of my strength, my refuge is in God. Trust in Him at all times, O people; pour out your heart before Him; God is a refuge for us" (Ps. 62:5–8). Here waiting includes the idea of silence. Too many saints, when they wait, are vocal. They say, "I'm waiting on God but He sure seems like He is taking His sweet old time." They complain. If I have done everything I can, to the point of receiving counsel and even sharing with others, my recourse left is to wait in silence. Notice it says "for God only." By doing so, I enter into Him as my rock, salvation, stronghold. By this act of faith and obedience, I shall not be shaken.

"May those who fear You see me and be glad, because I wait for Your word" (Ps. 119:74). Biblical waiting becomes a testimony to others. Others are watching you as you are working, watching, and waiting for God. As a personal aside, while we are working, watching, and waiting, numerous people have given testimony to our posture in this process. It is a testimony to God's glory.

"I wait for the Lord, my soul does wait, and in His word do I hope. My soul waits for the Lord more than the watchmen for the morning Indeed, more than the watchmen for the morning" (Ps. 130:5–6).

The watchman eagerly waited for the sunrise to drive back the darkness of night and expose what he could not see. The watchman was the first to see clearly what the day would reveal. He waited for the dawn's first light. This is our type of waiting. A knowledge, that just as the sun rises each morning, so too the Lord's answers will come and we will see clearly what was the delay and why.

"But if we hope for what we do not see, with perseverance we wait eagerly for it" (Rom. 8:25). Waiting includes perseverance—the dogged determination that motivates me to rise each day to work, watch, and wait. Today, we remind ourselves, is the day it could happen. In the movie, *Angels in the Outfield*, one of the foster boys has a saying, "It could happen." Yes, with God all things are possible!

Here are some biblical examples of this concept. Hannah was married to Elkanah as one of his two wives. Elkanah had several other children by his other wife. But Hannah's womb was barren. Yearly they went to Shiloh to worship the Lord. And yearly, Hannah would petition God for a child. And yearly, she would return home barren. But this year's trip was different. Her wait was over. God's perfect timing would be revealed. She would conceive this year. No other time would have been perfect like this time; for Hannah, Elkanah, Eli, and the nation of Israel.

David was anointed as the next king over Israel. Saul was a disappointment to God. He was filled with self and pride. He was unrepentant and disobedient. Samuel anointed David in the presence of his father and brothers to be the next king. It would be many years before he would realize God's promise. During those years, Saul hounded, persecuted, pursued, and sought to destroy David through numerous murderous plots. David lived in caves; hid like an outlaw; cared for 600 men like himself—outcasts to the political kingdom; was nearly captured twice; was betrayed by others; had two opportunities to become king—all he had to do was kill Saul. But David waited for God's timing. He endured the hardships by clinging to God's Word.

Here are some questions to ask yourself in reflection and application of this material.

1. Take time now to list the additional steps you would like to take regarding a situation you feel you should do more about. Review your list and ask yourself if any of them are sinful. Would God be pleased? Do any of them push you away from trusting God? Has Christ given you clearance to proceed? How would God be honored and glorified?

2. Are there things you know you should be doing, but you are not because you are discouraged? What areas of daily living are you neglecting? As you think of this question, remember you are a whole person. Areas you maybe neglecting can be mental, emotional, physical, and spiritual. What responsibilities do you need to resume? How will you return to performing your tasks as unto the Lord? Plan your work, and work your plan. Do you need an accountability partner to begin?

3. Make a list of things you would like God to do about your situation. As you re-read your list, add the fingerprints of God that are required to fulfill the larger answer. What do you think are some smaller miracles God could do that could lead to the handprint of God's miracle? Develop a God Hunt Log. Record daily how you see God working on your behalf. It might not be directly related to that for which you are watching and waiting. But recognizing His fingerprints can encourage your heart that if God is expressing His loving concern in another area of your life, He surely knows and is working on this thing for which you are watching and waiting.

An old hymn written by Katharina Von Schlegel, translated by Jane L. Borthwick, summarizes much of this tape's truths. "Be still my soul, the Lord is on thy side. Bear patiently the cross of grief or pain. Leave to thy God to order and provide; in every change He faithful will remain. Be still my soul, they best, they heavenly Friend through thorny ways leads to a joyful end. Be still my soul, thy God doth undertake, to guide the future as He has the past. Thy hope, thy confidence let nothing shake; all now mysterious shall be bright at last. Be still my soul, the waves and wind still know His voice who ruled them while He dwelt below."

Work, watch, wait. When you have done everything biblically and you cannot do any more.

Smack Down, Tap Out

Wrestling with God:
"I Will Not Let You Go Until You Bless Me"

Historical Setting

The settling in which we read these words, "I will not let you go until you bless me," begins all the way back in Genesis 25:19 where two boys are wrestling within the womb of Rebekah. We know the story. It has theological implications in Romans 9 with regards to the sovereignty of God, His purposes, and why He does what He does.

God predicted that Esau would serve Jacob. Esau was the first born. This divine prediction was culturally offensive. The younger always served the older. God had His reasons as outlined in Romans 9. That's another message for another time.

During the labor and delivery, Jacob's hand reached out and grabbed the heel of his brother (25:26). Each boy grew healthy and strong. Esau was a hunter, Isaac's favorite (25:28). Jacob was a homebody and Rebekah's favorite (25:28).

Isaac was growing older and nearing death. It was customary for the father to give his final blessing to the oldest. From Isaac's perspective, this was Esau (27:1-4). In God's economy, He had already predicted that Jacob would receive the blessing of the firstborn. But God was eliminated from fulfilling His purpose because Rebekah took matters into her own hand (27:5–17). As she saw her husband's health fail, she convinced Jacob to participate in an evil and deceptive plan. She dressed Jacob up like Esau, and he entered his father's tent seeking the blessing. Jacob deceived and lied to his father (27:18–24). He secured the blessing and a one-way ticket to his uncle's home. When Esau found out what had occurred, he wept and pleaded with his father for some type of blessing (27:34). When there was none to give, he vowed he would kill his brother (27:41). Jacob fled for his life (27:42–45).

The Bible says be careful what you sow. For what you sow, you will surely reap (Gal. 6:7). Jacob fell in love with a beautiful girl named Rachel. He struck an agreement with his Uncle Laban to work seven years for young Rachel. Those years passed like the wind (29:16–20). The time came for him to take Rachel to be his bride. The honeymoon suite must have been extremely dark, for when he woke in the morning he discovered that Uncle Laban deceived him. Here he was in bed with Leah—the weak-eyed older daughter! Laban stated that it was culturally unacceptable for the younger to be blessed in marriage before the older (sound familiar?). If Jacob would work another seven years, he could have Rachel (29:23–28). So he worked another seven years. His love for her was intense and passionate that these next seven years also were like the wind. After fourteen years, he had two wives. Now we know the problems with one wife, let alone two! This is not double your pleasure, double your fun; double mint, double mint, double mint gum!

Jacob agreed to stay on. God began to bless his wives with children. God blessed Jacob's flocks and they multiplied (30:25–43). After six years of disagreements, suspicions of Uncle Laban, and intra-family fighting, Jacob had enough. He would steal away in the evening hours and return home. Jacob left one set of problems for another set—facing his brother Esau.

Jacob trusted himself. He was still attempting to control the outcome. As he headed home, the words of his brother began to ring afresh. "The days of mourning for my father are near, then I will kill my brother." With each step, with each mile, these words echoed in his mind, even after twenty years. He began to think what his brother might be like. Had anything changed? "After tricking him out of his birthright, after deceiving and lying to their father, after twenty years, what can I do to assess the situation?" Jacob devised a plan to send a specific message to his brother. He wanted to assure Esau that God had blessed him and he was not a threat to Esau's family inheritance (32:3–5). He was hoping to find favor. What he discovered was his brother coming to meet him with 400 men. Jacob translated this as an inevitable massacre (32:6–8).

In trouble again, Jacob turned to God in prayer (32:9–12). He reminded God of His promise to bless and protect him. He admitted he was not worthy of such favor. He pleaded for deliverance from the hand of his brother. He then began to plan for the inevitable. He arranged for five gifts of animals. Five hundred and fifty animals and their drovers were sent in stages. He hoped that the size of the gift and the timing would appease his brother's wrath (32:13–20). He then divided his immediate family in two segments; Leah, and her children and concubines in the first entourage, with Jacob, Joseph, and Rachel at the rear (33:1–3).

What are some general principles I can learn from Jacob's experience of wrestling with God?

First, this entire vignette addresses a singular topic in Jacob's life and in ours. What is that topic? The topic is, "Who's in charge?"

Jacob was usually in charge. When I am in charge I am found wanting. What I strive to gain I cannot secure. James 4 says we lust for but do not have; we are envious, but cannot obtain.

Jesus speaking about true Kingdom saints in Matthew 7 that not everyone who calls Him "Lord, Lord" will enter into the Kingdom of Heaven. Calling Christ "Lord, Lord," is not the same as living life in which Christ is "Lord, Lord."

The following words are from an old engraving on a cathedral in Labeck, Germany:

> Thus speaketh Christ our Lord to us:
>
> You call Me master and obey Me not.
>
> You call Me light and see Me not.
>
> You call Me the Way and walk Me not.
>
> You call Me life and live Me not.
>
> You call Me wise and follow Me not.
>
> You call Me fair and love Me not.

You call Me rich and ask Me not.

You call Me eternal and seek Me not.

If I condemn thee, blame Me not.

When we truly have Christ as Lord of our lives, what people will see is different. Our focus is different, and therefore our pursuits in life will be different. We will not be like the Gentiles, but we will be seeking the Kingdom of God and His righteousness first (Matt. 6:33)

The Bible reminds us that Joshua challenged the elders about whom they were going to serve.

> Now, therefore, fear the Lord and serve Him in sincerity and truth; and put away the gods which your fathers served beyond the River and in Egypt, and serve the Lord. If it is disagreeable in your sight to serve the Lord, choose for yourselves today whom you will serve: whether the gods which your fathers served which were beyond the River, or the gods of the Amorites in whose land you are living; but as for me and my house, we will serve the Lord (Josh. 24:14–15).

Elijah called upon Israel to decide. If Baal is god, serve him; if Jehovah is God, serve Him. "Elijah came near to all the people and said, 'How long *will* you hesitate between two opinions? If the Lord is God, follow Him; but if Baal, follow him.' But the people did not answer him a word" (1 Kings 18:21). Other Scriptures are:

> He must increase, but I must decrease (John 3:30).

> I have been crucified with Christ; and it is no longer I who live, but Christ lives in me; and the life which I now live in the flesh I live by faith in the Son of God, who loved me and gave Himself up for me. I live this life in the flesh by faith in the Son of God (Galatians 2:20).

> And He was saying to them all, "If anyone wishes to come after Me, he must deny himself, and take up his cross daily and follow Me" (Luke 9:23).

> Or do you not know that all of us who have been baptized into Christ Jesus have been baptized into His death? Therefore we have been buried with Him through baptism into death, so that as Christ was raised from the dead through the glory of the Father, so we too might walk in newness of life (Romans 6:3–4).

The outcome of wrestling with God is to submit and to yield. "Submission" means getting under authority. It also implies while under authority to move in the same direction. "Yield" means to give way, to relinquish my rights to one who is superior in deference.

Paul had to learn who's in charge. He learned the lesson on the road to Damascus when God asked Paul why he was kicking against the goads. The NASB says, "Whom you are persecuting"; warring against, wrestling with. Paul was at war with God about who was in charge. "And he said, 'Who are You, Lord?' And He said, 'I am Jesus whom you are persecuting'" (Acts 9:5).

Submission brings the peace of God that passes all understanding. I no longer have to be in control and strive, manipulate, plot, or scheme to control the outcome.

> And the peace of God, which surpasses all comprehension, will guard your hearts and your minds in Christ Jesus (Phil 4:7).

Floyd McClung cleverly identifies two significant ingredients in life's drama: "the game of life" and "the Lord of life." The question is, are we willing to play according to His rules? (Floyd McClung, *Holiness and the Spirit of the Age*, p. 105.)

Second, Jacob is wrestling with the pre-incarnate Christ. Our battles are not of human origin.

> For our struggle is not against flesh and blood, but against the rulers, against the powers, against the world forces of this darkness, against the spiritual forces of wickedness in the heavenly places (Eph. 6:12).

Therefore, our resources are not of human origin.

> For though we walk in the flesh, we do not war according to the flesh, for the weapons of our warfare are not of the flesh, but divinely powerful for the destruction of fortresses (2 Cor. 10:3–4).

There are previous appearances of the pre-incarnate Christ with Abraham, Lot, and Sodom and Gomorrah. What is significant about this? Did Jacob know with whom he was wrestling? This is significant,

I believe, because Jacob had to realize that no one else could help him. His tiny, unarmed band would be no match for Esau's army of 400 men. There was no one else to whom he could appeal. His father and mother are dead. He could not enlist anyone to help. He had been gone for twenty years. Who would remember him and want to lend him aid? He could not recruit anyone to help. He could not hire anyone to protect. Esau evidently had gained mastery over the land where Jacob sojourned. No one in his or her right mind would venture out against Esau. No amount of money could hire a band of mercenaries.

Like the woman with the issue of blood, exhausting all of her resources, she found that no human being could bring relief. She needed Jesus, she found Jesus, and Jesus healed her.

While attending college, a student visited a psychiatric institution with a group of students to observe various types of mental illness. The experience proved to be very disturbing. I remember one man who was called "No Hope Carter." His was a tragic case. A victim of venereal disease, he was going through the final stages when the brain is affected. Before he began to lose his mind, the doctors told this man that there was no known cure for him. He begged for one ray of light in his darkness, but had been told that the disease would run its inevitable course and end in death. Gradually his brain deteriorated, and he became more and more despondent. When I saw him in his small, barred room about two weeks before he died, he was pacing up and down in mental agony. His eyes stared blankly, and his face was drawn and ashen. Repeatedly he muttered these two forlorn and fateful words: "No hope! No hope!"

That is why Christ wrestled with Jacob. So Jacob could exclaim, "Whom have I in heaven but You? and besides You, I desire nothing on earth." John 6:68 says, "Simon Peter answered Him, 'Lord, to whom shall we go? You have words of eternal life.'"

Third, when all of Jacob's efforts and plans were in place, with little confidence that they would work, he wrestled with God. Why is it that we usually wrestle with God as the last resort? Like Jacob, we *look to control the situation.* There is something innate in each human heart that fears being out of control. Not necessarily emotionally, but feeling like the ability to make choices is removed or the sense of having to rely upon another and be dependent. I know some people who will not carpool to an event, because they want to make the decision when to leave or how long to stay.

Like Jacob, *we seek to manipulate circumstances* for our own personal gain and benefit. If we have to depend upon another for a decision that will affect us, we become apprehensive that their decision will be made in light of themselves, not for whom they should be making the decision.

Like Jacob, *we are fearful if we relinquish full control to God,* we will not be happy with the outcome. Is it possible for God to make a decision that would be so displeasing to the recipient? Yes, because that recipient is not walking by, led by, taught by, or filled by the Spirit! It's the age-old lie spoken in the Garden that God will somehow make my life miserable and He cannot be trusted.

Often, if we can turn to someone else first other than God, we will. We often turn to a spouse, a close trusted friend, pastor, spiritual mentor, or others.

The Bible reminds us, "But in everything by prayer and supplication let your request be made known to God. Be anxious for nothing, but in everything by prayer and supplication with thanksgiving let your requests be made known to God" (Phil 4:6). "Men ought always to pray." "Pray without ceasing" (1 Thess. 5:17).

Moses, when faced with so many difficulties, turned to God in prayer. Nehemiah, when opposed in doing the will of God, was a man who turned to prayer.

Fourth, Jacob's plans were futile and did not inspire hope. Jacob's plan had large gaping holes. He could not account for all the variables. There were too many unknowns Jacob had not considered. He couldn't anticipate with precision what or how Esau would react. Esau was coming with 400 men. Even if Esau began to massacre the initial parties, Jacob could not escape. He sent gifts to appease his brother. Did it work? He divided his possessions. He couldn't out run Esau. He would soon be lame. All unknowns are intimidating to us. We want to know so we can control. But all unknowns are known to God, and to Him alone. What we cannot see, He has seen and is looking at right now.

Fifth, when we wrestle with God we are usually alone. It is an individual time. It is a time of isolation.

Christ was by Himself when He wrestled with His Father in the Garden. The disciples were fast asleep and couldn't even stay awake for one hour to help our Lord intercede. Don't rely upon people. They will often fail you. Christ was by Himself for forty days during the Temptation utterly dependent upon God so as not to fall, and to be fully prepared for His earthly ministry. Christ was by Himself after ministering to the crowds. He went alone to pray.

It can be a blessed, joyful, quiet, and peaceful time to be alone with God. We need not fear being alone with God. He invites us to come.

> Come now, and let us reason together, says the Lord (Isa. 1:18).

> And again, Come to Me, all who are weary and heavy-laden, and I will give you rest (Matt. 11:28).

He welcomes us with open loving arms. We should not fear unless we attempt to hide sin from His all-seeing eye. It is usually during some dark moment (night) when no human support is available and no human resources can be found, just the divine—you and God.

The Bible seems to have a lot to say about those dark moments. These dark moments are a time for us to meditate.

> But his delight is in the law of the Lord, and in His law he meditates day and night (Psalm 1:2).

> When I remember You on my bed, I meditate on You in the night watches (Psalm 63:6).

Wrestling with God: "I Will Not Let You Go Until You Bless Me"

> My eyes anticipate the night watches, that I may meditate on Your word (Psalm 119:148).

These dark moments are a time for instruction.

> I will bless the Lord who has counseled me; indeed, my mind instructs me in the night (Psalm 16:7).

These dark moments are a time for introspection.

> You have tried my heart; You have visited me by night; You have tested me and You find nothing, I have purposed that my mouth will not transgress (Psalm 17:3)

These dark moments are a time to gain knowledge.

> Day to day pours forth speech, and night to night reveals knowledge (Psalm 19:2).

These dark moments are a time to offer praise.

> The Lord will command His lovingkindness in the daytime; and His song will be with me in the night, a prayer to the God of my life (Psalm 42:8).

These dark moments are a time to lift up our petitions.

> O Lord, the God of my salvation, I have cried out by day and in the night before You (Psalm 88:1).

These dark moments are a time to express our confidence in God.

> You will not be afraid of the terror by night, or of the arrow that flies by day (Psalm 91:5).

> If I say, "Surely the darkness will overwhelm me, and the light around me will be night," even the darkness is not dark to You, and the night is as bright as the day. Darkness and light are alike to You (Psalm 139:11–12).

It is usually shrouded in a measure of fear. What is fear? Fear is a dominating feeling of dread of a supposed harmful situation or event. Fear has no power—only the power we give it. We have not been given the spirit of fear, but of love, discipline and a sound mind (2 Tim. 1:7). The foundation of fear is often hypotheses, "What if?"

We are commanded forty-six times, "Do not be afraid." We are commanded fifty-seven times, "Do not fear." Jacob feared Esau. His memory of Esau was twenty years old. He had no present frame of reference. It was the past.

We come and wrestle with God because of some fear. We can fear the unknown such as our heath, employment, finances, layoffs, downsizing, or having an accident while we travel. We can fear consequences such as punishment, natural disasters, or personal harm. We can fear—fear. We can become so absorbed and preoccupied with a thought, without any factual information, that it can paralyze us. We reject the facts and live by emotions. "I just know I'm going to get cancer because my mother, my mother's mother were all diagnosed with cancer at my age!"

It will take great effort, great strength, and unhurried time. Jacob wrestled throughout the night—depending upon when the last hour was used in sending his family across the brook, it probably was at least four hours if not more. Remember Jews did not like water or the dark. So it is reasonable to believe Jacob's immediate family had crossed well before darkness fell. This means that the length of wrestling may have been closer to six or seven hours.

The Hebrew word for "wrestling" means getting dusty. Wrestling means attempting to pin your opponent to the ground. Can you see the Second Person of the Trinity getting dusty with Jacob? It could be pictured like the old childhood game called King of the Hill, where you attempted to wrestle off the top of a hill the one who laid claim to it. Can you allow your mind to envision this scene? Back and forth. And again back and forth. Then they rested. Then back and forth.

Christ had His reasons in allowing this event to persist through the night. Jacob had his motivation to persevere. Christ wanted Jacob to come to the end of himself. Jacob wanted God to bless him. Christ would bless Jacob when he surrendered.

Sixth, we often become physically, mentally, emotionally and spiritually fatigued and exhausted when we wrestle with God. Here Jacob's thigh was touched. This took his advantage of strength away. The text implies that he clung to his opponent. He would not be able to stand and wrestle. So Jacob wrapped himself around Christ. Despite his disadvantage, he persisted.

What are some common disadvantages we wrestle through? *The passing of time*; hours turn to days, and days turn to weeks, and weeks turn to months, and months turn to years, and years turn to decades—cling to God. Abraham never did live in the Promised Land, but he clung to God's covenant. Noah turned years into decades (twelve, in fact) while he clung to God and built the Ark. The lack of results—cling to God. The weeping prophet had no converts, no results from his faithful service of forty years. Yet, he clung to God and faithfully performed his duties.

The seemingly changeless situation—cling to God. The psalmist echoes the words, "How long, O Lord?" But as you read Psalm 13, with only six verses, he clung to God in hope of rejoicing and seeing God's answer in his day. There are several important ways to cling to God while you wrestle with God about a matter. One is to lay hold of His promise like Jacob. Another is to remind yourself of His purpose for this time. A third is to be a person of praise and worship

Seventh, the pre-incarnate Christ would have taken Jacob with His breath. Christ does not want you to let Him go. He wants you to cling to Him. Christ does this so our faith will increase.

> You shall fear the Lord your God; you shall serve Him and cling to Him, and you shall swear by His name (Deut. 10:20).
>
> You shall follow the Lord your God and fear Him; and you shall keep His commandments, listen to His voice, serve Him, and cling to Him (Deut. 13:4).
>
> But you are to cling to the Lord your God, as you have done to this day (Josh. 23:8).

Eighth, when we wrestle with God, something happens to our situation and us. We come to know that God is compassionate. God longs to be compassionate to us.

> Therefore the Lord longs to be gracious to you, and therefore He waits on high to have compassion on you. For the Lord is a God of justice; how blessed are all those who long for Him (Is. 30:18).
>
> For the Lord your God is a compassionate God; He will not fail you nor destroy you nor forget the covenant with your fathers which He swore to them (Deut. 4:31).
>
> For the Lord your God is gracious and compassionate, and will not turn His face away from you if you return to Him (2 Chron. 30:9).
>
> Light arises in the darkness for the upright; He is gracious, compassionate, and righteous (Ps. 112:4).

God hears. You will never get an answering machine when you talk with God. He is always available. You are never a disturbance to Him. He makes time to listen to you.

> But know that the Lord has set apart the godly man for Himself; the Lord hears when I call to Him (Ps. 4:3).
>
> The righteous cry, and the Lord hears and delivers them out of all their troubles (Ps. 34:17).
>
> For the Lord hears the needy and does not despise His who are prisoners (Ps. 69:33).
>
> I love the Lord, because He hears my voice and my supplications (Ps. 116:1).

God answers. Since God hears and listens, He answers. And how He answers is always good, just, perfect, and acceptable. At times, His answers are "Yes." We like the "Yes" answers. At other times, His answers are "No." We struggle with this answer. We question if He has really analyzed all the data as we have. We question how He could arrive at such an answer, when we concluded the answer should be "Yes." His "No"s means He *knows*—He knows something we do not and He sees something we cannot see. How wonderful He prevents us from going off half-cocked, straight into harm's way. And sometimes His answer is "Wait" or "Not now."

God is wise. God has complete and full knowledge of things actual and things possible. He is infinite in wisdom. His wisdom is a personification of His righteousness. His wisdom is based and rooted in Himself, the author of perfect knowledge. His source is absolute, unlike our finite and subjective comprehension. "As a blind man has no idea of colors, so have we no idea of the manner by which the all-wise God perceives and understands all things" (Sir Isaac Newton, 1642–1727).

God is loving. From His love, He listens, answers, decides, shows compassion, and is holy, just, fair, kind, and benevolent. God is loving and none of His actions are harmful or destructive.

> God is love, not, God is loving. God and love are synonymous. Love is not an attribute of God, it is God; whatever God is, love is. If your conception of love does not agree with justice, judgment, purity, and holiness, then your idea of love is wrong (Oswald Chambers, 1874–191??).

Because He is loving, even His pruning is done with tenderness and thoughtfulness. We are the object of His love and of all His good intentions. His love is beyond intellectual capacity. If we ever toy with the idea that God does not love us, we are asking for something He is unwilling to give us because He loves us. We are asking for something inferior compared to what His abundance desires to give us.

"God is love and God is sovereign. His love disposes him to desire our everlasting welfare, and His sovereignty enables him to secure it" (A.W. Tozer, 1897–1963).

A farmer printed on his weather vane the words "God is love." Someone asked him if he meant to imply that the love of God was as fickle as the wind. The farmer answered: "No, I mean that whichever way the wind blows, God is love. If it blows cold from the North, or biting from the East, God is still love just as much as when the warm South or gentle West winds refresh our fields and flocks. God is always love."

We are changed. Jacob's name was changed from Supplanter to one who wrestles with God. When we wrestle God and see Him face-to-face, as Jacob proclaims, something happens to us. Like Isaiah, "And one called out to another and said, "Holy, Holy, Holy, is the Lord of hosts, the whole earth is full of His glory. And the foundations of the thresholds trembled at the voice of him who called out, while the temple was filling with smoke. Then I said, 'Woe is me, for I am ruined! Because I am a man of unclean lips, and I live among a people of unclean lips; for my eyes have seen the King, the Lord of hosts." Or Peter, "But when Simon Peter saw that, he fell down at Jesus' feet, saying, 'Go away from me Lord, for I am a sinful man, O Lord!'" (Luke 5:8).

We see God in a fresh way. Jacob said, "No, please, if now I have found favor in your sight, then take my present from my hand, for I see your face as one sees the face of God, and you have received me favorably" (Gen. 33:10). When Jacob fully surrendered and in his heart proclaimed God as sovereign King, he was able to see God through Esau's actions. Now, Esau remained a godless and immoral man according to Hebrews 12. But Jacob had a new perspective on trusting God and allowing God to govern his life. This new perspective opened Jacob's eyes to see Esau, not as a vengeful bloodthirsty brother, but as an agent of God's answer to Jacob's prayer and wrestling with God. Oftentimes, after wrestling with God, the very thing we fear becomes the instrument God uses to bless our lives.

Concluding his book, *Born Again*, Charles Colson writes: "It was that night in the quiet of my room that I made the total surrender. 'Lord, if this is what it is all about,' I said, 'then I thank You. I praise You for leaving me in prison, for letting them take away my license to practice law, yes—even for my son being arrested. I praise You for giving me your love through these men, for being God, for just letting me walk with Jesus.' With those words came the greatest joy of all—the final release, turning it all over to. He went on to found Prison Fellowship and several affiliate ministries. What was feared was used by God in a greater way than the fear itself.

Jacob learned the hard way to surrender to God's will. He lost twenty years of life. He himself was deceived by a family member. He lived with fear. He was not home when his father and mother died. We lose so much when we think we know better than God does.

C.S. Lewis writes, "Surrendering to God is different: harder, and easier. Christ says, 'Give me All. I don't want so much of your time and so much of your money and so much of your work: I want You. I have not come to torment your natural self, but to kill it. No half-measures are any good. I don't want to cut off a branch here and a branch there, I want to have the whole tree down. I don't want to drill the tooth, or crown it, or stop it, but to have it out. Hand over the whole natural self, all the desires, which you think innocent, as well as the ones you think wicked—the whole outfit. I will give you a new self instead. In fact, I will give you Myself: my own will shall become yours.'"

William Booth, founder of the Salvation Army Movement, at age fifteen is quoted to have said, "God shall have all there is of William Booth."

Can you make such a statement? Will you make such a commitment today? For what do you need to cling to God? What have you let slip through your grasp? Won't you return today? Won't you surrender to the good, perfect, and acceptable will of God? Will you tell God today, "I will not let you go until you bless me"?

I Can Count on One Hand How Many of My Friends Don't …
The Case for Abstinence

Abstinence—the very vocalization of the word conjures up images in my mind. Does it for you? For example, one image that comes to mind would be a woman wearing an ankle-length black dress with a high-buttoned collar, no jewelry or makeup, and her head adorned with some type of covering. I see her daughter dressed like her mother. I see a man wearing a starched white shirt buttoned to the neck, a neatly trimmed long beard, a round brim hat, dark pants, and an overcoat. I see his son looking like his father.

This scene is reinforced by our twenty-fifth wedding anniversary in which we took a trip to an Amish community in Wisconsin. We observed horse-drawn wagons/coaches clipping along the busy two-lane highway, those same carriages parked behind the local mercantile, homes with no electricity, and religious home meetings only for those within the community (no outsiders—we couldn't attend if we wanted to).

Those are the images that come to my mind. What about you? And inside perhaps we snicker at such a primitive lifestyle. To us it is technologically deficient. But to those who have committed themselves to this way of life, based on their convictions, they view technology as the devil's tool. They have withdrawn to avoid exposure to and influence by those things deemed as destructive. You may say that this is an extreme example of abstinence.

How about someone who says "no" to your offer of a second piece of caramel silk supreme pie? Or one who abstains from purchasing more than they know they can afford? Or … and the examples can be endless. In some senses, whether we recognize it or not, most human beings abstain from something on a regular basis. But what I fear the most is that abstinence is only momentary, without forethought as to why.

Abstinence is driven by motivation. So what is the motivation to forego that second piece of caramel silk supreme pie? Is it diet, fear of man, getting sick, or for appearance sake? Isn't it possible if these motivations can be addressed, we could find room for that second piece of caramel silk supreme pie? Or at least get it to go?

As a biblical counselor, I want to reexamine the word "abstinence." It is a word that is rarely used. When was the last time you heard the word? It possesses an archaic ring. Its cousin, "abstain," is equally shunned from our daily speech, let alone using it in a sentence, or even spelling it! It seems like these words have been kicked to the curb and replaced with an ideology of tolerance and acceptance, a new spiritual liberty that embraces anything and everything without guidelines or boundaries.

Since we have removed these words from our vocabulary, close behind are the words purity and holiness. Abstinence and abstain flow from inner convictions of personal purity and holiness.

Abstinence is a difficult word to conceptualize. We will have to work hard at seeing how it got lost and rejected over time, and why we need to rediscover its power for holy living.

I will attempt to develop a biblical paradigm that can be applied to any area of Christian living. When we think of abstinence, we usually associate it with alcohol, sex, or drugs. The "Just Say No" campaign comes to mind. But it is not my attempt to become so narrow in the application of abstinence, but provide a wider scope of this concept for application.

Defining abstinence

The dictionary defines abstinence as "to hold back" or "the denial of the appetites." Abstain is derived from the Middle English roots meaning "to avoid" or "to refrain from something voluntarily."

Abstinence is primarily used in secular literature in the realm of sex. Of the nearly two million websites and nearly 250,000 informational websites, this is what the word is related to. The word is associated with alcohol but with infrequent use.

Today's literature, websites and self-help books have watered down the understanding of abstinence. They have removed the objectivity of abstinence and promote it as someone's personal and subjective decision. You and I know that this breeds situational ethics and relativism.

The organization Campaign for Our Children (CFOC), promotes the definition of abstinence as "waiting to choose the right person, setting and time in your life to be sexually active. Only you can decide what is best for you." They suggest ten reasons for practicing abstinence:

1. I want to follow my family's values
2. I want to respect myself
3. I want to respect others
4. I want to have a good reputation
5. I do not want to feel guilt
6. I am not ready for marriage
7. I do not want to get pregnant
8. I am not ready to be a parent
9. I do not want to be infected with a sexually transmitted infection
10. I do not want HIV

How new is abstinence?
Abstinence is as old as the Garden of Eden. God told Adam to abstain from eating from the tree of the knowledge of good and evil.

Joseph had an abstinence stand in the area of morality when he refused to succumb to the sexual advances of Potiphar's wife (Gen. 39).

In Numbers 6:1–8, God clearly speaks of abstinence for anyone taking a Nazarite vow when Moses records:

> Again the Lord spoke to Moses, saying, Speak to the sons of Israel and say to them, "When a man or woman makes a special vow, the vow of a Nazirite, to dedicate himself to the Lord, he shall abstain from wine and strong drink; he shall drink no vinegar, whether made from wine or strong drink, nor shall he drink any grape juice nor eat fresh or dried grapes. All the days of his separation he shall not eat anything that is produced by the grape vine, from the seeds even to the skin. All the days of his vow of separation, no razor shall pass over his head. He shall be holy until the days are fulfilled for which he separated himself to the Lord; he shall let the locks of hair on his head grow long. All the days of his separation to the Lord, he shall not go near to a dead person. He shall not make himself unclean for his father or for his mother, for his brother or for his sister, when they die, because his separation to God is on his head. All the days of his separation, he is holy to the Lord."

In Judges 13:4–5, Samson's mother was commanded to abstain from any strong drink and wine, and to refrain from eating any unclean thing.

In Jeremiah 35:2–10 another example of abstinence is recorded.

> "Go to the house of the Rechabites and speak to them, and bring them into the house of the Lord, into one of the chambers, and give them wine to drink." Then I took Jaazaniah the son of Jeremiah, son of Habazziniah, and his brothers and all his sons and the whole house of the Rechabites, and I brought them into the house of the Lord, into the chamber of the sons of Hanan the son of Igdaliah, the man of God, which was near the chamber of the officials, which was above the chamber of Maaseiah the son of Shallum, the doorkeeper. Then I set before the men of the house of the Rechabites pitchers full of wine and cups; and I said to them, "Drink wine!" But they said, "We will not drink wine, for Jonadab the son of Rechab, our father, commanded us, saying, 'You shall not drink wine, you or your sons, forever. You shall not build a house, and you shall not sow seed and you shall not plant a vineyard or own one; but in tents you shall dwell all your days, that you may live many days in the land where you sojourn.' We have obeyed the voice of Jonadab the son of Rechab, our father, in all that he commanded us, not to drink wine all our days, we, our wives, our sons or our daughters, nor to build ourselves houses to dwell in; and we do not have vineyard or field or seed. We have only dwelt in tents, and have obeyed and have done according to all that Jonadab our father commanded us."

Daniel held to an abstinence policy when he refused to eat the king's rich meat and drink the wine (Dan. 1). In Acts 15, one of the conclusions of the first Christian synod was for Gentiles to abstain from things contaminated by idols, from fornication, and from what is strangled and from blood.

Paul abstained from eating meat if it would cause his younger brother to stumble. In fact, Paul provides some biblical guidelines for abstinence in Romans 14 and 1 Corinthians 6 and 8–10. We should abstain if our actions will put a stumbling block in our brother's way. We should abstain, even if lawful, if it is not profitable. We should abstain, even if lawful, if the activity can gain mastery over us. We should abstain, if it will defile our body as the Temple of the Holy Spirit. We should abstain, if it causes our brother to stumble. We should abstain, even if lawful, if it does not edify. We should abstain if it gives offense to the unbeliever or the church of God. Paul writes in 1 Thessalonians 4:3, "that you should abstain from sexual immorality for this is the will of God."

So throughout biblical literature, abstinence was commanded by God and taught by God-fearing authority figures.

There are negative connotations that have developed throughout Christendom. Church history and our forefathers put a spin on abstinence, which taken at face value coupled with their practice of it, the majority of humanity has rejected. Below is an extensive historical study showing the deviant development of abstinence. One does not have to wonder why this word and its potency have been lost, and how the church has abdicated its authority to teach this to the federal and state governments who sit in our rightful seat.

With regards to the letter written to the Gentiles after the Jerusalem Council in Acts 15, we read, "The decree was restrictive and conservative on questions of *expediency* and comparative indifference to the Gentile Christians. Under this aspect, it was a wise and necessary measure for the apostolic age, especially in the East, where the Jewish element prevailed, but not intended for universal and permanent use. In Western churches, it was gradually abandoned. It imposed upon the Gentile Christians as abstinence from meat offered to idols, from blood, and from things strangled (as fowls and other animals caught in snares).

The strange manners and institutions of the Jews, such as circumcision, Sabbath observance, abstinence from pork and meat sacrificed to the gods whom they abhorred as evil spirits, excited the mingled amazement, contempt, and ridicule of the Greek and Roman historians and satirists. Whatever was sacred to the heathen was profane to the Jews. They were regarded as enemies of the human race.

During the earthly ministry of Christ, the Pharisees were accustomed to fasting twice in the week, on Monday and Thursday. Christians appointed Wednesday and especially Friday as days of half-fasting or abstinence from flesh, in commemoration of the passion and crucifixion of Jesus.

As the Gospel spread across the Roman Empire, the spiritual depravity seemed to engulf many new believers. Some preached total abstinence. We read, "Nor should the excesses of asceticism blind us against the moral heroism of renouncing rights and enjoyments innocent in themselves, but so generally abused and poisoned, that total abstinence seemed to most of the early fathers the only radical and effective cure. So in our days some of the best of men regard total abstinence rather than temperance, the remedy of the fearful evils of intemperance."

One author writes,

> Asceticism in general is a rigid outward self-discipline, by which the spirit strives after full dominion over the flesh, and a superior grade of virtue. It includes not only that true moderation or restraint of the animal appetites, which is a universal Christian duty, but total abstinence from enjoyments in themselves lawful, from wine, animal food, property, and marriage, together with all kinds of penances and mortifications of the body. In the union of the abstractive and penitential elements, or of self-denial and self-punishment, the catholic asceticism stands forth complete in light and shade; exhibiting, on the one hand, wonderful examples of heroic renunciation of self and the world, but very often, on the other, a total misapprehension and perversion of Christian morality; the renunciation involving, more or less a Gnostic contempt of the gifts and ordinances of the God of nature, and the penance or self-punishment running into practical denial of

the all-sufficient merits of Christ. The ascetic and monastic tendency rests primarily upon a lively, though in morbid sense of the sinfulness, of the flesh and the corruption of the world; then upon the desire for solitude and exclusive occupation with divine things; and finally, upon the ambition to attain extraordinary holiness and merit. It would anticipate upon earth the life of angels in heaven. It substitutes all abnormal, self-appointed virtue and piety for the normal forms prescribed by the Creator; and rarely looks down upon the divinely-ordained standard with spiritual pride. It is a mark at once of moral strength and moral weakness. It presumes a certain degree of culture, in which man has emancipated himself from the powers of nature and risen to the consciousness of his moral calling; but thinks to secure itself against temptation only by entire separation from the world, instead of standing in the world to overcome it and transform it into the kingdom of God.

Some early church fathers viewed asceticism as heretical. They write, "The beginnings of which are resisted in the New Testament itself (1 Tim. 4:3; Col. 2:16 Cf: Rom. 14), meets us in the Gnostic and Manichaean sects. It is descended from Oriental and Platonic ideas, and is based on a dualistic view of the world, a confusion of sin with matter, and a perverted idea of God and the creation. It places God and the world at irreconcilable enmity, derives the creation from an inferior being, considers the human body substantially evil, a product of the devil or the demiurge, and makes it the great moral business of man to rid himself of the same, or gradually to annihilate it, whether by excessive abstinence or by unbridled indulgence. Many of the Gnostics placed the fall itself in the first gratification of the sexual desire, which subjected man to the dominion of the Hyle.

Abstinence touched the institution of marriage in the church. Clement of Alexandria is the most reasonable of all the fathers in his views on this point. He considers eunuchism a special gift of divine grace, but without yielding to it on this account preference above the married state. On the contrary, he vindicates with great decision the moral dignity and sanctity of marriage against the heretical extravagances of his time, and lays down the general principle that Christianity stands not in outward observances, enjoyments, and privations, but in righteousness and peace of heart. Of the Gnostics he says, that, under the fair name of abstinence, they act impiously towards the creation and the holy Creator, and repudiate marriage and procreation on the ground that a man should not introduce others into the world to their misery and provide new nourishment for death. He justly charges them with inconsistency in despising the ordinances of God and yet enjoying the nourishment created by the same hand, breathing His air, and abiding in His world.

At the Ecumenical Council of Nicaea (325) an attempt was made, probably under the lead of Hosius, bishop of Cordova, to elevate the Spanish rule to the dignity and authority of an ecumenical ordinance, that is, to make the prohibition of marriage after ordination and the strict abstinence of married priests from conjugal intercourse the universal law of the Church; but the attempt was frustrated by the loud protest of Paphnutius, a venerable bishop and confessor of a city in the Upper Thebaid of Egypt, who had lost one eye in the Diocletian persecution, and who had himself never touched a woman. He warned the fathers of the council not to impose too heavy a burden on the clergy, and to remember that marriage and conjugal intercourse were venerable and pure. He feared more harm than good from excessive rigor. It was sufficient if unmarried clergymen remain single according to the ancient tradition of the church; but it was wrong to separate the married priest from his legitimate wife, whom he married while yet a layman. This remonstrance of a strict ascetic induced the council to table the subject and to leave the continuance or discontinuance of the married relation to the free choice of every clergyman. It was a prophetic voice of warning.

Abstinence of wine touched the Eucharist. The practice of using mere water for wine in the Eucharist was condemned by Clement of Alexandria, Cyprian, and Chrysostom, and forbidden by Theodosius in an edict of 382. A certain class of modern abstinence men in America, in their abhorrence of all intoxicating drinks, has resorted to the same heretical practice, and substituted water or milk for the express ordinance of our Lord.

The Hindoo monks or gymnosophists (naked philosophers), as the Greeks called them, live in woods, caves, on mountains, or rocks, in poverty, celibacy, abstinence, silence: sleeping on straw or the bare ground, crawling on the belly, standing all day on tiptoe, exposed to the pouring rain or scorching sun with four fires kindled around them, presenting a savage and frightful appearance, yet greatly revered by the multitude, especially the women, and performing miracles, not infrequently completing their austerities by suicide on the stake or in the waves of the Ganges.

Even in the most favorable case, monasticism falls short of harmonious moral development and of that symmetry of virtue, which meets us in perfection in Christ, and next to Him in the apostles. It lacks the finer and gentler traits of character, which are ordinarily brought out only in the school of daily family life and under the social ordinances of God. Its morality is rather negative than positive. There is more virtue in the temperate and thankful enjoyment of the gifts of God, than in total abstinence; in charitable and well-seasoned speech, than in total silence; in connubial chastity, than in celibacy; in self-denying practical labor for the church, than in solitary asceticism, which only pleases self and profits no one else.

So we can conclude over time that abstinence went from honoring and pleasing God to an outward show and demonstration of spirituality. If you did such prescribed activities, deemed by men as holy, then you were holy. You see, motivation is essential to your reasons for abstinence.

Abstinence without the proper motivation is asceticism—the very act Martin Luther practiced. Oswald Chambers writes, "Asceticism is the passion of giving up things and is recognizable in a life not born again of the Spirit of God. It is all very well if it ends in giving up the one thing God wants us to give up, namely our right to ourselves, but if it does not end there, it will do endless damage to the life."

Newell Dwight Hillis (1858–1929), evaluating his day in which asceticism was largely practiced, wrote, "The black shadow of asceticism spread over the sky of the Puritan Fathers. Given two coats, they chose the ugliest one. Given two colors for the woman's garb, they chose the saddest and soberest. Given two roads, they chose the one that held the most thorns and cutting rocks. Given two forms of fear and self-denial, they took both. The favorite text of asceticism is 'deny yourself.' The favorite color of asceticism is black, its favorite music, a dirge; its favorite hour is midnight; its favorite theme is a tombstone. The mistake of asceticism is in thinking that it has a moral value."

Reasons why abstinence declined
Poor role models
How someone is raised can have a profound impact on his or her thinking and behavior. If a child/teen is raised in a home where Dad displays anger toward his wife and the wife, to avoid domestic abuse, leaves her husband alone, that child sees that anger has a positive effect. Dad was left alone. Unless someone shows this young person the powerful negative effects, you have the breeding grounds for a second generation. In biblical counseling, this is called preconditioning. A role model is anyone to whom someone looks up. He or she can be a parent, teacher, principle, Hollywood celebrity, sports figure, or neighbor. When role models do not live with self-control, have standards, abstain from societal evils, their influence can make an impression the next generation.

Diluted abstinence philosophy
As mentioned earlier, because the church has [1] portrayed an abstinence policy of legalism, and [2] because the federal and state governments have interceded, the brand of abstinence is relative. The prevalent abstinence teaching either by locale or by program drives any rule of conduct or behavior. In the Bible-belt, it may contain a higher value, while in other parts of the country it is not as important. This subjectivism shapes the standard of abstinence and any resulting practices.

Lack of parental teaching
Rocky Mountain Family Council writes, "Can parents make a difference in helping their kids choose abstinence? Definitely. Studies show that parents can have the most dramatic impact on their children's behavior if they clearly define what they expect their children to do, and not to do." It continues, "It is best to share these family guidelines in the context of everyday life and not during some specially orchestrated sex talk. As a parent, when you see a moment to share truth with your kids, take advantage of that moment. Those moments

may include talking after attending a wedding or explaining a bad example you see in the media. Abstinence is best taught in the context of everyday, family life." Sounds like Deuteronomy 6:6–7, which says, "These words, which I am commanding you today, shall be on your heart. You shall teach them diligently to your sons and shall talk of them when you sit in your house and when you walk by the way and when you lie down and when you rise up."

Single parent homes
God designed homes to consist of two opposite sex parents—a mom and dad, male and female. God designed marriage to be permanent. God says He hates divorce. Single parent homes may be at an all time high in our day. And most of the single parent homes are female. Mom is called to be the bread winner, disciplinarian, educator, coach, and teacher, besides working full time and even holding a part-time job to make ends meet. Fatigue sets in, coupled with bitterness and anger that her "ex" is living the high life with his girlfriend. She reaches out for assistance. She finds the school with its pre- and after-school programs and everything in between; one being Sex or Abstinence Education. She is thankful that "someone" will teach her children about this so they don't learn it on the street or from their friends.

Influence of the media
What the schools or friends do not convey, the media will. The media is a good actor. It plays to the audience. Some audiences need only a little influence, a little skin, touching, or scantily dressed actresses, while other audiences have graduated and require more stimulation, nudity and more. Media is television, cable, videos, DVDs, music, and whatever those who use these tools to sell their version of abstinence to a targeted audience.

Culturally defined standards
Students are taught, "It's your choice." "Only you know when it's right." Why one student may wait until they are twenty-two and another indulges at fourteen is determined by what they have come to believe as influenced by false teaching and others' experiences.

Mockery of abstinence
Carol Everett, who formerly operated several abortion clinics, says that when she spoke at public schools, "The first thing was to get the students to laugh at their parents. That way, they won't go home and tell their parents what I told them."

Who has taken over the role of abstinence teaching and are they effective? The federal and state governments sponsor abstinence training. Since 1997, when federal government became involved, Congress has authorized nearly one-half billion dollars in abstinence training programs. Over the past five years, $250 million dollars have been distributed to each of the continental United States. For every $1 spent on abstinence education, $4.50 is spent on sex education. President Bush has asked for an unprecedented $273 million dollar increase for abstinence education in his 2005 budget.

The programs available are too numerous to specific. To qualify for federal funding, the program must have as their "exclusive purpose, teaching the social, psychological, and health gains to be realized by abstaining from sexual activity." Among other conditions, abstinence-only programs must also convey that "a mutually faithful monogamous relationship in [the] context of marriage is the expected standard of human sexual activity" and that "sexual activity outside of the context of marriage is likely to have harmful psychological and physical effects."

Their approach seems twofold. They use scare tactics by portraying the horrific details of sexually transmitted diseases, unwanted pregnancy, never fulfilling personal life goals, being a single parents, and possible poverty. They say that knowledge is power. Knowing what we will reap before we sow can be an effective tool. But in this area is it?

Thirty years ago, doctors recognized only two STDs—syphilis and gonorrhea. Both are curable. Today, there are over 25 STDs, generating more than thirteen million new cases annually. Half are incurable.

In 1998, Kaiser Family Foundation reported, "By age twenty-four, at least one in three sexually active people are estimated to have contracted an STD. Trichomoniasis is the most common STD in young sexually active women in the US. An estimated 45 million new cases occur each year."

The other approach is to promote safe sex. If you are going to be sexually active, as most sex educators think, then let's show you how to have safe sex to prevent STD and unwanted pregnancy. This is taught as a means of abstinence. However, we must understand this more as a result rather than the mindset that affects decisions.

Is abstinence education working? Sex education has been the prevalent norm for a number of decades, ever since the federal and state governments took over the role of the family and the church. They taught how to have safe sex and passed out condoms. Abstinence education teaches abstinence and why a young person should wait until marriage. Ari Fleischer, former White House Press Secretary, January 27, 2003 wrote, "Abstinence is more than a sound science—it is a sound practice. Abstinence has a proven track record of working."

According to the Rocky Mountain Family Council, "When abstinence education is presented to teens within the correct context, the results are staggering. One study reports that participants in an abstinence-based program are five times less likely to engage in intercourse than those who have not received the abstinence counseling. The message is clear—we should expect more virtue from our teens and they should expect more godly counsel from us."

A study representing over 2,000 physicians said about the decline in teen pregnancy, abortion, and birth rates in the 1990s: Programs in safer sex education and condom distribution have not reduced the out-of-wedlock birthrates among teens.

For years, Rhea County, Tennessee, had the worst rate of teen pregnancy in the state. But Cahti Woods, the director of a local crisis pregnancy clinic, started a new abstinence program for teens. Cathi encouraged open discussion, but she never shied away from telling them the consequences of premarital sex. Her results: in just three years. Rhea County went from #1 in teen pregnancy in the state to #64 (*Christianity Today*, 1999).

San Marcos Junior High in San Marcos, California, adopted an abstinence only curriculum developed by Teen-Aid, Inc., titled, Sexuality, Commitment, and Family. The year before the curriculum was implemented, 147 girls were reported pregnant. But two years after the program's adoption only 20 girls became pregnant.

Federally funded abstinence programs have built-in limitations. Morality cannot be legislated. First, there is no universally acceptable definition for morality. Second, Paul reminds us "against such there is no law," referring to the command to show the fruits of the spirit. Third, to be able to legislate a moral society (as Calvin thought he could do) is to suppress the free will of man for a time of rebellion. The righteous reign of Christ to the rebels is a time to conform. In the end, the rebels revolt.

There is not enough money to orchestrate abstinence. Even with the millions of dollars spent each year on abstinence education, the success rate, though marginally improved, is not any more significant in comparison to the dollars being spent. It would be interesting to conduct a study on the cost of abortions and federal/local government monies for unwanted pregnancy, treatment of sexually transmitted diseases, and other associated ills for the balance of people who do not abstain.

Then you have everyone doing that which is right in his or her own eyes. Instead of spending the federal funds for which they were distributed, you have states wanting to divert the funds from abstinence education to abstinence advertising using billboards, subway signs, and media advertising. One state's governor proposed such an act and it was voted down 104 to 44.

So we either have apathy or we provide an alternative. The statistical information on abstinence education is not impressive for the federal dollars poured into this government program. There is no denying improvements can be cited, but are they that significant to justify its continuation at the present success rate? Or is there another alternative?

We read from literature the cry for parental involvement in this area. Some studies cite marked improvement when parents teach abstinence in the home within the family structure.

We briefly reviewed the biblical literature from the first writings of Moses that God was the originator of abstinence training. As with anything dealing with the human heart, you have God's plan and man's. This is as old as the Garden itself.

Let's take a moment, consider God's plan, and ask ourselves some questions. In answering these questions, one will discover facts in which an informed decision can be made. What are some of these questions?

Why did God speak of abstinence to Adam? Wasn't Adam made in God's image? Wasn't he perfect—without sin? God spoke to Adam about abstinence because God created him for fellowship. God is holy. Adam was created in His image and perfect, sinless. For Adam to have unbroken and intimate fellowship with God, Adam needed to maintain a certain lifestyle. Adam was free to eat of any of the tress God supplied for him. But one tree was off limits. Adam, to have fellowship with God, was commanded to abstain from the Tree of the Knowledge of Good and Evil. God told him what would happen if he did not obey. Adam would die. He would die spiritually and physically.

Abstinence was a condition of fellowship. Abstinence guards unity and oneness of mind. Without it, how can two walk as one? Paul refers to this union build on abstinence when he writes in 1 Cor. 6:14–16, "Do not be bound together with unbelievers; for what partnership have righteousness and lawlessness, or what fellowship has light with darkness? Or what harmony has Christ with Belial, or what has a believer in common with an unbeliever? Or what agreement has the temple of God with idols?"

Fellowship is based on the concept of abstinence. This is the basis for our sanctification, namely that we abstain from every appearance of evil. First John reminds us that as we walk in the light as He is in the light and we have fellowship with one another and the blood of Jesus cleanses us from all sin (1:7).

> i. Are there any incentives in following God's pattern for abstinence?
>
> ii. Are there any warnings and consequences if someone does not follow God's pattern for abstinence?

Can anyone follow God's pattern for abstinence? Abstinence is a matter of belief. Our source of belief determines the persistence of one's abstinence. Why would a young person abstain from sexual activity until marriage? Because of the teachings of his parents? Because of societal mores? To avoid contracting a sexually transmitted disease? Because he/she is not ready to be a parent?

If any of these are the major deterrent to participating in sex, and the person could justify or avoid the unwanted consequences, the probability of participating becomes greater. A person dead in their trespasses and sins is not capable of a consistent abstinence policy. We can also conclude that a person with a redeemed relation to Christ as Savior but not Lord cannot develop a consistent abstinence policy because they are taken captive to their fleshy lusts. Only the spirit-controlled saint can develop a consistent abstinence policy. I am not saying that the struggle will not be within them. Paul alludes to this when he pens his struggle in Romans 7, "For I know that nothing good dwells in me, that is, in my flesh; for the willing is present in me, but the doing of the good is not. For the good that I want, I do not do, but I practice the very evil that I do not want." But he continues when he writes, "Wretched man that I am! Who will set me free from the body of this death? Thanks be to God through Jesus Christ our Lord!" Struggles are part and parcel of abstinence. Victory in abstinence of an area of my life comes from a solid, true, infallible, inerrant absolute source.

Does God tell us why abstinence is so difficult for His creation? If we return to the first failure of abstinence, we quickly discover the difficulty. Adam and Eve were selfish. This is a bit astounding, but we must not be too hard on them. We would have acted precisely as they did.

Let's think about this. Adam was made in the image of God. This means he was capable of rationally, emotionally, and volitionally living life like His creator. He was created in a perfect universe. He was given every blessing under Heaven. He was instructed, warned, and blessed. Why was abstinence so difficult for him?

I think we find the answer in Genesis 3. Abstinence is eliminated when the basis of truth is questioned, denied, and replaced. Adam knew God's abstinence policy. So did his wife, because Adam instructed Eve. But the serpent began the abstinence erosion campaign by casting dispersion upon God's character. The serpent called into question God's goodness and fairness. Why couldn't Adam and Eve enjoy the fruit from the Tree of the Knowledge of Good and Evil? They were permitted to eat from every other tree. What did God know that He didn't want His creation to know? Why did it seem like God was withholding something good from them? He made them; He made all the trees—even this tree under prohibition!

Why do I have to wait before marriage? What is wrong with a beer? It's only a dollar on the lottery. It's only a cup of coffee in a public place—nothing will happen! Once Eve began to think on this lofty thought the serpent raised up against the knowledge of God, Eve was more susceptible to believe the serpent's next statement. They would surely not die if they ate of the tree. The serpent called God a liar. God wouldn't kill you because He withheld something good from you. God is just threatening you to keep you in line. How could God punish you for something that He is doing that is unfair? That would be more unfair! What kind of God is that? It's only one drink. It can't possibly affect me. I hug all my female friends. There's nothing to it. She's comfortable with it, and we are using protection. We're adults! It's almost eliminated. But it's still kind of edgy. I need some justification before I proceed. I need to be convinced so I can convince others. You shall be like God, knowing good from evil; and your eyes will be opened. Need any more justification to abandon abstinence? There you have it. It's all there. You don't need anything more.

Abstinence is difficult because we are our own worst enemy. We are selfish. We want our way more than God's way. We think we are smarter than God is. We convince ourselves that we know better than God does. "All of us like sheep have gone astray; each of us has turned to his own way" (Isa. 53:6). "Beloved, I urge you as aliens and strangers to abstain from fleshly lusts, which wage war against the soul" (1 Peter 2:11). "So as to live the rest of the time in the flesh no longer for the lusts of men, but for the will of God" (1 Peter 4:2). "Now those who belong to Christ Jesus have crucified the flesh with its passions and desires" (Gal. 5:24). "Instructing us to deny ungodliness and worldly desires and to live sensibly, righteously and godly in the present age" (Titus 2:12).

In everything, we should want Him who alone is beautiful. "That I may know Him and the power of His resurrection and the fellowship of His sufferings, being conformed to His death" (Phil 3:10). "By this, we know that we have come to know Him, if we keep His commandment" (1 John 2:3).

Are there any crucial factors that would help someone maintain a life of abstinence?

Thinking
Proverbs instructs us that as a man thinks so he is. What a person thinks about directly guides his footsteps of actions. A biblical example would be that of Isaac in Genesis 26. Remember that he was fearful that Abimelech would kill him because of the beauty of his wife. Let me read the verse: When the men of the place asked about his wife, he said, "She is my sister," for he was afraid to say, "my wife," *thinking*, "the men of the place might kill me on account of Rebekah, for she is beautiful. Notice the emotions (fear). Notice the action (he lied). Notice what precipitated the feelings and behavior—his thinking. This is why Paul commands us in 2 Cor. 10:4–5 to take captive every thought unto the obedience of Christ. Amy Knicely says, "You

feel what you feel and do what you do because of the way you think." To maintain a life of abstinence you must think biblically.

Feeling

Then Jonathan said to David, "The Lord, the God of Israel, be witness! When I have sounded out my father about this time tomorrow, or the third day, behold, if there is good *feeling* toward David, shall I not then send to you and make it known to you? Do you find this passage interesting? Jonathan sought to understand the depraved mind of his spiritually insane father through intuition! Jeremiah reminds us that the heart is desperately wicked and deceitful. Who can trust it? To maintain a life of abstinence, we must shun feelings that influence our utter belief that we serve a good and great God, and that what He does is always for His glory and our ultimate benefit. We must shun the testimonial feelings of others whose experience becomes their point of validation for accepting a sinful practice. The majority in the Bible was never right about anything—ever! To maintain a life of abstinence you must subjugate your feelings to truth.

Behavior

The volitional choice to act in accordance with God's declared Word. Elijah's words echo to us, as they did on the mountains of old, "How long will you halt between two opinions? If Baal is god, then serve him; but if God is God, serve Him!" Unlike our first father, who was so richly blessed, we too are richly blessed and are faced daily with decisions of abstinence. The decisions we make are the display of what we believe.

What is at the core of abstinence? The Bible commands that we have no other gods before us. We are not to make any graven images. We are to love the Lord God with all of our heart, mind, soul, and strength. The Apostle John wrote that he must decrease and Christ must increase. Jesus tells us to die daily and take up our cross. Paul says that we have been crucified and the life we live now by faith in the Son of God who loved me. Paul reminds us that we have been baptized into the death, burial, and resurrection of Jesus Christ.

What is the core of abstinence? *It is what or whom you love most.* The core of abstinence is a superlative. It is a comparison between values, goals, and aspirations. It is all about focus. "Looking for the blessed hope and the appearing of the glory of our great God and Savior, Christ Jesus." "For he was looking for the city which has foundations, whose architect and builder is God." "Considering the reproach of Christ greater riches than the treasures of Egypt; for he was looking to the reward." "Looking for and hastening the coming of the day of God, because of which the heavens will be destroyed by burning, and the elements will melt with intense heat! But according to His promise, we are looking for new heavens and a new earth, in which righteousness dwells." All these verses deal with focus. Abstinence is a contrast between eternal and temporal things.

God calls us to be holy like He is holy. God lives out His own abstinence policy. His call to us is possible, just like it was for Adam. Like Adam, we have a choice. Like the first Adam, we can love something or someone more than loving God. But in the second Adam, we are blessed with all spiritual blessings in the heavenlies. We have everything pertaining to life and godliness. We can meditate on His precepts and regard His ways. We can walk in liberty because we seek His precepts. We can understand more than the experts can because we observe His precepts. From His precepts, we get understanding so we can hate very false way. We can esteem right all *Your* precepts concerning everything, so I hate every false way.

Is there any area of your life right now in which you need to practice abstinence? Have you strayed from God's law? Are you drifting from the moorings and shelter of truth? Have you allowed others to use their experience to convince you to compromise your values and beliefs? Will you heed God's voice today and recommit your life to abstinence in the area He is showing you? Here are three steps to begin a life of abstinence.

Acknowledge in prayer that you have rejected God's patterns for your life. Repent and ask God's forgiveness. Humbly acknowledge that His ways are better for your life than the empty cisterns from which you have been drinking.

In a paragraph, write out God's pattern for this area of your life. What does God's Word say? How does God describe this pattern? Is there a biblical example I can study and follow? What does God promise to those who abstain? What resources does God make available to me?

Press forward. Paul says we are to forget the past and press forward for the high calling, which is in Christ Jesus. How can I translate God's pattern into my life? Is there someone I need to avoid? Should I take a different route home? Where can I go to spend uninterrupted time with God alone? How can I appropriate God's truth so I can effectively deal with those influences in my life that try to erode my commitment to abstinence? Do I need an accountability partner? Should I seek some informal counseling? Do I need to be discipled or mentored in this area?

This material may be brand new to you. Maybe your interest has been piqued by its content. Maybe there is a strange warming in your heart—something you have not experienced before. It could be that the Holy Spirit is trying to get your attention. And He is trying to tell you that you need to have a personal relationship to Jesus Christ.

Many people think they are "okay" with God because they view themselves as good people. They pay their taxes, are good providers, better than average employees, and they do not deliberately hurt anyone. They try harder every year to be better than the previous year.

But the Bible tells us that not according to our works, but according to His own purpose and grace, which was granted us in Christ Jesus from all eternity (2 Tim. 1:9). What seems frightening to me is how would a person know if they have enough works to get into Heaven? Is there some earthly scale one can go to on a weekly basis for personal measurement? That way the person knows whether he is ahead of the game or has to perform extra works to make up for last week's deficit.

Friend, Jesus—the second person of the Trinity—God very God, was born of a Virgin, lived a perfect life, suffered, and died on a Roman cross for our sins—yours and mine. The good news is not only did

He love us so much to take our place, but also He is alive today. He rose from the grave. Because He rose from the grave, He conquered death. Death is the result of sin. Therefore anyone who believes these truths, from a sincere heart, will be saved and have the power to live a powerful and holy life.

Have you ever made this personal commitment? Would you like to right now? Consider repeating this prayer:

> Dear God, I have come to understand that I have lived my life in direct opposition to what You have prescribed in Your Word. I am a violator, a sinner. I have heard that Your Son, Jesus, took my place at Calvary for my sinful life and actions. I now pray and ask You to cleanse me from all my sin because of Jesus. I personally want to receive Him into my life as Savior and Lord. I commit myself to live, with your help and empowerment, in such a way to please you the rest of my days. Amen.

It Seems Like Nothing Is Going Right for Me

What to Do When Surrounded by Suffering

How do you know if it's going to be a bad day? You wake up face down on the pavement. You call suicide prevention, and they put you on hold. You see a *60 Minutes* news team waiting in your office. Your birthday cake collapses from the weight of the candles. You turn on the news, and they're showing emergency routes out of the city. Your twin sister forgets your birthday. You wake up to discover that your waterbed broke and then realized you don't have a waterbed. Your horn goes off accidentally and remains stuck as you follow a group of Hell's Angels on the freeway.

Someone wrote, "Don't complain and talk about all your problems—80% of people don't care; the other 20% will think you deserve them!"

On a more serious note, are you going through a hard time? Maybe these words from a song sung by Kristine Wyrtzen will help you. The song is called "The Fire."

> I've been through a fire that has deepened my desire to know the living God more and more. It hasn't been much fun, but the work that it has done in my life has been worth the hurt. You see sometimes we need the hard times to bring us to our knees, otherwise we do as we please and never heed Him. For He always knows what's best, and it's when we are distressed that we really come to know God as He is.

Charles Spurgeon (1834–1892) wrote, "I owe more to the fire and hammer and the file than to anything else in my Lord's workshop. I sometimes question whether I have ever learned anything except through the rod. When my schoolroom is darkened, I see the most."

In the pictures of the ancient Roman method of threshing grain, one man is always seen stirring up the sheaves while another rides over them in a crude cart equipped with rollers instead of wheels. Sharp stones and rough bits of iron were attached to these cylinders to help separate the husks from the grain. This simple cart was called a tribulum—from which we get our word "tribulation." When great affliction comes to us, we often think of ourselves as being torn to pieces under the cruel pressures of adverse circumstances. Yet as no thresher ever yoked up his tribulum for the mere purpose of tearing up his sheaves but to disclose the precious grain, so our loving Savior never puts us under the pressure of sorrow and disappointment needlessly.

What are some causes of suffering? We often thing that suffering is created by our boss, spouse, children, neighbors, circumstances, the auto mechanic, in-laws, etc. I believe those people, places, or things we point to as objects of suffering fall into three basic sources of suffering. Let's examine them together.

First, we suffer because we are involved in a spiritual battle. The Christian lives in two worlds; the earthly world and the heavenly world. Each world has a thought system. Paul describes this as setting our minds on things above, not things below. He further describes what happens as a result of what we think. When we set our minds on the flesh, it breeds hostility and death. If a Christian sets his or her mind on things above, the result is peace. This dichotomy is the tension with which a saint lives. It is a spiritual battle. Who or what are the enemies of the saint? They are the world, flesh, and the devil.

The world is the saint's first opponent. Consider these verses.

> If you were of the world, the world would love its own; but because you are not of the world, but I chose you out of the world, because of this the world hates you (John 15:19).

> These things I have spoken to you, so that in Me you may have peace. In the world you have tribulation, but take courage; I have overcome the world (John 16:33).

Why does the world war against us? Because our salvation removed us from the family of the world, the way it thinks and acts. Paul often reminds the saint that they were "formerly" like the world. The world loves it own—those who think, feel, and act like the world. Salvation makes me a threat to the world because we are light and the world is darkness. The world is terrified of exposure of its wickedness. Jesus honestly tells us that the saint will have tribulation, and the source of the tribulation is the world.

The world's economy stands in utter contrast to the way a saint now thinks, feels, and acts. The world justifies its sinful behavior; the saint confesses his or her sinful behavior. The world blames others for its faults; the saints accepts responsibility for his or her sins. The world rationalizes its unjust practices; the saints humbly accepts the just rewards for his or her practices.

A practical example would be the life of King Saul. Here is a man anointed as Israel's first King. He started well, but finished poorly. What went wrong? When Saul disobeyed the Lord, he rationalized his behavior. He blamed others. He pointed to unbearable pressures others placed upon him. Saul never did accept responsibility for his willful rebellion and spirit of divination.

The world engages the saint in battle by attacking the mind. The world throws hypothetical questions at the saint, those "what if" questions. At times, the world speaks softly to persuade the saint's mind of the acceptableness of a sinful action. At other times, the world speaks boldly against a biblical principle embraced by the saint to intimidate, threaten, or mock.

The flesh is our second enemy. Consider what Paul writes in Romans 7:18–21.

> For I know that nothing good dwells in me, that is, in my flesh; for the willing is present in me, but the doing of the good is not. For the good that I want, I do not do, but I practice the very evil that I do not want. But if I am doing the very thing I do not want, I am no longer the one doing it, but sin which dwells in me. I find then the principle that evil is present in me, the one who wants to do good.

Do you hear Paul's struggle? He desires to do the right thing. He longs to please the Lord. He knows what is right and what is wrong. Yet Paul humbly admits that he understands all too well his willful choice of selfishness and pride in doing his own thing. He knows decisions motivated by lust break God's heart and violate biblical patterns of holiness. Paul cries out that he comprehends this awful, serious ongoing battle between what the flesh craves and what a saint must do to please the Savior and Lord. He accurately labels this battle. Paul battles with the sin nature or the flesh. Other names for this monster are the old nature, the Adamic nature, the old man, and the first Adam.

What are some practical examples? "A gentle answer turns away wrath, but a harsh word stirs up anger" (Prov. 15:1). You struggle between exercising self-control and losing your cool. "Poor is he who works with a negligent hand, but the hand of the diligent makes rich" (Prov. 10:4). I choose to be negligent or to be diligent in what I do. And we could offer a plethora of other examples.

There is a prime way the flesh battles with the saint. The flesh uses our emotions. The flesh stirs up feelings of resentment, bitterness, anger, pity, and the like to persuade the mind that contemplation of subsequent sinful actions are justified. "Well, he yelled at you first." "Who else do you see working like a dog? And what are you getting out of it?"

The devil is our third enemy. Read the following verses.

> Be of sober spirit, be on the alert. Your adversary, the devil, prowls around like a roaring lion, seeking someone to devour (1 Peter 5:8).

> You are from God, little children, and have overcome them; because greater is He who is in you than he who is in the world (1 John 4:4)

Peter portrays the devil as our adversary. An adversary is someone who opposes another with animosity. This enemy is pictured as a lion on the prowl. He hunts me down. He stalks me. He lies in wait for the right opportunity to pounce. He lurks in the shadows anticipating when I am vulnerable.

The devil is also pictured in the Bible as an angel of light (misrepresentation and deception) and a serpent (subtlety and lies). His basic "MO" (*modis operendi*) is misrepresentation or denial of truth. The world attacks our mind, the flesh our emotions, and here the devil attacks the truthfulness, reliability, and trustworthiness of what God says.

So suffering can come because of a spiritual battle in which we are involved. We may be battling with staying true to God's Word because the world is attempting to erode our convictions by appealing to our minds. We may be battling with staying true to God's Word because the flesh is attempting to erode our convictions by appealing to our emotions. We may be battling with staying true to God's Word because the devil is attempting to erode our convictions by misrepresenting or denying the truth.

We suffer because of another's sinful choices. Let's review the life of Joseph for a moment. Joseph was the youngest son born to Jacob and Rachel. He was Jacob's pride and joy, so much so that Jacob placed Joseph in a precarious position by giving Joseph that famous coat of many colors.

God took a special interest in Joseph by granting two visions to Joseph about the future of him and his family. Joseph shared these divine revelations, but his family was displeased. His brothers were angry.

Joseph was sent to check on his brothers. Jacob knew the sinfulness of his sons from a previous problem they had with the Shechemites. Joseph obeyed, which opened the door of revenge for his brothers. They stripped Joseph of the coat, sold him to the Midianites who in turn sold him to the Egyptians. He served in Potiphar's house until he was falsely accused by Potiphar's wife of sexual misconduct. He was imprisoned and later released to interpret the Pharaoh's dream. Because of God's hand upon Joseph's life, he rose to the second most powerful man in Egypt. All of this occurred, from a human perspective, because of the sinful actions of his brothers.

Let's review the life of Daniel. Daniel was a righteous man who became an exile in Babylon. He died in Babylon never seeing his homeland. Why? Because of the sinfulness of his nation. Israel's idolatry and intermarriage provoked God's jealousy, and in God's holiness, He punished them by moving Nebuchadnezzar to destroy Jerusalem and take its citizens into captivity.

Other's actions can create very difficult, hard situations in our life. We did not do anything wrong or sinful. This is what James refers to when he reminds the saints that while traveling through life don't be surprised when trials leap upon you (1:3). Joseph and Daniel experienced this.

What we need to remember is that God is sovereign. With this difficult moment in life, He is working out His purposes and good intentions for my good. Reflecting on Joseph and Daniel's lives, we, in our hindsight, know of God's good intentions for them and through them.

We suffer because of our own sinful choices. Then we can suffer because of our own sinful choices. Now I want to take a moment to help you understand a very significant biblical truth. When we suffer from our own sinful choices, it is not really suffering in the biblical sense of the world. Suffering is related to the results I am experiencing because of the actions of another. My sinful choices do not result in suffering because it is something I did. Therefore, what I am experiencing is not suffering but the consequences of my choices.

Why am I straining at a gnat to swallow a camel? I believe there is a noteworthy difference in counseling. Dealing with true suffering will focus on the sovereignty of God and yielding to His good intentions and purposes. Dealing with the results of a sinful action demands repentance, confession, forgiveness, and perhaps restitution. Do you see the difference?

Are there biblical examples of people who lived with the consequences of their own sinful choices? Let me provide you with four. Cain's murderous act of Abel resulted in a life of a vagabond. David's adultery and first-degree murder resulted in deep ongoing family problems. Solomon's use of God's great gift resulted in a life of despair, hopelessness, and frustration. Jonah's disobedience and grudge-holding resulted in three days and nights all-expense-paid holiday at the Whale's Inn.

A general observation about the sources of suffering: in a spiritual battle, choices of another, and my own choices, no matter what the source of suffering is and the scenario, nine times out of ten people are watching you and me. How will I respond? Will I display humility and repent? Will I remain faithful to the Word of God? Will I cling to its truthfulness?

Suffering is observable and often leaves an indelible impression. In a positive way, the story is told of Adoniram Judson, the renowned missionary to Burma, who endured untold hardships trying to reach the lost for Christ. For seven heartbreaking years, he suffered hunger and privation. During this time, he was thrown into Ava Prison, and for seventeen months was subjected to incredible mistreatment. As a result, for the rest of his life, he carried the ugly marks made by the chains and iron shackles that had cruelly bound him. Undaunted, upon his release he asked for permission to enter another province where he might resume preaching the Gospel. The godless ruler indignantly denied his request, saying, "My people are not fools enough to listen to anything a missionary might say, but I fear they might be impressed by your scars and turn to your religion!"

Are there any guidelines on how to get a handle on suffering? I believe what you have previously taught about the sources of suffering. In fact, Rick, I have experienced each of them in my life. But I have to be honest, I did not do such a great job when any of them attacked me. In fact, I failed miserably. I even questioned my own salvation! I was angry, miserable, spiteful, a poor testimony, and people did not want to be around me. After the suffering subsided, close friends rebuked me, telling me how unpleasant I was.

Here are some guidelines. I call them "Grip Principles" to get a handle on suffering.

Grip Principle #1: Saints are never exempt from suffering.
How does a saint reach the conclusion that he or she is exempt from suffering? Or that he or she should not have any difficulties in life they cannot handle? In a moment we will consider Job and things he could have pointed at to exempt him from suffering.

But first, here is a partial list of New Testament saints who suffered. Remember the words of our Lord to His disciples when He reminded them, "A pupil is not above his teacher; but everyone, after he has been fully trained, will be like his teacher" (Luke 6:40).

1. Matthew suffered martyrdom by being slain with a sword at a distant city of Ethiopia.

2. Mark expired at Alexandria, after having been cruelly dragged through the streets of that city.

3. Luke was hanged upon an olive tree in the classic land of Greece.

4. John was put into a cauldron of boiling oil, but escaped death in a miraculous manner, and was afterwards banished to Patmos.

5. Peter was crucified at Rome with his head downward.

6. James the Greater was beheaded at Jerusalem.

7. James the Less was thrown from a lofty pinnacle of the temple, and then beaten to death with a fuller's club.

8. Philip was hanged up against a pillar at Heiropolis in Phrygia.

9. Bartholomew was flayed alive.

10. St. Andrew was bound to a cross, where he preached to his persecutors until he died.

11. Thomas was run through the body with a lance at Coromandel in the East Indies.

12. Jude was shot to death with arrows.

13. Matthias was first stoned, and then beheaded.

14. The Jews at Salonica stoned Barnabas of the Gentiles to death.
15. Paul after various tortures and persecutions, was at length beheaded at Rome by the Emperor Nero.

What could Job point to as reasons why he should be exempt from suffering? He was blameless. The Hebrew word is *tam*, which means complete, morally innocent, having integrity, one who is morally and ethically pure. From a human perspective, there were no grounds of accusation against his character, conduct, or lifestyle.

He was upright. The Hebrew word is *yashar*, which means straight, straightforward, proper, and fitting. There was no deviation, hint of wickedness or evil in Job.

He feared God. This means Job centered his life on God. He worked hard at thinking like, feeling like, and acting like God would act. God was the center of Job's life, not Job.

He turned away from evil. This means Job turned aside, departed from, removed himself from anything that was viewed as causing distress or misery.

He had many children. The text tells us he had seven sons and three daughters. He had many possessions. The text tells us he had 7,000 sheep, 3,000 camels, 500 yoke of oxen, 500 female donkeys. His possessions also included the hired staff to care for such material blessings.

He interceded for his children and their wives. Job often seemed to be impressed by the Spirit that his children might have in some way offended Jehovah. Understanding his role as a patriarch, he would offer sacrifices and intercede for them.

So, why would God single out Job? One would think that the blessings of God would be an indicator that God favored Job. God wouldn't subject such a blessed servant to such oppression. Or, Job's character was a shining beacon to his family and community. God wouldn't bring adversity into this pristine saint's life would He?

If someone could convince God that they were exempt from suffering, then another could come along and challenge the exclusiveness of God's decision. The person could raise the question of including his or her exemption. Then you have a problem of degrees of the item pointed to as exemplary. "I endured longer," or, "I had cancer, this other person only had kidney failure." You see how ridiculous this line of reasoning is?

Grip Principle #2: Suffering is one way God expresses confidence in me. Take a moment and read chapters 1 and 2 of Job. As you read, note how specifically God expresses His confidence in Job as God permits this time of suffering in his life.

In chapter 1, God expresses His confidence this way. God asks if Satan considers the challenge of tempting Job. Satan did not find anyone challenging to his attacks. All evidently gave in. God says in effect that Job is different. God continues by reading Job's divine resume. He points to Job's as blameless, upright, fearing God and turning from evil. God points to the inward character of the man, not the outward displays that Satan could misconstrue. When God is challenged as to Job's motivation why he serves God, God responds appropriately by giving Satan permission to cause suffering. God does not need to defend Job verbally. God expresses His confidence in Job's faithfulness through complete and thorough knowledge that Job would act biblically when this unknown onslaught occurs.

In chapter 2, God expresses His confidence this way. God returns to reminding Satan that Job was unlike any other man. Other men God created would have collapsed under such trials Satan threw at him in chapter 1. God says in effect, "Job is still standing. He remained faithful to me. I told you he would not capitulate." He again reminds Satan of Job's inner beauty by saying again that Job is blameless, upright, fearing God, and turning from evil.

Satan retorts that because Job was not personally touched he could portray an air of spiritual smugness. However, Satan says, "if you let me directly afflict him, he will recant." Again, God doesn't reprove Satan with words, but grants permission knowing Job will remain

What to Do When Surrounded by Suffering

faithful even when he is personally touched. You see, how could Satan even propose that Job was not touched personally by the loss of sons, daughters, servants, and possessions? When you examine Satan's accusations, they never make spiritual or logical sense.

When I experience suffering, when life's every turn is seasoned with difficulties, pain and sorrow, I remind ourselves that God is expressing His uttermost confidence in me that whatever is taking place, I can endure and come forth shining as gold. Charles Swindoll wrote, "God's wisest saints are often people who *endure* pain rather than *escape* it." "If God sends us on stony paths, he provides strong shoes" (Corrie Ten Boom).

Grip Principle #3: Suffering clarifies why I serve God.
Suffering reveals the human heart like no other time in our life. It exposes our understanding of this divine relationship and its purposes. Is God serving me or am I serving God?

Job served God because he loved God. He tells his wife (2:10), "Shall we indeed accept good from God and not accept adversity?" Job knew that there was purpose in the adversity he was experiencing. Although he did not know the exact reasoning and divine purposes, "he did not sin with his lips," (2:10) nor "through all this Job did not sin nor did he blame God." (1:22)

You see before God granted permission for the first trial, Satan accused Job of only serving God because, "Have you not made a hedge about him and his house and all that he has on every side? You have blessed the work of his hands, and his possessions have increased in the land. But put forth Your hand now and touch all that he has; he will surely curse You to Your face." Satan is saying you don't bite the hand that feeds you. Why wouldn't anyone worship and serve you when times are good? "Remove the good times, and you will see the manipulated human heart and its real relationship to you, God."

When the first trial passed, and the outcome was not that which Satan expected, and God kind of rubbed it in Satan's face, Satan retorted that because Job was not personally touched by the tragedy, why wouldn't he worship Jehovah? Job was willing to give up all of his children, possession, and most of his servants. But if you allow suffering to attack his body, for him to feel the sensations of pain, to hear the accusatory statements of close friends that he has some hidden sin in his life, "he will curse You to Your face."

When we fail to have the inner attitude of Job and speak the words of Job ("Naked I came from my mother's womb, and naked I shall return there. The Lord gave and the Lord has taken away. Blessed by the name of the Lord."), the motivation of our heart for serving God is unmasked. The word that uncovers our motivation is the word "why." The actions that expose my heart are complaining, criticizing, bartering with God, anger, and fear.

If what I just said is not our motivation for serving God when suffering, then what does suffering reveal about our heart of service? Many serve God because they want to avoid health issues. Many serve God because they want to avoid rebellion in their children. Many serve God so they can point to their badges, not their scars, and remind God of their faithfulness.

Each trial and subsequent suffering is an opportunity to declare privately and publicly, "This is why I serve God. Because God is good all the time and all the time God is good, I can trust Him. Yes, I can trust Him, for He does all things well according to the kind and good intentions of His heart and will!"

Grip Principle #4: Suffering is a divinely controlled experience.
When you and I enter the valley of the shadow of death, we are looking for the "5:15 Express" out of the valley. We want out, and we want out yesterday! If the suffering goes on for any length of time, we feel like God has forgotten us. He has forgotten to watch the "timer" of our suffering! Our minds convince ourselves that we can't take any more. "Enough is enough! When is this going to end?" When we become ensnared in our emotions, begin to whine and complain, our heart is saying, "God, I don't trust you. I question if you really know what You are doing. I think you might have made a mistake. This is Rick, remember?"

Go back and look at Job chapters 1 and 2. Can you spot the divine controls? In the first trial, God places the limitations on the suffering when He says, "Behold, all that he has is in your power *only* do not put forth your hand on him." In chapter 2, God said, "Behold, he is in your power, *only* spare your life."

The problem with this reality (suffering is a divinely controlled experience) is we want to know what the limits are that God set. We would like to know, but it is not necessary for us to know to respond biblically. The singular truth we need to know and believe is that God is in control. He is watching the "timer." He has the leash. There is no runaway truck or train. The plane is not going to ditch in the ocean. God's great compassion only allows that which His sovereign omniscience determined is enough to accomplish His good intention and purpose.

Remember this: all suffering ends. And whatever you suffer authentically, God has suffered from it first (Meister Eckhart, 1260–1327)

Grip Principle #5: Suffering does not block out the Son (not sun).
We have all heard or read the story entitled, "Footprints." It is the story of a man who was complaining to God about all the hard and difficult times he endured. He protested to God that God was not there. He was left to weather these storms by himself. He even showed Jesus that there was only one set of footprints walking along the beach, not two! And we know how the story ends. Christ tells the man that the reason there was only one set of footprints is because Christ was carrying the man.

Suffering does not block out the Son. In a valley, the density of the forest floor, the towering trees, block out the sun. But the sun is still shining. You may not be able to feel the sun. You may not be able to see its brilliance and brightness. But each and every day the sun rises in the east and sets in the west. God has ordained it to be so, and it is true. Our feelings or circumstances cannot change that scientific and creation truth.

Likewise, suffering does not block out the Son. Circumstances may loom large. The pathway we travel may be overgrown with critical people, unchanging situations, and voices of despair and discouragement. We may not be able to feel the Son. He may seem uncaring and inattentive. But the biblical fact is the Son is near and dear. He never sleeps nor slumbers. He is always alert, and His eye is continually guiding us. He is ever present. He has not left us as orphans. Theologically this is known as His omnipresence. Christ is everywhere. He has no restrictions.

Grip Principle #6: Suffering does not deny human emotions.
Some Christian sects advocate a "grin 'n bear it" portrait. They believe that Christians should not show emotions like tears, weeping, disappointment, or anger. The saint's life should be filled with "Praise the Lord," "God is good," and other positive thinking and speaking phrases. However, this is contrary to the great saints, and even our Lord Himself, who shed tears, cried, wept, and even became angry!

God did not rebuke Job for his emotions at the loss of family and possessions. Job was not denied his tears, torn robe, shaved head, and sitting in an ash heap.

Because we are made in the image of God, like God and our wonderful Savior, we can express emotions. How we express determines their sinfulness or truthfulness. Were Job's emotions truthful? Yes, because he continued to trust and act righteously as heard from his lips.

I think to deny our emotions, to mask them, to pretend they are not there, to resort to super-spiritual colloquialisms may go as far as to interfere with God's good intentions and purposes.

Grip Principle #7: Suffering expresses my confidence in God.
This is the flip side of the coin where suffering is God's way to express confidence in us. Suffering is a way we express confidence in God

Before his wife, remaining servants, a community of observers, and his three closest friends, Job expressed boldly, bravely, courageously, daringly, gallantly, fearlessly, unflinchingly, valiantly, unashamedly, and confidently God's goodness, mercy, righteousness, providence, sovereignty, and purposes.

There are times during suffering when this is the only thing you can do. You cannot discern the purpose for the suffering. You cannot comprehend the reasons for the circumstances. You cannot perceive God's intent. But you must tell yourself, "God, I completely trust You. I do not even remotely fathom what You might be doing. But I do know with certainty that You do not allow things arbitrarily. So in faith, I thank You for Your active work in my life through the gift of suffering."

One writer of verse put it this way: "Today Lord, I have an unshakable conviction, a positive, resolute assurance that what you have spoken is unalterably true. But today, Lord, my sick body feels stronger and the stomping pain quietly subsides. Tomorrow, and then tomorrow, if I must struggle again with aching exhaustion and twisting pain until I am breathing, until I am utterly spent, until fear eclipses the last vestige of hope. Then Lord, then grant me the enabling grace to believe without feeling, to know without seeing, to clasp your invisible hand and wait with invincible trust for the morning."

We need to address the "why" question. All too often, the first word out of our mouth when suffering assails us is the word "why." We are searching for a reason for what is transpiring in our life. "Why is this happening? Why am I going through this? Why does this have to happen now? Why is God allowing this to me?"

"Why" is used 392 times in NASB. "Why" means for what purpose, reason or cause, for which or on account of, cause or intention underlying a given action or situation, whys and wherefores, and it is used to express mild indignation, surprise, or impatience.

When we ask "why" it reveals something about our heart. We are searching for answers, but we are searching for answers that we can or will accept. "Why" is the type of question that demands accountability. "Why" is looking for justification for what is happening. "Why" demands satisfactorily answers. And "why" keeps asking the same questions until "why" is satisfied with the responses. Until then, "why" keeps asking.

Do you have a hard time envisioning this? Let's say you have a teenage son or daughter. You have worked hard at establishing a reasonable and amendable curfew. But your son or daughter regularly breaks the curfew. At first, it was just a few minutes. Lately, it has been as much as one hour. You have a sit-down with him or her. You ask, "Why are you breaking curfew?" Your son or daughter gives you a reason that you deem as lame. You repeat yourself. He or she offers another reason. This one is worse than the first. You ask again and again and again until you hopefully secure an answer you are either looking for or makes sense to you.

Christians have the same tendency with Christ when it comes to suffering. We want to know why. We demand answers. And when Christ responds, if He does, and we do not like what we hear, we ask again. We whine, plead, beg, and get angry. Stop and think about this picture. To whom are you speaking? Aren't you speaking to God? Remember, omniscient, omnipotent, sovereign, Lord, merciful, holy, infinite, just, and fair? And remind yourself who you are—finite, selfish, limited, restricted, saved, and in the process of sanctification, which means your intellect, emotions, and will are tainted and being purged with each biblical step of obedience. So, let's get this again. You are asking God to explain Himself?

"Why" demands reasons to determine if cooperating is beneficial. "What" is asking for purpose, seeking understanding in order to cooperate believing in God's kind intentions of His will and purpose.

Here are some purposes behind suffering. Purposes are God's "whats" for the saint. I am confident you can find more purposes for suffering. I simply offer you five.

A wife tells the following story.

> A peach tree stands in our back yard. Unpruned, the tree grew big and leafy. And it was loaded with peaches, although the fruit was disappointingly small and tasteless. The year he was out of work, Larry went to work on

the tree. When I came home from school one day and saw how far back he had pruned it, I stared in shock. "You've killed it," I cried. "Now we won't have any peaches at all." I was wrong. That spring the pruned branches burst forth with a beautiful blanketing of pink blossoms. Soon little green peaches replaced the blossoms. "Leave them alone," I begged. Larry ignored me and thinned the fruit. By the end of the summer the branches were so heavily laden, they had to be propped up. And the peaches—oh, how large and sweet and juicy they were. There was no denying it: the tree was far better off for the painful cutting it endured under Larry's pruning shears. No one wants to go through troubles, suffering, and pain. But looking back, Larry and I can only say, "Thank you, Lord, for pruning us. Thank you for teaching us to trust you. Thank you for drawing us together as a family and welding us in a way that never happened in happier times. Thank you, that after seeing each other at our worst, we still want to be together.

In the center of Main Street in Enterprise, Alabama, stands one of the strangest monuments in the world. It's a memorial to an insect! Handsomely carved in stone is the likeness of a boll weevil. Many believe that divine providence was involved in the circumstances that led to the erection of this unusual statue. In early plantation days, almost everyone in the community raised cotton. But as the years rolled on, a serious pestilence infested the area in the form of a small beetle that punctured the boll of the plant. As a result, it became almost impossible to bring a season's growth to maturity. George Washington Carver, along with several other scientists, became deeply concerned about the situation and began intensive studies to see if any substitute crop could be grown in that part of the country. Raising peanuts was the answer, for they could be planted and harvested with very little loss. In time, cotton gins were forgotten in that region, and it became known as an outstanding peanut center of the world. Soon the farmers' profits far exceeded what they had earned from their best cotton yield. In the end, they realized that the destructive insect they had feared had actually triggered the research that brought them prosperity. The Lord often allows trials to unsettle our lives for a blessed purpose. Perhaps we are trying to "grow cotton" when we should be "raising peanuts." If so, the delays and disappointments we experience are just the gracious "boll weevils" sent to redirect us so that we will plant the crop of God's choosing.

First, suffering can produce a deeper understanding of God. Because suffering comes from God, who is purposeful in all that He does, one benefit of suffering is gaining a deeper understanding of God. "I have heard of You by the hearing of the ear; but now my eye sees You" (Job 42:5)

Remember from Job 1 and 2, how God described Job? He depicted Job as a man who was blameless, upright, fearing God, and turning away from evil. God could see into the heart of Job and this is what God saw. How could Job say that after this intense time of suffering he sees God?

Suffering is one of God's special ways to impress upon my life a divine lesson, a lesson about Him and myself, that becomes indelible and in which this lesson could be learned no other way. Jesus did not come to explain away suffering or remove it. He came to fill it with His presence (Paul Claudel, 1868–1955).

Job said that he learned of God through hearing. If you please, Job had an academic faith, head knowledge. He was taught. He absorbed. He could recite.

But after his suffering, Job gained a new and fresh perspective on his relationship with God. It went deeper. Job's level of intimacy swam in the clear depths of pure joy and intense rest.

When life is rosy, we may slide by with knowing about Jesus, with imitating him and quoting him and speaking of him. But only in the fellowship of suffering will we know Jesus. We identify with him at the point of his deepest humiliation. The cross, symbol of his greatest suffering, becomes our personal touch-point with the Lord of the universe (Joni Eareckson Tada).

Job moved from hearing only to seeing clearly. Intimacy sharpens one's spiritual vision. The recognition of the divine in all of daily life is heightened. Seldom is an act of God missed because of busyness or carelessness.

Someone has written, "I rejoice in knowing that there is no oil without squeezing the olives, no wine without pressing the grapes, no fragrance without crushing the flowers, and no real joy without sorrow."

Second, suffering may result in an unimaginable wider ministry. The saint knows not why he suffers as he does, yet he comprehends with a knowledge that passes knowledge that all is well (Oswald Chambers, 1874–1917). Consider these words from Philippians.

> Now I want you to know, brethren, that my circumstances have turned out for the greater progress of the gospel, so that my imprisonment in the cause of Christ has become well known throughout the whole praetorian guard and to everyone else, and that most of the brethren, trusting in the Lord because of my imprisonment, have far more courage to speak the word of God without fear. Some, to be sure, are preaching Christ even from envy and strife, but some also from good will; the latter do it out of love, knowing that I am appointed for the defense of the gospel; the former proclaim Christ out of selfish ambition rather than from pure motives, thinking to cause me distress in my imprisonment. What then? Only that in every way, whether in pretense or in truth, Christ is proclaimed; and in this I rejoice (1:12–18).

Where is Paul? He is in prison. In fact, this is a prison epistle and his imprisonment is at Rome. He is writing back to these saints from a Roman cell. It appears that a part of the New Testament Christians felt that the spread of Christianity would soon end. Why? The great missionary diplomat was in jail facing death. How would the Church advance without his efforts? He singlehandedly moved throughout the Roman Empire sowing the seeds of the Gospel, planting churches and training men. Now in jail, what would happen to the Church and the Gospel?

These discouraged saints, unable to see what God was doing, needed encouragement. Paul reminds them that because of his incarceration many saints were coming to the forefront. Many saints were becoming more actively involved. Many saints were boldly standing up for and preaching the gospel. This must have been so uplifting for Paul. Remember that most of Paul's ministry was difficult and challenging.

At times, Paul was near submitting his resignation to God. While in Ephesus, God had to remind Paul (Acts) not to be discouraged. God has prepared many souls for the harvest. Paul could point to the troublesome church at Corinth. He could single Demas who return to serving the world. Paul even writes to Timothy that no one stood with him at his trial but Dr. Luke.

But Paul's life was not a zero. It was not useless. Paul's life greatly impacted countless others. And most of all, through Paul's suffering God was developing an unimaginable wider ministry.

Suffering tries to convince you that the pain and heartache is hindering you from doing great work for God. This is such a lie. Often the greatest work accomplished for God comes through suffering. Remember Hebrews 12:2, the suffering of our Lord Jesus? The result? Eternal life for Jews and Gentiles!

The other day, I was walking and talking with God. I was going through some hard times. I felt my life had little impact. My life accounted little for the Kingdom. As I spoke, the Spirit brought to mind this truth. My heart was strengthen, uplifted and my joy returned.

Paul's faithfulness in life meant he handed off the spiritual baton to others. He puts it this way, "The things, which you have heard from me in the presence of many witnesses, entrust these to faithful men who will be able to teach others also" (2 Tim. 2:2).

The marks of suffering can become a powerful gospel message. The story is told of Adoniram Judson, the renowned missionary to Burma, endured untold hardships trying to reach the lost for Christ. For seven heartbreaking years, he suffered hunger and privation. During this time, he was thrown into Ava Prison, and for seventeen months was subjected to almost incredible mistreatment. As a result, for the rest of his life he carried the ugly marks made by the chains and iron shackles which had cruelly bound him. Undaunted, upon his release he asked for permission to enter another province where he might resume preaching the Gospel. The godless ruler indignantly denied his request, saying, "My people are not fools enough to listen to anything a missionary might say, but I fear they might be impressed by your scars and turn to your religion!"

Third, suffering can refocus a distracted life. Consider Genesis 22:1–13.

> Now it came about after these things, that God tested Abraham, and said to him, "Abraham!" And he said, "Here I am." He said, "Take now your son, your only son, whom you love, Isaac, and go to the land of Moriah, and offer him there as a burnt offering on one of the mountains of which I will tell you." So Abraham rose early in the morning and saddled his donkey, and took two of his young men with him and Isaac his son; and he split wood for the burnt offering, and arose and went to the place of which God had told him. On the third day, Abraham raised his eyes and saw the place from a distance. Abraham said to his young men, "Stay here with the donkey, and I and the lad will go over there; and we will worship and return to you." Abraham took the wood of the burnt offering and laid it on Isaac his son, and he took in his hand the fire and the knife. So the two of them walked on together. Isaac spoke to Abraham his father and said, "My father!" And he said, "Here I am, my son." And he said, "Behold, the fire and the wood, but where is the lamb for the burnt offering?" Abraham said, "God will provide for Himself the lamb for the burnt offering, my son." So the two of them walked on together. Then they came to the place of which God had told him; and Abraham built the altar there and arranged the wood, and bound his son Isaac and laid him on the altar, on top of the wood. Abraham stretched out his hand and took the knife to slay his son. But the angel of the Lord called to him from heaven and said, "Abraham, Abraham!" And he said, "Here I am." He said, "Do not stretch out your hand against the lad, and do nothing to him; for now I know that you fear God, since you have not withheld your son, your only son, from Me."

Romans 1 states, "For they exchanged the truth of God for a lie, and worshiped and served the creature rather than the Creator, who is blessed forever (1:25). It is so easy to love the gifts of God and forget to love the Giver of the gifts. Suffering becomes one way in which God tests our affections.

After waiting twenty-five years for God's promise, Isaac is now eighteen to twenty-two years old. This father and son delighted in each other. I am confident that Abraham told and retold the story of Jehovah's appearance to them, Isaac's mother laughing, and the joy of his conception and birth.

Life for this family settled into a routine. There had not been any tests, troubles, or poor decisions. Life was good, tranquil, and normal. Day after day was the same. And with each passing day, God looked into Abraham's heart and saw straying affections, misplaced affections. God's great gift was enjoyed and cherished more than he cherish. The gift was replacing Abraham's affection for Giver.

Thus, God tested Abraham. The Scriptures clearly state the purpose for this time of suffering. Imagine being asked to sacrifice your son. And the son of promise. The son you had waited for for so long!

But the response of Abraham is exactly what God wanted. The text can be summarized by two words: instant obedience. No delays, no hesitation, no seeking counsel, unlike other times in which God spoke to Abraham.

After binding Isaac, lifting him upon the altar, answering his son's questions in faith, he brings his arm up with knife in hand, prepared to plunge it into his son's heart. But the angel of the Lord stops the time of testing and suffering, saying that He (God) knows that Abraham fears or love Him.

James tells us that all good and perfect gifts come down from the Father of Lights. God's gifts are often an answer to a longstanding prayer. God's gifts are often the reward of faith and obedience. God's gifts reflect and represent God Himself. And if we fall more in love with the gift, God will ask for it back. Like Abraham, God asked for Isaac back. Abraham had no idea that God would intervene. He was prepared to give the gift back. He believed that God would either replace the gift or return the gift.

Abraham was not slow to open his hand. Many of us are slow to open our hand. And if we are, God loves us so much He will greatly begin to pry open our clenched fist, and if need be break every finger on our hand to release the idol of the gift to return to worshiping and loving the Giver.

Suffering is one way God helps us to refocus our distracted lives. The result is always good because God's kind intentions of His will are in operation. The sooner we open our hand, the quicker we will show God how much we love Him and the earlier we will enjoy the result of this time.

Fourth, suffering may preserve the work and Word of God. You should take a moment to review Genesis 39–50 for this principle. I will summarize these chapters.

- Joseph has been sold to the Egyptians by the Midianites.
- Joseph biblical work ethics results in his promotion to being the head steward in Potiphar's home. Nothing is withheld from him except Potiphar's wife.
- Potiphar's wife is physically attracted to Joseph. She attempts to seduce him. Joseph resists, even to the point of fleeing her aggressive and physical attacks, leaving his coat behind.
- She cries rape. Potiphar has Joseph arrested and put into the royal prison. If you do not know this point, this means Potiphar did not believe his wife's accusation. Had he, Joseph would have been placed in the prison for criminals.
- Joseph demonstrates righteous abilities and as a prisoner runs the prison. After two years, he is called before Pharaoh to interpret a troubling dream. God is with Joseph. He successfully interprets the dream and proposes a wise plan. God's favor upon Joseph's life results in his being named second in command over all of Egypt.

Joseph's suffering preserved the work and Word of God. What work of God was in danger? Joseph was used by God to fulfill His promise to Abraham, Isaac, and Jacob. That promise? Genesis 12:1–3—land, seed, and blessing. The Abrahamic covenant.

What was happening in the "land"? There was a famine. Famine often results in death of the weak. Joseph's family numbered seventy persons in all. They were nomadic. They grazed sheep, maybe sunk some wells. But did not stay long in any one place. When such natural (or divine) disasters arose, they would simply move on. They would pack up their belongings, tents, gather the children and sheep, and move one.

This time was different. The famine seemed to be more generalized, not localized. Had it been localized, they would have relocated. But this generalized famine meant no one had food for himself or herself, let alone to sell. Perhaps the citizens were hoarding what food was available.

And we know the rest of the story: How Jacob commanded his sons to go to Egypt and buy food. How Joseph recognized his brothers, put the gold coins in the grain bags, kept Benjamin, and the subsequent return of Jacob's sons with the revelation of Joseph to his brothers.

We then see the truth of suffering. Suffering may preserve the work and Word of God. Had not Joseph been in such a position and favor with Pharaoh, the line of Jacob would have surely been extinguished because of the famine.

Do you think Joseph recognized he was working with the sovereignty of God in preserving his family? Yes, I do. Why? Because God had already shown him how He would care for his family in the vision of the moon and stars bowing to the sun, and the fat and skinny sheaves.

It may be true that you and I cannot see how our suffering preserves the work of God. It would be nice to see this and know this. But whether we recognize the greater work involved, God may be using your suffering to preserve His work through you. Our biblical response to suffering will assure the outcome of this truth if it is what God is seeking to accomplish.

Fifth, suffering strengthens your character and convictions. You should take time to consider reading Daniel 1–6. Again, I will summarize.

- Daniel was living in Judah at the time of Nebuchadnezzar's invasion. Being nobility, he was the first to be deported to Babylon.
- The mentality of foreign captors was to indoctrinate the nobility and royalty in the ways of their new captors so when the worker was finally deported, they would see the nobility

and royalty and accept the new environs, and hopefully this would prevent revolt by the workers when they got into the new land.

- Daniel entered Babylon at a young age. Daniel died in captivity. He never returned home. We know that Daniel was near eighty when he was put into the lion's den in Daniel 6. We say this because he had lived through three world empires: the Babylonian, the Medes, and the Persian empires.

We see Daniel developing convictions very early in his life. In fact, I believe that Daniel was a very astute and spiritually sensitive young man. He heard the prophets' prediction of the impending captivity. He knew it was because of the nation's idolatry. He knew he would be taken first. I believe he also knew several things that would take place, such as changing his name, dress, language, reading materials, and diet. I believe Daniel meditated on these matters during the nearly 540 miles trip from Jerusalem to Babylon. Daniel 1:8 says he purposed in his heart not to defile himself with the king's meat.

Daniel made up his mind. Then Daniel was given an opportunity to explain the king's dream. As a result, he was made one of the satraps. His influence on his three friends emboldened them not to bow down before the great image of Nebuchadnezzar on the plain. Daniel knew of the decree not to pray to anyone else but the Persian king, but he still knelt before his window, with shutters open, daily. Arrested and thrown into the lion's den, Daniel held to his convictions.

God is the Master Artist. And there are aspects of your life and character—good, quality things—He wants others to notice. So without using blatant tricks or obvious gimmicks, God brings the cool, dark contrast of suffering into your life. That contrast, laid up against the golden character of Christ within you, will draw attention—to Him. Light against darkness. Beauty against affliction. Joy against sorrow. A sweet, patient spirit against pain and disappointment—major contrasts that have a way of attracting notice. You are the canvas on which He paints glorious truths, sharing beauty, and inspiring others. So that people might see him (Joni Eareckson Tada).

How did God paint in the canvas of Daniel's life? All three world emperors recognized Daniel's God because Daniel had convictions. Daniel's friends were bold and fierce in the face of compromising times because Daniel had convictions.

Convictions are not stagnant. They should be growing, maturing, and developing. A conviction is something I truly believe and am willing to make any and all sacrifices for it. The source from which the conviction is derived makes it an absolute. There is only one source for such absolutes. That is the Word of God. Daniel knew the Word and Christians have the Word of God.

Convictions are not related to a time in our life. Convictions are ageless, timeless, and universal. Eating laws for Daniel were applicable if he were in Jerusalem or Babylon. They remained applicable whether he was twenty, thirty, fifty, or eighty years old. They were applicable whether he was living in the Babylonian, Mede, or Persian culture. Convictions are culturally relevant but not determined by culture.

Suffering can strengthen and develop our convictions and character if we know the truth, embrace the truth, and allow the truth to sustain us in and during the crucible of suffering.

Let's make this instruction as practical and useful as possible. Taking the truths you've heard, let's develop a matrix.

    a. First, when you are surrounded by suffering, you must identify your source of suffering.

    b. Second, you must remind yourself of the "grips" for grappling with suffering and utilize the grip most powerful now. The grip may change from day to day.

    c. Finally, prayerfully ask God to show you which purpose He is working out in your life. Make a list of ways that purpose may be accomplished. Ask God for daily strength to allow His to complete the good work through this suffering to bring forth the greatest harvest in your life.

No One Cares. No One Understands Me!

Cutting, Self-Mutilation

What is cutting or self-mutilation? It is defined as deliberate, repetitive, impulsive non-lethal harm.[1] It is a deliberate damaging of body tissue without the intention of suicide.[2]

Self-injury is an intentional act done to the self, it includes some type of physical violence, and it is not undertaken with the intent to kill oneself.[3]

Self-injury involves self-inflicted bodily harm that is severe enough either to cause tissue damage or to leave marks that last several hours.[4]

It is also injuring yourself on purpose by making scratches or cuts on your body with a sharp object enough to break the skin and make it bleed. Areas most common for cutters are the arms, wrists, legs, and bellies. Experts call cutting an unhealthy coping mechanism.[5]

Tracy Alderman's[6] definition is concise and includes harm done to oneself by oneself, physically violent, intentional, and not suicidal.

What other terminology is used for cutting? Self-mutilation, self-harm, self-abuse, self-injurious behavior syndrome, self-inflicted violence, delicate self-cutting, and course self-cutting.

The statistic information is astounding. One out of ten adolescents have deliberately harmed themselves[7]. This was concluded after 6000

---

[1] www.facetheissue.com
[2] ibid
[3] Arizona Adolescent Health Coalition, 2000
[4] www.depression.about.com
[5] www.kidshealth.org
[6] Alderman, Tracy. *The Scarred Soul. Understanding and Ending Self Inflicted Violence.* Oakland, CA. New Harbinger, 1997
[7] BBC news: Centre for Suicide Research at Oxford University. www.newsvote.bbc.co.uk: 11/23 *British Medical Journal*

students aged fifteen to sixteen were interviewed from forty-one schools across England. In England, girls were four times likely to engage in self-harm as boys. Researchers from this BBC study concluded that over half of those who self-harmed were on medication, while less than twenty percent were receiving counseling.

The National Mental Health Association (NMHA) cites that those who do so are usually middle to upper class background, average to high intelligence. Fifty percent report physical or sexual abuse during childhood. Nearly ninety percent report they find it difficult to express their emotions or to deal with problems.[8]

Wendy Lader, Ph.D., estimates that one percent of the U.S. population as a whole resorts to self-injury.[9] Lader says this is nothing new, but the awareness of this has contributed to teens looking for new ways to express their rebellion. It is harder for kids to get noticed as individuals and they don't have the words for it, so they show it even if it's just to themselves because it makes it real for them. It's almost as if their body becomes a bulletin board on which to notch their pain.[10]

According to the Lysamena Project on Self Injury, two to eight million Americans per year are cutting, or one to three percent of the population.[11]

What are the signs of a cutter? Unexplained frequent injury including cuts and burns. Wearing long pants and sleeves in warm and hot weather. Difficulty handling or expressing feelings. Relationship problems. Poor functioning at school and home.

How does self-injury occurs? Cutting,[12] scratching, picking scabs, or interfering with wound healing, burning with matches or cigarette, punching self or objects, inserting objects in body openings, bruising or breaking bones, or some forms of hair pulling.

---

[8] www.nmha.org
[9] www.webmd.com, Lader, Wendy, *Bodily Harm*
[10] Lader, Wendy. *Bodily Harm*
[11] www.selfinjury.com
[12] Major means for SI

What are the etiologies (causes or origins) according to psychology? Specific etiology[13] has not been identified. What psychology has done is comprise a list of associated problems that teens cite as the reason they cut. Those reasons are feelings of guilt, feelings of hopelessness, feelings of hatred, feelings of anger, feelings of failure, feelings of loneliness, sexual abuse, domestic violence, parents, death of a loved one, lack of care as a child, family alcoholism, being criticized by authority figure, feeling strongly disliked, difficulty putting their feelings into words, acting out their emotional pain,[14] hypersensitivity to rejection, high levels of aggressive feelings, impulsiveness, being driven by the mood they are in at the moment, lacking direction, feeling like they cannot cope with the problems or stresses of life, feeling out of control or controlled by another, or affects of peer pressure.[15] This is quite a list from which psychology can draw.

What are some reasons cited by teens who cut? They were pressured into it. Some other teen was cutting and suggested they try it. To avoid ridicule or being ostracized, they participate. Initially it may carry with it some pain, and depending on the need for acceptance, the person may refuse next time or it will become a habit.

Some say it is to let out inner pain or emotions they are unable to talk or discuss with someone.

Someone has suggested the connection with endorphins. When the body is injured, neurotransmitters called endorphins are released. Endorphins that are also released when the pain is dulled and the person is given a general feel-good sensation. Some theorists believe that people get addicted to these endorphins.[16] It gives release, like a drug or alcohol addiction.

---

[13] Etiology means cause or the source for the behavior
[14] Arizona Adolescent Health Coalition, 2000
[15] ibid
[16] www.selfinjury.org

What are the proposed treatment options[17] for the wide range of possible causes for someone who cuts? Outpatient therapy[18] is prescribed. Cognitive behavioral therapy is being used. Medication treatment (antidepressants).[19] Medications such as antidepressants, moody stabilizers, and anxiolytics may alleviate the underlying feelings that the patient is attempting to cope with via SI.[20]

Does the Bible have anything to say about cutting? What hope can we give to someone who elects to cut himself or herself when life gets difficult? What are the biblical responses?[21]

What are some basic facts we know? People who cut themselves agree that cutting is not a good way to get the relief they are seeking. They know the relief doesn't last.[22]

Many people think that cutters are attempting suicide. This is a myth. Cutting infrequently leads to suicide. Cutting is not an attempt to commit suicide. Cutters frequently end up in the emergency room. Cutters hide this practice by wearing long-sleeved clothing and by doing this in private. Most teens cite some seemingly overwhelming problem for which they cannot find a solution for, that they don't know how to fix, and they don't understand how to deal with (psychology would say, "cope with"). Cutting is not some new concept. It has been around for centuries. The Bible even speaks of cutters in 1 Kings 18:28.

---

[17] I find it very interesting that a legal advertisement is found on the SI websites (Levitte Law Group) that deals with auto claims and Workers Compensation Third Party. I think this is saying that self-injury is someone else's fault.

[18] Most research revealed that the "experts" do not see any value in hospitalizing a cutter. It is better to leave the teen within the home and school environment unless the cutting is suicidal.

[19] Self-injury is not yet a classification of the DSM. However, psychology associates self-injury with numerous mood disorder problems.

[20] This report speaks of teaching the counselee coping mechanisms to deal with the underlying problems.

[21] The BBC research concluded their report with the following statement. "Clearly, the underlying reasons for people self harming are not being addressed." So the Bible must have answers!

[22] www.kidshealth.org

Here are some counseling issues when dealing with someone who cuts. First, communication. Some claim they do not have the ability to talk about their feelings, hurts, or grievances. They assert they others cannot or do not understand the pain they are experiencing. If someone cannot or does not understand precisely what they are experiencing, then, they ask, how can they really help me?

Is it absolutely necessary that another person is able to identify with the particular issue a cutter is encountering? How would someone having the same problem help the cutter? Where is hope found in "misery loves company"? To accommodate this thinking is practicing either pragmatism (if it works it must be right), or multiculturalism (only those of similar race, age, issues offer the most beneficial counseling).

No human being can ever fully identify with another's deepest hurt, pain, and sorrow. We might have had a similar occurrence that provides a loose common bond, but the exact nature of the event eludes us. We hear the details of another's pain and we can relate with parts of the story, but not so fully we can honestly say, "I understand."

So, from a human perspective, the cutter will endure loneliness and isolation. But from the divine perspective, we read these words in Hebrews.

> Therefore, He had to be made like His brethren in all things, so that He might become a merciful and faithful high priest in things pertaining to God, to make propitiation for the sins of the people. For since He Himself was tempted in that which He has suffered, He is able to come to the aid of those who are tempted (Heb. 2:17–18).

> For we do not have a high priest who cannot sympathize with our weaknesses, but One who has been tempted in all things as we are, yet without sin. Therefore let us draw near with confidence to the throne of grace, so that we may receive mercy and find grace to help in time of need (Heb. 4:15–16).

Hebrews 2:17–18 can be a wonderful comfort to the cutter. Christ completely understands human existence because He was made as we were. Why did Christ want to be made like a human being? So as a High Priest, He is able to be merciful and faithful pertaining to the things of God. Because of His position, we have the confidence to draw near to Him, to run to Him, to flee to Him for help. He is the only one that is able to provide mercy and grace in our deepest hour of need.

Instead of turning to cutting and the delusion that cutting can somehow provide comfort, the cutter needs to be shown how to turn immediately to Christ. This means the cutter has a personal relationship to Christ. Because Christ is his/her Brother, this family and familiar relationship promotes trust and desire to share with a family member. Inclusive is the statement that this family member offers grace (despite this reoccurring issue, I can still come to Him), and mercy (despite this reoccurring issue, He will help me live for Him).

Hebrews 4:15–16 is also an encouraging passage for the cutter. Jesus knows our struggles because He endured great struggles but did not sin in the process of dealing with those struggles. Again, this is where the cutter can find grace and mercy.

Self is another counseling issue. The focus of a cutter is upon themselves. Cutting is about how it makes them feel or how the cutting may solicit sympathy from others towards them. If the cutter is saved, several biblical injunctions need to be explained and made practical. John writes that, "He must increase and I must decrease." A cutter's motivation and actions must change. Instead of the desire to be served, Galatians 5:13 reminds the cutter he/she is to serve others in love.

Alone with the self, there are issues of selfishness. The act of cutting is intentional, not merely emotional. It is a selfish willful act to inflict a manageable level of pain and exposure of blood. As cited earlier, it may be to experience the release of endorphins (a feeling), sympathy, or attention. Cutters are not alone with wanting some sympathy or attention. For those brief moments, a cutter feels accepted, understood, and even bonded with a unique person of respect, but when life returns to "normal," the cutter often returns to self-destructive thoughts. Think about this. Many times when we experience a problem, someone has hurt us badly, or an unbearable event occurs, what do we do? We reach out to someone or something to find comfort. Because the etiology is so broad and vast and there is no consensus on the cause, a Christian young person cutting needs to be approach from a biblical worldview.

Relationships are another counseling issue. How to biblically deal with broken or damaged relationships may be one of the core counseling topics. These fractured relationships can be within the family such as a mother, father, or sibling. The splintered relationship may be external, outside the family, a friend, classmate, boyfriend, or girlfriend.

The cutter may struggle with possessiveness. The cutter may struggle with acceptance. The cutter may struggle with peer pressure or the opinions of others. The cutter has a difficult time when relationships go sour because the cutter has placed expectations upon the other person or themselves. When the expectation is not met, the cutter takes a measure of responsibility, if not all, and attempts to escape the pain through momentary acts of self-destructive behavior.

A more generalized counseling issue is problems in life. Everyone has problems. The cutter fails to follow a procedure to resolve the problem or does not have the ability to resolve the problem. Some cutters think the only resolution for the problem is for the other person to do what I want or say. Instead of avoiding or manipulating circumstances through cutting, they need to learn biblical problem-solving skills.

Finally, for our purposes, the issue of choices is a counseling topic. Several surveys indicate that someone becomes involved in cutting because of peer pressure. The cutter must be taught how to be an individual and stand up against peer pressure from friends to try cutting. Peer pressure can be overwhelming. If the cutter really wants to blend in, they will try cutting in order to be accepted or to avoid ridicule.

It is vitally important to gather good data. Here is a suggested list of beginning questions to ask the cutter.

1. When did the cutting first begin?
2. How does the teen cut?
3. What circumstances seem to bring on the desire to cut?
4. Is there a particular favorite place the teen cuts? (Bedroom, school bathroom, etc.)
5. How does the teen feel before, during, and after cutting?
6. How often during a given week, does the teen cut?
7. Are the parents aware of the teen's cutting?
8. What intervention has the parents, school, or friends provided?
9. Does the teen want to stop?
10. Describe what was happening before the last cutting episode.
11. Is the teen on any medication?
12. Is the teen undergoing any other counseling?
13. Has the teen every been hospitalized?
14. Has the teen ever cut so deeply that they were taken to the emergency ward? By whom? (Parents, school officials, police, paramedics, psych ward, etc.)
15. When the teen cuts, what does the teen hope for or desire, want or need that they believe cutting will provide for them?

Like any counseling situation, we must give much hope. Remind the cutter that no situation is so overwhelming that an answer cannot be found. Ask them if their present choice of coping provides lasting relief, or do they find themselves repeatedly turning back to the same habit?

Christ Jesus understands the emotional pain the teen is going through. The teen will want someone who has "flesh" on to understand what they are going through. As stated earlier, the one who has or is going through cutting probably is not the best counselor. Why? Because they probably can only offer sympathy. The teen wants to identify with someone who "knows." Who better than Jesus Christ (Heb. 2:17–18, 4:15–16). There is Someone who completely comprehends and desires to help (Christ). If no other human being understands or wants to become actively involved in providing help, there is One that sticks closer than a brother, and this One is always for the teen and will never desert the teen.

How should you begin to address the issues biblically? First, insure that biblical salvation is in place. Religion and religious practices are not evidence of genuine salvation. Get precise details of their conversion. What did they understand they were doing? Can they remember what they prayed? Was it a "group" experience? Matthew 7:14–23 clearly contrasts the professor with the confessor. Helping a cutter without the solid foundation of who Christ is and what He did is futile.

Assure the teen that they should neither question Christ's availability or ability (Matt. 8—leper). Many wonder if Christ really exists during this intense time. Some wonder if Christ cares. Or if He is all-powerful, why doesn't He stop this torment and provide relief? The leper, in Matthew 8, broke cultural, religious, and social perimeters to find Jesus. When the leper did, he did not question Christ about His ability. He heard of other miracles Christ performed. The leper was concerned about Christ's availability. Was his condition so repulsive that Christ would not want to provide aid? The cutter may feel this way. "Jesus is too busy with other 'good' Christians, He would not want to help me." But Christ came not to heal those who need no physician, but the sick.

They must make a commitment to want to be healed (John 5—man at the pool). If you read the first few verses of John 5, you will note that the lame man never answered Christ's question. Christ asks him if he wanted to be made well. The leper only offered excuses why he had not made himself better. The cutter often hedges truth and honesty in their commitment. If things are going well and they have not cut recently, the thought of bowing to Christ is not on their radar. However, if things begin down that dark sinister alley, they will cry out to God for relief. Immediate relief is not a bad thing. But that kind of commitment is a fleeting momentary cure. When the same feelings return, the likelihood of them returning to handling life through cutting is real. The result is an endless cycle of failures, of starts and stops.

The teen must make a commitment to allow Christ to establish His lordship in all areas of their life. It will be hard work. The journey will not be easy. The teen cannot balance the prospects of lasting change with the momentary pleasures of acceptance from others and will often choose the latter. When the surging feelings become too strong, speaking of victory in Christ will be odious. In their mind, Christ failed and that is why they returned to cutting. No, Christ did not fail. The teen experienced the weight relieved and thought he or she was cured. They returned to walking, sitting and standing in the counsel of the ungodly. They consented to listening to and participating with sinners.

Teach the teen that the way they have been handling their circumstances and life is displeasing to the Lord. It is sinful and must be confessed. Mere acknowledgement is not sufficient. Many people acknowledge they should diet and not eat so many sweets, but that mental assent lacks backbone. It is like a skeleton trying to stand against hurricane-force winds. Does the cutter believe that self-inflicted wounds are harming their body, which is the temple of the Holy Spirit? Do they really believe that their body is not their own to do with as they wish, but has been paid for with a very expensive price? Failure to see their body from God's perspective will only result in a type of counseling that deals with the present and ignores the past and future.

Show the teen he/she must be willing to completely abide by the instructions of God's Word to have victory and success in conquering cutting (Js. 1:25, Josh. 1:8–9, Eccl. 10:10). The blessings of God, God's solutions, are based on the hearer being a doer. These verses speak of the diligence, hard work, and tenacity that is required for complete victory. The ten percent that the cutter holds back on out of the one hundred percent is the little leaven that spoils the whole lump.

This commitment to God's way will involve radical amputation. Commitment to God's solutions is not like a doctor telling a cancer patient, "We think we got it all," only to have it reoccur months later. Our Great Physician says, "I will get it all if you follow My ways." This radical amputation may involve eliminating enabling friends, music, or forms of media that portray cutting as acceptable. It will involve a new diet that develops a whole new appetite. Bulking up on the Bible, prayer, church, youth activities, and loving service to others will purge any standing space for rebellious thoughts of wanting to cut.

We need to help the teen discern what the evil cravings and desires are and what the teen hopes to gain from cutting. They want something so badly, they are willing to rebel against God and harm their own bodies. What does this teen want? What does the teen crave? What does the teen believe they cannot live without? What does the teen think they must have? Once some of these things are identified biblically, you will be able to understand their thinking and help them to replace, or put on, righteous thinking that will be observed through godly character and conduct.

This topic, like many others today, is not a walk in the park. It will take faithfulness on the counselor's part and consistent obedience and warring against the wants of the cutter. Victory is possible. It s real. It is out there.

Epilogue

By Pastor Scott Sundin, Blue Ridge Bible Church, Missouri

As a pastor, I know and teach the Bible. I believe with my whole heart that God, in the form of the Bible and His indwelling Holy Spirit, has given us everything we need for life and godliness.

And as a pastor, I frequently find myself in unscheduled, unlabeled counseling situations. I know and believe the Bible, but I am sometimes left scratching my head as people describe the pickles they've got themselves in. I love Dr. Rick's *Tough Issues, Straight Answers*.

Dr. Rick not only thoroughly covers the Biblical teaching regarding tough issues in the lives of our people, but he provides very complete research and identification of the causes of those problems. In other words, while I know the Bible, Dr. Rick's book has helped me label the issues, understand the issues, and then see which principle or story in scripture applies to that specific issue. Whether your counselee is struggling with perfectionism or is the parent of a crack baby, Dr. Rick offers help, explanation and counsel that juxtaposes Biblical teaching with everyday life experiences.

About the Author

Dr. Thomas is the Founder and Executive Director of Mt. Carmel Ministries, a ministry dedicated to training, counseling, and equipping. You can access audio materials on a variety of counseling subjects by going to www.mtcarmelmin.org and click on resources. There you will find individual cassette tapes, cassette albums, CDs and printed study guides and booklets. Mt. Carmel Ministries also produces a free monthly newsletter dedicated to providing education to help men and women help others. Past issues of the newsletter (Today's *Biblical Counselor*) are available online at www.mtcarmelmin.org (click on library).

Dr. Thomas developed a correspondence course that when completed will start you on your way towards certification as a biblical counselor with the National Association of Nouthetic Counselors. You can learn about additional optional training opportunities at www.mtcarmelmin.org (click on training).

If you have questions for Dr. Rick, please email him at mcmbclsor@yahoo.com.

To locate a biblical counselor in your area, contact the National Association of Nouthetic Counselors at www.nanc.org. Then click on "NANC Counselors." You can search by last name or ZIP code.

Other works by Dr. Thomas
Worship: A Life in Tune with God
King David: God's Man with Feet of Clay
Restoring Truth to Counseling: Foundation for Change
Masturbation: Shattered Expectations for Sexual Gratification
You Can Make A Difference
PTSD (Post Traumatic Stress Disorder): Self-Study Manual for Re-Entry into Life and Living.
Preparing to Meet God: Your Commencement to Glory Personal Funeral Planner

Endorsements

"This volume containing truly Biblical analysis and answers to some of the most difficult issues facing Biblical counselors today will become an indispensable tool in the toolbox of the Biblical counselor. It's on my Biblical counseling shelf right next to Jay Adams *The Christian Counselor's Manual* and John MacArthur's *How to Counsel Biblically*. As a pastor and NANC certified counselor, I have already referred to this essential and practical resource many times. The Christian counseling community owes Dr. Thomas great thanks for compiling this timely and greatly needed resource for the truly Biblical counselor. Dr Richard Thomas pours many years of experience and countless hours of research into this volume, which will without doubt save the Biblical counselor many hours and change many lives through the unchangeable principles of God's Eternal Word that he expertly lays out so clearly for us all. Thanks not only to Dr. Thomas for all his hard work on our behalf, but many thanks to his wife Carolyn also for the sacrifice that compiling such a volume necessitates upon their spouse!" —*Pastor Joe Litton, NANC Certified Counselor, Montana*

Dr. Thomas has done the counseling community a huge favor! This book will be a regular resource in your counseling toolbox for years to come. The topics are broad. And it is an excellent reference manual. But it is more than that. Dr. Thomas loves and believes the Bible is the answer for man's problems. This is where you'll be served so well. He takes the old book and makes it plain and relevant for the average counselor. He brings the Bible stories to your living room and shows how they can apply to a broad range of people and problems. Read it for yourself! And then read it to serve your friends. —*Rick Thomas. President, The Counseling Solutions Group and NANC Fellow, South Carolina*

Made in the USA
Charleston, SC
11 September 2012